Reciprocity in Public International Law

There is a common perception of reciprocity as a concept that is opposed to the communitarian interests that characterise contemporary international law, or merely a way of denoting reactions to unfriendly or wrongful conduct. This book disputes this approach and highlights how reciprocity is instead linked to the structural characteristic of sovereign equality of States in international law. This book carries out an in-depth analysis of the concept of reciprocity and the elements that characterise it, before examining the various roles and articulations of reciprocity in a number of fields of public international law: the law of treaties, the treatment of individuals, the execution of international law, and the jurisdiction of international courts and tribunals. In all these areas, it analyses both more traditional and more contemporary examples to demonstrate how reciprocity is closely linked to the very structure of public international law.

ARIANNA WHELAN is currently First Secretary in the Department of Foreign Affairs of Ireland. She holds a Masters and PhD in international law from the Graduate Institute of International and Development Studies in Geneva, Switzerland.

CAMBRIDGE STUDIES IN INTERNATIONAL AND COMPARATIVE LAW: 173

Established in 1946, this series produces high quality, reflective and innovative scholarship in the field of public international law. It publishes works on international law that are of a theoretical, historical, cross-disciplinary or doctrinal nature. The series also welcomes books providing insights from private international law, comparative law and transnational studies which inform international legal thought and practice more generally.

The series seeks to publish views from diverse legal traditions and perspectives, and of any geographical origin. In this respect it invites studies offering regional perspectives on core *problématiques* of international law, and in the same vein, it appreciates contrasts and debates between diverging approaches. Accordingly, books offering new or less orthodox perspectives are very much welcome. Works of a generalist character are greatly valued and the series is also open to studies on specific areas, institutions or problems. Translations of the most outstanding works published in other languages are also considered.

After seventy years, Cambridge Studies in International and Comparative Law sets the standard for international legal scholarship and will continue to define the discipline as it evolves in the years to come.

A list of books in the series can be found at the end of this volume.

Reciprocity in Public International Law

Arianna Whelan
Graduate Institute of International and Development Studies

CAMBRIDGE
UNIVERSITY PRESS

CAMBRIDGE
UNIVERSITY PRESS

Shaftesbury Road, Cambridge CB2 8EA, United Kingdom

One Liberty Plaza, 20th Floor, New York, NY 10006, USA

477 Williamstown Road, Port Melbourne, VIC 3207, Australia

314–321, 3rd Floor, Plot 3, Splendor Forum, Jasola District Centre,
New Delhi – 110025, India

103 Penang Road, #05–06/07, Visioncrest Commercial, Singapore 238467

Cambridge University Press is part of Cambridge University Press & Assessment, a department of the University of Cambridge.

We share the University's mission to contribute to society through the pursuit of education, learning and research at the highest international levels of excellence.

www.cambridge.org
Information on this title: www.cambridge.org/9781108845588

DOI: 10.1017/9781108980173

First published 2023

A catalogue record for this publication is available from the British Library.

ISBN 978-1-108-84558-8 Hardback

Contents

Foreword

Reciprocity has a bad reputation in current times. It can be seen as a matter of selfishness, a way of taking into account one's own interests first, which in turn become the yardstick by which to measure what one is ready to accept from the other in exchange. On the contrary, progressive ideas are focused on communitarian interests, be they matters of human rights, protection of the commons, peoples' rights, or peace. At first sight, a reader may think that this work swims against the tide. Indeed, it does something different and more important than that. The book you have in your hands or on your screen challenges received ideas and proceeds with a concrete analysis, beyond superficial *a priori* takings of stance, unfortunately so in vogue today.

The subject of reciprocity has been addressed by the doctrine and to a certain extent, it can even be said, quite extensively. Nevertheless, it needed a contemporary, global, and specific study, and this is what Dr. Whelan has undertaken. This is a revised and updated version of her PhD thesis, brilliantly defended at the Graduate Institute of International and Development Studies of Geneva with the highest possible grades. She gives us a text of rather small dimensions, if we judge it in light of a current tendency to produce long pieces of work. Conciseness is therefore another merit of this text. Nothing in this book is superfluous or merely descriptive.

The working hypotheses are clearly presented and discussed. First, the author demonstrates that reciprocity is not in opposition to the increasing consideration by international law of community interests or subjects other than the State. Second, the still important role of reciprocity in international law nowadays is explained by the existence of sovereign equality as a fundamental principle of international law, one of its very structural factors.

The structure of the book is clear, and the text is readable in an agreeable manner. The first two chapters expound and analyze the role of reciprocity in society and in law in general, which then allows the author to frame the concept more correctly within international law. The following chapters relate to the main areas in which reciprocity plays its major role in international law: treaties, international organizations, the protection of the individual in its various forms, the implementation of the consequences arising from nonrespect of the law (which includes but goes beyond international responsibility), and finally the settlement of international disputes and more broadly the activity of international courts and tribunals.

The reflection was carried out and transpires in the text in a rigorous way. Only someone with an excellent knowledge of the subject matter, and also of law in general, is able to produce such an important contribution to the theory of international law. The case law considered is from many different areas and a variety of different courts and tribunals. Doctrinal works are critically appraised and, something remarkable in these times of exclusive use of English, were consulted and studied in several languages. Reciprocity allowed the author to make a cross-sectional study of the international legal system, which requires deep knowledge of the different "branches" of the discipline.

I am sure you will not only enjoy and benefit from reading this book but also, at the end, certainly come away with an enriched perspective on international law.

Marcelo Kohen, Professor of International Law
Graduate Institute, Geneva
Geneva, March 2022

Preface and Acknowledgments

This book is the revised version of a PhD thesis completed in 2017 at the Graduate Institute of International and Development Studies in Geneva, under the supervision of Professor Marcelo Kohen. It began its life a few years before then, from a curiosity about the idea of reciprocity in international law; during my time as a student in International Law at the Graduate Institute, I had the good fortune of being taught by Professor Pierre-Marie Dupuy shortly before his retirement. He first convinced me that not only was reciprocity an interesting topic but that it deserved to be the subject of a PhD thesis.

That initial idea of analyzing the role of reciprocity in international law gained in scope and complexity the more familiar the concept became. Reciprocity is something extremely concrete, and yet, up close, it proves almost frustratingly elusive, which at the very least makes it an excellent candidate for in-depth research. Perhaps because it feels so concrete, reciprocity is often considered a vestige of a classical system of international law that we have left behind with the advent of ideas such as community interests and peremptory norms. Nonetheless, it still crops up across public international law. The idea underlying that doctoral thesis – and this book – is that reciprocity is important in international law because it reflects a structural characteristic of the system, namely sovereign equality, and it is not just found in areas closely linked to the "old", classical international law.

I would most certainly not have found a path through the many questions, or the fuzzy contours of the concept, were it not for the careful supervision of Professor Marcelo Kohen. I was privileged to be the teaching assistant for his General Course of Public International Law for over three years at the Graduate Institute, which pushed me to reflect on the *tout organique* of international law and on reciprocity's role within it. Not only am I extremely grateful for his guidance over the years but also greatly honored that he has written the foreword for this book. The text also greatly benefited from the thoughtful comments of those who, alongside Professors Kohen and Dupuy, were members of the jury at my thesis defense, namely Judge Georg Nolte and Professor Eric Wyler.

Since 2017 the road has been long, and that initial thesis has undergone further work in preparation for its publication. I am deeply grateful to Cambridge University Press, and particularly Tom Randall, for agreeing to publish it and also for the guidance and patience during the process of revision. The text has also benefited greatly from the comments of its five (anonymous) reviewers, who pushed me to reflect and, I hope, improve it. Since completing the PhD in 2017, I have been working at the Department of Foreign Affairs of Ireland. It goes without saying that the views expressed in the present book are my own and do not represent those of the department.

If the ideas in this book have matured over time, it is also thanks to those who I worked with during my time as a teaching assistant at the Graduate Institute, the position that funded the original PhD – particularly Edward Kwakwa, Professor Jorge Viñuales, and Fuad Zarbiyev. Thanks also go to my friends and former colleagues Bérénice, Chiara, Dan, Elena, Elizabeth, Ginevra, Jason, Kendra, Kerim, Leon, Lorenzo, Sarah, and Vince, for (variously) their comments, insights, and assistance in accessing resources. Thanks also to Marcin Kaldunski for inviting me to discuss my work with his research group. I am also particularly grateful to the staff of the Graduate Institute Library and the Peace Palace Library in The Hague. Completing work on this book without access to a university library, and with the restrictions of the Covid-19 pandemic, would have been impossible if not for the many resources available remotely through their networks.

Finally, thanks to my family – particularly my parents, Gerard and Silvia, and my sister, Antonia. This book is dedicated to them, and to the memory of my grandfathers, Eugenio and Anthony.

Introduction

Reciprocity is a deceptively simple concept that in reality has a complex and elusive nature. Emmanuel Decaux wrote in describing reciprocity, "*Intuitivement, chacun croit la connaître, avec cette force de l'évidence qui exclut toute definition. Mais, s'agit-il de l'analyser, la réciprocité devient floue, incertaine, évanescente.*"[1] [Intuitively, everyone believes they know it, with the force of the obvious that excludes any definition. But when it comes to analyzing reciprocity, it becomes blurry, uncertain, evanescent] "Reciprocity" is often used to describe some kind of return, of dependence of conduct. In the context of international law, its use also often takes on negative connotations: reaction, reprisals, retortion. It implies lawlessness, private justice, symmetrical reactions: the famous maxim of "an eye for an eye, a tooth for a tooth." But reciprocity may also have positive connotations when used to mean returning kindness with kindness, comity, and positive returns. All these, however, still fall short of the label of law. It is this elusive nature of reciprocity that constitutes the main challenge when analyzing its role in international law.

It is particularly the negative connotations of reciprocity and its link to conduct-based responses in a lawless context that have led to a juxtaposition of reciprocity with community interests, institutionalization, and the existence of objective legality. This opposition between reciprocity and community is, like the concept of reciprocity itself, deceptively simple. Intuitively, it makes sense: to have stable legal relations in a wider interest than the bilateral, even selfish, reactions of one State to the conduct of another, then international relations simply cannot be based on reciprocity.

[1] E. Decaux, *La réciprocité en droit international*, Paris, Librairie générale de droit et jurisprudence, 1980, p. 2.

The aim of this book is to go beyond reciprocity merely as a description of conduct, to look at the *legal* concept of reciprocity as exists in international law. As the reader will see, reciprocity is found in many areas of public international law; it underlies numerous mechanisms of the law, and turns up even where we might not expect to find it, including in areas of public international law that concern rules of interest to the international community as a whole, and in obligations *erga omnes* that are owed by States to the international community.

The question addressed here is thus: What explains the role of reciprocity in contemporary, communitarian public international law, and is it antithetical to community interests and obligations – indeed, to the existence of an international community itself? The answer advanced here is that reciprocity in public international law is not antithetical to community interests and obligations but that its importance is explained by a structural factor: the sovereign equality of States. This explains and predicts where reciprocity will be relevant and where it will find its limits. Reciprocity will predictably be important as a default means of regulation in areas closely connected to the exercise of sovereign power by the State, where an imbalance in obligations can most easily impair equality. But it is its relevance in the horizontal legal obligations between States, regardless of content, which explains why we find reciprocity even in areas relating to human rights and community interests. Its application is instead limited in obligations owed by States to individuals, where the legal relationship has a vertical element, and legal inequality between the subjects of the rule makes reciprocity inapplicable. Reciprocity is not something limited to bilateral obligations, but it also works in multilateral obligations and those whose focus is an interest of the international community as a whole. Reciprocity is therefore a structural factor in international law, fundamental to the operation of a horizontal system of law based on the *legal*, if not always factual, equality of States.

Many scholars across the social sciences view the notions of reciprocity and community as antithetical. There is widespread recognition among authors that reciprocity has a fundamental importance in international law; yet reciprocity is almost invariably contrasted with the idea of an international community and of community obligations; reciprocity is therefore generally viewed as a characteristic of a "classical" international law that is primarily bilateral in operation.

On the other hand, views that consider reciprocity as the basis on which the international legal system rests often see international law as the sum of mutual renunciations made by States[2] – what may be termed a voluntarist viewpoint that sees international law as no more than a series of contractual undertakings.[3] This view is difficult to reconcile with concepts such as community interests, *erga omnes* obligations, and the existence of peremptory norms of international law.[4] Reciprocity is also considered fundamental by those who consider international law a result of coexistence between antagonists, particularly theorists from the time of the Cold War. Georg Schwarzenberger, for example, underlined the "reality" of international law as reciprocal, expressed through the principle of State sovereignty.[5] In these approaches, reciprocity is understood as tit for tat, or conduct dependent on the actions of another subject.

Still others consider reciprocity as being proper to legal systems that are less developed or institutionalized, of which, so the argument goes international law is a clear example. For example, in his separate opinion in the *Former Yugoslav Republic of Macedonia* v. *Greece* case before the International Court of Justice (ICJ), Judge Simma stated:

> Reciprocity constitutes a basic phenomenon of social interaction and consequently a decisive factor also behind the growth and application of law ... The lower the degree of institutionalization of a legal order, however, the more mechanisms of direct reciprocity will still prevail as such.[6]

2 Combacau, for example, at one point describes *ius cogens* as a "useless notion"; J. Combacau and S. Sur, *Droit international public*, 10e ed., Paris, Montchrestien, 2010, p. 162.

3 See G. Scelle, "La doctrine de Léon Duguit et les fondements du droit des gens," *Archives de philosophie du droit et de sociologie politique*, nos. 1–2, 1932, pp. 84–85; D. Anzilotti, *Corso di Diritto Internazionale*, Padova, Cedam, 1955, p. 46.

4 Combacau and Sur, *Droit international public*, p. 162.

5 G. Schwarzenberger, "The Fundamental Principles of International Law," *Collected Courses of the Hague Academy of International Law*, vol. 87, 1955, p. 225. The basis of coexistence between States from the beginning of the Cold War was to be based on the five principles of Panch Shila, later also echoed among the principles in the Declaration on Friendly Relations and Co-operation among States of 1970; these include mutual respect for territorial integrity and sovereignty, mutual noninterference in internal affairs, equality and mutual benefit, and peaceful coexistence: See Agreement (with exchange of notes) between the Republic of India and the People's Republic of China on Trade and Intercourse between Tibet region of China and India, 29 April 1954, 299 U.N.T.S. 57, preamble; General Assembly Resolution 2625 (XXV), Declaration on Principles of International Law concerning Friendly Relations and Co-operation among States in accordance with the Charter of the United Nations, 24 October 1970; M. Virally, "Le principe de réciprocité dans le droit international contemporain," *RCADI*, vol. 122, 1967, p. 8.

6 Application of the Interim Accord of 13 September 1995 (the *Former Yugoslav Republic of Macedonia* v. *Greece*), Judgment of 5 December 2011, ICJ Reports 2011, Separate Opinion of Judge Simma, p. 699.

International law is sometimes considered to be an example of a primitive system of law that, lacking a centralized enforcement mechanism, allows self-help and retaliation in response to wrongdoing. The idea that a reciprocal form of retaliation must be available in a legal system lacking a centralized enforcement mechanism is present in many of the explanations according to which a "state of nature" exists at the international level.[7] "Primitive" in this case refers to the lack of centralized organization in the international legal order and more precisely to the absence of a centralized mechanism to make rules and impose sanctions.

But it seems limiting to write off as "primitive" the international legal system, even as it changes and develops, merely because it is a system in which States are legally equal, rather than subject to a higher, centralized lawmaking body. If we accept that international law is, by virtue of its lack of centralized enforcement, a "primitive" system of law, then we are essentially saying that internal law is the only possible, developed legal system – or "the only finalised form law can take, and its only finality."[8] There may be those who agree, and look forward to the day a world State exists. However, it is perhaps more useful in the international legal – and political – system as we know it to see international and domestic law as *different*, rather than as different stages of evolution of the only form a legal system can take.

Those views that consider international relations and indeed international law as something similar to a "state of nature" at the international level also only describe a situation in which there are no legal rules – which is not an accurate depiction of the international legal system, in which certain very well-defined consequences exist when rules are broken, as will be seen in the examination of State responsibility in Chapter 5.[9] Furthermore, the absence of any punitive element to the consequences of breaching rules of international law, firmly rejected during the codification of the rules on States responsibility, limits the

[7] For example, international economic law analyses; see, for example, F. Parisi and N. Ghei, "The Role of Reciprocity in International Law," *Cornell International Law Journal*, vol. 36, no. 1, Spring 2003, p. 1. In game theory, reciprocity is indicated as an ideal strategy to ensure cooperation over repeat interactions between States – but only where there is an advantage to be drawn from such cooperation; see ibid., p. 11.

[8] R. Kolb, *La bonne foi en droit international public*, Paris, PUF, 2000, p. 167; see also M. Virally, "Sur la prétendue 'primitivité' du droit international," in *Le droit international en devenir: Essais écrits au fil des ans*, Paris, PUF, 1990, pp. 91–101.

[9] These are set out in the law of State responsibility; see Section 5.2.

possible comparisons with another commonly considered view of reciprocity, that of "an eye for an eye," the *lex talionis*.

This separation between classical, reciprocal and contemporary, non-reciprocal international law, which either considers international law itself as primitive, or considers reciprocity to be extraneous to community interests and obligations, seems to give an inordinate amount of importance to the execution of the law and particularly to the absence of a centralized public power that can enforce the observation of rules. This book instead aims to show how it is the horizontal structure of international law that provides the ideal conditions for reciprocity to operate: equality and independence of the subjects of the law, and the absence of any superior power. Reciprocity in this sense is both a result of the sovereign equality of States,[10] which implies the need for a given State not to obtain a greater advantage or bear more obligations than another, and a means of ensuring that sovereign equality is maintained effectively.[11] But these structural characteristics do not change because a rule concerns a given subject matter that is of particular importance to the international community. It is not sufficient to look at reciprocity in international law through the prism of classical versus modern or bilateral versus communitarian. Therefore, the analysis here will juxtapose "classical" and "contemporary" domains of international law, looking at how reciprocity operates to see where it might encounter limitations, and why. The analysis focuses in particular on whom obligations are owed to, and what the consequences of their violation are – that is, the *structure* of international legal obligations, rather than their content or object. The aim throughout is to look closely at areas that might generally be considered to escape the operation of reciprocity, to see whether this is really the case, and if not, then why.

While the analysis here focuses on reciprocity in international law, the starting point in Chapter 1 is a socio-philosophical approach, looking at the relationship between reciprocity, psychology, and morality, to see how reciprocity is a concept that is closely linked to the existence of a

[10] P.-M. Dupuy, "L'unité de l'ordre juridique international: Cours général de droit international public," *Collected Courses of the Hague Academy of International Law*, vol. 297, 2000, p. 54.

[11] Parisi and Ghei, "Role of Reciprocity in International Law," p. 41. This same idea is put forward by Michel Virally, when he underlines that, by virtue of reciprocity, sovereignty limits sovereignty, so that to each obligation for one State, there corresponds an obligation for another State; but also, for each obligation of one State, that same State can claim a corresponding right from others. M. Virally, "Panorama du droit international contemporain," *RCADI*, vol. 183, 1983, p. 84.

community, but also, in its deepest sense, to fairness and equality. Chapter 1 also goes on to analyse the origins of reciprocity in the Roman law of contracts, as well as more modern applications in contract law, and other examples of the operation of reciprocity in domestic law. This look at domestic legal systems shows not only that reciprocity in fact can, and does, exist within "institutionalized" domestic law but also shows the close link between reciprocity and sovereignty, giving an important initial indication of the use made by national legal systems of reciprocity as a basis on which to limit the State's sovereignty.

The issue of defining reciprocity is the focus in Chapter 2, alongside establishing the legal nature of the concept and the functions it can have within the law – in norm-creation, as a condition of application of the law, and in ensuring execution of the law. "Reciprocity" can have many possible meanings, and many are used in different fields of the sciences and social sciences, as examined in Chapter 1. However, as the topic being dealt with here is public international law, for present purposes, the meaning given to reciprocity is that of the legal interdependence of the corresponding rights and obligations States mutually owe each other. Therefore, it does not cover mere factual conduct but relates to the structure of international rights and obligations. The functions of reciprocity identified in Chapter 2 are the frame of reference for the analysis of positive law that follows in Chapters 3–6. In discussing public international law, it is also important to situate reciprocity with respect to the doctrine of sources of international law, and in particular general principles and customary international law. Reciprocity is particularly relevant as a dynamic basis of cooperation in the creation of rules of customary international law.

Having examined the background of reciprocity as a concept, establishing its nature as relevant to community relations, intrinsically linked to fairness and equality, and its uses in domestic law as well as a conceptual background in international law, the remaining chapters carry out an analysis of reciprocity in public international law and practice.

With the aim of examining whether reciprocity is still relevant in community-focused obligations of international law, and seeing where limitations to reciprocity arise, the first focus of the analysis in Chapter 3 is on treaties. The law of treaties is a fertile ground in which to easily compare the functioning of reciprocity in a variety of legal obligations. The drafting history of the Vienna Convention on the Law of Treaties (VCLT), particularly in relation to reservations to treaties, sets out the reciprocity underlying how treaty obligations work. The outline that begins to emerge from examining different kinds of treaty, particularly where human rights are concerned, is that limitations to mechanisms of reciprocity appear when obligations are owed to individuals. The study of treaties of the integral type shows that it is not the subject matter or the existence of a collective or community interest on which the obligation focuses that limits the applicability of reciprocity but rather this existence of a vertical legal relationship within the obligation.

This is however not a sufficient point at which to stop in examining reciprocity in the functioning of treaties; after all, the argument that reciprocity is linked to sovereign equality and therefore characterizes horizontal legal relations would be invalidated if reciprocity were absent from treaties that created objective regimes, or put in place differentiated obligations. The remainder of Chapter 3 therefore looks at how reciprocity works in treaties that have differentiated obligations, those founding international organizations, or where treaties have effects beyond the parties. For all these kinds of treaty, reciprocity again follows the pattern described above, being more limited where rights are conferred upon entities that are not in a relationship of sovereign equality to States. Distinctions as to bilateral or multilateral obligations, or the content of the obligation itself, do not have an effect on the relevance of reciprocity.

A closer analysis of how reciprocity functions in rules concerning the treatment of individuals in public international law is the subject matter of the analysis in Chapter 4. Here again, the point is to examine whether it is the *content* of the norm – that is, the fact that it concerns an individual, or the international protection of an individual – or its *structure* that dictates whether reciprocity will be limited within a given rule. Therefore, the analysis looks both at "classical" standards of treatment of individuals, such as the international minimum standard, national treatment, or most-favored nation (MFN) treatment, and compares these with contemporary international humanitarian law, human rights law, and investment law. Here again, the same pattern emerges, of reciprocity finding its limitations when rules have a vertical element in that they give rights directly to individuals, and reciprocity instead playing a more important role when there is an inter-State dimension to a rule, even when such a rule concerns a collective interest.

Reciprocity in the execution of rules is another crucial function and one in which the tension between the view of reciprocity as a negative reaction to some form of wrongdoing and that advanced here, of a structural feature of a legal system based on sovereign equality, can most easily be seen. It is after all in this area that we might expect to find the greatest relevance of reciprocity because of the lack of a central enforcement mechanism in international law. Chapter 5 therefore looks at how reciprocity functions in the execution of international law, in the law of treaties, and the law of State responsibility. Rather than finding any "pure" reciprocity, or principle of reciprocity, in this area of international law reciprocity has the greatest variety of meanings and is expressed in a number of specific mechanisms. Chapter 5 compares the classical mechanisms of responsibility and nonperformance in response to a breach of the law to the regime around peremptory and *erga omnes* rules, to see whether rules that are designed to protect a matter of collective interest to the international community escape the functioning of reciprocity in execution. It finds that the different types of obligation that exist in international law (bilateral, interdependent, integral) all still function on the basis of reciprocity, as does the law of State responsibility in its entirety. In the inter-State domain of the rules of international responsibility, reciprocity remains a structural factor.

In contemporary international law, it is not only the rules of State responsibility that dictate the consequences of a breach, but there exist a number of dispute settlement mechanisms and courts to which States, and individuals, can have recourse. Chapter 6 therefore finally looks at the jurisdiction of a variety of international courts and tribunals, including human rights mechanisms. Reciprocity plays an important role in the context of dispute settlement, and is particularly important in the jurisdictional requirements of the ICJ and the dispute settlement system under Part XV of the UN Convention on the Law of the Sea (UNCLOS). It is also still required in inter-State complaints mechanisms under human rights treaties. However, in individual–State complaint mechanisms, reciprocity is simply inapplicable. Once again, the existence of a relationship of legal equality between the two subjects concerned in a dispute is the key. The chapter ends with some considerations on the extension of the jurisdiction of investment arbitral tribunals on the basis of the MFN clause.

Throughout the pages that follow, and attempt will be made to highlight both the structural consequences of reciprocity in international law and the specific meanings that it may have in given contexts or in given roles. The end result will hopefully be to paint a picture of reciprocity in public international law that shows both a general landscape and – like trees, rivers, and villages on a canvas – the different manifestations of reciprocity and the roles it may fulfill within that landscape.

1 Reciprocity at the Basis of Law and Society

The study of reciprocity has not been restricted to the field of international law – far from it. Reciprocity is a concept of some importance in philosophy, psychology, and sociology, in explaining human behavior, and indeed in the formation of law. Reciprocity is relevant not only in international law but also in certain branches of domestic law – a point that goes some way toward disproving the view of reciprocity as a characteristic of "primitive" or prestate legal systems. Notably, reciprocity is of fundamental importance in the law of contracts and in the relationships between entities of federal states, as well as being a basis for respecting international law in domestic constitutions.

A study of reciprocity in public international law would miss out on some important insights into the nature of reciprocity if it were to limit the analysis exclusively to the field of international law. The analysis in this book will therefore begin with a wider background to the concept of reciprocity, which will give a deeper comprehension of its significance. This will highlight the importance of reciprocity as a concept that is fundamental to human behavior, intrinsic to the existence of law, and foundational to notions of fairness.

1.1 The Formation of Law and Society

Reciprocity has been the object of significant attention in philosophy, ethics, and sociology. There are many interesting questions that could be addressed here, but the analysis will focus on the characteristics of reciprocity that are most useful to the study of its role in international law: the relationship between reciprocity and community, reciprocity's relationship with justice, and its importance in the formation of legal rules.

1.1.1 *Philosophical Approaches to Reciprocity*

Some of the basic questions regarding the nature of reciprocity in philosophical thought mirror the issues we encounter in international law: Is reciprocity limited to bilateral and self-interested relationships, such as those that may arise from a contract? Or does it have a greater role to play in human community?[1]

It can be hard to imagine how the concept of reciprocity could be compatible with the idea of community if understood as "tit for tat," or returning cooperation or defection for like behavior. If we presuppose that in a community there exist absolute obligations owed by each member regardless of the conduct of the others, it seems completely incongruous to accept that each subject may modulate its conduct in response to the behavior of others. Intuitively, if "tit for tat" is the rule in social relations, other principles have presumably already fallen by the wayside; any idea of community would appear to have already broken down.

But this depends on our understanding of reciprocity. Hiskes, for example, is one author who argues that "tit for tat" is not the same as reciprocity but rather a pattern of behavior that diminishes reciprocity.[2] According to this point of view, reciprocity is a wider ethical principle that cannot be reduced to reactive responses to conduct. In any case, reciprocity operates in a distinctly intersubjective manner, regardless of its ethical significance or of whether it is operating between two individuals or in a community. I cannot reciprocate toward myself; I need another person, or a collective, with whom to enter into a relationship of reciprocity. Reciprocity by necessity implies social relations.

But in order to enter into such a relationship with another, a second requirement exists: I need to recognize that other subject as capable of being bestowed with rights and obligations, and of offering some kind of exchange. Even considering a simple exchange of goods between two persons, the effect of reciprocity is to create correlative rights and obligations for the two persons involved. A prerequisite for reciprocity is therefore mutual recognition between two or more subjects.[3]

[1] See, e.g., R. P. Hiskes, *The Human Right to a Green Future*, Cambridge, Cambridge University Press, 2009, pp. 50–51.

[2] Ibid., p. 52.

[3] On the function of justice as providing relationships of mutual recognition, see J. Robbins, "Recognition, Reciprocity and Justice," in M. Clarke and M. Goodale, eds., *Mirrors of Justice: Law and Power in the Post–Cold War Era*, Cambridge, Cambridge University Press, 2010, pp. 187–188.

If reciprocity is viewed as a relationship of exchange, I must recognize the other as a person with whom I can enter into a relationship that will fulfill the specific aim I am seeking. As Darmstädter explains, "the will is directed not only to the object, but also the fact that he is faced with another will, the will of someone who is willing to give."[4]

Recognizing the intersubjectivity of reciprocity is the first step toward establishing whether it can apply bilaterally or also within a community. Darmstädter explains that it is the very aspect of man as a member of society that both reciprocity and community have in common.[5] The difference between reciprocity and community lies in the fact that reciprocity requires a meeting of wills that are mutually exclusive and incompatible, which rely on each other as far as is advantageous until they reach their ends, and a community requires an agreement of wills, "tending to a collective aim": the "objectivisation of the common will."[6] Therefore, reciprocity requires opposing but complementary ends, and community a single commonly held end. However, this difference is no reason for reciprocity and community to be mutually exclusive.

Some have recognized reciprocity as a principle that is not only socially useful within a community but also lies at the very basis of community relations. These approaches define reciprocity as doing or returning good, or as "sharing and mutual concern between the members of a ... moral community."[7] In this view, the "moral community" in question is not based on a contract but rather based on "mutual esteem and concern, friendship, general affection, and concern for one's partner" that predates any contractual arrangements.[8] Indeed, in Plato's Myth of Protagoras, the god Zeus gives to mankind *aidôs* and *diké*, which may be translated as "respect" and "justice," and it is on this basis that reciprocity between men, and therefore human community and cities, can be founded.[9] Reciprocity requires the existence of moral and ethical principles among members of a society, that is, a preexisting social basis, to operate successfully. Rather than being a mode of interaction where no community exists, it is instead applicable within a community.

[4] F. Darmstädter, "La réciprocité et la communauté considérées comme catégories juridiques," *Archives de philosophie du droit et de sociologie juridique*, no. 1, 1935, p. 102. This description closely recalls the Hegelian explanation of recognition as a prerequisite not only for any form of social living but also for the concretization of the will itself; G. W. F. Hegel, *Phenomenology of Spirit*, Oxford, Oxford University Press, 1977, paras. 178–184.

[5] Darmstädter, "Réciprocité et la communauté considérées," p. 95.

[6] Ibid., pp. 95–96, 110. [7] Hiskes, *Human Right*, pp. 55–57. [8] Schumaker, in ibid.

[9] Plato, *Protagoras*, transl. B. Jowett, New York, Liberal Arts Press, 1956, pp. 19–20.

The two understandings of reciprocity, as a bilateral and fundamentally self-interested concept, or as a communitarian concept, can be seen in the ancient distinction, first made by Aristotle, between distributive and commutative justice: Distributive justice "has to do with the distribution of honour, wealth and other things that are divided among the members of the body politic," and commutative justice is the kind that "has to give redress in private transactions."[10] While commutative justice implies in essence a contractual, private law relation, distributive justice requires a community.[11] More specifically, distributive justice deals with distribution to each according to their needs and possibilities. It therefore implies a proportional relationship between the members of a community.[12] Reciprocity in distributive justice is therefore interdependence between the members of the community, rendering to each his due within the society.[13] There is an underlying recognition that the community exists first and foremost, that what one is due can only be determined by reference to the other members of the community. Rights and obligations are therefore owed between individuals and the community. Punishment of transgressors belongs to distributive justice; for Vattel, as well as for many others, upon entry into a social relation, the right to private punishment is relinquished to the collective.[14]

Commutative justice, however, is closer to the commonly held idea of reciprocity as a synallagmatic obligation. It is the relation of private justice, between particular persons, and has to do with the rights and obligations owed between them, in a relationship of strict equality where the obligation of each depends on fulfillment of the bargain by the other.[15] Instead of a preexisting community upon which the very existence of rights is based, it posits the absolute power and freedom of each individual, which can be limited only on the basis of an equivalent exchange.[16] Contract is therefore a fundamental tool to achieve any agreement between two subjects that enjoy complete freedom.[17] Commutative justice requires absolute equivalence and balance in

[10] Aristotle, *Nichomachean Ethics*, 3rd ed., London, Kegan Paul, 1886, p. 148.

[11] See R.-J. Dupuy, "Communauté internationale et disparités de développement: Cours general de droit international public," *Collected Courses of the Hague Academy of International Law*, vol. 165, 1979, p. 115.

[12] Aristotle, *Nichomachean Ethics*, p. 148; A. Papaux, *Introduction à la philosophie du "droit en situation,"* Geneva/Basel/Zurich, Schulthess, 2006, pp. 37, 55; Saint Thomas Aquinas, *Summa Theologica*, Chicago, Benton, 1952, p. 1926.

[13] Aquinas, *Summa Theologica*, p. 1911.

[14] E. Vattel, *The Law of Nations*, Indianapolis, Liberty Fund, 2008, Book 1, ch. XIII, para. 169.

[15] Papaux, *Introduction à la philosophie*, p. 55. [16] Ibid., p. 108. [17] Ibid., p. 109.

exchange. It is something given for something received, and includes retaliation, and concern for equal repayment of loss.[18]

The two different conceptions of reciprocity based on the two conceptions of justice both presuppose intersubjectivity and recognition. While they differ in considering whether reciprocity only applies in private relations, and whether it requires proportionality or strict equality, there do not emerge any compelling reasons to consider that reciprocity could be incompatible with the existence of a community.

1.1.2 *Reciprocity, Morality, and the Influence on Individual Conduct*

Reciprocity has also received extensive attention in psychological and economic studies. Psychological studies have shown that reciprocity has a deep influence on human conduct. This is due to its success in eliciting cooperative behavior in others (as shall be seen in game theory, with interesting ramifications for public international law) and its close links with what is considered to be fair and just. Reciprocity is the Golden Rule of ethics, instantly and universally recognizable as a moral norm. It is this particularity that makes it so important as a basis for society and the formation of law.

1.1.2.1 Reciprocity and Human Behavior

Reciprocity has proven to be a powerful psychological tool with significant influence on human behavior. In psychology, the norm of reciprocity has been defined thus: "You should give benefits to those who give you benefits" and "you should make concessions to those who make concessions to you."[19] It is interesting to note that reciprocity does not emerge as being as closely linked to selfish or self-interested behavior as one might intuitively expect. It has been noted that

> [r]eciprocity means that in response to friendly actions, people are frequently much nicer and much more cooperative than predicted by the self-interest model; conversely, in response to hostile actions they are frequently much more nasty and even brutal .... People repay gifts and take revenge even in interactions with complete strangers and even if it is costly for them and yields neither present nor future material rewards.[20]

[18] Aquinas, *Summa Theologica*, pp. 1936–1939.

[19] R. B. Cialdini et al., "Reciprocal Concessions Procedure for Inducing Compliance: The Door-in-the Face Technique," *Journal of Personality and Social Psychology*, vol. 31, no. 2, 1975, p. 207.

[20] E. Fehr and S. Gachter, "Fairness and Retaliation: The Economics of Reciprocity," *The Journal of Economic Perspectives*, vol. 14, no. 3, 2000, p. 159.

While reciprocity means contingent actions, and responding to how one is being treated, this is not the same as acting in a manner that is self-interested. Fehr and Gachter noted in a study that, when acting reciprocally, individuals actually go beyond what would be beneficial for them, using reciprocity to enforce social norms.[21] This raises the intriguing point that reciprocity's success in influencing behavior may not be explained so much by its appeal to personal advantage as by its role as a social tool. It is not merely a pattern of behavior that can reap a favorable outcome for social relations but is truly a social *obligation* – the "imbedded obligations created by exchanges of benefits or favors among individuals."[22] What we are looking at is a notion with normative value – only, in this context, socially rather than legally normative value.

The norm of reciprocity in social behavior can be extremely influential, to the point where methods based on reciprocity can induce compliance and cooperation in persons who had no previous intention to provide it.[23] It would seem that when a concession is made in their favor, humans feel obliged to respond with a concession of their own – to the point of two authors describing the behavior of their test subjects as resembling that of "automatons."[24] Even giving a gift can be seen as being a means of creating an obligation, or engaging in an exchange, rather than aiming to improve welfare while expecting nothing in return.[25]

The reasons why reciprocity is so incredibly effective at altering individual behavior seem to go beyond self-interest to something that has far more to do with social control and social norms. Reciprocity appears to resonate with individuals as a means of ensuring fairness, as strikingly illustrated in another experiment in which it was demonstrated that the

[21] "[T]he power to enhance collective actions and to enforce social norms is probably one of the most important consequences of reciprocity"; ibid., p. 160.

[22] Gouldner, cited in Y. Chen, X. Chen, and R. Portnoy, "To Whom Do Positive Norm and Negative Norm of Reciprocity Apply? Effects of Inequitable Offer, Relationship, and Relational Self-Orientation," *Journal of Experimental Social Psychology*, vol. 5, 2009, p. 24.

[23] In one experiment conducted by Cialdini et al., one group of students were asked to act as counselors for juvenile delinquents two hours a week for a period of two years; when they refused, they were then asked to chaperone juvenile delinquents on a single trip to the zoo. A second group of university students was directly asked to assist in the zoo trip. None of the students in the first group agreed to the large request, but 50 percent agreed to the smaller request. In contrast, of those only asked the smaller favor, only 16.7 percent agreed. Cialdini et al., "Reciprocal Concessions Procedure," pp. 208–209.

[24] Ibid., p. 214.

[25] R. Axelrod, *The Evolution of Cooperation*, New York, Basic Books, 1984, p. 135; Robbins, "Recognition, Reciprocity and Justice."

perceived fairness of an offer depended on how much the person making it had to sacrifice.[26] Put in Aristotelian terms, in the human mind, reciprocity involves a proportion, and not arithmetic equality. In social situations, one "tend[s] not to find the kinds of precise quid pro quos that are suggested by models of reciprocity as mutual gain or equal exchange."[27] The ideal of fairness implied by reciprocity is not a perfectly equal give-and-take between two individuals but one that takes into account other circumstances, notably those of the other person in the relationship.[28]

Indeed, it has been suggested that it is the very "imbalances" in the tally of obligations owed on either side that give reciprocity its stabilizing nature and propensity to forge long-term relationships. After all, it is "inexpedient to break off relationships with those who have outstanding obligations to you," and "morally improper to launch hostilities against those to whom you are still indebted."[29]

Reciprocity has also been extensively analyzed in economics, specifically in game theory. A competition for game theorists devised around 1980 by Robert Axelrod found that the most successful computer program at eliciting cooperation was tit for tat, namely "starting with cooperation and thereafter doing what the other player did on the previous move."[30] Reciprocity, or tit for tat, allowed both players to do well and, indeed, more so than any other strategy.[31] The simplistic context of a computer game with two participants may seem far removed from complex real-life situations, let alone from contemporary international law. However, it does raise some interesting points.

[26] For example, an offer benefiting the test subject more than the person offering was not deemed reasonable if it put the person making the offer in a relatively disadvantageous position: A. Falk and U. Fischbacher, "A Theory of Reciprocity," *Games and Economic Behavior*, vol. 54, 2006, p. 297. Similar results regarding "fairness" required of offers for test subjects to reciprocate is detailed in Fehr and Gachter, "Fairness and Retaliation," pp. 161–164.

[27] J. Woodward, "Cooperation and Reciprocity: Empirical Evidence and Normative Implications," in H. Kincaid, ed., *The Oxford Handbook of Philosophy of Social Science*, Oxford, Oxford University Press, 2012, p. 597. See also R. Ellickson, *Order without Law: How Neighbors Settle Disputes*, Cambridge, MA, Harvard University Press, 2005.

[28] This is an interesting point to bear in mind when considering subjects such as common but differentiated responsibility, or the special treatment given to least-developed nations. Reciprocity has also been explained as returning inequitable treatment, whether favorable or unfavorable. Chen et al., "To Whom Do Positive Norm and Negative Norm of Reciprocity Apply?," p. 25.

[29] A. W. Gouldner, "The Norm of Reciprocity: A Preliminary Statement," *American Sociological Review*, vol. 25, no. 2, April 1960, p. 173.

[30] Axelrod, *Evolution of Cooperation*, p. viii.

[31] Ibid., p. 112.

Reciprocity allows antagonists to cooperate in a mutually beneficial manner,[32] and indeed leads to repeat interactions that can generate trust.[33] Even if we consider individuals (or, for present purposes, States) as essentially selfish, having conflicting interests, and being hostile toward one another, reciprocity can work as a basis not only for cooperation but also for closer, stable social relations to thrive. In eliciting cooperation, reciprocity shows itself to be a principle of social self-regulation: It is the prospect of mutual rewards that ensures continued cooperation, rather than any additional threat in the case of defection.[34] But even without having to subscribe to the view that States are antagonist entities, it is useful to recognize that reciprocity plays a role in encouraging cooperation rather than defection.

One aspect of the results of Axelrod's experiment that is of particular interest for present purposes is that reciprocity works best in a "prisoner's dilemma" situation; that is, it manages to bind the strategies of players that cannot know exactly the intentions of their counterparts.[35] This makes the analysis particularly interesting for international law, where the lack of an overarching legislator or enforcement mechanism means that States must rely on each other's choices to conclude and fulfill agreements. In fact, it is this very characteristic of international law, of existing between independent entities that cannot control each other's conduct and would in most cases benefit if they could defect unilaterally, that has made it into a field of interest for game theory analyses.[36] Reciprocity can actually obviate the lack of foreseeability of the actions of other parties when it has legal effects. For example, a State may know that if it adopts a certain course of conduct – such as making a reservation to a treaty – the consequence is that the same will be invoked

[32] Ibid., p. 87.

[33] J. B. Silk, "Forum," in M. Tomasello, ed., *Why We Cooperate*, Cambridge, MA/London, MIT Press, 2009, p. 119. The tit-for-tat strategy also has ramifications in the real world; Tomasello also views children's adoption of reciprocity as a social norm at a certain stage of development as an example of the adoption of the tit-for-tat cooperation strategy; Tomasello, *Why We Cooperate*, p. 35.

[34] Axelrod, *Evolution of Cooperation*, p. 179. It has been posited that this form of self-regulation can only exist in the context of very simple social relations: R. Kolb, *Réflexions de philosophie du droit international: Problèmes fondamentaux du droit international public: théorie et philosophie du droit international*, Brussels, Bruylant, 2003, p. 310.

[35] Parisi and Ghei, "Role of Reciprocity in International Law," p. 2; A. Sykes, "When Is International Law Useful?," NYU Law and Economics Research Paper, no. 13-23, June 2013, http://lsr.nellco.org/nyu_lewp/348, p. 8.

[36] See, e.g., Parisi and Ghei, "Role of Reciprocity in International Law."

against it. Therefore, reciprocity can be used to simply remove the possibility of unilateral defection,[37] creating interdependence between obligations.

1.1.2.2 Reciprocity and Morality

Having seen the extent to which reciprocity can affect and influence human behavior, it is perhaps not surprising that reciprocity also has a moral value. The "Golden Rule," that of treating others as we ourselves would wish to be treated, is commonly referred to as a basic rule of ethics,[38] and is an embodiment of a commandment of reciprocity similar to that contained in the social norms mentioned above. But instead of being a socio-psychological rule to which we are all pushed to conform, it is posited as a rule of how we *ought* to behave. Interestingly, the operation of reciprocity as a moral or ethical precept differs to some extent from patterns of behavior that reward giving and punish defection. In Confucian thought, in which reciprocity is one of the basic precepts, it is posited that injury should be met with "justice," rather than vengeance. Grotius, in contrast, places the necessity to meet evil with evil among the natural laws.[39]

Some definitions describe reciprocity as the duty to return a kindness, and the duty or obligation to help others, and consequently help those who have helped you.[40] The structure of reciprocity in this case may be distinguished from what we might term legal reciprocity. As a social norm, reciprocity is explained as the right of A toward B, implying that A has a duty toward B, and the right of B toward A, implying that B also has a duty toward A. Reciprocity in the legal sense could best be described as the right of A toward B, implying that B has a correlative duty toward A, and vice versa.[41]

Reciprocity is not universally recognized to be sufficient as a rule of ethics, however. Kant argued against it as a universal principle, as it "does not contain the ground of duties toward oneself" and is not suffi-

[37] Ibid., pp. 22–23; F. Parisi, "The Cost of the Game: A Taxomony of Social Interactions," *European Journal of Law and Economics*, vol. 9, no. 2, 2000, p. 105.

[38] S. Liu, "The Principle of Reciprocity and Globalization of Law in Relation to the Golden Rule," *Persona y Derecho*, vol. 60, 2009, p. 20; L. T. Hobhouse, *Morals in Evolution: A Study in Comparative Ethics*, 5th ed., New York, Henry Holt & Co., 1925, p. 533.

[39] Hobhouse, *Morals in Evolution*, pp. 533–534; Hugo Grotius, *The Rights of War and Peace: Book 2*, ed. R. Tuck, Indianapolis, Liberty Fund, 2005, ch. XX, §1. For an overview, see S. Fard, *Reciprocity in International Law*, Abingdon, Routledge, 2016, ch. 1.2.1.

[40] Gouldner, "Norm of Reciprocity, pp. 161 (cit. Cicero), 173.

[41] Ibid., p. 168.

cient to ensure "duties of love toward others."[42] For Hobhouse, reciprocity "sets the standard," but includes no compulsion for individuals to give anything, which explains the need for legal obligations in a society.[43]

Reciprocity may very well not be sufficient to set a rule for one's internal moral compass. However, in applying to others the standards that we would like to see used toward ourselves, we are necessarily recognizing others as equals,[44] rather than as competitors to exploit to our own advantage.[45] Indeed, reciprocity creates equality between the members of the social group that, to quote Hart, "offset[s] the inequalities of nature."[46] This equality is one of the basic reasons why reciprocity is considered a fundamental element of justice.[47]

1.1.3 Reciprocity in Law Formation

Reciprocity also plays a crucial role in law formation. First, in binding individuals together in social relations, it casts the foundations for a legal system to be formed. Reciprocity creates interdependence in rights and duties, as well as between the subjects themselves. This places subjects in a situation in which their roles are interchangeable.[48] Furthermore, the fact that reciprocity requires prior recognition of the other as an equal adds normative force to the rules of conduct it prescribes. It has been observed that children recognize social rules expressed by other children on the basis of reciprocity as having binding force because they recognize their peers as equals.[49] A parallel may here be made with legal orders: In a similar way to children, the force of norms can come either from a higher authority or an equal; either from a state-like, centralized legal order, or from reciprocity, in a legal order whose subjects are equal to one another.

[42] I. Kant, *Groundwork for the Metaphysics of Morals*, transl. A. W. Wood, New Haven, CT/ London, Yale University Press, 2000, Ak 4:430.

[43] Hobhouse, *Morals in Evolution*, p. 16.

[44] Kolb, *Réflexions de philosophie du droit international*, p. 317.

[45] L. Martins Zanitelli, "A reciprocidade nos contratos: Uma analise expressivista," *Revista de direito privado*, no. 42, April–June 2010, p. 160.

[46] H. L. A. Hart, *The Concept of Law*, Oxford, Oxford University Press, 2012, p. 160.

[47] S. Jorgensen, "Individual Rights and Contract (Freedom and Reciprocity in Contract Law)," *Washington University Law Review*, vol. 65, no. 4, 1987, p. 730; Hugo Grotius, *The Rights of War and Peace: Book 1*, ed. R. Tuck, Indianapolis, Liberty Fund, 2005, ch. I, § III: "that which is *just* takes Place either among Equals, or amongst People whereof some are Governors and others governed, considered as such"; the same is indicated by Hume and Rawls, cit. in Hiskes, *Human Right*, pp. 6, 11.

[48] Tomasello, *Why We Cooperate*, pp. 58, 91–92.

[49] Ibid., pp. 35–36.

Second, reciprocity makes social interaction possible where rules have not yet been created: Making a concession or extending a benefit to another can create obligations relative to a specific object. Gouldner observes that it is the succession of exchanges of this type that gives rise to eventual long-term cooperation between individuals.[50] Such a long-term view of reciprocity reinforces its normative aspects and its role as a principle of social organization, by allowing for reciprocal action even when this is not advantageous in the short term.[51]

It has also been suggested that it is this mechanism that gives force to precedent, through which society thus transforms an isolated event into a "continuing relationship, an essentially bargaining relationship."[52] This is done through the mechanism of reversibility: The possibility that the same situation may be applicable to all members of the society at some point in the future stabilizes and gives predictability and force to their interactions. Reciprocity therefore allows interactions to spread into the future. It makes subjects themselves forward-looking; knowing that one precedent of conduct allows the same conduct in exchange, subjects must take into account the significance of their actions for the future. As Fisher points out, nowhere is this more evident than in international law, where the legal equality of States necessarily means that they can all claim the same rights.[53]

Third, the equality necessary for reciprocity to operate makes it antithetical to relations based purely on power. As such, reciprocity is used as an explanation for the formation of law and society in the theory of social contracts.[54] While contractualism is a fictional construct, it is conceptually interesting that reciprocity should be the justification for the construction of a State. It is almost as if the intrinsic quality of

[50] Gouldner, "Norm of Reciprocity," pp. 175–178.

[51] T. M. Franck and E. Weisband, "The Role of Reciprocity and Equivalence in Systemic Superpower Interaction," *New York University Journal of International Law and Politics*, vol. 3, 1970, pp. 267–269 .

[52] Ibid.

[53] Fisher, cit. in ibid. This point is demonstrated by the fact that one State cannot claim a right that another does not have. The operation of this is illustrated by the steps that led to the creation of the Exclusive Economic Zone in the Law of the Sea, and to a certain extent also by States' reactions to justifications for the use of force.

[54] Most notably in the theories of Hobbes and Rousseau; H. Hobbes, *Leviathan or the matter, forme and Power of a Commonwealth ecclesiasticall and Civil*, Oxford, Blackwell, 1957; J.-J. Rousseau, *The Social Contract; and the First and Second Discourses*, New Haven, CT/London, Yale University Press, 2002; Kolb, *Réflexions de philosophie du droit international*, p. 311; F. Ost , *Du Sinaï au Champ-de-Mars: L'autre et le même au fondement du droit*, Bruxelles, Lessius, 1999, examples at pp. 28, 59–61, 107.

fairness that reciprocity possesses is necessary to justify humankind living in a structure in which individuals are subjected to the decisions of a higher body. Reciprocity applies as a guarantee that the standards set out in the law will be applied to citizens if they respect the rules.[55]

Theoretically, then, there are good arguments for reciprocity to function as a means of law formation. However, "strict" reciprocity in punishment does not appear to occupy as extensive a place in the history of the development of legal systems as it might at first seem.[56] There are disagreements concerning the extent to which the talionic law, "an eye for an eye," was truly an institution in legal history. In his analysis, Diamond, analysing ancient laws, concluded that "there is never at any stage of law … a regular application of 'an eye for an eye.'" Through history, in any case, he notes that a shift occurs toward punishment of wrongdoers with the aim of deterrence, rather than punishment as private justice for the victim. Parisi in his analysis of liability in ancient law notes that the "eye for an eye" rule was not always the expression of talionic justice. Instead, the talion imposed a limit to the punishment that could be imposed, which, it is supposed, could otherwise be left to the discretion of the victim.[57] The limit imposed was however only quantitative, and only bore an indirect relationship to the harm suffered.[58] Rules requiring identity of punishment gradually gave way to those requiring some kind of equivalence between harm and compensation.[59] While the common explanation for why reciprocity belongs to primitive legal systems is the very existence of mechanisms of justice such as that incorporated in the Hammurabi Code, it appears instead that reciprocity in the consequences of the breach of a legal rule, understood as equivalence between a violation and the punishment meted out for it, appeared if anything at a later stage of development of the more ancient systems of punishment.

Reciprocity was undeniably a salient characteristic of what may be identified as the first international agreements, such as the Treaty of Kadesh in 1270 BC, concluded to put an end to the war between Egyptians and Hittites, based on mutual recognition and renunciation

[55] L. L. Fuller, *The Morality of Law*, rev. ed., Delhi, Universal Law, 2009, p. 39 (cit. Simmel).

[56] A. S. Diamond, *Primitive Law Past and Present*, London, Methuen & Co., 1971, pp. 85, 98, 339–340; Parisi notes such a shift to centralization of punishment away from self-help occurring in Roman law: F. Parisi, "The Genesis of Liability in Ancient Law," *American Law and Economics Review*, vol. 3, no. 1, 2001, pp. 120–121.

[57] Parisi, "Genesis of Liability in Ancient Law," p. 83.

[58] Ibid., pp. 86–88.

[59] Ibid., p. 118.

of invasion, and on strictly synallagmatic obligations.[60] In his analysis, Pierre-Marie Dupuy insists that decentralisation is a structural characteristic both of the particular system of the Treaty of Kadesh, and international law in general,[61] a point that is undoubtedly true.

However, it is not because reciprocity was at the basis of the system established by the Treaty of Kadesh that it is a characteristic of primitive legal systems. Contracts are still used today in all areas of private law, but it seems counterintuitive to write off all areas of law based on contractual arrangements as "primitive" merely because contract is one of the most ancient forms of legal obligation. The Treaty of Kadesh by itself set up a legal system, based on reciprocity of rights and duties; but this cannot be compared to the scope and complexity of international legal rules that exist today, and similarities cannot be drawn merely by virtue of the fact that in both systems reciprocity plays an important role. The more logical conclusion is that reciprocity is important in a legal system that can be described as *decentralised*, rather than *primitive*. The distinction between "primitive" and somehow more "evolved" legal systems is simply not helpful when we look at international law.

A similar agreement including mutual renunciations, and therefore based on reciprocity, was concluded in 813 between Charlemagne and the Byzantine emperor Nicephorus I. The treaty put an end to a war that had begun in 805 after the imperial crown was presented to Charlemagne. The treaty contained a renunciation by Charlemagne to his claims over the Venetian and Dalmatian regions, and a renunciation by the Byzantine emperors to recognition of the Carolingian empire, and agreement by the sovereigns to consider themselves as equals.[62] No such agreements were concluded between the Roman Empire and "barbarian" tribes, but bilateral agreements that did bear the hallmarks of equality and reciprocity were concluded by the Romans with other empires around the Mediterranean.[63] The key to reciprocity's presence

[60] See P.-M. Dupuy, "L'unité de l'ordre juridique international: Cours général de droit international public," *Collected Courses of the Hague Academy of International Law*, vol. 297, 2000, pp. 81–82.

[61] Ibid., pp. 96 ("On peut donc dire que loin d'être un obstacle à la creation et au développement du droit international, la souveraineté constitue, du fait de son égale diffusion entre les États, la cause première de ce droit") and 137.

[62] R. Ago, "Pluralism and the Origins of the International Community," *Italian Yearbook of International Law*, 1977, vol. 3, pp. 11–12.

[63] R. Ago, "The First International Communities in the Mediterranean World," *British Yearbook of International Law*, 1982, vol. 53, pp. 231–232.

in the formation of law, and the history of the world's legal systems, therefore seems to lie in the equality of its subjects.

1.2 The Contractual Aspect of Reciprocity

Perhaps the most significant role played by reciprocity is in the field of contracts. This arises directly from reciprocity's role in creating obligations. In fact, in the Roman law of obligations, which systematized the different legal relationships that could exist in Roman society, we find not only structures of obligation based on reciprocity, or reciprocal in nature, but also many features that allow parallels to be drawn with international law. This section will analyze whether the role played by reciprocity is specific to the Roman law of obligations by looking at the law of contracts throughout history and in different legal systems. The question will then be addressed of how far it is possible to draw parallels between the law of contracts and public international law.

1.2.1 Reciprocity in the Roman Law of Obligations

The Roman law of obligations concerned the duties arising between parties, which bound (*ligare*) one party to a performance of some kind, and exposed them to liability in the case of a failure to fulfill such a duty.[64] Obligations could arise out of delict or contract.[65] An obligation was considered to be a tie: in fact, the execution of obligations in Roman law was termed *solutio, liberatio*: dissolving, freeing.[66] It would be far beyond the purview of this book to explain the different classes of obligation existing in Roman law.[67] However, there are many aspects of this field of Roman law that cannot be overlooked in conducting an analysis of reciprocity.

Reciprocity is most readily recognizable in "innominate" contracts of Roman law, in which one party was bound to perform something in return for a counterperformance.[68] These contracts were not restricted to exchanges of goods, but could concern performance of any kind (*dare*,

[64] R. Zimmermann, *The Law of Obligations: Roman Foundations of the Civilian Tradition*, Oxford, Clarendon, 1996, pp. 5, 7.

[65] P. Bonfante, *Corso di diritto romano, vol. 4: Le obbligazioni*, Milano, Giuffrè, 1979, p. 10.

[66] E. Betti, *La struttura dell'obbligazione romana e il problema della sua genesi*, Milano, Giuffrè, 1985, p. 32.

[67] See in general Bonfante, *Corso di diritto romano*, and Grotius, *Rights of War and Peace: Book 2*, Ch. XII, § II, III.

[68] Bonfante, *Corso di diritto romano*, p. 279. In fact, the most often cited representation of reciprocity is that of *do ut des*.

facere, praestare), and could be enforced once the initial performance had been rendered.[69] Herein lay the synallagma: duties were reciprocal, and conditioned upon one another. If one party did not carry out its side of the agreement, the other was not held to carry out its own: the *exceptio non adimpleti contractus*.[70] These agreements made both parties simultaneously debtors and creditors, that is, they gave each party at the same time both a right to expect a counterperformance, and an obligation to perform. The obligations were therefore mutual.[71] This type of Roman obligation is therefore used to exemplify a reciprocal obligation, where not only are the rights and duties of the parties interdependent but their performance depends on fulfillment of contractual duties by the counterparty.

But reciprocity in the Roman law of obligations should not be considered merely as a specific category in a wider social reality. Perhaps it is the extensive categorization of all transactions in Roman law, which considered the entirety of social relations to be exhausted in the concept of obligation, that has led some authors to consider social life in Roman times as nothing other than a series of reciprocal obligations.[72] Obligations could not be divorced from social reality but were instead its vital principle. Obligations were also actions *in personam*, concerning relationships between persons.[73] An obligation was a tie to another person; something that brought two parties closer. Although imposing a duty upon one or more parties to perform a specific act, it was not equivalent to completely subjecting one person to the aims of another, in what would have been a relationship of servitude.[74] Only free citizens, that is, equals, could enter into obligations. Although the obligation concerned an imposition of a given performance upon a person, its essentially temporary nature preserved the equality of the parties.[75]

Reciprocal contracts such as innominate contracts in Roman law were clearly bilateral. However, there were other classes of contract that, although not synallagmatic, gave rise to some reciprocal rights and obligations. Bilateral imperfect contracts, for example, imposed performance

69 Zimmermann, *Law of Obligations*, p. 534; Bonfante, *Corso di diritto romano*, p. 457.

70 Bonfante, *Corso di diritto romano*, p. 285.

71 B. Schmidlin and C. A. Cannata, *Droit privé romain 2: Obligations, successions, procédure*, 2e éd. revue et corrigée, Lausanne, Payot, 1991, pp. 30, 119.

72 Perozzi, in Bonfante, *Corso di diritto romano*, p. 23.

73 Bonfante, *Corso di diritto romano*, pp. 10, 15; Schmidlin and Cannata, *Droit privé romain 2*, p. 11.

74 Bonfante, *Corso di diritto romano*, pp. 21–22.

75 Betti, *Struttura dell'obbligazione romana*, pp. 53–55.

upon one of the parties but not necessarily upon the other. However, it is interesting to note that the party not bearing a duty in the relationship could rely upon the same action in exacting what it was due, such as payment.[76] Further, Constantine classified donations, too, as bilateral acts immediately executed.[77] It seems that the relational nature of the obligation in question – its taking place among two persons – was sufficient, in some situations at least, to give rise to a reciprocal right even when duties were imposed asymmetrically, that is, principally upon one party.

1.2.2 *The Law of Contracts*

Eventually the Roman Empire fell, but its legal system lived on, forming a basis for most of the legal systems in modern-day Europe and, with the extension of the modern nation-state, colonialism, and legal transplantation, much of the rest of the world. Reciprocity in the law of obligations, too, lived on by other names. This is most notable in the area of contract law, to which we will now turn. But it would be wrong to analyze reciprocity in this context merely as a remainder of a Romanic heritage. Instead, it is suggested that reciprocity in contract law is of particular importance due to certain structural characteristics of contractual obligations.

The importance of reciprocity in contracts may be exemplified by what has been termed the "functional basis of contract in its wider sense": an exchange of some sort between individuals,[78] a meeting of wills, an agreement containing a promise to do something in exchange for something else.[79]

Reciprocity is at the basis of all contracts for which there is some form of exchange or counterperformance – that is, unless the contract is one of donation, where the undertaking or promise is made unilaterally and not upon any condition or performance given in exchange. The question of the relationship between unilateral acts and reciprocity is one that will arise repeatedly; for the moment, it will suffice to note that within a single, specific instrument that only confers rights, and does not establish corresponding obligations, it is difficult to establish how reciprocity (defined as interdependence of mutually exchanged rights and obligations) may exist. Contracts of donation aside, it is difficult to envision a

[76] Schmidlin and Cannata, *Droit privé romain* 2, p. 119.
[77] Zimmermann, *Law of Obligations*, p. 492.
[78] Jorgensen, "Individual Rights and Contract," p. 723.
[79] L. Fin-Langer, *L'équilibre contractuel*, Paris, LGDJ, 2002, p. 20.

contract in which an exchange of any sort takes place without reciprocity; reciprocity is the main motor of the contract, its raison d'être or functional basis.[80]

One of the main misconceptions relating to reciprocity is that it means two parties carrying out exactly the same thing in relation to one another: what Niboyet classifies as reciprocity *trait pour trait*, which establishes a rigorous balance of performance.[81] There may indeed be contracts that require such a form of exchange. But terming this strict exchange "reciprocity" would seem to mistake the manifestation for the cause. Reciprocity is in the exchange of promises of performance, and the resulting set of interdependent rights and obligations. The content and structure of the exchange may vary. But in general, in terms of the exchange contained within the contract, the commonly held view is that it should be more or less equivalent or balanced.

This basic view of the fundamental importance of reciprocity in contract law is reflected in contemporary contract law, and not only that of the Roman tradition. For example, in the law of contracts in common law, this is contained in the concept of "consideration," which must be the counterpart of performance in a contract,[82] and is what makes the contract enforceable.[83] The classic definition of consideration in the common law in *Currie* v. *Misa* is that "a valuable consideration, in the sense of the law, may consist either in some right, interest, profit or benefit accruing to the one party, or some forbearance, detriment, loss or responsibility given, suffered or undertaken by the other."[84] However, while *something* needs to be exchanged in order for a contract to be enforceable under the common law, what is exchanged must be sufficient but need not be of equal, equivalent, or adequate value.[85] Therefore, reciprocity, even in the classic example of contracts, need not mean strict equivalence between what the parties have promised.

80 J.-P. Niboyet, "La notion de réciprocité dans les traités diplomatiques de droit international privé," *Collected Courses of the Hague Academy of International Law*, vol. 52, 1935, pp. 264–266; P. Lagarde, "La réciprocité en droit international privé," *Collected Courses of the Hague Academy of International Law*, vol. 154, 1977, p. 189.

81 Niboyet, "Notion de réciprocité," p. 310.

82 Jorgensen, "Individual Rights and Contract," p. 724.

83 M. Eisenberg, *Foundational Principles of Contract Law*, Oxford, Oxford University Press, 2018, p. 29.

84 *Currie* v. *Misa* (1875) LR 10 Ex 153; E. McKendrick, *Contract Law*, 13th ed., London, Macmillan, 2019, p. 74.

85 McKendrick, *Contract Law*, p. 76; Eisenberg, *Foundational Principles of Contract Law*, p. 48; see the example in *Lindner* v. *Mid-Continent Petroleum*, 252 SW2d 631 Ark. 1952.

While the need for consideration is what makes a contract enforceable, the source of the obligation in a contract is the promise made by the parties.[86] There is a difference, however, between common and civil law systems as to what exactly creates that obligation. In the common law, it is the promise of performance; in civil law systems, rather than the performance, it is the promise of a certain behaviour.[87]

Similarly to natural law theories, and dissimilarly to Roman law, Islamic law does not require agreements to fit into any specific categories to be valid. It does, however, recognise the *exceptio non adimpleti contractus* for synallagmatic contracts, as well as the maxims that "injury may not be met by injury" and that "an injury cannot be removed by the commission of a similar injury."[88] It therefore seems justified to say that the relevance of reciprocity in contract law is not a vestige that is limited to legal systems of Romanic extraction.

Some questions arise here as to what conditions are required for reciprocity to exist. Notably, questions arise as to its bilateral nature. If reciprocity is a necessary element in a contract, it must follow that it should be between two persons who promise each other something. In natural law thinking this was not necessary, as the fact of the promise itself was enough to make such agreements obligatory.[89] The specific promise existed within a framework that gave it force: natural law rules of honesty. Similarly, in ancient Greece, oaths were made before gods, who were also "depositaries" of agreements entered into by human persons. Any breach would be sanctioned by the gods – effectively, a third party. The obligations in question appeared to be triangular in nature, rather than only bilateral, with the contract or agreement being embedded within an obligation undertaken toward a higher entity, without making a difference as to the unilateral, bilateral, or other

[86] McKendrick, *Contract Law*, p. 3. In the *Hannah Blumenthal [1983] 1 All ER 34,3* Lord Diplock stated that "to create a contract by exchange of promises between two parties . . . what is necessary is that the intention of each as it has been communicated to and understood by the other."

[87] J. W. Carter, *Carter's Breach of Contract*, 2nd Hart ed., London, Hart, 2018, section 2-13; J. Basedow, "Towards a Universal Doctrine of Breach of Contract: The Impact of the CISG," *International Review of Law and Economics*, vol. 25, 2005, pp. 487–500, at p. 496.

[88] See S. Habachy, "Property, Right, and Contract in Muslim Law," *Columbia Law Review*, vol. 6, no. 3, March 1962, pp. 450–473, especially pp. 451, 465.

[89] R. Lesaffer, "The Medieval Canon Law of Contract and Early Modern Treaty Law," *Journal of the History of International Law*, vol. 2, 2000, pp. 183, 187; Jorgensen, "Individual Rights and Contract," p. 731.

nature of the contract.[90] Contracts have not therefore always been limited to two parties.

In the case of a promise whose enforcers are the gods, however, any undertaking is by necessity unilateral. Instead, in Roman obligations or modern contract or treaty law, particularly for those categories of contract that are called synallagmatic, it is the exchange of performance between the parties that gives rise to the binding force of the agreement. This explains the possibility of not carrying out one's side of the bargain where there has been no performance by the other party, including in the case of contracts with dependent obligations – where the obligation of performance by one party is not dependent on performance by the other – where there is a possibility for the party not in breach to abandon performance of its obligations in response.[91]

The possibility of withholding performance in response to nonperformance is explained differently in different legal systems, and is dictated by the type of obligations at issue,[92] and requires specific conditions to be fulfilled. One of these is the requirement of sufficient seriousness of the breach. French case law has explained this requirement by way of the concept of good faith; the condition that nonperformance be "serious" ensures that there is no disproportionate application of the exception, as well as ensuring that the provision does not open the possibility of using nonperformance of "a relatively secondary obligation in order to escape from a fundamental obligation."[93] The same test applies in German law.[94] The recourse to the notion of good faith shows how, even in the case of a synallagmatic contract, where reciprocity could be understood in its strictest sense, while there must be dependence between the obligations of both parties, and an equivalence of importance between the obligations that are not being performed, it is not necessary to have strict equality or equivalence in terms of the obligations themselves.

While the exception of nonperformance is most usually associated with civil law systems, the right of withholding performance also exists

[90] E. Wyler and A. Papaux, "Le mythe structurant de l'humanité: La communauté international vivante," in D. Alland et al., eds., *Unité et diversité du droit international: Écrits en l'honneur du Professeur Pierre-Marie Dupuy*, Leiden, Nijhoff, 2014, p. 187.

[91] McKendrick, *Contract Law*, p. 366; Carter, *Carter's Breach of Contract*, section 1-08.

[92] Specifically, it is available for synallagmatic contracts: H. Beale, B. Favarque-Cosson, J. Rutgers, and S. Vogenauer, *Cases, Materials and Text on Contract Law*, 3rd ed., Oxford, Hart, 2019, eBook locations 1174, 1192.

[93] Ibid.

[94] Bürgerliches Gesetzbuch [BGB] [Civil Code], § 320, www.gesetze-im-internet.de/englisch_bgb/index .html (Ger.); see Beale et al., *Cases, Materials and Text*, eBook location 1181.

in English law. Similarly to the case of civil law systems, the possibility is explained by reference to conditional obligations.[95] The nonperformance need also not even be total in order to give rise to the right to withhold performance, as long as the breach is significant and of an essential obligation.[96]

The consequences of a breach of contract, that is, failure to perform a contract without a lawful excuse,[97] are also particularly illustrative of the continued relevance of reciprocity in the law of contracts. While a breach of contract can have a number of consequences, including the possibility for the innocent party to claim damages, or the impossibility for the party who is in breach to sue to enforce the obligations of the innocent party under the contract,[98] of particular interest for present purposes is the case of termination. This is not exactly the same thing as the exception of nonperformance; a party to a contract may refuse to perform its obligations in the face of a breach, but this is not the same as terminating the contract, particularly as, in the first case, the original breach may be at least to some extent "cured" by a resumption of performance.

In modern contract law, it is generally possible to terminate a contract following a breach, within certain limits.[99] Different legal systems take different views as to the nature of termination,[100] admit different possibilities such as anticipatory breach, or place different requirements on termination. In general, however, some similar characteristics apply.

The first is that termination is a right, or an option, of the innocent party, rather than an automatic effect of a breach; there is no require-

[95] "The promise to complete the work is construed as a term of the contract, but not as a condition. It is not every breach of that term which absolves the employer from his promise to pay the price, but only a breach which goes to the root of the contract," *Hoenig* v. *Isaacs* [1952] EWCA Civ 6. In *Kingston* v. *Preston*, Lord Mansfield made reference to "mutual conditions to be performed at the same time": *Kingston* v. *Preston* [1773] 2 Doug KB 689.

[96] Beale et al., *Cases, Materials and Text*, eBook locations 1176, 1180.

[97] McKendrick, *Contract Law*, p. 364; P. M. Furmston, "Breach of Contract," *The American Journal of International Law*, vol. 40, no. 3, Summer 1992, pp. 671–674, at 671.

[98] See i.e. McKendrick, *Contract Law*, p. 365.

[99] H. N. Schelhaas, "A *lex mercatoria* for Remedies of Breach of Contract?," in A. Hutchison and F. Myburgh, eds., *Research Handbook on International Commercial Contracts*, Cheltenham, Elgar, 2020, pp. 57–85, at 70.

[100] For example, in French law, termination is considered a sanction for nonperformance; see Beale et al., *Cases, Materials and Text*, eBook location 1201; McKendrick, *Contract Law*, p. 371.

ment to terminate a contract in this situation.[101] If the innocent party chooses to affirm the contract, then the contract remains in force and both parties will be bound to continue performance.[102] This possibility of renouncing a right to terminate the contract exists both in common and civil law.[103]

A second point of commonality is the nature of the breach that can give rise to termination. In all systems, a breach must be sufficiently serious. In English law, for example, termination is only available for terms that are "conditions" of the contract, or for sufficiently serious breaches of terms known as "innominate." A condition is an essential term, one which goes to the root of the contract.[104] In the case of a breach of a condition, the innocent party has the option to terminate the contract and claim damages or, if it so chooses, to affirm the contract.[105] In the case of the breach of an innominate term, the situation is slightly more complicated. In this case, the innocent party has a right to terminate the contract only when the breach of the term has had sufficiently serious consequences for it.[106]

In the civil law, while there is no distinction made between categories of contractual term, the same principle of a right to terminate in the case of fundamental breach still operates.[107] In fact, the requirement for a breach to be fundamental is also reflected in the International Institute for the Unification of Private Law (UNIDROIT) Principles of International

[101] See *Photo Production Ltd* v. *Securicor Transport Ltd* [1980] AC 827; McKendrick, *Contract Law*, 365; Schelhaas, "*Lex mercatoria* for Remedies of Breach," p. 71.

[102] McKendrick, *Contract Law*, p. 370, although as noted in *Safehaven* v. *Springbok* [1998] 71 P & CR, continued repudiatory conduct after the first breach may be treated as a fresh act of nonperformance, giving right to a further right to terminate.

[103] See Beale et al., *Cases, Materials and Text*, section 25.10.A, eBook location 1279.

[104] McKendrick, *Contract Law*, p. 194; Schelhaas, "*Lex mercatoria* for Remedies of Breach," p. 71; Beale et al., *Cases, Materials and Text*, section 25.3.C, eBook location 1212. The test was set out by Diplock LJ in *Hong Kong Firs* (at 64):

> The test whether an event has this effect or not has been stated in a number of metaphors all of which I think amount to the same thing: does the occurrence of the event deprive the party who has further undertakings still to perform of substantially the whole benefit which it was the intention of the parties as expressed in the contract that he should obtain as the consideration for performing those undertakings?
>
> (*Hong Kong Fir Shipping Co Ltd* v. *Kawasaki Kisen Kaisha Ltd* [1962] 2 QB 26.)

[105] McKendrick, *Contract Law*, p. 194; Carter, *Carter's Breach of Contract*, section 1-20; see also Lord Diplock in *Photo Production* v. *Securicor Ltd.*(at 7).

[106] See Diplock LJ in *Hong Kong Fir*, at 70; McKendrick, *Contract Law*, pp. 201–202.

[107] Schelhaas, "*Lex mercatoria* for Remedies of Breach," p. 71.

Commercial Contracts (UPICC) at Article 7.3.[108] Of course, some differences between legal systems remain, with German law in particular having a less demanding test for the seriousness of a breach than other systems. In French law, where the possibility of unilateral termination of a contract in case of a "sufficiently serious" breach was admitted in the 2016 reform of French contract law, the decision to terminate also remains subject to judicial review, with the possibility remaining for a court to determine whether termination was well founded.[109]

The possibility of termination, like the exception of nonperformance. which will be addressed below, shows how reciprocity of rights and obligations is inherent in contracts, and the importance of mutuality and interdependence of obligations within them. For present purposes, the consequences of a breach of contract in domestic law are particularly interesting because they also reflect to a large extent the provisions in the VCLT. The consequences of a breach of international law, and the exception of nonperformance, will both be analyzed further in Chapter 5. In the meantime, it may be noted that, similarly to domestic systems, in VCLT Article 60.1, a "material" breach of a bilateral treaty gives rise to a right for the other party to invoke the breach as a ground for termination or suspension of the treaty. Again, similarly to "fundamental breach" in domestic systems, a "material breach" is defined as either a repudiation of a treaty in Article 60.3 (a), or "the violation of a provision essential to the accomplishment of the object or purpose of the treaty," in Article 60.3 (b). Similarly to domestic legal systems, a breach must have a sufficient degree of "seriousness," or impact the root of the agreement itself, in order to give rise to a right of termination. However, unlike the operation of termination in contract law, a material breach under the Convention does not give rise to a right for the other party to pronounce that the treaty is terminated. As the Commentary to the Articles makes clear, the wording "invoke as a ground" indicates that if a party to a treaty considers that there has been a material breach, it is instead required to settle the dispute peacefully.[110]

[108] UNIDROIT Principles of International Commercial Contracts (UPICC) 2016, Article 7.3. For an overview, see Schelhaas, "*Lex mercatoria* for Remedies of Breach," p. 79.

[109] Ordonnance n° 2016-131 du 10 février 2016 portant réforme du droit des contrats, du régime général et de la preuve des obligations, Article 1224; Beale et al., *Cases, Materials and Text*, eBook location 1206; on German law, see ibid., section 25.4.C, eBook location 1225.

[110] ILC, Draft Articles on the Law of Treaties, with Commentaries, *Yearbook of the International Law Commission*, vol. II, 1966, pp. 254–255.

The similarities between domestic contract law and international law are not limited to the consequences of a material breach of agreements. In relations of private law, as in international law, parties are in a relationship of equality to one another. Reciprocity allows this equality to be reflected in their undertakings, which is why it also requires some element of balance. This is not to say that whatever is exchanged within an agreement must be exactly equivalent or identical. However, the idea of balance of undertakings is pervasive; the equality of parties in contracts has been deemed a requirement of natural law.[111] This is also why unconscionability makes a contract unenforceable; accepting otherwise would be tantamount to accepting that the parties to a contract are in a situation of inequality, or placed therein by the contract – which is perhaps even worse. The balance in question should be general, concerning the overall "economy" of the contract. This may be either a proportion, or direct equivalence.[112]

If reciprocity is a mechanism used to ensure balance and reflect the legal equality of contractants, what then will be the role for reciprocity in a situation in which there is no equality between the parties to a contract? An interesting example is that of administrative contracts, that is, contracts between a private person and a public body.[113] In most legal systems, the public power that is a party to the contract has the power to unilaterally modify the contract, which may not be suspended by reason of nonexecution.[114] These unilateral prerogatives are justified by the fact that the public power is protecting the public interest and is in a situation of inequality with respect to the other party to the obligation.[115] This is clearly contrary to "the principle of equality of the parties" in contracts, where the parties do not have the capacity to unilaterally modify their undertakings.[116]

111 Grotius, *Rights of War and Peace: Book 2*, Ch. 12, § VIII.

112 Fin-Langer, *Équilibre contractuel*, pp. 160–161, 217–219, 224.

113 Distinctions regarding this sort of agreement are already present in the writings of Grotius: Grotius, *Rights of War and Peace: Book 2*, Ch. 14, §§VI–IX.

114 R. Chapus, *Droit administratif général*, 9e éd., Paris, Montchrestien, 1995, p. 424; J. Waline, *Droit administratif*, 23e éd., Paris, Précis Dalloz, 2010, p. 448.

115 G. Langrod, "Administrative Contracts: A Comparative Analysis," *The American Journal of Comparative Law*, vol. 4, no. 3, 1955, p. 330; Fin-Langer, *Équilibre contractuel*, pp. 6–7; J. Chevallier, "L'obligation en droit public," *Archives de philosophie du droit*, vol. 44, 2000, pp. 181–183. Chevallier goes on to indicate that this is true not only of administrative contracts but also any form of obligation between individuals and the State, by reason of the principle of sovereignty.

116 Not only, but in interpreting administrative contracts, it is not the will of both parties, but rather the statutory will that is taken into consideration: Langrod, "Administrative Contracts," p. 331; Waline, *Droit administratif*, p. 435.

A notable exception is Islamic law, in which even public bodies are on a footing of equality with private contractants and have no exorbitant powers.[117] Otherwise, despite differences in approach and characterization in the various legal systems,[118] the inequality between contracting parties and the need to protect public interests mean that these types of agreement depart from some of the basic principles normally applicable in contract law. Some examples of the actions that the administration may take in the public interest in French law include placing the private party under the authority of the public person; allowing the administration to act unilaterally in modifying the terms of the contract; or even unilaterally terminating it.[119] These actions are of the kind that may completely upset the original exchange that gave rise to the contract.[120]

However, this is not to say that the administration is completely unfettered in its actions. In French law, the private party will have the right to indemnification in the case of a unilateral termination, as well as in the case where a unilateral modification of a contract by the public authority makes their contractual obligations more onerous.[121] There is therefore a right to reestablish a balance by way of compensation. However, while the contractual form still sets out a reciprocal exchange of rights and obligations, which are interdependent, the exorbitant unilateral powers essentially give a unilateral right to one of the parties to the agreement, which is incompatible with reciprocity of rights and obligations. Recovering financial outlays cannot change the fact that there is a fundamental inequality in legal position and prerogatives of both parties, which makes any real reciprocity in this type of contract impossible. The very possibility that the public administration may make use of these powers automatically upsets the balance of the agreement. The working of contracts between a private individual and a public authority therefore more closely resembles that of unilateral norms, which rather than setting out rights and obligations, attribute powers to a subject.[122]

117 Habachy, "Property, Right, and Contract," pp. 460–465.

118 See notably the doubts as to the legal character of such acts in Germanic legal systems: Langrod, "Administrative Contracts," p. 355.

119 Chapus, *Droit administratif général*, pp. 492, 1960; Waline, *Droit administratif*, p. 447.

120 However, even this original exchange is often imposed unilaterally by the administration: Waline, *Droit administratif*, p. 445.

121 Chapus, *Droit administratif général*, pp. 160, 1065.

122 E. Cannizzaro, *Il principio della proporzionalità nell'ordinamento internazionale*, Milano, Giuffrè, 2000, p. 29.

The Germanic approach, which classifies all administrative acts as unilateral in nature, therefore makes sense. Private individuals cannot act in the same way with the State as the State acts with them; they do not have the right to the prerogatives of public bodies in their dealings with others. Their positions in this regard are not reversible, and they cannot enter into a truly reciprocal exchange with State bodies, although this does not remove the obligation of public bodies to also observe the law.[123]

1.2.3 *Parallels with International Law*

Historically, the synallagmatic form of contract was used as a working principle for the very first treaty generally considered susceptible of being called such, that is, the Treaty of Kadesh. As seen above, there are also parallels in the possibility of terminating agreements in both legal systems following a material or fundamental breach. Questions still remain, however, as to the appropriateness of the analogy between contract law and public international law. Considering reciprocity to only be applicable in synallagmatic agreements leads to the conclusion that it is only relevant in treaties that impose bilateral obligations on parties (that is, either treaties that are bilateral or multilateral treaties whose obligations are bilateralisable). In other words, following the distinction often made between contractual treaties and normative treaties (*traités-contrat* and *traités-loi*), this approach can lead to rejecting reciprocity as being inapplicable for treaties that are "normative." However, the contractual/normative distinction between treaties is of dubious utility; most treaties will contain a mix of obligations that are both "normative" and strictly "contractual".[124] It seems difficult to therefore divide treaties into those that operate reciprocally, and those that do not, merely based on this distinction.

Other divisions are however proposed regarding the various types of obligation existing at the international level – indeed, in any legal order. One such distinction is that made in the Germanic tradition (also relevant in the field of administrative law) between *Vertrag* and *Vereinbarung*. The former are what we may call typical contracts, between two persons

[123] Chevallier, "Obligation en droit public," pp. 182–183.

[124] This point was put forward in the Oral Statements of both the UN Secretary-General and Israel in the *Reservations to the Convention on the Protection and Punishment of Genocide* Advisory Opinion before the ICJ. *ICJ Pleadings, Reservations to the Convention on the Prevention and Punishment of the Crime of Genocide, Advisory Opinion*, Part II (1951), pp. 315–316, 334–339.

with opposing interests, but whose aims intersect with each other at a point in which they will agree to an exchange, for each to fulfill their own specific aim; this is a manner to satisfy different, opposing but corresponding aims.[125] Triepel further explains that *Vertrag* can only ever be bilateral,[126] and cannot be a means to create law.[127]

A *Vereinbarung*, instead, does not result from the meeting of opposing wills but is instead a fusion of wills having a common content, tending toward a common aim. When parties want different things from each other, they will enter into a contract; when they all want the same thing, they will enter into a *Vereinbarung*,[128] which creates an obligation for the parties to carry out an act that is similar or common for all. There may be an unlimited number of parties in a *Vereinbarung*, as no specific exchange takes place, but rather a collective undertaking.[129]

For Triepel, a *Vereinbarung* is the only means by which international law may be created.[130] Consequently, because a *Vereinbarung*, which is in any case a form of contractual agreement, can only bind the members who created it, no rule of international law created in such a way can apply outside the circle of the States that agreed to it.[131] According to this view, there is therefore no general international law susceptible of binding all States that have not participated in creating it.[132] There are also important consequences for the unilateral acts of States: because a *Vereinbarung* was created by a common will, it is not possible to unilaterally declare it to be terminated; only another similar agreement can replace the original one.[133]

While this distinction seems to capture the difference between what may be termed synallagmatic treaties and "true" (that is, non-bilateralisable) multilateral treaties, the explanation provided is not entirely satisfying. Much in the same way that a contract is inscribed within a legal system that gives it force and sets out the consequences of its breach, treaties also derive their force from underlying general rules of international law.[134] Indeed, it would not seem that a *Vereinbarung* can

[125] H. Triepel, *Droit international et droit interne*, Paris, Editions Panthéon-Assas, 2010, p. 43. Triepel explains these agreements as "des declarations de contenu opposé mais visant un même but extérieur," p. 44. This would seem to indicate commonality of aim, and therefore differentiate *Vertrag* from *Vereinbarung* merely on the basis of the content of the expressed will. However, a situation might be envisaged in which two parties express two opposing wills in a contract, to achieve two separate aims: for example, in an insurance contract.

[126] Ibid., p. 57. [127] Ibid., p. 68. [128] Ibid., p. 51. [129] Ibid., p. 57.

[130] Ibid., p. 82. [131] Ibid., p. 74. [132] Ibid., p. 82. [133] Ibid., p. 87.

[134] J. L. Brierly, *The Basis of Obligation in International Law*, Oxford, Oxford University Press, 1958, p. 10.

"make law" any more than a contract can; it is difficult to see how a rule that is not applicable generally, but instead only to those parties who agreed to it, could be any more legally binding than a rule that is entered into by two parties to a contract for a specific purpose. Therefore, the distinction offered by Triepel identifies different forms of agreement, but it isn't immediately clear, following his own conclusions, why one should have more normative force than the other. If we did follow him, then we should recognize that all international law is only based on the will of States expressed in a *Vereinbarung*. However, there are rules of customary international law, for example, that bind all States; but there was no *Vereinbarung* that ever decided upon them. At most, the rules created by *Vereinbarung* are those of treaties setting up international organizations.[135] But even so, this would not be sufficient for there to even exist an international legal system; any analysis could very well stop here.

This brings us to another distinction between, in French, *obligations consenties* and *obligations assumées*. The first category is that of contractual obligations, to which States have consented. According to Pierre-Marie Dupuy, for this category of obligations, reciprocity operates to ensure their observance. Reciprocity here is considered as the synallagma, the "built-in" enforcement mechanism of obligations in which performance by one party depends on performance by the other. Each has an interest to respect their obligations because this is the means by which they will ensure that the other party's side of the bargain is carried out;[136] these obligations are therefore self-enforcing.

The idea of the *obligation assumeé*, however, is that of an undertaking, rather than a synallagmatic obligation. The obligation is taken on unilaterally, that is, without requiring a counterperformance, but rather recognizing the legal validity of the obligation in itself.[137] While not requiring an approach as voluntarist as that for a *Vereinbarung* for such obligations to become binding, States do however have to acknowledge the existence of the obligation for it to apply.[138] The manner in which reciprocity may apply in this kind of obligation, which is explained as being essentially undertaken unilaterally by the State, will be the subject of further analysis, notably in Chapters 3 and 5, in relation to multilateral treaties and community obligations.

[135] Wyler and Papaux, "Mythe structurant de l'humanité," p. 193.
[136] P.-M. Dupuy, "L'obligation en droit international," *Archives de philosophie du droit*, vol. 44, 2000, p. 218.
[137] Ibid., p. 224. [138] Ibid.

In the meantime, it is safe to say that the contractual analogy can certainly be used for those treaties that are bilateral and synallagmatic in nature. However, in all forms of agreement, whether bilateral or collective, there is reciprocity of rights and obligations, and there must be for these agreements to work. Whereas in bilateral contractual agreements obligations are exchanged whose execution is conditioned upon performance by the other party, and therefore rest upon the internal balance of the agreement, an exchange of rights and obligations also takes place in *Vereinbarung*-type agreements. In the latter, each party must be legally equal to the others, and will have rights and obligations that are relative to all others. Otherwise, it would be possible both to withdraw unilaterally, and to make these rules generally applicable outside the circle of subjects that created them. Rights and obligations are therefore interdependent, and reversible – they can potentially apply to all subjects equally. Not only, but there must be a balance in undertakings – for *Vereinbarung*-type agreements, this must mean that all parties' undertakings are the same.

The difference between *Vertrag* and *Vereinbarung* lies in what is exchanged, rather than in the fact of the exchange. This is also reflected in some national practice. For example, it has been indicated that the condition of reciprocity in Article 55 of the French Constitution, which subjects the superior authority of treaties over national laws to their application by the other party,[139] is fulfilled if, in a multilateral treaty of the type that sets out fundamental rules and principles, all States have undertaken this obligation in common, and not by looking, as would be the case of a synallagmatic treaty, at whether other States parties have executed their obligations.[140] As will be seen below, reciprocity is also an important factor in explaining the creation of customary international law. Reciprocity, therefore, does not require the form of a contractual agreement.

1.3 Other Roles of Reciprocity in Domestic Legal Systems

In domestic law, reciprocity is not only relevant in private law relationships and the law of contracts. It also plays a role that, even in a domestic legal system, is linked closely with sovereignty and equality. These

[139] "Les traités ou accords régulièrement ratifiés ou approuvés ont, dès leur publication, une autorité supérieure à celle des lois, sous réserve, pour chaque accord ou traité, de son application par l'autre partie." France, Constitution du 4 octobre 1958, Article 55.

[140] Waline, *Droit administratif*, p. 267, citing Stirn.

functions include being the constitutional basis on which respect for international law is founded within a State, and in a number of applications in the relations between units of a federal State.

1.3.1 *Reciprocity as a Condition for Accepting Limitations to Sovereignty Domestically*

There exist a number of examples of States that use reciprocity as a condition within their constitution for their acceptance of international law. Not all constitutions use the term "reciprocity," but in most cases, the wording of relevant clauses has been interpreted as meaning "reciprocal." For example, the Italian constitution refers to "conditions of parity with other States."[141] A similar concept is expressed in the preamble of the French Constitution, but this time using the term "réciprocité."[142] Article 55 of the French Constitution also conditions the superiority of treaties over municipal law on their application by other parties.[143] Similar language is employed in the Constitution of Cyprus.[144] The Portuguese Constitution places a condition of reciprocity on further deepening European cooperation,[145] as does the Constitution of Greece in its Article 28.3.[146] These kinds of provisions are the domestic

141 *Costituzione della Repubblica Italiana*, Gazz. Uff. n. 298 del 27/12/1947, Article 11: "*consente, in condizioni di parità con gli altri Stati, alle limitazioni di sovranità necessarie ad un ordinamento che assicuri la pace e la giustizia fra le Nazioni*"; see the analysis in *Frontini*, Corte Costituzionale, *Frontini*, Sentenza n. 183/1973, Gazz. Uff. n. 2, 2 gennaio 1974, paras. 4,5.

142 "Sous réserve de réciprocité, la France consent aux limitations de souveraineté nécessaires à l'organisation et à la défense de la paix."

143 "*Les traités ou accords régulièrement ratifiés ou approuvés ont, dès leur publication, une autorité supérieure à celle des lois, sous réserve, pour chaque accord ou traité, de son application par l'autre partie.*"

144 Constitution of Cyprus, Article 169.3, "treaties, conventions and agreements concluded in accordance with the foregoing provisions of this Article shall have, as from their publication in the official Gazette of the Republic, superior force to any municipal law on condition that such treaties, conventions and agreements are applied by the other party thereto." See in general D. Dero, *La réciprocité et le droit des Communautés et de l'Union européennes*, Bruxelles, Bruylant, 2006, p. 95.

145 Constitution of the Portuguese Republic, Article 7.6

> Subject to reciprocity . . . and with a view to the achievement of the economic, social and territorial cohesion of an area of freedom, security and justice and the definition and implementation of a common external, security and defence policy, Portugal may enter into agreements for the exercise jointly, in cooperation or by the Union's institutions, of the powers needed to construct and deepen the European Union.

146 Greece shall freely proceed by law passed by an absolute majority of the total number of Members of Parliament to limit the exercise of national sovereignty, insofar as this is dictated by an important national interest, does not infringe upon the rights of man

legal basis on which powers may be transferred to international organizations,[147] without compromising the sovereignty of the States concerned.

The consequences of this for international law may not be particularly extensive; after all, a State may not justify its lack of observance of international legal rules on the basis of its domestic law.[148] A State could not therefore invoke the existence of a provision in its constitution requiring limitations to sovereignty to be accepted on condition of reciprocity to justify a violation of rules of international law. The role played by such provisions is however twofold. Internally, they provide a basis on which rules of international law may be observed. This gives a good insight into the close relationship that exists between reciprocity and sovereignty; any limitations of sovereign power are deemed acceptable only if other States equally limit their sovereignty. Secondly, and more concretely, such formulations may result in a State not undertaking an international obligation if it perceives this as occurring on the basis of a lack of reciprocity.

This point requires two further considerations. Firstly, there arises a question as to the meaning of "reciprocity" in this context. Secondly, there is a connected question of what type of agreement or rule of international law could fall short of the condition in national constitutions. French observers have noted that, at least in the case of a bilateral treaty, a lack of application by the other party would entail the inapplicability of the treaty in internal law.[149] It has also been suggested that the meaning of "reciprocity" may change depending on the agreement in question. For a bilateral treaty, the fact of a lack of observance by the other party would mean that the condition of reciprocity is not fulfilled. However, for a multilateral treaty comprising undertakings with respect to general principles, as would be the case in a human rights treaty, the condition of reciprocity would not require *actual* execution of the treaty by all other parties but rather the commonality of the undertaking in that group of States.[150] Decisions of the

and the foundations of democratic government and is effected on the basis of the principles of equality and under the condition of reciprocity.

Article 28.1 of the Greek constitution also provides that "the rules of international law and of international conventions shall be applicable to aliens only under the condition of reciprocity."

[147] Dero, *Réciprocité et le droit*, p. 185.

[148] Articles on Responsibility of States for Internationally Wrongful Acts, 2001, GA Res. 56/83 of 12 December 2001, Article 3.

[149] Waline, *Droit administratif*, p. 267.

[150] Ibid., citing Stern.

French Constitutional Court have gone in this direction and considered the condition of reciprocity to be fulfilled by the exchange of consent. Some slightly different interpretations are possible: In its decision on the constitutionality of France's ratification of the Statute of the International Criminal Court (ICC), the Constitutional Court found that the condition of reciprocity in Article 55 of the Constitution did not apply, because the obligations relating to international peace and security applied to States independently of whether the other States parties executed their obligations.[151] This could imply that reciprocity in French law is a condition of reciprocity *in execution*, and may be inapplicable by virtue of the type of treaty concerned.

Reciprocity is also used as a basis for the adherence of States to the EU. This may be surprising because EU law, while still international law, is considered in the holdings of the European Court of Justice (ECJ) to be a field in which reciprocity is not applicable, due to its significant institutional development.[152] However, it has been laid out in cases before both domestic and European courts that the system of EU law is based on reciprocity, and that this is both the condition on which States have adhered to it and the reason for its superiority over national laws. In *Costa* v. *ENEL*, the ECJ stated that "the integration into the laws of each Member State of provisions which derive from the Community [. . .] make it impossible for the States, as a corollary, to accord precedence to a unilateral and subsequent measure over a legal system accepted by them on a basis of reciprocity."[153] Similarly to what is stated in national constitutions, reciprocity has therefore been considered as the basis on which it is possible to place an international agreement above national law. Also similarly to the law of contracts, what is also at stake here is the balance in rights and obligations. Any unilateral measure taken by a State would upset this balance.[154] Such analyses have also been undertaken before national courts, notably in the *Frontini* case, where the cession of certain powers to the organs of the EEC was found not to have

[151] France, Conseil Constitutionnel, Décision 98-408 DC 22 janvier 1999, para. 12. See also Dero, *Réciprocité et le droit*, p. 197.

[152] *Commission of the E.E.C.* v. *Grand Duchy of Luxembourg and Kingdom of Belgium*, Cases Nos. 90 and 91/63, Judgment of 13 November 1964, p. 631; *NV Algemeine Transport* v. *Netherlands Inland Revenue Administration*, Case No. 26/62, Judgment of 5 February 1963, p. 12.

[153] *Flaminio Costa* v. *E.N.E.L.*, European Court of Justice, Case No. 6-64, Judgment of 15 July 1964, pp. 593–594; Dero, *Réciprocité et le droit*, p. 157.

[154] Dero, *Réciprocité et le droit*, p. 159.

been made unilaterally, and therefore not in breach of Article 11 of the Italian Constitution.[155]

Reciprocity is therefore used as a domestic legal justification for transfer of powers to international organizations; its meaning is interpreted either as reciprocity in the execution of the international obligations in question – in which case it will not be deemed applicable to agreements that are not synallagmatic – or as equality of undertaking of all States parties to the agreements in question, which therefore cannot be upset by unilateral action. In both cases, this highlights States' view of reciprocity as a mechanism for safeguarding their sovereignty.

1.3.2 Reciprocity in Federal States

The working of reciprocity in federal States is of particular interest for present purposes. In federal States, international law is often applied by analogy when there are gaps in the regulation provided by intra-federal law.[156] In areas of intra-federal law that are not governed by the national constitution, recourse is sometimes made to reciprocity.

In the United States, there exist a number of examples of reciprocal legislation, which can be divided into reciprocal and retaliatory legislation. Both have been explained as being "branches of interstate comity, which, by analogy with international practice, may be defined as an observance of interstate privileges beyond the requirements of the federal constitution."[157] Reciprocal legislation enters into operation if the legislature of the other US state concerned also enacts legislation setting out the same requirements: It is "conditional or contingent legislation, since it depends for its full effect upon an event beyond the control of the enacting legislature, that is, the passage of a similar act by a foreign legislature," and is "mutual or correlative action."[158] It therefore requires some similarity or uniformity between the two pieces of state legislation.[159]

[155] Italy, Corte Costituzionale, *Frontini*, Sentenza n. 183/1973, Gazz. Uff. n.2, 2 gennaio 1974.

[156] W. Rudolf, "Federal States," *Max Planck Encyclopedia of International Law*, May 2011, para. 39.

[157] J. R. Starr, "Reciprocal and Retaliatory Legislation in the American States," *Minnesota Law Review*, vol. 21, 1937, p. 372.

[158] Ibid. See also A. Lenhoff, "Reciprocity: The legal aspect of a perennial idea", *Northwestern University Law Journal*, vol. 49, 1954–1955, p. 640.

[159] Starr, "Reciprocal and Retaliatory Legislation," p. 373.

This mechanism is usually used to regulate licensing of trades and professions, whereby one state recognises the licenses of another state on condition that the same treatment is afforded its own licensees, and on the basis of equality in standards.[160] However, it has also been used in fields connected to criminal law, such as granting extraterritorial powers to police forces of another state on the basis of the same advantage being granted to one's own police force.[161] Similarly to the role reciprocity plays in national constitutions, here too reciprocity can provide a basis on which to allow limitations or derogations from some of the exclusive powers federated states have in matters such as enforcement. Retaliatory legislation, however, often used in the fields of insurance and tax law,[162] is a "legislative threat of the imposition of penalties upon the citizens of other states which impose penalties upon the citizens of the enacting state."[163]

These examples show how reciprocity is not completely alien to constitutionally ordered legal systems. The important characteristic of the entities that enter into relationships of legal reciprocity is that they must be legally equal, as indeed is the case in federal States.[164] However, unlike in international law, states in a federation are subordinated to a higher authority. While this accounts for the limited degree to which reciprocity can be applicable in their legal relations, it also disproves the point that reciprocity is inapplicable in a constitutionalised or institutionalized order. Reciprocity is useful when the subjects concerned are in a relationship of equality to one another, and is seen, in domestic systems, as the condition on which limitations to sovereignty can be accepted.

[160] Ibid., p. 375. Reciprocity is also used for gun licenses. For an illustration, see www.usacarry.com/concealed_carry_permit_reciprocity_maps.html. This reciprocal basis for relationships between federal entities is not exclusive to the United States; in Switzerland, for example, reciprocal legislation exists notably in matters of taxation; see, e.g., Canton de Vaud, Loi 648.11 concernant le droit de mutation sur les transferts immobiliers et l'impôt sur les successions et donations (LMSD) du 27 février 1963, Article 20; Accord 670.93 de réciprocité entre les cantons de Vaud et Bâle-Ville en matière d'exonération de l'impôt sur le revenu et la fortune (A-rR-BS) du 30 juin 1959; Accord 670.99 de réciprocité entre les cantons du Tessin et de Vaud en matière d'exonération d'impôt sur les successions et donations du 21 novembre 2012.

[161] Starr, "Reciprocal and Retaliatory Legislation," pp. 389–390.

[162] See Lenhoff, "Reciprocity," p. 634.

[163] Starr, "Reciprocal and Retaliatory Legislation," p. 375.

[164] As set out, concerning the states of the United States, in *Kansas* v. *Colorado* ([13 May 1907] 206 US 46, para. 94.

1.4 Conclusion

This analysis of reciprocity in the social sciences and domestic contexts sheds light upon some of its fundamental characteristics.

Firstly, reciprocity is not incompatible with the existence of a community. It necessarily requires a social relation; after all, two subjects are required in order to reciprocate. Reciprocity has a normative value that goes beyond mere self-interest and can serve as a way of enforcing social norms. As illustrated by game theory, it creates the conditions for repeat interactions and predictability in a system where there is no overarching legislator or enforcement mechanism, as is the case in international law. It also has a role to play in law creation.

Secondly, one of the defining characteristics of reciprocity is its relationship with equality. This does not mean that it requires a strict *quid pro quo* but only proportionality in the aggregate; reciprocity is not the same thing as "an eye for an eye." In Roman law, there are examples of reciprocal obligations that are asymmetrical. Reciprocity also implies equality, and is a way of reflecting the equality that exists between parties. For this reason, reciprocity continues to play a role in the modern-day law of contracts, in ways that are similar to what we can find in international law. It is also this characteristic that explains why States use reciprocity as a justification to accept limitations to their sovereignty within the domestic legal system. This relationship with equality explains why reciprocity is also relevant in federal systems, between legally equal entities.

Rather than being a negative concept, based on occasional and discontinued instances of interaction on the basis of reactions to conduct, reciprocity is a concept fundamental to the existence of social relations and inherent to ideas of justice and fairness.

2 What Is Reciprocity?

It will hopefully be clear from Chapter 1 that reciprocity is an important concept not only in international law but also in many other areas of social sciences. But for all the discussions on its uses and roles, in legal terms, what is reciprocity? This chapter will seek to expand on the concept of reciprocity, looking at how it can be defined, its key characteristics, and the three key functions it plays: in norm creation, as a condition, and in execution of the law.

2.1 Definitions of Reciprocity

Before explaining the different uses of reciprocity, and its relationship to related concepts and principles, it will be helpful to put forward some of the definitions of reciprocity that have been offered by authors in the field of law, and international law most notably, as well as addressing the question of its legal nature. After all, "the differences in meaning depend on the legal situation in which reciprocity is invoked (the creation, observance or sanction of legal obligations), on whether it is understood in a formal rather than material way, and on the other principles with which it is combined."[1]

2.1.1 *Reciprocity of Conduct versus Reciprocity of Obligation*

Definitions of reciprocity vary on a series of crucial points. The first of these is whether the "reciprocity" in question is that of conduct or of legal obligation. Both of these meanings may be legally relevant, although they take into account two different things. The definition of

[1] G. Wils, "The Concept of Reciprocity in EEC Law: An Exploration into These Realms," *Common Market Law Review*, vol. 28, 1991, p. 246.

reciprocity as the dependence of the obligations of one upon the material conduct of another is most often used when addressing reciprocity as inherent to primitive legal systems and incompatible with generalized obligations. Gouldner offers a definition of this type of reciprocity as "two related assumptions: (1) that B reciprocates A's services, and (2) that B's service to A is contingent upon A's performance of positive functions for B."[2] This definition also relates to the second main point of differentiation: whether reciprocity is viewed as a transaction or as a more widely and systemically applicable concept. Lenhoff gives such a definition of reciprocity as a transaction with regards to international law, explaining reciprocity as making a legal norm dependent upon the observation of certain conduct by governments.[3]

A second approach considers the legal dependence of an obligation upon the fulfillment of the obligation by another party. This is similar to the structure of the Roman synallagma.[4] The definition given by Simma goes in this sense: "the status of a relationship between two or more States in which the conduct of one is in some way or other juridically dependent upon the conduct of the other party, in most instances but not all amounting to equivalent treatment."[5] In this case, conduct is still relevant, but it is *legally* relevant; the focus is no longer on the material effects of reciprocity of conduct (that is, A doing something for B will then require B to do something for A). This definition of reciprocity for the most part ends up reducing the meaning of reciprocity to that of a reprisal or suspension of an obligation. In fact, following this definition, Paulus then goes on to refer to the "tit for tat of classical international law."[6]

2.1.2 *Characteristics of Reciprocity: Proportionality, Relativity, and the Question of Applicability outside Bilateral Obligations*

Not all international obligations fit this synallagmatic model, and it is asserted here that reciprocity can also be found in legal obligations that

[2] Gouldner, "Norm of Reciprocity," p. 163.

[3] Lenhoff, "Reciprocity," p. 628; the same definition, referring to "treatment or conduct" is also used by Frigo: M. Frigo, "Le reciprocità nell'evoluzione del diritto del commercio internazionale," *Comunicazioni e studi*, vol. IXX–XX, 1992, p. 418.

[4] A. L. Paulus, "Reciprocity Revisited," in U. Fastenrath, ed., *From Bilateralism to Community Interest: Essays in Honour of Judge Bruno Simma*, Oxford, Oxford University Press, 2011, pp. 116–118.

[5] B. Simma, "Reciprocity," in R. Wolfrum, ed., *The Max Planck Encyclopedia of Public International Law*, Oxford University Press, 2008–, para. 2.

[6] Paulus, "Reciprocity Revisited," p. 114.

are not of this type. Other definitions of reciprocity take a wider view of it as a concept uniting ideas of mutuality and proportionality, while still maintaining a distinctly contractual nature; a "certain correspondence between sacrifices required and advantages accorded."[7] Black's legal dictionary defines "reciprocal" as something "given or owed mutually as between two persons; interchanged" and "reciprocity" as "mutuality."[8] Consequently, this approach defines reciprocity by an exchange or correspondence in obligations, rather than mere conditionality. Hiskes places the differentiation between mutuality and reciprocity on the level of the difference between individual and community obligations. Giving the example of human rights, mutuality means recognizing that each has the same rights against me as I do toward others, while reciprocity is inherent to a community of rights.[9]

However, reciprocity is not coextensive with mutuality. Virally defines reciprocity as being mutual advantage, together with a certain correspondence in what is given or exchanged.[10] This adds an element of proportionality in the corresponding, mutual obligations. Proportionality has been defined as "balancing the effects of measures chosen against the objective sought, taking into account whether those effects are excessive according to those most affected."[11] The proportion within reciprocity ensures equality of its subjects.[12] Proportionality is always present in reciprocity, as an additional element to the exchange of obligations. This definition of reciprocity places its interpretation within the realm of distributive, rather than commutative, justice.[13] The emphasis is not on the transaction, but on the right measure between the obligations borne by each party.

This distinction is reflected in what Keohane identifies as "specific" and "diffuse" reciprocity. While "specific reciprocity" is reflected in conditions or conditionality of conduct, such as in conditional most-

[7] Martins Zanitelli, "Reciprocidade nos contratos," p. 161.

[8] J. Nolan et al., eds., *Black's Law Dictionary*, 6th ed., St. Paul, MN, West, 1990, pp. 1269–1270. The eighth edition of the dictionary defines reciprocity as "mutual or bilateral action," or "mutually conceded advantages"; B. A. Garner, *Black's Law Dictionary*, 8th ed., St. Paul, MN, West, 2004, p. 1299.

[9] Hiskes, *Human Right*, pp. 23–24, 54.

[10] Virally, "Principe de réciprocité," p. 9.

[11] E. Crawford, "Proportionality," *Max Planck Encyclopedia of International Law*, May 2011, para. 2.

[12] V. Porto, "A aplicação do princìpio da reciprocidade no Direito Internacional Pùblico: Do bilateralismo à supranacionalidade," *Direito publico*, no. 26, mar–apr 2009, p. 89.

[13] Wyler and Papaux, "Mythe structurant de l'humanité," p. 198, cit. E. Decaux, *Réciprocité en droit international*, p. 344.

favored nation treatment in the field of trade, "diffuse reciprocity" is conformity "to generally accepted standards of behaviour";[14] this latter type of "diffuse" reciprocity "can be maintained only by a widespread sense of obligation" because of the lack of direct rewards for the conduct of the parties.[15] Again, this emphasizes the difference between the transactional and systemic approaches of reciprocity.

This brings us to a set of definitions that emphasize another essential aspect of reciprocity, and one which can include both specific and diffuse, or transactional and systemic, aspects: that of interdependence of obligations. This definition requires us to look at the nature of the obligations in question and how they function, instead of the conduct of the parties. According to Dero, reciprocity is the "symmetry of legal causes,"[16] requiring two elements: exchange, and identity or equality of rights and obligations.[17] Reciprocity is thereby a characteristic of the type of legal obligations that are owed by one subject to another. This definition is also used by Provost in the field of international human rights and humanitarian law: "[O]bligations are reciprocal if their creation, execution and termination depend on the imposition of connected obligations on others," adding that "international law, being a system based on the formal equality and sovereignty of states, has arisen largely out of the exchange of reciprocal rights and duties between States."[18]

Far from being only a transactional concept, or a characteristic of a rule that permits reaction to a breach, reciprocity can therefore properly be applied in a systemic manner, and within a communitarian setting; as interdependence and proportionality, it is not limited to the bilateral context.[19]

2.1.2.1 Equality and Equivalence

Reciprocity is closely tied to the equality of the parties to an obligation, all the more so in international law. Insofar as States are sovereign (that is, there is no power above them), they are also legally, or formally, equal. They are therefore entitled to the same rights, and also to the

[14] R. O. Keohane, "Reciprocity in International Relations," *International Organization*, vol. 40, no. 1, December 1986, p. 4.

[15] Ibid., p. 20.

[16] Dero, *Réciprocité et le droit*, p. 165, "*symétrie de causes juridiques*" in the original French.

[17] Ibid., p. 11.

[18] R. Provost, "Reciprocity in Human Rights and Humanitarian Law," *British Yearbook of International Law*, vol. 65, 1994, p. 383.

[19] Hiskes terms "reflexive reciprocity" that which brings together both mutuality and the shared beliefs that create a community. Ibid., pp. 62–63.

same treatment (including owing the same obligations), as all other States.[20] This is a structural element of the international community,[21] and it is a necessary characteristic of the system, which accounts for a number of rules – notably those that impede the exercise of authority by one State within the territory of another. Another consequence of the particular structure of international law is that no State can be placed at a disadvantage, or obtain more advantages than other States, although all States may decide to cede or restrict some of their rights.[22] This legal equality, or equality in the condition of States, necessarily gives a particular importance to reciprocity.[23] Reciprocity can be seen as a manifestation of sovereign equality, as well as a mechanism for ensuring sovereign equality is maintained. The legal equality of States in international law means that one State cannot unilaterally create an obligation for another,[24] in any case not one to which the first State will not itself also be subject.[25] In the context of norm creation, it also means that States can only claim rights that they will accept to see generalized;[26] it is not possible for one State to claim a right to the exclusion of all others. The role of reciprocity is therefore of particular importance in international society, a society of legal equals, in encouraging agreements to be maintained and in effectively permitting the exercise of State prerogatives.[27]

[20] Dupuy, "Unité de l'ordre juridique international," pp. 98–99; M. Byers, *Custom, Power and the Power of Rules: International Relations and Customary International Law*, Cambridge, Cambridge University Press, 1999, pp. 11–12; J. Crawford, "Chance, Order, Change: The Course of International Law," *RCADI*, vol. 365, 2014, p. 263; N. Politis, *Les nouvelles tendances du droit international*, Paris, Hachette, 1927, p. 30; "by a necessary consequence of that equality, whatever is lawful for one nation, is equally lawful for any other; and whatever is unjustifiable in the one, is equally so in the other," Vattel, *The Law of Nations*, para. 19.

[21] C. Tomuschat, "Obligations Arising for States without or against Their Will," *RCADI*, vol. 250, 1994, p. 221, 292–294.

[22] A. Cassese, *International Law in a Divided World*, Oxford, Clarendon, 1986, pp. 130–131; Niboyet, "Notion de réciprocité," p. 271.

[23] This point has been picked up by a number of authors: Byers, *Custom, Power and the Power of Rules*, p. 36; Virally, "Panorama du droit international contemporain," p. 84; Kolb, *Réflexions de philosophie du droit international*, pp. 11, 27–33, 92; Dupuy, "Unité de l'ordre juridique international," pp. 95, 399; Frigo, "Reciprocità nell'evoluzione," p. 431.

[24] Brierly, *Basis of Obligation in International Law*, p. 46; Cassese, *International Law in a Divided World*, p. 130.

[25] Treaty law in this connection will be discussed in Chapter 3.

[26] Byers, *Custom, Power and the Power of Rules*, p. 90.

[27] Kolb, *Réflexions de philosophie du droit international*, pp. 309, 313; Dero, *Réciprocité et le droit*, p. 7; "Le principe de l'égale souveraineté des États, qui conduit à ce qu'aucun État ne bénéficie de plus d'avantages qu'un autre, fait en effet de la réciprocité une règle

The inequalities between States in terms of size, resources, and power have led some to claim that reciprocity is not possible in relations between States that have very different levels of development,[28] or even that these factual differences negate any equality between States. However, we are speaking here of legal equality, that is, equality under international law and in the rights and obligations in general that are imposed upon States: the possibility of freely consenting,[29] and of opposing the same right to another State that it recognizes for itself. Further, States may place differing values on receiving a given counterperformance. Therefore, it may not immediately be clear to an outside observer whether the rights and duties incorporated in, for example, an agreement on trade, are of equivalent or even equal value to the parties. Finally, as we have seen, reciprocity is tied up with the idea of proportionality; expecting less from a State that can give less would therefore fully respect the requirements of reciprocity. It has been said that "la notion de reciprocité implique toujours l'idée d'équilibre. Toutefois, elle n'indique nullement ni les modalités de cet équilibre, ni son contenu."[30] [The notion of reciprocity always implies the idea of balance. However, it does not indicate the modalities of this balance, nor its content.] Looking at the behavioral aspect of reciprocity, what is an acceptable reciprocation for each State will depend on its interests and perceptions.[31]

The question is how to work out exactly what kind of standard is required by reciprocity. The subjective element of equivalence makes it difficult to establish when an exchange gives an equivalent advantage to both sides. It is proposed here that in legal relationships, reciprocity will be of two types. The first is reciprocity in undertaking identical obligations, for example in a multilateral convention, including one to which reservations are possible, or in the acceptance of the jurisdiction of a body such as the ICJ, where the scope of the obligations entered into

fondamentale de ce droit": P. Serrand, "Réciprocité," in D. Alland and S. Rials, eds., *Dictionnaire de la culture juridique*, Paris, PUF, 2003, p. 1300.

28 Dero, *Réciprocité et le droit*, p. 171; this is also one of the points made by Virally, "Principe de réciprocité" (see, e.g., pp. 73–74).

29 In fact, coercion results in invalidity of a treaty under articles 51 and 52 of the Vienna Convention on the Law of Treaties. The case in which inequality of undertakings does render reciprocity impossible is one in which one State forces the other to benefit it with no reciprocity (see, e.g., Gouldner, "Norm of Reciprocity," p. 164).

30 Serrand, "Réciprocité," p. 1302.

31 Franck and Weisband give the examples of the Soviet invasion of Czechoslovakia as the asserted "equivalence" of the United States' right to invade the Dominican Republic, Franck and Weisband, "The Role of Reciprocity and Equivalence," pp. 265, 271.

must be identical for both parties.[32] The other involves exchanging different undertakings that amount to an equivalent exchange; these may be in a transactional setting such as a bilateral treaty, or indeed a multilateral treaty of the type that differentiates obligations for States according to criteria such as their status (as we may consider is the case in nuclear disarmament treaties) or their capacities (as would be the treatment of developing nations in environmental treaties, or developing and least developed nations in trade agreements). In all these cases, the quantitative element of reciprocity is in the idea of proportionality. In matters in which the States in question must be considered equal, identity of obligations will be necessary for these obligations to be defined as reciprocal; where matters relate to concrete measures that depend on the real situation of the States in question, and their capacity to carry out certain obligations, then proportionality suggests that the undertakings may be modulated to take these differences into account, without affecting the reciprocal nature of the agreements and rules in question.[33]

2.1.2.2 Relativity

Another characteristic of reciprocity is its link with relativity. Reciprocity operates on the intersubjective level between two subjects. The conduct or obligations it requires will vary depending on the circumstances of that relationship. In international law, it is not sufficient to look at a State's observance of a rule in the absolute; rules of international law need to be viewed not as imposed upon States in isolation but within the wider context of which States an obligation applies to, whether in terms of the rule's creation, or in the consequences of its violation. This is a structural factor in international law. As rules are not imposed from above, they must be owed to one or more other States.[34] It follows that, in case of a breach, other States may demand compliance and take action to that end.[35] This point has consequences, which will be seen in subsequent chapters, notably concerning the law of treaties; it is not possible for States to impose

[32] S. Torres Bernárdez, "Reciprocity in the System of Compulsory Jurisdiction and Other Modalities of Contentious Jurisdiction Exercised by the International Court of Justice," in E. G. Bello and A. A. Bola, eds., *Essays in Honour of Judge Taslim Olawale Elias*, vol. 1, Dordrecht/Boston, Nihoff, 1992, p. 292.

[33] There is also an argument to be made as to the reciprocal basis of the law of treaties, which will be addressed in Chapter 3.

[34] S. Sur, "Quelques observations sur les normes juridiques internationales," *Revue générale de droit international public*, vol. 89, no. 4, 1985, pp. 904–910, 914.

[35] Paulus, "Reciprocity Revisited," p. 122.

treaty obligations upon third States when these have not accepted them; treaty obligations are consent-based and relative, and, as we shall see, governed by reciprocity.[36] In more general terms, international law, being a horizontal system of law, is also a form of relational law, and by definition reciprocal.[37]

2.1.3 *Rule, Principle or Meta-Rule? The Structural and Structuring Nature of Reciprocity*

Having analyzed the various definitions of reciprocity, and its key characteristics, it is time to turn now to its legal nature. The idea that reciprocity, in its general sense, may be considered a rule can be set aside. Specific rules, may, of course, contain a reference to reciprocity and be conditioned upon reciprocal application or execution of the obligations contained in the rule. However, particularly with reference to public international law, we cannot affirm that there is a "rule of reciprocity." Even considering reciprocity as conditionality of conduct (rather than in legal obligations), there is no general rule in international law that conditions observance of rules on the conduct of the other State or States; affirming the existence of such a rule would amount to denying the existence of international law. So reciprocity can be a component of a rule but not a rule in itself.

Doctrinal approaches can be distinguished between those that consider reciprocity to be something less than a legal concept and those that consider reciprocity to be a general principle of law. For example, Keohane considers reciprocity to be a "convention"; that is, an "informal institution with implicit rules and understandings, that shape[s] the expectations of actors" and allows actors to coordinate their behavior without explicit rules.[38] Therefore, reciprocity allows agreement and coordination of action, and actors conform to this norm of behavior because not doing so would entail a cost for them.[39] In international law, a "convention" in the sense used by Keohane would not be legally binding but States would conform to it due to economic considerations of some kind.[40] This is an interesting approach, which may be relevant when considering the role of reciprocity as a convenient basis upon which to conduct relations when there are no other legal obligations in place. Parisi and Ghei consider reciprocity to be a "meta-rule" of

[36] C. Campiglio, *Il principio di reciprocità nel diritto dei trattati*, Padova, CEDAM, 1995, p. 66.
[37] Porto, "Aplicação do princìpio da reciprocidade," p. 94 (cit. Decaux).
[38] Keohane, "Reciprocity in International Relations," p. 27. [39] Ibid. [40] Ibid., p. 28.

international law,[41] that is, a concept essential to its functioning. Again, this addresses reciprocity's role as encouraging the formation of international law.[42] In their analysis, however, the emphasis still remains on the economic expediency of reciprocity, rather than what its role in law may be.

On the other hand, there are some authors who quite clearly consider reciprocity to be a general principle of public international law[43] or, similarly, a "fundamental structural feature of the international community."[44] Simma differentiates reciprocity in general from reciprocity as a "maxim" or principle (used interchangeably) prescribing that "a State basing a claim on a particular rule of international law must also accept that rule as binding upon itself."[45] While we may accept this as a rule of international law, it is unclear which principle makes this maxim applicable in international law. Is it reciprocity, or is it the sovereign equality of States? The requirement for States to accept that other States may be entitled to the same rights they claim appears, rather than being a principle of reciprocity, to be instead a manifestation of the sovereign equality of States, which is indeed a fundamental, structural rule of international law.

In public international law, reciprocity appears to be the mechanism whereby the sovereign equality of States is preserved. This accounts both for reciprocity in its sub- or paralegal character, as a convention or metalegal rule, and in its normative role, as requiring reversibility of obligations and mutuality of State claims. Reversibility in this sense means that to each right of one State there corresponds an obligation of another but that the latter State also enjoys the same rights as the first. Sovereignty itself therefore sets legal limits to sovereignty.[46] Indeed, attaching reciprocity to sovereign equality in this manner helps to understand its requirements of proportionality or equality; these do not apply in the abstract. We cannot say that reciprocity requires identity rather than equivalence, for it may require both in different

[41] Parisi and Ghei, "Role of Reciprocity in International Law," pp. 2, 20.

[42] In fact, Parisi and Ghei illustrate their point with reference to the birth of the exclusive economic zone in the law of the sea, ibid., pp. 26–27.

[43] Porto, "Aplicação do princìpio da reciprocidade," p. 94 (cit. Decaux); Frigo, "Reciprocità nell'evoluzione," p. 429.

[44] Tomuschat, "Obligations Arising for States," p. 276.

[45] Simma, "Reciprocity," para. 2.

[46] Virally, "Panorama du droit international contemporain," p. 78.

contexts. Reciprocity entails that which is necessary to ensure the sovereign equality of States is preserved.

2.1.4 Legal Reciprocity or the Interconnection of Obligations

The hypothesis advanced here is that reciprocity in international law is not antithetical to community interests and obligations, but its importance is explained by a structural factor: the sovereign equality of states. By virtue of this fact, reciprocity is relevant as a default means of regulation, in areas closely connected to the exercise of sovereign power by the State, where an imbalance in obligations can most easily impair equality, and in inter-State obligations, even those relating to human rights and other community interests. Its application is instead more limited in obligations owed by States to individuals, or where States seek to establish a regime that is somehow "objective."

Reciprocity is a necessary consequence of the legal equality and sovereignty of States,[47] and it makes limitations on sovereignty acceptable to States. In order to function, reciprocity requires the equality of the subjects of the law. In a relationship of *sovereign* equality, the activities of one legal person are subject only in a limited manner to the aims of another. Otherwise, we would be faced with a situation of dependence, as opposed to the independence that is by definition inherent in sovereignty.[48] Therefore, firstly, the aims of States are not delegated to a higher organ in the same manner as they might be within the legal orders of the States themselves. This does not mean the States are not subject to international law; however, they are not subjected to another legal person.

This fact has some particular consequences for the structure of obligations and legal rules. In domestic legal systems, these are imposed from above. In international law, however, rights and obligations must be agreed upon and created by States. This accounts for the importance of reciprocity in this field of law. It was seen how the fundamental elements required by reciprocity are equality and relativity; in international law, the creation, application, and execution of rules necessarily take place among States; no world government exists that may impose rules. Rights and obligations are therefore by necessity owed by one State to another – or to a number of other States.

[47] Michel Virally, among others, highlights the close connection between reciprocity and legal equality: Virally, "Principe de réciprocité," p. 50.

[48] Bonfante, *Corso di diritto romano*, p. 22.

The definition of legal reciprocity that will be used throughout this book is distinct to the definition of reciprocity as the sole act of extending mutual advantages or disadvantages. Reciprocity means the interdependence of rights and obligations of States: mutually dependent rights and obligations are owed between one another. This interdependence is geared toward maintaining the condition of legal equality between States. This has two important implications. First, each right will have a corresponding obligation. Second, a State must accept that any right it claims is equally available to all other States; what is more, it must accept that, by claiming a right, that same right is also opposable to it.

2.2 The Functions of Reciprocity

There are some distinctions to be made regarding reciprocity in international law that have been proposed by numerous authors. Material reciprocity relates to the content of an obligation; formal reciprocity regards the manner in which an agreement comes into force;[49] and reciprocity in application concerns parties' execution of their obligations.[50] "Formal reciprocity" has been used in the same way that the expression "legal reciprocity" is used here: a legal notion with effects at the legal level, linked to ideas of equality and balance.[51] Reciprocity may be internal, when it is contained within an agreement; it may also be external, even systemic, where counterperformance is to be found in a different instrument.[52] Further divisions may be made as to what reciprocity may concern: reciprocity is identical when it requires the parties to carry out the same thing, and otherwise it is equivalent.[53] "Real" or "material" reciprocity, instead, is extralegal.[54]

Preiswerk suggested other divisions, distinguishing diplomatic or conventional, legislative, and factual reciprocity. Diplomatic or legislative reciprocity would therefore be of the type found in a treaty, in which a balance of obligations is sought, the *do ut des* of aiming to obtain a counterperformance (which therefore need not be identical to the performance sought) in exchange for a concession, or as a condition for application of a treaty. Legislative reciprocity is primarily concerned with the treatment of foreign nationals, in which a right is granted to

[49] Serrand, "Réciprocité," p. 1300; Campiglio, *Principio di reciprocità*, p. 48.
[50] Serrand, "Réciprocité," p. 1300. [51] Campiglio, *Principio di reciprocità*, p. 325.
[52] Ibid., p. 48; Virally, "Principe de réciprocité," p. 46.
[53] Serrand, "Réciprocité," p. 1301. [54] Virally, "Principe de réciprocité," p. 34.

the nationals of one State if that State grants the same advantages to the nationals of the first State. In this case, therefore, the right or more generally obligation in question needs to be identical as far as possible.[55] The third type is factual reciprocity, that is, the treatment States accord one another in the absence of a specific law or treaty.[56]

Similar subdivisions may be found in most studies of reciprocity.[57] Here, following the divisions proposed by authors such as Serrand and Decaux,[58] the distinction that will be used is that between the three key roles reciprocity can play. The first is reciprocity's role in the creation of legal obligations. This includes reciprocity's use as a basis for cooperation in the absence of legal obligations, and its role in the formation of legal rules. The second is the role of reciprocity as a condition within specific legal rules. The third is reciprocity in execution of the law, that is, in the consequences of the nonobservance of a legal obligation.

2.2.1 *A Basis for Cooperation in the Creation of Legal Obligations*

Some mention has already been made, in Chapter 1, of reciprocity's importance as a basis for the formation of law and, indeed, of society. It is possible to further subdivide two equally important roles of reciprocity in this connection. The first is to provide a basis for cooperation when there are no legal obligations in place. The second is reciprocity's role in the formation of legal rules.

In a situation where there are no legal rules applicable, reciprocity functions as a norm of conduct to which parties will conform their behavior, according to which parties may do to others what has been done to them.[59] Without having to subscribe to views of the intenational system as "lawless" or exclusively voluntarist, reciprocity can play an important role in the international legal system in this way. Even recognizing that there exist general principles and general rules in international law that can regulate the conduct of States in the absence of a specific legal rule on a given matter, reciprocity is still used as a standard

[55] This is also the definition of reciprocity used by the United States; see Keohane, "Reciprocity in International Relations," p. 3.

[56] Campiglio, *Principio di reciprocità*, p. 50.

[57] See, e.g., Niboyet, "Notion de réciprocité," 1935.

[58] Dero, *Réciprocité et le droit*, 8; R. Preiswerk, "La réciprocité dans les négociations entre pays à systèmes sociaux ou à niveaux économiques différents," *Journal du droit international*, vol. 94, no. 1, 1967, pp. 7–8. In his study, Emmanuel Decaux divides reciprocity into three roles, the creation, execution, and sanction of obligations; Decaux, *Réciprocité en droit international*, p. 13.

[59] Parisi, "Cost of the Game," p. 106.

when there are no specific rules applicable or when States undertake cooperation or extend treatment that goes further than what is required by law.[60]

Secondly, reciprocity is of fundamental importance in the formation of legal rules in international law.[61] Reciprocity allows concessions to be made and accepted, and agreement to be found. These concessions and the repeated behavior that follows from them may subsequently take the form of either a treaty or of a customary rule of international law.[62] In the formation of both treaty and customary rules, reciprocity creates expectations that a given course of conduct will be observed in response to concessions by one party. It is these expectations that give legal significance to specific conduct or practice.[63] The expectation of reciprocal conduct allows putative new rules to emerge and consolidate, particularly in customary international law.[64] The balance reciprocity creates allows legal rules to be formed in a context in which it is not possible for them to be imposed from above. Reciprocity does not only function organically to form rules but it also makes new limitations on, or manifestations of, State sovereignty acceptable, as these will be applicable in the same manner to all States,[65] according to the requirement for States to recognize to all other States the same rights that they themselves claim.[66]

Reciprocity in the context of law formation or in regulating situations where no existing rules are applicable should be understood as the interdependence of equivalent and mutual conduct or responses, rather than in terms of legal obligations, for the simple reason that in this context, no legal obligations are applicable.

2.2.2 *Reciprocity as a Condition: Its Operation within Legal Rules*

The second role reciprocity can play is as a condition or an element of a legal rule, for example, when the content of a rule requires it to be carried out "on the basis of reciprocity." In such a formulation, reciprocity adds the requirement of equal application of the rule, and may

60 Simma, "Reciprocity," para. 12. 61 Virally, "Principe de réciprocité," p. 11.
62 Lagarde, "Réciprocité en droit international," p. 189.
63 Wils, "Concept of Reciprocity in EEC Law," p. 248.
64 Campiglio, *Principio di reciprocità*, pp. 12, 15.
65 Lenhoff, "Reciprocity," p. 624, and Section 2.3.1.
66 Parisi and Ghei, "Role of Reciprocity in International Law," p. 41; Niboyet, "Notion de réciprocité," p. 272.

allow the standard set by the rule to be modulated according to the parties' conduct.[67]

What exactly fulfills this condition of reciprocity will depend on the type of obligation in question. For example, the rule may require either specific conduct or more vague action, such as "cooperation on the basis of reciprocity."[68] In the latter case, there will be no minimum standard the parties must observe to fulfill the obligation. It may not even be necessary for both parties to carry out exactly the same things for the condition of reciprocity to be fulfilled; in this case, the rule will more closely resemble a transaction, that is, exchanging equivalent performance. Using reciprocity as a condition can therefore either put in place cooperation where it is difficult to obtain, or put in place a legal rule where the content of the rule is not certain.[69] Reciprocity's role as a condition is closely connected to States' "psychological justification" for accepting limitations to sovereignty; placing such a condition of reciprocity within a given rule may therefore permit cooperation on matters that may otherwise be considered too closely connected to State sovereignty for such agreement. The point with such provisions is to ensure a very strict equality in the burden of obligations of the parties, whether the standard of conduct is set out in the rule or modeled on the conduct of the parties. The effect may also be to ensure that lack of execution will not automatically entail a breach of the rule, as performance is conditioned on reciprocal counterperformance, and not held against an absolute standard which, if not realized, will give rise to a breach.

2.2.3 *Reciprocity in Application and Execution of the Law*

The third role of reciprocity, in the application and execution of the law, may appear to be similar to that of reciprocity as a condition. However, while reciprocity as a condition is part of the requirements set out in a specific rule, reciprocity in execution relates to the continued observance of rules and the consequences of a violation. This can also be explained as reciprocity applying in the third stage of the "life" of a rule; in the first stage, it applies in the rule's creation; secondly, within the rule itself, in how the parties fulfill the obligation it lays out; and thirdly, at the point of performance, or the consequence of nonperformance or breach by one

[67] Frigo, "Reciprocità nell'evoluzione," pp. 422, 430.

[68] As, for example, set out in treaties on cooperation such as the Agreement on Cultural Cooperation between the Government of the Republic of the Philippines and the Government of the Russian Federation of 12 September 1997, Art. 1.

[69] B. Conforti, *Diritto internazionale*, 4th ed., Napoli, Milano, Scientifica, 1995, p. 369.

of the parties. The role of reciprocity in execution of obligations is often treated as if it were coextensive with reciprocity itself. However, again, this does not explain the entirety of the concept of reciprocity, and instead fixates on one of its possible uses.

It was seen in Chapter 1 that reciprocity in execution is an effective way of ensuring cooperation. If there is a possibility for one party to respond to a defection by discontinuing their observance of the rule, this will make noncompliance far less attractive. Reciprocity used in this way can be seen as an enforcement mechanism.[70]

Reciprocity in execution can be divided into two main mechanisms. The first is that of a reprisal or, in the examples of ancient laws, that of talionic retaliation. This unites the idea of a response to a breach of a rule with that of equality in response. In talionic law, the retaliation to a breach had to be identical (the well-known "an eye for an eye"); in public international law, for example, it consists in the proportionality that must be observed in taking countermeasures.

The second mechanism is related to the synallagma, the *exceptio non adimpleti contractus*. Here, in an obligation in which performance by each party depends on the other's counterperformance, it is possible for a party not to carry out its side of the bargain if no performance is forthcoming. This again is an example of a self-enforcing rule, one in which the penalty, and the mechanism for discouraging defection, is provided by the structure of the obligation itself.

2.3 Reciprocity and the Sources of International Law

Some mention has already been made of the relationship of reciprocity with certain principles or in the creation of customary rules of law. The final point to examine in answering the question "what is reciprocity?" is to look at its relationship with the sources of international law.

For this purpose, the sources of international law enumerated in Article 38(1) of the Statute of the ICJ, which traditionally are considered to encapsulate the sources of international law, will be taken as a starting point.[71] Treaties will be addressed extensively in Chapter 3,

[70] L. B. Childs, "Shaky Foundations: Criticism of Reciprocity and the Distinction between Public and Private International Law," *New York University Journal of International Law and Politics*, vol. 38, nos. 1 and 2, 2006, p. 229.

[71] While there exist other views as to the sources of international law and their hierarchy, for reasons of space and relevance for the present subject matter, the traditional view of the doctrine of sources will be used.

and leaving aside judicial decisions and the teaching of the most highly qualified publicists in Article 38(1)(d), which are a subsidiary means for the determination of the rules of law, the current section will therefore take a closer look at the relationship between reciprocity and, first, international custom, as evidence of a general practice accepted as law *per* Article 38(1)(b), and second, the general principles of law recognized by civilized nations *per* Article 38(1)(c).

2.3.1 Reciprocity and the Creation of Rules of Customary International Law

While the role of reciprocity is not as readily apparent in the operation of the rules of customary international law as it is in the law of treaties, this is not to say that it does not play an important role in custom as well, primarily linked to its role in the creation of customary rules in a system of legally equal entities. This section will therefore first look at the role of reciprocity in comity and in the creation of rules of customary law, before looking at whether reciprocity still plays a role in customary rules that apply only between a group of States, as is the case in local custom, and at whether the role of specially affected States in the formation of customary rules calls into question the importance of reciprocity in customary international law formation.

2.3.1.1 Comity

Before a look at customary law, the analysis would not be complete without making reference to what is more a category of conduct than a category of legally binding rules – namely, comity. Action on the basis of comity is a good example of an area in which reciprocity is used as a basis to regulate conduct, in the absence of a true legal obligation, and has parallels to the creation of customary rules.

The concept of comity is most widely used in relation to the treatment of foreigners or as a basis for the mutual recognition and application of judgments and national laws of foreign States. It is also used by some States as a justification for the extension of privileges and immunities.[72] In its operation, and in the mutuality that underlies it, comity is based on the idea of reciprocity. States will extend a certain treatment to foreign laws, decisions or nationals, with an expectation that the foreign

[72] G. I. Tunkin, *Theories of International Law*, transl. W. E. Butler, 2nd ed., London, Wildy, Simmons, & Hill, 2003, p. 20; Conforti, *Diritto internazionale*, p. 370.

State will extend a similar treatment to their laws or nationals.[73] The role of reciprocity in comity is to allow for cooperation in the extension of a treatment that goes beyond that which is required by law, setting the standard for the treatment that each State expects,[74] and for retorsion in case the treatment granted is not reciprocated.[75] For example, reciprocity is widely used as a basis for extradition in the absence of an extradition treaty between two States.[76] It may also be used as a basis for the provisional application of a treaty between States having ratified it, prior to its entry into force.[77] Its role, however, remains that of a basis of cooperation in the absence of an obligation.

2.3.1.2 Reciprocity's Role in the Creation of Customary Rules

Reciprocity operates clearly in comity as a basis on which to extend a given treatment, in the absence of a legal obligation. Reciprocity's rule in the creation of customary international law rules may be less immediately obvious, as these are, in the wording of Article 38(1)(b) of the ICJ Statute, evidence of a "general practice accepted as law" rather than a bilateral extension of specific treatment. However, what is of interest in the formation of customary international law is the build-up of claims and their acceptance that manifests itself through State conduct, providing reciprocal responses to each action.[78] Reciprocity also functions to ensure that any State that does not wish to be bound by a new rule is not placed at any advantage; one State cannot assert a right, or enjoy the benefits of the application of a new rule against other States, if it does not accept the operation of that same rule against itself.[79] Because of the sovereign equality of States, and by virtue of reversibility and the

[73] Lagarde, "Réciprocité en droit international," p. 116.

[74] Lagarde makes a historical analysis of reciprocity's increasing use as a basis for retorsion; ibid., p. 189.

[75] Ibid., p. 117.

[76] See, in general, F. Rezek, "Reciprocity as a basis of Extradition," *British Yearbook of International Law*, vol. 52, 1981, pp. 171–203.

[77] See, for example, Agreement in the Form of an Exchange of Letters between the European Community and the Republic of Uzbekistan amending the Agreement between the European Economic Community and the Republic of Uzbekistan on Trade in Textile Products initialed on 8 June 1993, as last amended by an Agreement in the form of an Exchange of Letters initialed on 4 December 1995, Letter from the Council of the European Union, para. 2.7(5).

[78] Paulus calls this the "informal process of tit-for-tat," Paulus, "Reciprocity Revisited," p. 119; Frigo, "Reciprocità nell'evoluzione," p. 419.

[79] Byers, *Custom, Power and the Power of Rules*, pp. 103–105.

interdependence of rights and obligations, a right asserted by one State is, if accepted, a right of all.

But is reciprocity sufficient to explain customary international law? While it can account for the patterns of conduct necessary to create a rule, can it make up the requisite psychological element, or *opinio iuris*? Some authors, such as Campiglio, recognize in reciprocity the *opinio necessitatis* of customary rules.[80] This point of view would require States to feel that they are under an obligation to reciprocate the given conduct or concession, rather than just responding or cooperating out of convenience, or, as outlined above, on the basis of mere comity. If we consider reciprocity to only be applicable and have legal effects bilaterally, this standard seems rather difficult to attain. If, instead, reciprocity can apply multilaterally, that is, not just between two States, it is possible to accept that a State may reciprocate any given assertion (in any given way) in the belief that this is a right or obligation that weighs not only on it, but also on all other States. In fact, in customary international law, where all States feel they are concerned by a unilateral assertion of a right, they will respond consequently – and not just on a bilateral basis. Parisi and Ghei give the example of the Truman Proclamation and subsequent developments in the law of the sea as an example: a situation in which all coastal States could make the same claim, and in which all of them stood to gain.[81] A similar alignment of interests and acceptability of a claim as a general rule has also been used to explain extensions in the rights of coastal States to enforce pollution prevention measures outside their territorial sea.[82] Reciprocity therefore functions in custom formation to preserve the legal equality of States, and allow the general extension of a rule.

2.3.1.3 The Cases of Local Custom and Specially Affected States

However, not all customary rules are either formed or apply universally. ICJ jurisprudence has confirmed that customary rules may also apply between a subgroup of States – for example in a given geographic area – or even bilaterally.[83] The existence of bilateral custom was most notably

[80] Campiglio, *Principio di reciprocità*, p. 14.

[81] Ibid., pp. 91–92; Parisi and Ghei, "Role of Reciprocity in International Law," pp. 26–27. The authors also identify role reversibility and repeat interactions as essential elements for this type of reciprocity, p. 34.

[82] Byers, *Custom, Power and the Power of Rules*, pp. 92–95.

[83] *Case concerning Right of Passage over Indian territory (Portugal* v. *India)*, Preliminary Objections, Judgment of 26 November 1957, ICJ Reports 1957, p. 125; *Asylum Case*

set out in the Judgment in the *Right of Passage* case of 1960.[84] In its work on the identification of customary international law, the International Law Commission (ILC) has further noted that there is no reason why such rules of particular customary international law could not also develop among States that are linked by a common cause or activity; that is, special, local or particular rules of custom can exist among a subgroup of States to deal with issues that are not generalizable, and do not bind third States without their assent.[85] In the case of local or special custom, the "general practice accepted as law" in Article 38(1)(b) of the ICJ Statute is general among those States to which the particular rule applies.[86] This has translated into a strict application of criteria to identify the existence of such rules, particularly in terms of uniformity of practice; this has led to views that consider local or special custom to be more akin to a tacit agreement than general customary international law.[87]

What the ICJ has sought when establishing whether a rule of local customary law exists has been whether there exists practice and *opinio juris* among the States concerned, and the existence of a right and of a correlative obligation.[88] The requirement of reciprocity, in terms of mutuality, is therefore also present when the customary rules in question are not applicable generally, but only among a subset of States, and

(Colombia/Peru), Judgment of 20 November 1950, ICJ Reports 1950, p. 266. See also Report of the International Law Commission on the Work of Its Sixty-Eighth Session, 2 May–10 June and 4 July–12 August 2016, ILC Report A/71/10, pp. 115–116; K. Guliyev, "Local Custom in International Law: Something in between General Custom and Treaty," *International Community Law Review*, vol. 19, 2017, pp. 47–67, at 49; A. D'Amato, "The Concept of Special Custom in International Law," *American Journal of International Law*, vol. 63, 1969, pp. 211–223, at 212; ILC, Third Report on Identification of Customary International Law, by Michael Wood, Special Rapporteur, ILC Doc. No. A/CN.4/682, *Yearbook of the International Law Commission*, 2015, p. 56.

84 *Right of Passage over Indian Territory*, p. 39.

85 See ILC Doc. No. A/71/10, at pp. 115–116; ILC Doc. No. A/CN.4/682, at p. 56, and D'Amato, "Concept of Special Custom," pp. 212–213.

86 ILC Doc. No. A/71/10, at p. 117; Guliyev, "Local Custom in International Law," pp. 52–53.

87 The application of criteria to establish these types of customary rule can be found in ILC Doc. No. A/CN.4/682, at p. 57; for an overview of positions on the matter, see Guliyev, "Local Custom in International Law," pp. 53–56.

88 "The Court is, in view of all the circumstances of the case, satisfied that that practice was accepted as law by the Parties and has given rise to a right and a correlative obligation," *Right of Passage* case, p. 40; "it has not shown that the alleged rule of unilateral and definitive qualification was invoked or . . . that it was, apart from conventional stipulations, exercised by the States granting asylum as a right appertaining to them and respected by the territorial States as a duty incumbent on them," *Asylum Case*, p. 277.

both in the case of a bilateral custom – as in *Right of Passage* – and a regional custom, as in the *Asylum* case.

The question remains, however, whether the mechanism in this type of customary rule affects the point made in the previous section, that a right asserted by one State is, if accepted, one that can be invoked by all States, and which must also be recognized to all other States. In the case of special or local custom, the specificity or regional circumscription of a rule is included in its scope. There is not therefore an assertion by a group of States of greater rights in relation to a matter than others; the scope or content of the rule is itself limited to a given area. Within the subgroup of States concerned, there still needs to be generality and reversibility, granting a specific right and imposing a correlative obligation to all States concerned.[89]

Another doctrine that raises questions in relation to the "general practice" of custom, and the relevance of reciprocity, is the requirement, set out by the ICJ in the *North Sea Continental Shelf* cases, that State practice should include the practice of States that are specially affected.[90] The doctrine itself has not been relied upon by the ICJ since then and has only been invoked by a very small number of States.[91] While the idea that the practice of some States could have more weight than others in the formation of customary rules of law has been seen as a challenge to sovereign equality,[92] the requirement to *include* the practice of States that are specially affected to ensure that practice is "widespread and representative"[93] would appear more, as Heller argues, a recognition that not all States have the same interest in the same rules, or are affected by them in the same way than granting more rights to some States than to others.[94] Firstly, all States can find themselves in the

[89] The specific mechanism will depend on the content of the rule. In *Right of Passage*, the rule operates as a simple right held by one State with a correlative obligation held by the other. In the case of a regional practice, then all States concerned may have the same rights and obligations as against each other in relation to the rule.

[90] North Sea Continental Shelf cases (Federal Republic of Germany/Denmark; Federal Republic of Germany/Netherlands), Judgment of 20 February 1969, ICJ Reports 1969, p. 3, para. 74; S. Aviv Yeini, "The Specially-Affecting States Doctrine," *American Journal of International Law*, vol. 112, 2018, pp. 244–253; K. J. Heller, "Specially-Affected States and the Formation of Custom," *American Journal of International Law*, vol. 112, 2018, pp. 191–243, at 194.

[91] See Heller, "Specially-Affected States," pp. 192, 196, 203.

[92] See Aviv Yeini, "Specially-Affecting States Doctrine," p. 245; Heller, "Specially-Affected States," pp. 200–202.

[93] North Sea Continental Shelf cases, Judgment, para. 73.

[94] Heller, "Specially-Affected States," p. 202.

position of "specially affected," even if it is not in relation to exactly the same rules; there is no serious iniquity inherent in the requirement. Secondly, the fact that the practice of specially affected States is taken into account in establishing whether "general practice" exists is also not the same as saying that only specially affected States can create customary rules; when faced with the assertion of a right, the reaction of other States is also relevant. Thirdly, a State may not be specially affected and therefore may not be engaged in a specific practice but may be perfectly happy to assert those same rights, as is the case in general customary international law, even if it did not have a hand in creating the rule. This point is where reciprocity is to be found and where the legal equality of States comes into play.

2.3.2 *Reciprocity and General Principles of Law*

Ahead of the examination of the law of treaties in Chapter 3, there remains one source of international law to examine: that of general principles of law, as set out in Article 38(1)(c) of the Statute of the ICJ. Conceptions of what exactly is meant by "general principles of law recognised by civilised nations" in this paragraph of the Statute have differed since its drafting. However, the preparatory works and the manner in which Article 38(1)(c) has since been applied in jurisprudence indicate that it includes both general principles found in domestic legal systems and principles that are proper to international law itself.[95] "General principles" have also been recognized as not only being those recognized by domestic legal systems but axiomatic principles of the international legal system itself, such as would be the case of the principle of the sovereign equality of States in international law; structural principles underlying the system that cannot be pinpointed in a specific treaty or customary rule of law.

Reciprocity is occasionally referred to as such a general principle of international law. However, this statement requires some further examination. The following section will therefore examine whether reciprocity bears the characteristics of a general principle, any links it may have with other general principles, and its interaction with the fundamental principles of international law.

[95] For an overview, see J. Crawford, *Brownlie's Principles of Public International Law*, 9th ed., Oxford, Oxford University Press, 2019, pp. 32–34; J. R. Leiss, "The Juridical Nature of General Principles," in M. Andenas et al., eds., *General Principles and the Coherence of International Law*, Leiden, Brill, 2019, pp. 84–85; Kolb, *Bonne foi en droit international public*, p. 19.

2.3.2.1 A General Principle under Article 38(1)(c) of the Statute of the ICJ?

The first question to answer in determining whether reciprocity fits within the category of general principles of law within the meaning of Article 38(1)(c) of the Statute of the ICJ is to look at whether it has been recognized as such in the ICJ's jurisprudence. Two cases in particular are usually used to as references for a "principle" of reciprocity. The first is the *Right of Passage* case, examined above in relation to bilateral custom, and the second is *Interhandel*.[96] Here, however, the "principle of reciprocity" relates to declarations of the acceptance of the jurisdiction of the Court, rather than a general principle of reciprocity applicable in the legal dispute; the legal force of reciprocity in this case comes from an agreement, the Statute of the Court, with no indication that it draws any legal force from its nature as a general principle separate to a treaty or customary rule of international law. The case of reciprocity in the acceptance of the jurisdiction of the Court will be examined in Chapter 6. Aside from the case of jurisdiction, however, there is no other case in which the Court has recognized reciprocity as a general principle of law in the meaning of Article 38(1)(c).

Reciprocity is certainly not unknown in domestic legal systems – as examined in Chapter 1. However, the very specific instances in which it is used, usually as a domestic basis for the acceptance of rules of international law, or as a basis for recognition of laws among states in a federation, are not so established or universal as to constitute what we might consider a general principle of law, in the same manner as the principle of good faith, to cite one well-established example. One principle that is based on reciprocity and could better fit in the category, due to its widespread presence in domestic legal systems as seen in Chapter 1, is the *exceptio non adimpleti contractus*.[97] The next question to address may therefore be whether reciprocity could be considered as a general principle as embodied in the *exceptio*. The analysis here, again,

[96] *Interhandel Case (Switzerland* v. *United States of America)*, Preliminary Objections, Judgment of 21 March 1959, ICJ Reports 1959, p. 23; *Right of Passage over Indian Territory*, Preliminary Objections, pp. 147–148; see also M. Dordeska, *General Principles of Law Recognised by Civilised Nations (1922–2018): The Evolution of the Third Source of International Law through the Jurisprudence of the Permanent Court of International Justice and the International Court of Justice*, Leiden, Brill, 2020, pp. 94, 97.

[97] The *exceptio* was suggested as an applicable principle by Judge Anzilotti in the Permanent Court of International Justice (PCIJ), *Diversion of Water from the Meuse*, Judgment of 28 June 1937, PCIJ, No. A/B 70, p. 210.

indicates that it is not. Firstly, while reciprocity underpins the *exceptio*, functioning as a condition for contractual rules, the two are not coextensive. As seen above, reciprocity cannot only be reduced to its function in the execution of legal rules, and to contractual rules at that. Secondly, as Fontanelli argues, the *exceptio* itself is best seen as a norm of the law of obligations, rather than a universal principle.[98] The fact that it may be considered a principle in domestic law would also not automatically make it applicable as a general principle in international law. International law contains its own secondary rules, including the conditions under which rules may be suspended following a breach. These are found in the rules on State responsibility; in relation to treaties, they are codified in Article 60 of the VCLT, both of which will be examined in Chapter 5. Given the existence of specific treaty and customary rules governing the cases in which the *exceptio* could apply, and given that both regimes have their specific characteristics that are not exactly coextensive with the *exceptio*, the latter cannot be said to constitute a general principle in international law.

The final question to be addressed is whether reciprocity could be considered a principle applicable in the absence of other rules. To avoid a *non liquet*, that is, could recourse be made to a principle of reciprocity? Here, the specific link of reciprocity with conduct poses a difficulty to accepting it as a principle of law having this function. As seen in Section 2.2.1, reciprocity can and does play an important role as a basis for cooperation in the absence of legal rules. However, this is not the same as ascribing normativity to reciprocity, or asserting that States must act on the basis of reciprocity in the absence of other applicable rules of law.

2.3.2.2 Reciprocity as an Element within Certain General Principles of Law?

While there is no general principle of reciprocity in international law, reciprocity still has an important link to several principles. It can however be envisaged that reciprocity of conduct in the absence of applicable legal norms could bring into play the applicability of principles such as good faith, which, as noted by Kolb, can play the role of extending the

[98] F. Fontanelli, "The Invocation of the Exception of Non-Preformance: A Case-Study on the Role and Application of General Principles of International Law of Contractual Origin," *Cambridge Journal of International and Comparative Law*, vol. 1, no. 1, 2012, pp. 119–136, at 126.

reach of law to areas where no firm legal rule has been established,[99] or acquiescence.[100]

Reciprocity also has a close link with equity, which is a wide notion that covers a multitude of principles and has a multitude of roles. It can be used to settle cases outside the law or to temper the application of legal rules to ensure they are consonant with justice. Equity has been described as "legally recognized qualification and modification of the law by considerations of morality and fairness."[101] In this respect, it bears similarities with reciprocity in its intrinsic links with considerations of fairness.[102] Equity ensures fairness through balance of the needs and rights of the parties and requires a degree of proportionality rather than a strictly transactional division; it has been noted that rules based on reciprocity require "no more than equity."[103]

But what is the relationship between the two? Reciprocity could be considered a part of equity and could even fulfill similar functions, for example in the absence of legal rules. But while equity is strictly tied up with judgment, and apportioning, and is in a sense retrospective in its application, reciprocity relates instead to the course of future events and the extent of obligations undertaken, whether as a catalyst for rule formation or as a condition in legal rules. Reciprocity may be within the realm of equity, but it is concerned either as a social norm, with a course of future conduct, or as a legal norm, with the functioning of rights and obligations incumbent on the parties.

For example, the clean hands principle can be seen as closely linked to reciprocity. Cases in which clean hands has been raised before the ICJ (even if not ultimately the basis on which a decision has been made) have raised arguments underpinned by reciprocity. A recent example is the assertion made by Iran in the *Certain Iranian Assets* case before the ICJ.[104] The clean hands doctrine differentiates itself from the *exceptio* in not

[99] Kolb, *Bonne foi en droit international public*, p. 685.

[100] On the general principle underlying acquiescence, see *Maritime Delimitation in the Indian Ocean (Somalia* v. *Kenya)*, Judgment of 12 October 2021, paras. 51–52.

[101] C. Grauer, "The Role of Equity in the Jurisprudence of the World Court," *University of Toronto Faculty of Law Review*, vol. 37, 1979, pp. 101–102.

[102] See Section 2.1.2.2, and R. N. Snyder, "Equity in the World's Legal Systems: A Comparative Study Dedicated to René Cassin," in R. A. Newman, ed., *Equity in the World's Legal Systems: A Comparative Study Dedicated to René Cassin*, Brussels, Bruylant, 1973, pp. 39–40.

[103] Axelrod, *Evolution of Cooperation*, p. 137.

[104] Certain Iranian Assets (*Islamic Republic of Iran* v. *United States of America*), Preliminary Objections, Judgment, ICJ Reports 2019, p. 7, paras. 120–121.

requiring conduct to meet the threshold of illegality, but otherwise a similar mechanism underpins it.

Overall, the relationship of reciprocity with certain other principles of international law does not add much to an understanding of its nature; it is relevant as a basis for certain principles, not all of which find an application in international law. The final point to address is therefore to look at the relationship between reciprocity and the fundamental, structural, or axiomatic principles of international law.

2.3.2.3 Reciprocity and Fundamental Principles of International Law

There is a further category of principles whose relationship to reciprocity deserves examination. These are what have variously been termed "fundamental" or axiomatic principles of international law. While there may be some overlap, what is meant by this term is not coextensive with the peremptory norms of international law, which are customary rules that are nonderogable in character, and which will be examined more closely in Chapters 3 and 5.

Fundamental principles of international law pertain to the structural characteristics of the legal system, or to logical necessities of the law.[105] Examples of these principles are *pacta sunt servanda*,[106] or the sovereign equality of States in international law. They are the basic principles on which the structure of international law rests, "assumptions" of the system that are different in nature to the general principles in the meaning of Article 38(1)(c).[107]

Reciprocity is best understood within this context of the structural principles of international law. By itself, it does not have the normative function that would be required of a principle of international law While it is possible to say that "States must keep their agreements," an assertion that "States must act on the basis of reciprocity" has, as will be seen in subsequent chapters, too many exceptions and is insufficiently clear as a logical premise to characterize reciprocity as a fundamental

105 Kolb, *Bonne foi en droit international public*, p. 57; Dordeska, *General Principles of Law*, p. 59.

106 Fontanelli, "Invocation of the Exception of Non-Preformance," p. 126; U. Lindefalk, "General Principles as Principles of International Legal Pragmatics: The Relevance of Good Faith for the Application of Treaty Law," in M. Andenas et al., eds., *General Principles and the Coherence of International Law*, Leiden, Brill, 2019, pp. 114–116.

107 D. Costelloe, "The Role of Domestic Law in the Identification of General Principles of Law under Article 38(1)(c) of the Statute of the International Court of Justice," in M. Andenas et al., eds., *General Principles and the Coherence of International Law*, Leiden, Brill, 2019, pp. 181–182.

principle of international law. Reciprocity fits far more clearly in the principle of the sovereign equality of States. Its functions in international law, it is argued here, are those of an implementing mechanism for the legal equality of States – the main subjects of international law. The precise roles and manifestations of reciprocity, and the limits to it in international law, are dictated primarily by the connection to legal equality.

2.4 Conclusion

A multitude of answers have been provided to the question "what is reciprocity?" depending on whether or not the term is being used to describe conduct that is legally relevant. The examination in the next chapters of how reciprocity operates in international law will refer to legal reciprocity, defined as the interdependence of mutual rights and obligations States owe each other, which are geared toward the maintenance of legal equality.

It is this relationship with the structural characteristic of sovereign equality in international law that explains many of reciprocity's roles and characteristics. Reciprocity does not require absolute equality in undertaking (although it can) but rather a measure of proportionality. Its application is not limited to a bilateral setting, but because of its intersubjective nature, it can also apply in a multilateral legal obligation in international law. While not itself a rule of international law, it can be an element or a condition within rules; it can also provide a basis for cooperation in the absence of legal rules, or in law formation, playing a role in the formation of customary rules, and in execution of the law. While not a general principle, it is intrinsically linked to the fundamental principle of sovereign equality in international law.

3 Treaties

Following an overview of the role of reciprocity in relation to custom and general principles above, the remaining source of international law to be examined, international agreements, requires an in-depth analysis. Analyzing how reciprocity works in the law of treaties is also key to answering the question of whether and why reciprocity might still exist in the rules of international law dealing with community interests and obligations. This chapter will therefore compare bilateral obligations and treaties to multilateral and integral obligations, in fields which address interests of the international community such as human rights or the environment. The analysis will begin by assessing the relationship between reciprocity and treaties in general, before analyzing reservations and some examples of bilateral treaties. These are all areas in which it can be expected that reciprocity will play a key role. The analysis will then focus on multilateral treaties, both bilateralizable and integral in type. Finally, the chapter will address three types of treaty that are commonly considered to be strictly nonreciprocal: those establishing differentiated obligations, those establishing international organizations, and "objective regimes."[1] While in all these examples there will be some differences with "normal" bilateral or multilateral treaties, it is argued here that none of them fully escape the functioning of reciprocity. The fact that obligations in a treaty may be differentiated has no consequence for the reciprocity of rights and obligations, unless the imbalance is such as to affect the legal equality of the parties; in this case, however, the validity of the treaty will be affected. Some of the traditional mechanisms of reciprocity, such as reservations, may also operate differently in treaties establishing, or established by,

[1] Virally, "Principe de réciprocité," p. 41.

international organizations; however, these are to a significant extent examples of institutionalized reciprocity. Finally, treaties cannot impose any rights or obligations upon third States without some form of acceptance on their part; in fact, reciprocity may be a basis on which to extend rights and obligations to third States, whether explicitly or implicitly.

3.1 Reciprocity and Treaties

The treaty in its bilateral form has been used since ancient times. In fact, until the Congress of Vienna in 1815, this was the exclusive form in which treaties were concluded.[2] Where it was necessary to regulate matters between a number of States or, before the emergence of the modern conception of sovereign State, between different entities or kingdoms, a plurality of parallel treaties would be concluded, rather than a single instrument. One example is the Peace of Westphalia, in which the Treaties of Münster and Osnabrück were concluded in parallel. The treaty was therefore based on a strict conception of reciprocity, as two sets of concessions made by contracting States.[3] The relatively recent shift toward the use of multilateral treaties in which consent of multiple States could be exchanged within the same instrument is a significant evolution in treaty law.

The question of the degree to which treaties can be compared to contracts has been the object of debate, and is related to which definition of treaty one accepts. In the Vienna Convention on the Law of Treaties (VCLT), a treaty is "an international agreement concluded between States in written form and governed by international law, whether embodied in a single instrument or in two or more related instruments."[4] The crucial point as to what constitutes a treaty is its nature as an agreement. Already in 1953, Hersch Lauterpacht as Rapporteur to the ILC on the Law of Treaties indicated that "the consensual – the contractual – nature of treaties constitutes their principal characteristic" and that, further, even for supposedly lawmaking treaties, whatever form of legislation

[2] Dupuy, "Unité de l'ordre juridique international," p. 46; Campiglio, "Principio di reciprocità," p. 62.

[3] Dupuy, "Unité de l'ordre juridique international," p. 49; Campiglio, "Principio di reciprocità," p. 62. As explained above, this form of reciprocity was the basis of the first known example of a treaty, the Peace of Kadesh. See G. Schwarzenberger, *The Dynamics of International Law*, Milton, Professional Books, 1976, p. 48.

[4] Vienna Convention on the Law of Treaties, 1969, Article 2.1(a).

they might contain was still subject to a contractual form.[5] This point is highlighted by the existence and function of reservations, addressed below. The exchange of agreement constitutes the very basis of treaties; indeed, the exchange of instruments of ratification makes treaties binding for States.[6]

A question therefore arises concerning the degree to which agreement in a treaty may be unilateral or not. This is important in order to understand whether this might constitute a first exception to reciprocity. Firstly, the definition of a treaty in the VCLT specifies that the written agreement in question may be present in more than one instrument. A seemingly unilateral undertaking may actually be part of an agreement that is strictly reciprocal in nature, such as in the case of declarations under the Optional Clause system of the Statute of the ICJ.[7] This is the case for all instruments containing an acceptance of previous or subsequently existing obligations in a separate treaty.[8] Secondly, the act in question may be "unilateral" in the sense that there is no apparent exchange of obligations among States parties; instead, as is the case in most human rights treaties, each State may make an undertaking in terms that are absolute. Despite appearances, it cannot be said that the obligations in question are strictly unilateral. They are still incorporated into a treaty and formalized by an exchange of ratifications.

A connected problem is the view that opposes contractual and lawmaking treaties (*traités-contrats* and *traités-loi*). Contractual treaties are described as being reciprocal treaties and in turn equated to bilateral treaties.[9] The term "lawmaking treaty" is instead shorthand for a multilateral treaty in which general obligations are set out that all parties must observe, and which cannot be reduced to a series of bilateral undertakings – and therefore which may also exclude any reciprocity.

The usefulness of this distinction has however long been questioned, both in the work of the ILC[10] and in State submissions to the ICJ in the *Reservations to the Convention on the Prevention and Punishment of the Crime of*

[5] ILC, Report on the Law of Treaties by Mr. H. Lauterpacht, Special Rapporteur, Doc. No. A/CN.4/63, *Yearbook of the International Law Commission 1953*, vol. II, p. 94.

[6] G. G. Fitzmaurice, "Some Problems Regarding the Formal Sources of International Law," in F. M. van Asbeck et al., eds., *Symbolae Verzijl*, The Hague, Nijhoff, 1958, p. 176.

[7] ILC, Doc. No. A/CN.4/63, p. 97.

[8] Ibid., p. 102.

[9] Campiglio, "Principio di reciprocità," p. 321.

[10] ILC, Fifth Report on the Law of Treaties by Sir Humphrey Waldock, Special Rapporteur, Doc. No. A/CN.4/183 and Add.1-4, *Yearbook of the International Law Commission 1966*, vol. II, p. 35.

Genocide Advisory Opinion of 1950.[11] The fundamental point against the distinction is that in any treaty, there will be both articles that are "lawmaking" in character, including abstract and general obligations, and those that are "contractual," which involve a more obvious exchange between the parties – usually final provisions and particularly those relating to dispute settlement. This makes it difficult to distinguish a contractual from a lawmaking treaty and raises questions as to where the line between the two is to be drawn. It is impractical to distinguish between "contractual" and "lawmaking" treaties for anything other than descriptive purposes. Introducing different rules of treaty law for different parts of the same treaty would mean separating treaty provisions from each other and cause more practical problems than it would solve.[12]

It might therefore be concluded that the unity of the regime of treaty law, and the unity of treaties themselves, reflects the acceptance of a treaty as a negotiated instrument, whose different articles, although they may be structured differently in terms of obligations, taken together constitute an exchange of undertakings by the States parties.[13]

A further distinction discussed by the ILC in its work on codifying the law of treaties was based on the number of parties to a treaty and the generality of their obligations. "Plurilateral" treaties were considered similar to what would today be termed interdependent treaties. That is, plurilateral treaties laid down matters of concern for the parties, rather than general regulations[14] and were constituted by a plurality of sides, rather than one common "side" with the same interest in the regulation of a common problem.[15] It was finally recognized that these differences did not have any legal consequences insofar as the rules

[11] See particularly the comments by Rosenne and Kerno, *Reservations to the Convention on the Prevention and Punishment of the Crime of Genocide*, Minutes of the Public Sittings held at the Peace Palace, The Hague, on 10–14 April and on 28 May 1951, pp. 333 and 316 respectively [hereafter "Genocide Convention Case"].

[12] Comments by Kerno, ibid., p. 315, and Rosenne, ibid., p. 334.

[13] The point is also made by Sir Gerald Fitzmaurice that this reflects the fact that treaties cannot ever be "law" in the common sense but are instead only sources of rights and obligations. It is therefore consent and the principle of *pacta sunt servanda* that give the treaties the character of law, rather than the content of any one of their specific provisions. Fitzmaurice, "Some Problems Regarding the Formal Sources," pp. 157, 173.

[14] ILC, Summary Records of the Fourteenth Session, 24 April–29 June 1962, *Yearbook of the International Law Commission*, vol. I, 1962, p. 77. The term was used by Portugal in both the Application and its Memorial in *Case Concerning East Timor (Portugal* v. *Australia)*. See *Case Concerning East Timor (Portugal* v. *Australia)*, Judgment, ICJ Reports 1995, para. 10.

[15] Ibid., p. 79.

regarding treaties are concerned, as "they are all based on agreement, and derive their legal force from its existence."[16] However, in relation to reservations, a specific rule exists in the VCLT in respect of "plurilateral" treaties.[17]

It is suggested here that this unified approach reflects the formally reciprocal nature of all treaties. It is quite simply not necessary to enquire whether the specific treaty at issue is or is not "contractual" in nature or whether it is multilateral or bilateral. There need not be any obvious exchange taking place in the treaty for it to be regarded as contractual.[18] By the very fact that a treaty constitutes an agreement between States, it is formally reciprocal. There is a correlation between every legal obligation and the subjective right of other parties to see these rights observed.[19] Whereas in some treaties there may be an obvious balance of rights and obligations for the parties, and it may be easy to identify the counterpart of each right the parties have agreed upon, this correspondence of rights and obligations will still be present even in treaties in which it may appear that States have only assumed obligations, or that grant no apparent benefit to States parties. Each State has a right: to see that other parties will respect their undertakings.[20]

In this sense, reciprocity governs and is a guarantee of the execution of treaties. Each party to a treaty has the legal right to expect

[16] ILC, Report on the Law of Treaties by Mr. G. G. Fitzmaurice, Doc. No. A/CN.4/101, *Yearbook of the International Law Commission 1956*, vol. II, pp. 107–108.

[17] See Section 4.2.2. [18] ILC, Doc. A/CN.4/63, p. 101.

[19] In Roberto Ago's second report on State responsibility, he observed that, indeed, this correlation between rights and obligations was true of all rules of international law. This will be examined in more detail in Chapter 5, on State responsibility. ILC, Second Report on State Responsibility, by Roberto Ago, Special Rapporteur, Doc. A/CN.4/233, *Yearbook of the International Law Commission*, 1970, vol. II, p. 193.

[20] [T]he intention is that the performance by one party of its obligations will confer on the other party (or parties) a benefit which the latter can legally claim; and this is normally reciprocal. Even in those cases where a treaty appears to involve nothing but obligations for one or more, or all, the parties, nevertheless each party (although it may itself receive no direct benefit therefrom) has a right to claim the performance of the obligation by every other party (ILC, Fourth Report on the Law of Treaties, Sir Gerald Fitzmaurice, Doc. No. A/CN.4/120, *Yearbook of the International Law Commission 1959*, vol. II, Part Two, pp. 53, 54.)

Virally also takes the position that, as all treaties incorporate undertakings toward all other parties, it can be said that reciprocity is the essence of a treaty. However, he bases this affirmation on the fact that in practice there exist few treaties that exclusively impose obligations and remains of the view that reciprocity retains the meaning of symmetry of treatment. Virally, "Principe de réciprocité," pp. 22, 40–43. Simma also views reciprocity in its formal sense as governing all treaties. Simma, "Reciprocity," para. 4.

compliance.[21] This is a legal, rather than merely moral, right or obligation.[22] In international law, therefore, there is a link between the fundamental reciprocity of treaties and the principle of *pacta sunt servanda*. After all, the reason why the *pactum* is to be observed is the parallel engagement with the other parties; the legal right to expect this performance is given by the very existence of reciprocity, in other words by the fact that every party is legally entitled to performance by virtue of the engagement of the others. The reciprocity of treaties is the intersubjective aspect of the fundamental general obligation to observe agreements entered into, the principle that *pacta sunt servanda*.

A second important dimension underlying the reciprocity of treaties, and the link with *pacta sunt servanda*, concerns the subjects that conclude them. After all, treaties cannot be merely equated to a contract but are something more; treaties concluded by States are concluded by entities that are sovereign and equal to one another. The sovereign equality of States also dictates the particular necessity to maintain equality within treaty relations, notably demonstrated in the mechanism of reservations.

Reciprocity is also important in treaty negotiations. Reciprocal concessions are what drive negotiations.[23] The initial aim or expectation of counter-concession in the negotiation phase is therefore extralegal.[24] Even an apparently unilateral undertaking in a treaty, or one in which there are no obvious benefits, may in fact be the result of a series of concessions, or otherwise mask a balance of interests that goes further than the treaty itself. This is often the case with treaties of a commercial nature, or those relating to investment protection. The expectation of performance is therefore not necessarily connected to the actual content of the treaty in terms of the balance of benefits and burdens, nor even of rights and duties. Instead, it is an expectation that arises from the operation of reciprocity: in a psychological or political sense before the treaty is concluded and in a legal sense once it is ratified.

If reciprocity is a basic characteristic of treaties, a question arises regarding reciprocity and treaty interpretation. Frigo asserts that the reciprocal character of treaties must be taken into account in their

21 Paulus, "Reciprocity Revisited," p. 117.

22 Lijnzaad sees it as the "morality of obligation," L. Lijnzaad, *Reservations to UN Human Rights Treaties: Ratify and Ruin?*, Dordrecht/Boston, Nijhoff, 1995, p. 109.

23 Frigo, "Reciprocità nell'evoluzione," p. 433.

24 Preiswerk, "Réciprocité dans les négociations entre pays," p. 8; Campiglio, "Principio di reciprocità," p. 52; Lijnzaad, *Reservations to UN Human Rights Treaties*, p. 68.

interpretation.[25] The question has been treated by courts as an issue linked to the question of reciprocity in treaty negotiation. The Inter-American Court of Human Rights (IACHR), in its Opinion 3/83, stated that "objective criteria of interpretation that look to the texts themselves are more appropriate than subjective criteria that seek to ascertain only the intent of the Parties," because human rights treaties cannot be assimilated to the "traditional" type of treaty that only accomplishes an exchange of rights for the benefit of contracting States.[26] Two observations can be made. First of all, "subjective criteria" are not the first port of call in interpreting a treaty. Preparatory works, which are the subjective means of interpretation *par excellence*, are, according to VCLT Article 32, only a supplementary means of interpretation. The criteria of ordinary meaning in light of the object and purpose of the treaty are in any case the most appropriate for interpreting *any* treaty. Secondly, it is argued here that the difference with human rights treaties is that they endow individuals, and not just States, with rights and also retain an inter-State dimension of reciprocity. It is this aspect that can explain certain limitations to reciprocity, but it does not make the treaty fundamentally different.

A slightly different problem is that which arose before the Permanent Court of International Justice (PCIJ) in the *Meuse* case already mentioned in Chapter 2. In this case, the Netherlands objected to the construction of channels in Belgian territory that could potentially have been used to divert water from the Meuse River, claiming a violation of a bilateral treaty between the two States. The Court noted that accepting this contention "necessarily implies that the Treaty of 1863 intended to place the Parties in a situation of legal inequality by conferring on the Netherlands a right of control to which Belgium could not lay claim," because the Netherlands did not accept that Belgium could have a similar right to contest the legality of the construction work it carried out on its own territory. It found that "[i]t would only be possible to agree with the contention of the Netherlands Agent that the Treaty had created a position of inequality between the contracting Parties if that were expressly indicated by the terms of the Treaty"[27] – which it was not. Grauer notes that it was the "equitable principle of equality" that was at

[25] Frigo, "Reciprocità nell'evoluzione," p. 207.

[26] Inter-American Court of Human Rights, OC-3/83, 8/9/1983, "Restrictions to the Death Penalty (Arts. 4(2) and 4(4) American Convention on Human Rights)," para. 50.

[27] PCIJ, *Diversion of Water from the Meuse*, p. 20.

the basis of the decision.[28] The reluctance of the Court to accept the assertions of the Netherlands may be read in a variety of ways, not least among them another reaffirmation of the ordinary meaning and object and purpose criteria. However, it is also interesting from the point of view of reciprocity; it indicates that, in a bilateral treaty at least, there is a presumption of reciprocity in the extent of the undertakings of the parties. It was the fact that the Netherlands did not accept a corresponding right by Belgium to control its building work relating to the channels around the Meuse that led the Court to decline the interpretation of the Treaty that was put forth by the Netherlands.

The aim of the next section of this chapter will be to examine whether there are limitations to reciprocity depending on the type of obligation and its substantive content; it will therefore first look at the rule of reservations to treaties, before looking at different examples of bilateral and multilateral treaty, and particularly the structure of obligations in human rights treaties, those that include differentiated obligations, and international organizations, before addressing the question of whether objective regimes or treaties that have effects beyond the parties escape the functioning of reciprocity.

3.2 Reservations to Treaties

It is in the rules on reservations that the contractual aspect of treaties is most evident, and also where reciprocity is most clearly at play. In Article 2 of the VCLT, a reservation is defined as "a unilateral statement, however phrased or named, made by a State, when signing, ratifying, accepting, approving or acceding to a treaty, whereby it purports to exclude or to modify the legal effect of certain provisions of the treaty in their application to that State." Therefore, a reservation is a statement made unilaterally with the aim of modifying some of the treaty's effects for the reserving State.

Unless the reservation is explicitly authorized by the treaty text,[29] or on the contrary impermissible under the treaty, its effects are determined by the attitude of other treaty parties. It would be incompatible with the consensual nature of treaties if it were possible for States parties to unilaterally determine the extent of their obligations. While it is made

[28] Grauer, "Role of Equity in the Jurisprudence," p. 103.
[29] Vienna Convention on the Law of Treaties, 1969, Article 19.1.

unilaterally, a reservation therefore requires some form of input from another party to the treaty to determine its effect.[30]

3.2.1 *Drafting History of the VCLT:* Unanimity *v.* the Pan-American Rule

The regime that was eventually codified in Articles 19 to 23 of the VCLT was not only the fruit of the creativity of the successive Rapporteurs to the ILC on the topic of the law of treaties. A variety of preexisting codification projects, case law, and importantly the ICJ's Advisory Opinion on *Reservations to the Genocide Convention* had also previously dealt with the issue.

Reservations had been the subject of lengthy discussions that turned around two opposing theoretical approaches. The first of these was the unanimity rule, according to which it was necessary for all States parties to a treaty to accept a reservation in order for it to have effect. The other approach, and that which eventually most influenced the regime in the VCLT, was the "Pan-American" rule, incorporated in the Convention on Treaties adopted by the Sixth International Conference of American States in 1928 (Havana Convention). According to Article 6 of the Havana Convention, reservations only have an effect in the relations between the reserving State and each of the other contracting States;[31] a State could still be a party to a treaty even if one or more States objected to its reservation.[32] The so-called Harvard Draft Convention on the law of treaties instead embodied the unanimity rule, whereby all States parties to a treaty had to accept a reservation for it to become effective. The two approaches were informed by an underlying difference in how reservations were considered. The unanimity rule held reservations to be unfavorable and possible upsets to the contractual balance struck by the parties in concluding the treaty. The Pan-American rule, instead,

[30] F. Horn, *Reservations and Interpretative Declarations to Multilateral Treaties*, Amsterdam/New York, North-Holland, 1988, p. 44; ILC, Guide to Practice on Reservations to Treaties, 2011, *Yearbook of the International Law Commission, 2011*, vol. II, Part Two, p. 53; Lijnzaad, *Reservations to UN Human Rights Treaties*, p. 38.

[31] Convention on Treaties adopted by the Sixth International Conference of American States at Havana, 20 February 1928, Article 6, available in *The American Journal of International Law*, vol. 29, Supplement: Research in International Law, 1935, pp. 1205–1207.

[32] J. M. Ruda, "Reservations to Treaties," *Collected Courses of the Hague Academy of International Law*, vol. 146, 1975, p. 121.

explicitly viewed reservations as favorable for treaty participation and a prerogative of States.[33]

A significant factor in the eventual acceptance of the Pan-American rule was the ICJ's Advisory Opinion on *Reservations to the Genocide Convention*, in 1950. Discussions in States' oral or written interventions centered around two policy-related points: should reservations be permitted, risking a dilution in the obligations set out in the Genocide Convention? Or should reservations be prohibited, possibly compromising universal participation in the Convention? Some States, such as the United Kingdom, considered that reservations to treaties of the lawmaking type should not be permitted; others, notably the United States and USSR, considered that making reservations was a sovereign prerogative and that it should not be for other States parties to limit participation in the Genocide Convention by objecting to reservations and therefore impeding the participation of reserving States.[34] Still others claimed that reservations should be permitted to some, but not all, the provisions of the treaty.[35] The Court eventually decided that reserving States could still be parties to the Genocide Convention so long as the reservation was compatible with the object and purpose of the Convention, and that States objecting to a reservation on the basis of incompatibility could consider the reserving State as not being a party to the treaty.[36] This in effect sees reservations as having the same bilateralizing effect as the rules of the Pan-American Convention.[37]

The development of the rule that reservations operate reciprocally was a less controversial point. That a reservation should operate both ways is embodied in Article 21.1 of the VCLT. The idea that one State party could avail itself of the reservation made by another in their mutual relations was recognized, rather conveniently for the Entente Powers, in Prize Courts set up by those same Powers during the First

[33] Havana Convention, Article 7; Dupuy, "Communauté internationale et disparités de développement," p. 98; Horn, *Reservations and Interpretative Declarations*, p. 30.

[34] "Genocide Convention Case," Written Statement of the Government of the United Kingdom, p. 48, Exposé écrit du gouvernement de l'Union des Républiques Socialistes Soviétiques, p. 21, Written Statement of the Government of the United States of America, pp. 30, 24, 43.

[35] Statement by Mr. Shabtai Rosenne (Representative of the Government of Israel) at the Public Sittings of 11–12 April 1951, p. 356, ibid.

[36] "Genocide Convention Case," Advisory Opinion of 28 May 1951, pp. 29–30.

[37] R. W. E. Edwards Jr., "Reservations to Treaties," *Michigan Journal of International Law*, vol. 10, 1989, p. 394.

World War – notably in the UK and France.[38] Other conventions in the 1950s and 1960s specifically allowed for reservations to operate in this fashion.[39]

3.2.2 *The Regime in the VCLT: Universality and Reciprocity*

The VCLT's reservations regime mirrors the ICJ's Advisory Opinion on the Genocide Convention in two main ways. Firstly, it is universally applicable to all types of treaty.[40] Secondly, it provides a compromise between the two opposing concerns that informed debates around reservations to the Genocide Convention. On the one hand, the general rule in Article 19 allows a reservation to be made unless it is expressly prohibited by the treaty (Article 19(a) and (b)), thereby promoting universal adherence to treaties. On the other hand, in excluding the validity of reservations that are contrary to the object and purpose of the treaty in question in Article 19(c), it allows the aims of the treaty to be safeguarded, dealing to some extent at least with concerns regarding the desirability of reservations to provisions of treaties such as – but not only – those relating to human rights.[41]

Once a reservation is made, Article 20 of the VCLT outlines three different scenarios. The first, in paragraph 1, is the case of a reservation expressly authorized by the treaty: in this case, it is not necessary for the other States parties to accept the reservation for it to come in to play in their relations with the reserving State. This stands to reason, as the required acceptance already exists within the treaty itself. In this connection, it is worth mentioning the Award in *Delimitation of the Continental Shelf* between the UK and France.[42] The tribunal found that the UK could not object to France subjecting its ratification of the Geneva Convention on the Continental Shelf of 1958 to reservations specifically permitted by the Convention – that is, reservations to any provisions except for Articles 1–3. Therefore, "the United Kingdom, when it ratified the

[38] Horn, *Reservations and Interpretative Declarations*, p. 145. [39] Ibid., p. 147.

[40] A. Pellet, "Article 19: Formulation of Reservations," in O. Corten and P. Klein, eds., *The Vienna Convention on the Law of Treaties: A Commentary*, Oxford, Oxford University Press, 2011, p. 424.

[41] See in this sense Dupuy, "Communauté internationale et disparités de développement," pp. 99–101; N. Bueno, "Analyse économique du droit international des traités: interpretation, reserve et violation revisitées," *Revue générale de droit international public*, vol. 116, no. 1, 2012, p. 101.

[42] Delimitation of the Continental Shelf between the United Kingdom of Great Britain and Northern Ireland, and the French Republic (UK, France), RIAA, Volume XVIII, Decision of 30 June 1977.

Convention in 1964, gave its express consent to the French Republic's becoming a party to the Convention subject to such reservations as the latter might make to any article other than Article 1, 2, or 3."[43]

According to Article 20.2, acceptance of the reservation by all parties to a treaty is required "[w]hen it appears from the limited number of the negotiating States and the object and purpose of a treaty that the application of the treaty in its entirety between all the parties is an essential condition of the consent of each one to be bound by the treaty."[44] This category of treaty was termed "plurilateral" in the ILC's preparatory discussions, which can today be identified as treaties embodying interdependent obligations. That is, for this type of treaty "a reservation would completely upset the balance of reciprocal rights and obligations achieved during the negotiations."[45] Ruda's use of the word "reciprocal" may be misleading; the issue with treaties referred to in Article 20.2 is not that they are based on reciprocity of rights and obligations but that it is obvious from their object and purpose that to allow free formulation of reservations would defeat the purpose of the treaty. Article 20.2 does not prohibit the making of reservations to this category of treaty but merely subjects the operation of reservations to acceptance by all States parties, reflecting the high degree of conditionality and interdependence that exists between the obligations set out in this type of agreement.

Finally, paragraphs 4 and 5 of Article 20 VCLT deal with the default operation of reservations. Acceptance of a reservation constitutes the reserving State a party to the treaty, even if only one other State accepts the reservation.[46]

If a State objects to a reservation, then two scenarios may present themselves, according to Article 20.4(c). The first is that the treaty enters into force between the reserving and objecting State. The second is that, if a contrary intention is "definitely expressed," the treaty does not enter into force between the two States. This is commonly referred to as a "maximum-effect objection."[47] The presumption is therefore that, when a reservation is objected to, the treaty will enter into force in any case.[48] Whereas the effect of an objection is to alter the obligations the reserving

[43] Ibid., para. 39. [44] Vienna Convention on the Law of Treaties, Article 20.2.

[45] Ruda, "Reservations to Treaties," p. 186.

[46] As per paragraph 5 of Article 20, acceptance is presumed if a State raises no objections to a reservation within twelve months. In practice, this is what most commonly happens.

[47] See for example the ILC's *Guide to Practice on Reservations*, p. 475.

[48] ILC, *Guide to Practice on Reservations*, Guideline 4.3.5; Lijnzaad, *Reservations to UN Human Rights Treaties*, pp. 52–54.

and objecting State are subject to under the treaty, a maximum-effect objection will, instead, mean that there is no treaty relationship at all between the two.[49] Of course, in both cases, the legal relationship with parties other than the objecting State will depend on the acceptance of the reservation. It could therefore happen that a reserving State is a party to a multilateral treaty, but that if half the parties to that treaty have raised a maximum-effect objection, it will only have treaty relations with the other half of the parties.

Regarding the legal effects of reservations, outlined in VCLT Article 21, the first is that, in the case of acceptance, the reservation modifies the provisions of the treaty to which the reservation relates *only* between the reserving and accepting States,[50] and this "to the extent of the reservation."[51] If a State wishes to exclude part of a treaty provision by means of a reservation, this only affects the part of the provision to which the reservation refers.[52]

Furthermore, the modification operates reciprocally, as per VCLT Article 21.1(b). The reservation does not only modify obligations under the treaty for the reserving State; the accepting State's obligations vis-à-vis the reserving State are also modified to the extent of the reservation. In their bilateral relations with respect to the treaty, the accepting State will not be held to the obligations it originally ratified but only those obligations as modified by the reservation. There are two ways of understanding this point. The commonly given explanation views reciprocity as a "reversal" of the reservation; if A is the reserving State and B the accepting State, then the reservation operates from A to B, but also vice versa from B to A.[53] Another way of looking at this is in terms of correlation of rights and obligations. If A restricts its obligations under the treaty by virtue of a reservation, then *its rights must also be restricted to the same extent*.

A similar mechanism applies regarding objections. VCLT Article 21.3 sets out the effects of an objection as being that "the provisions to which

[49] Ibid., pp. 474–475. [50] Vienna Convention on the Law of Treaties, Article 2.1.

[51] Vienna Convention on the Law of Treaties, Article 21.1(b).

[52] Vienna Convention on the Law of Treaties, Article 21.3; Delimitation of the Continental Shelf (UK, France), para. 61. In this case, France had made a reservation to the first two paragraphs of Article 6 of the 1958 Geneva Convention on the Continental Shelf, excluding the application of the equidistance principle for some specific circumstances, but not to the third paragraph of Article 6. The UK's objection therefore meant that only paragraphs 1 and 2 of Article 6 would be excluded.

[53] For example, see ILC, *Guide to Practice on Reservations*, p. 461, where it is mentioned that reservations "work both ways."

the reservation relates do not apply as between the two States to the extent of the reservation." It is easy to see how this may, in the case of a reservation whose aim is to exclude a certain provision, have the same effect as acceptance.[54] However, there will be a slightly different effect when the reservation purports to modify, rather than exclude, a provision of the treaty. In this case, an objection to the reservation would exclude the provision in the mutual relations of the States concerned, whereas acceptance would entail a modification of the obligations between the parties. A "normal" objection will therefore render the reservation non-opposable to the objecting State,[55] and indeed render inoperable the provision in question between the two States, while not affecting the remainder of the obligations under the treaty.

3.2.3 The Contractual Nature of Reservations

While the regime in the VCLT ensures flexibility in acceptance of the provisions of multilateral treaties, it means that the same multilateral treaty instrument can, by virtue of the effect of reservations, turn into a series of varying obligations.[56] In effect, the rules on reservations acknowledge the formally reciprocal structure of all treaties, without making distinctions as to whether they are "contractual" or "lawmaking."[57]

In the law of treaties, reservations are therefore "part of the bargain"[58] of the treaty. The basis of the reservations regime reflects the nature of international law, as based on the sovereign equality of States.[59] This explains the primary concern with acceptance of the reservation by other States parties. It means that, unless precisely specified in the

[54] Bueno, "Analyse économique du droit international des traités," p. 102.

[55] Lijnzaad, *Reservations to UN Human Rights Treaties*, p. 49.

[56] Bueno, "Analyse économique du droit international des traités," p. 101; Horn, *Reservations and Interpretative Declarations*, p. 31; D. Müller, "Article 21: Legal Effects of Reservations and Objections to Reservations," in *The Vienna Convention on the Law of Treaties: A Commentary*, Oxford, Oxford University Press, 2011, p. 543.

[57] J. Klabbers, "Les cimetières marins sont-ils établis comme des regimes objectifs? À propos de l'accord sur l'épave du *M/S Estonia*," *Espaces et ressources maritimes*, vol. 11, 1997, p. 777; *Pleadings*, "Genocide Convention Case," *Advisory Opinion*, Part II (1951), p. 202. As Ruda points out, however, a more strictly contractual explanation better suited the old unanimity rule for reservations; the current system is tailored to the specificities of international law. Ruda, "Reservations to Treaties," p. 212. The ILC *Guide to Practice on Reservations* described treaties as "a consensual instrument par excellence," ILC *Guide to Practice on Reservations*, pp. 472–473.

[58] ILC, Report on the Law of Treaties by J. L. Brierly, Special Rapporteur, Doc. No. A/CN.4/23, *Yearbook of the International Law Commission 1950*, vol. II, p. 241.

[59] Ruda, "Reservations to Treaties," p. 183.

treaty, a State must freely accept, and not have imposed upon it, any modifications in the consent expressed by other contracting States.[60]

3.2.4 *Reciprocity and Reservations*

The rule that reservations may be invoked reciprocally therefore derives from the consensual basis of both treaties and the acceptance of, or objection to, reservations. It may be defined as the rule that while a State may invoke a reservation it has made against other parties, these parties will also be able to invoke the same reservation in their relations with the reserving State.[61] Therefore, the reserving State may not invoke the provision of the treaty that it excludes by way of a reservation.[62]

It is argued here that this mechanism derives from the correlation between rights and obligations under the treaty,[63] with the aim of ensuring equality, or balance, between the parties.[64] If a reservation limits the obligations of one party, it must necessarily also limit that State's right to claim performance of the same obligation by other parties. If this were not the case, one State would be able to unilaterally claim more rights under the treaty than any other party. This would clearly affect the legal equality of the States parties.[65]

Aside from removing the possibility for any State to gain a unilateral advantage through the unilateral act of making a reservation, reciprocity of reservations also has a self-regulatory effect. It dissuades parties (at least to a certain extent) from making reservations to the treaty in the first place, as there is no possibility of obtaining any relative advantage by making a reservation.[66]

60 Written Statement of the Government of Israel, "Genocide Convention Case," pp. 208–209.

61 Ruda, "Reservations to Treaties," p. 117; ILC, *Guide to Practice on Reservations*, p. 461; Müller, "Article 21," p. 548; Lijnzaad, *Reservations to UN Human Rights Treaties*, p. 47.

62 Ruda, "Reservations to Treaties," p. 197.

63 Horn, *Reservations and Interpretative Declarations*, pp. 91, 148.

64 Dero, *Réciprocité et le droit*, p. 324.

65 ILC *Guide to Practice on Reservations*, p. 462; Müller, "Article 21," p. 549. It is a different problem when it is agreed upon in the treaty itself that there should be a differentiation in the rights and obligations of parties under the treaty; see Section 3.5.

66 Bueno goes further, arguing that reciprocity of reservations favors full ratification of the treaty by States that have a comparative disadvantage in ratification. Bueno, "Analyse économique du droit international des traités," pp. 104–105. The analysis has also been made that reservations foster cooperation in a Prisoner's Dilemma situation. See Parisi, Cost of the Game," p. 107.

3.2.5 *Limitations and Exceptions to the Reservations Regime: Human Rights and Individual Rights*

The regime outlined above does however have some limitations and exceptions. The first is that if a State unilaterally undertakes more obligations under the treaty than it is obliged to, then such an undertaking will not operate reciprocally. This has been termed an "extensive reservation,"[67] although in reality such undertakings are not treated as reservations but rather as autonomous unilateral acts that are not subject to the rules on reservations.[68]

The second exception to the general rule is indicated in VCLT Article 20.2, according to which a reservation requires acceptance by all parties "when it appears from the limited number of the negotiating States and the object and purpose of a treaty that the application of the treaty in its entirety between all the parties is an essential condition of the consent of each one to be bound by the treaty."[69] That is, where the obligations in the treaty cannot be separated into a series of bilateral relationships but instead represent a truly collective undertaking, and in effect a truly collective reciprocity. Where the condition of observance of the treaty is the participation of *all* other parties, obligations are effectively owed to *all* other States, rather than to each of the other States taken individually. All parties must therefore necessarily accept any modification in undertakings by way of a reservation.[70] While this maintains the distinction that was the subject of discussions in the ILC between plurilateral and multilateral treaties, in reality it follows the rationale of the object and purpose test.[71] The mechanism in Article 20.2 is therefore a "reciprocity plus" of sorts, and indeed shows that reciprocity is not only applicable to bilateral obligations.

The third limitation concerns international organizations. First, specific international organizations may prohibit the making of reservations in their constitutive treaties. Second, Article 20.3 of the VCLT, as well as of the Vienna Convention on the Law of Treaties between States and International Organizations or between International Organizations, sets out a specific regime of acceptance in the case of constitutive treaties of international organizations, whereby unless otherwise indicated,

[67] F. Majoros, "Le régime de réciprocité de la Convention de Vienne et les reserves dans les Conventions de la Haye," *Journal du droit international*, vol. 101, no. 1, 1974, p. 85.

[68] ILC, *Guide to Practice on Reservations*, p. 91.

[69] Reiterated in ibid., Guideline 4.1.2.

[70] Horn, *Reservations and Interpretative Declarations*, p. 123.

[71] ILC, *Guide to Practice on Reservations*, p. 443.

reservations must be accepted by the relevant organ of the organization. This again reflects the rationale of VCLT Article 20.2. As mentioned in comments to the ILC draft by the government of the United States, a treaty setting out the powers of an international organization does so "in terms so finely balanced and interrelated that a reservation disturbing that situation would seriously affect the powers, functions and procedures of the organization."[72] An international organization is intended to centralize decision-making by States; it would not be logical to defer to a decision by parties on an individual basis whether to accept a reservation or not when decision-making has been assigned to a central organ. It is also logical because international organizations have international legal personality; therefore, any reservation also affects the international organization itself.[73]

An argument has also been made with respect to limitations to the reciprocal operation of reservations in human rights treaties, based on the purported nonreciprocity of obligations in these treaties[74] – in the words of the ILC, "treaties establishing obligations owed to the community of contracting States."[75] While this is commonly taken to refer to human rights treaties, the ILC goes on to note that examples include treaties on "commodities, environmental protection, demilitarization or disarmament" and even uniform law treaties.[76] However, these types of treaty cannot easily be assimilated to one another. Specifically, the inclusion of the example of disarmament treaties belongs to the category of interdependent obligations, collective obligations characterized by a high degree of interdependence and collective reciprocity, as seen above. An instrument such as a human rights treaty will, instead, essentially consist of unilateral undertakings by States to respect the obligations outlined in the treaty, independently of the performance of other States parties.[77] In fact, it is precisely the unilateral nature of undertakings that supposedly affects the reciprocal applicability of reservations.

72 "Genocide Convention Case," Written Statement of the Government of the United States of America, p. 33.

73 Horn, *Reservations and Interpretative Declarations*, p. 152; D. Müller, "Article 20: Acceptance of and Objection to Reservations," in *The Vienna Convention on the Law of Treaties: A Commentary*, Oxford, Oxford University Press, 2011, p. 522.

74 The reason, as Horn puts it, is that "the reciprocal application of reservations presupposes the mutual operation of obligations and rights under the treaty," Horn, *Reservations and Interpretative Declarations*, p. 148.

75 ILC, *Guide to Practice on Reservations*, pp. 465–466.

76 Ibid., p. 467.

77 Although of course the consent of other States parties will be relevant insofar as the number of ratifications for entry into force are concerned.

In the case of a human rights treaty, in essence the State accepting a reservation is still held to observe its own obligations under the treaty. For example, Japan's reservation to the Convention on the Rights of the Child (CROC) excludes the application of the obligation to separate juveniles and adults in detention; this does not however mean that another party to the CROC that does not object to the reservation is entitled to equally not provide for such separation. However, it has been recognized that even if the accepting State must continue to observe its obligations, "it is clear that a State or international organization that has made a reservation cannot invoke the obligation excluded or modified by that reservation and require the other parties to fulfil it – even though the other parties remain bound by the obligation in question."[78]

This mechanism is an example of the operation of the reciprocity – understood as a correlation of rights and obligations – inherent in treaties and in the reservations regime. The reserving State cannot invoke performance by other parties of the obligation it has itself excluded. The impossibility in certain treaties for the accepting State to invoke the reservation springs from the type of unilateral undertaking they have made: It would not be possible to continue to respect the obligations of the treaty *in general* if they invoked the reservations made by other States.[79] It is also true that the type of treaty in question may involve a relationship that does not have a purely inter-State dimension, and this is notably the case for human rights treaties. This would mean limiting the rights granted to another entity – the individual – on the basis of an inter-State limitation of rights and obligations in a reservation.[80] Therefore, the reservation undertaken in the horizontal aspect of legal relations in a human rights treaty – the inter-State level – to which reciprocity applies cannot affect the State's obligations in the vertical relationship between the State and individuals in its jurisdiction.

[78] ILC, *Guide to Practice on Reservations*, p. 465. See the same argument in Müller, "Article 21," p. 551.

[79] Horn, *Reservations and Interpretative Declarations*, p. 151; Campiglio, "Principio di reciprocità," pp. 184–187.

[80] Simma makes this point concerning treaties that cannot be "performed 'between' their parties in any meaningful sense," B. Simma, "From Bilateralism to Community Interest in International Law," *Collected Courses of the Hague Academy of International Law*, vol. 250, 1994,, pp. 342–343. See Horn, *Reservations and Interpretative Declarations*, pp. 152 (making an example concerning international organizations) and 154; B. Simma and G. I. Hernández, "Legal Consequences of an Impermissible Reservation to a Human Rights Treaty: Where Do We Stand?," in E. Cannizzaro, ed., *The Law of Treaties beyond the Vienna Convention*, Oxford, Oxford University Press, 2011, p. 66. This is also a justification for the impossibility of making reservations in the ILO. See Chapter 4.

The example of human rights treaties is an interesting one to analyse further because of the large number of reservations made thereto by States. This begs the question of whether the structure of the obligations limits the effectiveness of reciprocity in ensuring full compliance with the treaty. The fact that human rights treaties place obligations on States to respect the rights of individuals on their territory increases the likelihood of an incompatibility with national law, which governments may wish to obviate by way of a reservation.[81] It also reduces the interest for other States parties to object to any reservations made. Indeed, apart from rare instances, reservations will not have much effect outside the State's internal order. Particular questions arise as to the effect of objections to reservations by States parties.

The first point relates to the particular effect of the objection to a reservation by a State party. According to Article 20.3(b) of the VCLT, an objecting State may preclude the entry into force of the treaty with the reserving State if it expresses this intention. It is interesting to note the position of the Inter-American Court of Human Rights (IACHR), in its Opinion 2/82, that the nature of the American Convention on Human Rights (ACHR), specifically its role granting right of petition to individuals[82] and the nature of its obligations as unilateral undertakings by States[83] meant that it was not necessary for other States parties to accept valid reservations before a reserving State could become a party to the treaty.[84] Considering the difference in the structure of obligations in human rights treaties, and because substantive obligations are owed to individuals rather than to other States parties, there is no reason why an objection to a reservation should preclude the entry into force of the treaty in the mutual relations of reserving and objecting States.

A second point concerns the effect of reservations that are contrary to the object and purpose of a human rights treaty. The ICJ in the *Reservations to the Genocide Convention* Advisory Opinion had indicated that, bilaterally, a State objecting to a reservation on the basis of its incompatibility with a convention could consider that the treaty was

[81] B. Simma, "Reservations to Human Rights Treaties – Some Recent Developments," in G. Hafner et al., eds., *Liber Amicorum Professor Seidl-Hohenveldern – In Honour of His 80th Birthday*, The Hague, Kluwer, 1998, p. 660.

[82] Inter-American Court of Human Rights, Advisory Opinion OC-2/82, of 24 September 1982 "The effect of reservations on the entry into force of the American Convention on Human Rights (Arts. 74 and 75)," para. 34.

[83] Ibid., para. 33. [84] Ibid., para. 37.

not in effect between itself and the reserving State, as no reservation could be effective against a State that had not accepted it.[85] Therefore, the question of the effect of an invalid reservation is left to the bilateral relations between States.

As mentioned above, the particularity of human rights treaties is that they usually have a treaty body that is capable of deciding on the validity of reservations made by States. The Human Rights Committee (HRC) in its General Comment 24 cited the "nonreciprocal" nature of the International Covenant on Civil and Political Rights (ICCPR) to justify its role in deciding on the validity of reservations, rather than leaving the decision to States. It further added that, contrary to other treaties, in the case of human rights treaties the effect of the invalidity of a reservation would not be that the reserving State is not a party but that "the reservation will generally be severable,"[86] meaning that the State may still be considered to have consented to the provision to which it had made an impermissible reservation. This position has however been nuanced by the ILC in its Guide to Practice, indicating that "[t]he assessment made by such a body in the exercise of this competence has no greater legal effect than that of the act which contains it,"[87] and in any case these bodies "may not substitute their judgment for the State's consent to be bound by the treaty."[88] The ILC also did not accept the explanation given by the European Court of Human Rights (ECtHR) and IACHR that human rights treaties were a special category for the purposes of rules regarding reservations, as these are not the only treaties that establish "higher common values."[89]

In the case of human rights treaties, reciprocity is limited in the vertical dimension between the State and the individuals on its territory, to whom it undertakes to accord the rights set out in the treaty. However, it still operates in the horizontal, inter-State dimension, limiting the possibility for the reserving State to invoke the rights it has reserved vis-à-vis another State. There being no equality or reciprocity between the State and the

85 "Genocide Convention Case," Advisory Opinion of 28 May 28 1951, ICJ Reports 1951, p. 21.

86 Human Rights Committee, General Comment 24: Issues Relating to the Reservations Made upon Ratification or Accession to the Covenant or the Optional Protocols Thereto, or in Relation to Declarations under Article 41 of the Covenant, CCPR/C/21/Rev.1/Add.6, Fifty-second session, 1994, paras. 17–18.

87 ILC, *Guide to Practice on Reservations*, Guideline 3.2.1.

88 Ibid., p. 395.

89 ILC, *Guide to Practice on Reservations*, p. 541.

individual under its jurisdiction, this latter relationship is instead excluded from the operation of reciprocity in reservations.[90]

3.3 Reciprocity and Bilateral Treaties

Whether reciprocity is understood strictly as a quid pro quo, or more widely as a correlation between rights and obligations, bilateral treaties should on the face of it be the type of international rule most clearly governed by reciprocity. It is in this type of agreement that the equality of contracting parties, and the relativity of obligations, are most obvious.

Historically, the emergence of bilateral treaties also signaled the emergence of international agreements as truly interdependent and synallagmatic obligations, agreed upon by both parties, and no longer as unilateral concessions granted in parallel.[91] It is clearest in bilateral treaties that the performance of the treaty by one party is the counterpart to performance by the other. This was illustrated by the tribunal in the *Gulf of St. Lawrence* arbitration, which identified the treaty between France and Canada as "*un échange de prestations de même nature entre les deux Etats contractants qui se concèdent mutuellement des droits de pêche dans des secteurs relevant de leur juridiction respective en la matière.*"[92] [an exchange of services of the same nature between the two contracting States, who mutually concede to each other fishing rights in sectors within their respective jurisdiction.] This may be why bilateral treaties are often used to regulate areas where the equality of conditions and access of the parties to the rights under the treaty is particularly important, either because the subject area concerned impacts upon national sovereignty, or because they regulate commercial matters – or, as is the case for air transport agreements, both.

This section will focus on two examples of bilateral agreement in which reciprocity could be expected to play a particularly important role. The first of these are air transport agreements, which regulate access by the airlines of each State party to routes and airports. This involves questions of sovereignty, such as access to land territory and airspace, as well as exemption from taxation and other commercial

90 Horn, *Reservations and Interpretative Declarations*, p. 155; Müller, "Article 21," p. 550; Campiglio, "Principio di reciprocità," p. 187.

91 P. Guggenheim, "Jus gentium, jus naturae, jus civile et la communauté internationale issue de la divisio regnorum intervenue au cours des 12e et 13e siècles," *Comunicazioni e Studi*, vol. VII, 1955, p. 64.

92 Filleting in the Gulf of St. Lawrence between Canada and France, Decision of 17 July 1986, *R.I.A.A.* vol. XIX, para. 29.

advantages. The second category is that of agreements relating to energy, and specifically research and development in energy matters.

3.3.1 *Reciprocity and Strict Equality: Air Transport Agreements*

The existence of bilateral air transport agreements finds its origins within the Convention on International Civil Aviation of 7 December 1944 ("Chicago Convention"), which sets out the rights of States with respect to flight over or into their territory by civil aircraft. The rights set out in this multilateral convention are implemented in bilateral air transport agreements between States, which set out the specific rights and duties of the civil aircraft of each State in respect of specific routes between the two States parties.

The reason air transport agreements are interesting from the point of view of reciprocity may also be found within the Chicago Convention. Article 1 of the Convention reads: "The contracting States recognize that every State has complete and exclusive sovereignty over the airspace above its territory."[93] The Preamble to the Chicago Convention states that the principles contained therein are intended to develop aviation "on the basis of equality of opportunity."[94] This informs a series of provisions both in the Chicago Convention and in a number of air service agreements that prevent special privileges being granted, or otherwise discriminating in favor of one State over another.[95]

Firstly, in bilateral air transport agreements ("ATAs"), rights are clearly granted by the contracting States "to each other" or "in their mutual relations." This is so even when the ATAs reiterate existing international legal obligations of the parties, including under multilateral treaties to ensure aircraft safety and prevent unlawful use of civil

93 In the Italy–US Air Transport Agreement Arbitration, Italy claimed that the agreement should be interpreted in the manner that least restricted the sovereignty of the States, although this was not accepted by the Tribunal. Italy–United States Air Transport Arbitration, Advisory Opinion of 17 July 1965, 45 ILR 393, at p. 395.

94 Fair opportunity of all States to operate airlines is also one of the stated aims and objectives in Article 44(f) of the Convention.

95 See, for example, within the Chicago Convention: Article 7, which prohibits granting of privileges to any State to service routes starting and ending within the territory of the same State party; Article 9, allowing restrictions to be put in place on use of airspace, on condition of nondiscrimination; Article 11, concerning nondiscriminatory application of national laws and regulations; Article 15, on openness of airports to all States regardless of nationality, and Article 44(g), stating nondiscrimination as an objective of the Convention.

aircraft.[96] Secondly, significant emphasis is placed on the equality of the rights granted by each party and the assurance of nondiscrimination,[97] regulation of the volume of air traffic passing between the two States[98] and, as seen in the Chicago Convention, application of national laws.[99] These provisions reflect the general concern to ensure equality in the economic advantages resulting from the performance of the ATA.[100] In the *France–US Air Transport Services Agreement* award, it was equally recognized that more extensive rights concerning routes could not be read into the treaty if the negotiators of the two States had not agreed on such an "exchange of reciprocal benefits."[101] In this connection, it is also reiterated in many ATAs that States parties cannot unilaterally alter the extent of the rights they grant, for example concerning the volume of air traffic.[102]

Thirdly, specific mention is made of reciprocity within these agreements. These references to reciprocity are of three main types: general references in the Preamble; conditions of reciprocity in the application of exemptions from the imposition of duties and levies; and recourse to reciprocity as a basis for undertakings on matters that fall outside the scope of the agreement.[103] References to reciprocity may also serve as a useful guide to interpretation, ensuring that one State does not claim

[96] Acuerdo entre el gobierno de la Republica de Colombia y el gobierno de los Emiratos Arabes Unidos en relación con servicios aéreos entre y más allá de sus respectivos territorios, 7 November 2012 ("Colombia–UAE ATA"), Article 12.1. For general examples of this language, see Air Transport Agreement between the government of the United States of America and the government of the State of Bahrain, 24 May 1999 ("US–Bahrain ATA"), Articles 2.1 and 7.1; Air Transport Agreement between the government of the United States of America and the government of the Republic of Costa Rica, 8 May 1997 ("US–Costa Rica ATA"), Article 7.3; Italy–US Air Transport Agreement Arbitration, p. 409; Colombia–UAE ATA, Article 2.1.

[97] See Colombia–Uruguay, Acuerdo de Transporte Aereo Comercial, 25 October 1979 ("Colombia–Uruguay ATA"), Annex, Section I.3. This is particularly evident in the provisions on regulation of fares: see, for example, Acuerdo sobre transportes aéreos entre el gobierno de los Estados Unidos Mexicanos y el gobierno de la Republica Argentina ("Mexico–Argentina ATA"), 14 May 1969, Article 7.

[98] See, for example, Mexico–Argentina ATA, Article 8.

[99] Air Transport Agreement between the government of the United States of America and the government of Canada ("US–Canada ATA"), 12 March 2007, Article 12.3.

[100] See US–Canada ATA, Article 5.1.

[101] Air Services Agreement of 27 March 1946 case (United States/France), 18 R.I.A.A. 416, Award of 9 December 1978, pp. 56, 67.

[102] See, for example, US–Costa Rica ATA, Article 7.3.

[103] For example, the Preamble of the Mexico–Argentina ATA refers to "bases equitativas de igualdad y reciprocidad." Reciprocity in conditions of competition is mentioned in the Colombia–UAE ATA, Article 5.1.

wider rights or privileges under the instrument than the other. The Annex to the Colombia–Uruguay ATA justifies the requirement for each contracting party to grant the same rights it is itself granted for air traffic under the Fifth Freedom of the Chicago Convention by reference to reciprocity. These references can be understood as the assertion of a duty of every State party to grant the other party to the agreement the rights it has itself under the ATA.

More specifically still, reciprocity is also used as a basis on which to grant specific privileges or rights under the agreement. One such provision in the Colombia–UAE ATA regards the selection by each contracting State of an agent for provision of services on the ground.[104] More commonly, exemptions of aircraft and their stores and parts from levies and duties are explicitly subjected to a condition of reciprocity in most agreements.[105] Such provisions go a step further than recognizing the reciprocity inherent in the exchange of rights and duties under the treaty itself. They essentially limit the obligation entered into by the two States parties, allowing the possibility of, in this case, not exempting, or not completely exempting, the other State from duties to the extent that it does not accord the same (or a similar) exemption itself.

Finally, references to reciprocity are also made for matters that are not the subject of obligations under the ATA but are related to it. One example may be found in the Canada–US ATA, which in its Annex III (C) states: "Each Party shall extend favourable consideration to applications by airlines of the other Party to carry traffic not covered by this Annex on the basis of comity and reciprocity."[106] On the one hand, the language used ("shall extend") is binding, while on the other hand neither State has an absolute right to have applications by its airlines to carry traffic falling outside the scope of the Annex accepted. The State might only be required to accept applications by airlines in these matters when it has already enjoyed such treatment itself. A specific course of conduct would therefore be required for any form of legal obligation to arise – in this case, an obligation to grant "favourable consideration" to

[104] Colombia–UAE ATA, Article 13.8.

[105] Mexico–Argentina ATA, Articles 7.3 and 7.4; US–Bahrain ATA, Article 9; US–Canada ATA, Article 10; US–Costa Rica ATA, Article 10; Colombia–UAE ATA, Article 6.1, which also refers to exemption from duties "en el mayor grado posible en virtud de sus leyes nacionales."

[106] Almost identical wording is found in the US–Costa Rica ATA, Annex II, Section II. Similar references to reciprocal agreements to be reached by airlines designated by the parties is present in the Annex, Section I.7(b) of the Colombia–Uruguay ATA.

the airlines of the other party in the same manner its own have received favourable consideration.[107] Referring to the distinction made in Chapter 2, this is a clear example of how reciprocity of *conduct* may be used to create a basis for the extension of a legal obligation outside the formal agreement itself.

The role of reciprocity in ATAs therefore illustrates its role in ensuring a balance not only in the extent of obligations undertaken between two States in an area closely related to sovereignty but also in terms of equality of outcome. Performance in ATAs will have effects that amount to a commercial advantage for the other party to the treaty, and reciprocity is used to ensure that this remains equal for both parties.

3.3.2 *Reciprocity and Equity: Bilateral Energy Agreements*

In the field of energy, cooperation between States, be this for joint development of petroleum deposits, transit, pipelines, or scientific cooperation, is primarily conducted through bilateral agreements. Bilateral agreements on research and development activities are of particular interest, as explicit references to reciprocity, equality, and mutual benefit may be found not only in the preamble but also in the text of the treaties themselves.[108] Further, these references are accompanied by requirements in specific treaty provisions to undertake sharing of benefits and distribution on an "equitable basis."[109]

These agreements are founded on cooperation on a basis that ensures equality in exchange and equity in distribution. At the same time, they deal with exchanges in scientific cooperation. The concern of governments in concluding such agreements therefore goes beyond the reciprocity of rights and obligations, to ensuring the *actual* exchanges that take place are equally advantageous for both parties – i.e., substantive

[107] It is doubtful in this case whether "favourable consideration" amounts to any obligation to actually accede to requests made.

[108] For example, the Agreement between the Department of Energy of the United States of America and the Ministry of Energy and Infrastructure of Israel Concerning Energy Cooperation, 1 February 1996 ("USA/Israel Energy Cooperation Agreement"), reads in its Article I: "The Parties shall conduct such collaboration on the basis of mutual benefit, equality, and reciprocity." Article I of the Agreement between the Government of the United States of America and the Government of Japan on Research and Development in Energy and Related Fields, 2 May 1979 ("USA/Japan Energy Cooperation Agreement") reads: "The two Governments will maintain and intensify their cooperation in research and development in energy and related fields on the basis of equality and mutual benefit."

[109] USA/Japan Energy Cooperation Agreement, Articles II.2 and VII.2.

equality in performance. This accounts for the focus on equity, equality, and mutual benefit written into the agreements.

However, there is a further point to be made. The term "reciprocity" is not used in all energy agreements and is used in addition to the terms "mutual benefit" and "equality." It therefore appears that reciprocity itself has an additional meaning that is not restricted to principles of equity and mutuality. Specific provisions requiring "reciprocity" within such agreements[110] suggest that cooperation on a specific point must be specifically equal; that is, one of the parties is not held unilaterally to fulfill the obligation in question without a similar performance on the part of the other. In general terms, however, it is less clear what the difference might be between requiring collaboration on the basis of "mutual benefit, equality and reciprocity" as opposed to "equality and mutual benefit" only. Requiring reciprocity in performance of the agreement seems to open an avenue to making performance by one party dependent on the specific conduct of the other party with respect to the agreement.

3.3.3 *Conclusion: Reciprocity Ensuring Equality*

In general, the importance of reciprocity in bilateral agreements is particularly marked when these emphasize the equality of States parties, and the concern with ensuring a balance in benefits – particularly economic – emerging from the treaty.[111] Whereas bilateral treaties are certainly reciprocal in the sense of a correlation between rights and obligations, agreements in certain specific areas of cooperation, particularly closely linked to matters considered of sovereign competence or related to access to the State's resources and amounting to an economic exchange, require actual equality or an equitable share in benefits arising under the treaty, and use the term "reciprocity" to ensure this.

3.4 Multilateral Treaties

As might be expected, reciprocity is particularly relevant in bilateral agreements and in the rules on reservations to treaties. While it is clear

[110] For example, Article VII(d) of the USA/Israel Energy Cooperation Agreement provides that "[e]ach Party shall provide for adequate accommodations for the other Party's staff or contractors (and their families) on a mutually agreeable, reciprocal basis."

[111] In response to a questionnaire by the ILC, States underlined that the question of oil and gas related to "essential bilateral interests" and it was not advisable to begin codification work on the topic; ILC, S. Murase, *Shared Natural Resources: Feasibility of Future Work on Oil and Gas*, 9 March 2010, UN Doc. A/CN.4/621.

that in bilateral treaties, obligations will be bilateral in nature, in order to establish the role of reciprocity in multilateral treaties, it becomes necessary to look at the structure of obligations under the treaty. A fundamental distinction may be made between treaties that are bilateralizable and those that are not. The obligations in a bilateralizable multilateral treaty will operate between pairs of States, despite being written into a single multilateral instrument. The Vienna Convention on Diplomatic Relations (VCDR) is a bilateralizable multilateral treaty *par excellence*, and one in which States can modulate some, but not all, of their obligations on the basis of reciprocity.

The second category is that of multilateral treaties that contain obligations that do not apply only between parties bilaterally. One class is that of interdependent obligations, which are proper treaties subjected to a form of collective reciprocity, in which performance by each State is conditioned on performance by every other party. An example is the Nuclear Non-Proliferation Treaty, which will be analyzed below. Integral obligations, instead, are those in which performance is owed to all other parties to the treaty.[112] In this latter category, undertakings may be assimilated to parallel unilateral engagements to observe a certain standard of conduct. This form of unilateralism has led to doubts about whether reciprocity operates at all in integral obligations. As the analysis below indicates, despite operating differently to bilateral or bilateralizable treaties, neither of these two types of treaty is nonreciprocal in nature.

3.4.1 *Bilateralizable Multilateral Treaties*

Bilateral obligations are not only found in bilateral treaties. Bilateral obligations may also arise is a multilateral treaty, where they are owed individually, that is, to take the language of the ILC in the commentary to the Articles on the Responsibility of States for Internationally Wrongful Acts (ARSIWA), "where particular performance is incumbent under the treaty as between one State party and another."[113] As might be

[112] Simma, "From Bilateralism to Community Interest," 1994, p. 336; A. Poch de Caviedes, "De la clause 'rebus sic stantibus' à la clause de revision dans les conventions internationales," *Collected Courses of the Hague Academy of International Law*, vol. 118, 1966, p. 121.

[113] ILC, Articles on Responsibility of States for Internationally Wrongful Acts, Commentary, p. 118; C. Chinkin, *Third Parties in International Law*, Oxford, Clarendon, 1993, p. 1, L.-A. Sicilianos, "The Classification of Obligations and the Multilateral Dimension of the Relations of International Responsibility," *European Journal of International Law*, vol. 13, no. 5, 2002, p. 1133.

expected, reciprocity continues to play an important role in this kind of multilateral treaty.

The VCDR is a good example of a bilateralizable multilateral treaty. By definition, diplomatic relations are bilateral, freely undertaken, and based on consent.[114] Prior to codification of the rules of diplomatic law into the VCDR, States regulated their bilateral diplomatic relations on the basis of reciprocity, a factor that explained the general reluctance to accept a general duty of nondiscrimination in the Convention.[115] This preference is reflected in the specific role played by reciprocity within the VCDR.

While it is a general, multilateral treaty that codifies rules of law on diplomatic relations, in its actual functioning not only does the VCDR operate bilaterally but it also allows for the restriction or more favorable application of certain provisions depending on the treatment granted by the other State in the bilateral relationship.[116] As such, it provides an excellent example of a general multilateral treaty that contains fully bilateralizable obligations.

The first example of a mechanism of reciprocity that subsists strongly in the VCDR is Article 9, which allows for a receiving State to declare that "any member of the diplomatic staff of the mission is persona non grata or that any other member of the staff of the mission is not acceptable." Upon such a notification, the sending State "shall, as appropriate, either recall the person concerned or terminate his functions with the mission."[117] It constitutes, in effect, a counterbalance to the privileges and immunities enjoyed by diplomats under the Convention,[118] and is used as a tool to respond to illicit activities of diplomats on a basis of reciprocity in execution. It may be understood as a form of inbuilt remedy

[114] Vienna Convention on Diplomatic Relations, 24 June 1964, 500 U.N.T.S. 95, Article 2.

[115] As was the case with Article 47; E. Denza, *Diplomatic Law: Commentary on the Vienna Convention on Diplomatic Relations*, 4th ed., Oxford, Oxford University Press, 2016, p. 406.

[116] Article 47 of the VCDR reads:

1. In the application of the provisions of the present Convention, the rec eiving State shall not discriminate as between States.
2. However, discrimination shall not be regarded as taking place:
   (a) Where the receiving State applies any of the provisions of the present Convention restrictively because of a restrictive application of that provision to its mission in the sending State;
   (b) Where by custom or agreement States extend to each other more favourable treatment than is required by the provisions of the present Convention.

[117] Vienna Convention on Diplomatic Relations, Article 9.1.

[118] Denza, *Diplomatic Law*, p. 64.

within the VCDR, which ensures that the reciprocity used in diplomatic relations is not channeled into a direct suspension of the immunities of the diplomats or the diplomatic mission. This point was made by the ICJ in the *Tehran Hostages* case, where it found that "diplomatic law itself provides the necessary means of defence against, and sanction for, illicit activities by members of diplomatic or consular missions."[119] Article 9 may be used as a measure of reciprocity even where there has been no wrongdoing, or as a measure of reciprocity in the strictest sense, of returning like for like, in response to a declaration of persona non grata of the State's own diplomats.[120]

The bilateralizable nature of obligations in this type of treaty also means that these can be modulated between pairs of States. For example, VCDR Article 47 allows the standards of treatment of the Convention to be tailored to the specific factual circumstances of a given bilateral relationship. It introduces a general rule of nondiscrimination in paragraph 1 but excludes differences in treatment between pairs of States from this duty in paragraph 2 where the differential treatment is either (a) a response to restrictive treatment or (b) constitutes more favorable treatment on the basis of separate agreements. Therefore, where there is discretion allowed under the Convention, States may vary its application on the basis of reciprocity. This however operates as reciprocity within the specific rule itself and does not amount to the possibility of *breaching* the VCDR on the basis of reciprocity.[121] This differentiation of obligations is however only possible on the basis of reciprocity of treatment. It still does not sanction any imbalance in the application of the treaty; in this sense, it does not grant a right to unilaterally restrict the application of the treaty but rather to ensure that equality in the application of standards is not undermined.

This example clearly illustrates how a bilateralizable multilateral treaty operates by creating a network of bilateral obligations, which, depending on the treaty in question, may be differentiated between pairs of States. The result is that a general, multilateral treaty can be split into a number of different bilateral relationships with distinctive obligations.

[119] *United States Diplomatic and Consular Staff in Tehran (United States of America* v. *Iran)*, Judgment of 24 May 1980, ICJ Reports 1980, para. 83.

[120] See the example of the United States declaring Singaporean and Nicaraguan diplomats persona non grata in response to an action under Article 9 by the two countries, ibid., p. 68.

[121] Such as, for example, with Articles 37 and 38 of the Convention; see Denza, *Diplomatic Law*, p. 407.

Unlike the case of interdependent and integral-type treaties that will be analyzed in the next section, their bilateralizable nature means that these differentiated obligations based on reciprocity do not affect the rights or obligations of other States parties.

3.4.2 *Multilateral Treaties Containing Interdependent Obligations*

A second type of multilateral treaty is that in which obligations are interdependent. In this type of treaty, legal obligations do not operate on a bilateral basis between one State party and other States taken individually, but rather observance of the obligations they contain is conditioned upon performance by all other parties. The most notable example is that of disarmament agreements, which embody a "global" reciprocity of engagement as well as of performance.

The Treaty on the Non-Proliferation of Nuclear Weapons (NPT) is an excellent example of an interdependent treaty, containing a form of collective reciprocity that goes beyond the correlation of rights and obligations to include conditionality of observance upon the continued performance of the treaty obligations by other States parties.

The NPT divides States parties into nuclear and nonnuclear weapon States. Nuclear weapon States are those having exploded a nuclear device before 1 January 1967, a definition intended to limit the nuclear weapon States to the five permanent members of the UN Security Council.[122] The treaty sets out different obligations for these different groups of States, effectively prohibiting those States that have not exploded a nuclear weapon before 1967 from acquiring one. Article I of the treaty outlines the obligations of nuclear weapon States, which must not

> transfer to any recipient whatsoever nuclear weapons or other nuclear explosive devices … or induce any non-nuclear-weapon State to manufacture or otherwise acquire nuclear weapons or other nuclear explosive devices, or control over such weapons or explosive devices.

Article II of the NPT sets out the obligations of nonnuclear weapon States in this regard. Nonnuclear weapon States must not

> receive the transfer from any transferor whatsoever of nuclear weapons or other nuclear explosive devices or of control over such weapons or explosive devices …

[122] J. Goldblat, "The Nuclear Non-Proliferation Régime: Assessment and Prospects," *Collected Courses of the Hague Academy of International Law*, vol. 256, 1995, p. 31. This definition has resulted in debates surrounding the status of States that exploded a device after 1967, such as India, and whether they should be treated as nuclear weapon States or not.

not ... manufacture or otherwise acquire nuclear weapons or other nuclear explosive devices; and not ... seek or receive any assistance in (their) manufacture.

The obligations weighing upon the two groups of States with respect to transfer are in effect the converse of one another: while nuclear weapon States must not transfer, nonnuclear weapon States must not receive transfers of any of the materials concerned by the articles of the treaty. The second part of Article II, however, sets out a further obligation that does not weigh on nuclear weapon States, that is, a prohibition on manufacture or acquisition of nuclear weapons.

There is, in turn, a further obligation weighing upon nonnuclear weapon States. Under Article III.1, "[e]ach non-nuclear-weapon State Party to the treaty undertakes to accept safeguards set forth in an agreement to be negotiated and concluded with the International Atomic Energy Agency." Nonnuclear-weapon States are therefore required to take on an additional obligation that includes onerous verification procedures, and which is not required of nuclear weapon States.

Some rights and obligations under the treaty weigh on all States parties regardless of their nuclear weapon status, such as Article III.2, relating to obligations on transfer of nuclear material; Article IV, recognizing the "inalienable right" of all States to peaceful uses of nuclear energy; and Article V, which states that "each Party" shall take appropriate measures to ensure that benefits from peaceful applications of nuclear explosions are made available to nonnuclear weapon States on a nondiscriminatory basis. Therefore, while purportedly applying to all States parties, in fact Article V imposes an obligation on nuclear weapon States toward nonnuclear weapon States.[123] Finally, Article VI also states that "each of the Parties" undertakes to pursue negotiations on nuclear disarmament.

In the case of interdependent-type multilateral treaties, such as the NPT, there is a real quid pro quo in the different obligations taken on by States parties. In the NPT, the benefits for nonnuclear weapon States under Article V are granted in exchange for the renunciation of the right to conduct nuclear tests, or indeed to possess nuclear weapons.[124] Nuclear weapon States' obligation to disarm is not only the counterpart of the obligations for nonnuclear weapon States not to acquire nuclear

[123] This provision is no longer relevant, as all five nuclear weapon States have signed the Comprehensive Test Ban Treaty, which prohibits nuclear testing.

[124] Goldblat, "Nuclear Non-Proliferation Régime," p. 47.

weapons,[125] but can also be seen as a way of achieving the same end by deferred means. The undertaking made by nuclear weapon States in the NPT can be understood as a promise to reach the condition of nonnuclear weapon States at an undetermined future date.[126]

It is also apparent that the rights and obligations under the NPT (indeed, even beyond it) are truly interdependent, in the sense that they apply to all parties all the time,[127] and are mutually dependent.[128] This also transpires from the conditions for withdrawal from the NPT. Article X states:

> Each Party shall in exercising its national sovereignty have the right to withdraw from the Treaty if it decides that extraordinary events, related to the subject matter of this Treaty, have jeopardized the supreme interests of its country .... Such notice shall include a statement of the extraordinary events it regards as having jeopardized its supreme interests.

In effect, this clause allows States to maintain the balance struck in the treaty by allowing for the possibility of withdrawal in case of events compromising their security interests. The appraisal of reasons for withdrawal is left to States,[129] and the formulation in Article X can notably cover noncompliance with the NPT;[130] however, this is not the only ground for withdrawal. The Conference on Disarmament also found Article X to cover "blatant disregard" for the treaty's aim of ceasing the nuclear arms race.[131] One example of withdrawal from the treaty was that of the Democratic People's Republic of Korea (DPRK) in 1993. The DPRK gave as reasons for withdrawal the US and South Korean joint military exercises, and a resolution of the International Atomic Energy Agency (IAEA) Board of Governors demanding a special inspection of DPRK military sites.[132]

[125] M. I. Shaker, "The Evolving International Regime of Nuclear Non-Proliferation," *Collected Courses of the Hague Academy of International Law*, vol. 321, 2007, p. 143.

[126] Goldblat makes a similar argument, "Nuclear Non-Proliferation Régime," pp. 48–49.

[127] ILC, Third Report on the Law of Treaties, Sir Humphrey Waldock, Special Rapporteur, Doc. No. A/CN.4/167 and Add. 1-3, *Yearbook of the International Law Commission*, 1964, vol. II, p. 39.

[128] A. Mahiou, "Interdependence," in R. Wolfrum, ed., *The Max Planck Encyclopedia of Public International Law*, Oxford University Press, 2008–, online edition, [www.mpepil.com], para. 4.

[129] Shaker, "Evolving International Regime of Nuclear Non-Proliferation," p. 95.

[130] Shaker indicates these as being among the possible reasons for withdrawal cited by US officials, ibid., p. 97.

[131] Ibid., p. 95.

[132] Letter Dated 12 March 1993 from the Permanent Representative of the Democratic People's Republic of Korea to the United Nations Addressed to the President of the Security Council, S/25407, Annex, 12 March 1993.

The NPT is not the only interdependent-type multilateral treaty in existence, and regional disarmament treaties also provide good examples in their withdrawal claues of the interdependence of obligations. For example, the Treaty of Tlatelolco allows for denunciation "if, in the opinion of the denouncing State, there have arisen or may arise circumstances connected with the content of this Treaty or of the annexed Additional Protocols I and II which affect its supreme interests or the peace and security of one or more Contracting Parties." The Treaty of Pelindaba refers to "extraordinary events, related to the subject matter of this Treaty, hav[ing] jeopardized [the Party's] supreme interests." The treaty of Rarotonga speaks of "a violation by any Party of a provision of this Treaty essential to the achievement of the objectives of the Treaty or of the spirit of the Treaty" by consequence of which "every other Party shall have the right to withdraw from the Treaty."[133]

In conjunction with the prohibition on making reservations present in all the abovementioned treaties, two characteristics of interdependent-type disarmament treaties become clear. First, all parties must accept the entirety of the provisions of the treaty, and second, continued performance rests on the observance by Parties not only of the provisions of the treaty but of conduct that does not frustrate the aims of the treaty or place States in a situation that may compromise their national security interests. This is logical, considering that disarmament treaties touch upon a subject matter that is both deeply connected to national security and State sovereignty, and of concern to the wider community of States.

The rights and obligations in interdependent multilateral treaties therefore cannot be split into bilateral relationships. It is only possible for the treaty to exist if all States parties observe its provisions. In this sense, therefore, they are subject to a form of collective reciprocity, which has a number of articulations. First, reciprocity in the strict sense of a quid pro quo exists within the treaty. This means that although obligations are differentiated, there is a clear exchange or bargain taking place. Second, the treaty is reciprocal in the sense that rights and obligations under it are clearly correlated: the obligation of each State party rests on the obligation of all other States parties, taken collectively. Third, and as a consequence of the nature of the treaty as a collective bargain, there is conditional reciprocity at work; continued performance

[133] Treaty for the Prohibition of Nuclear Weapons in Latin America and the Caribbean (Treaty of Tlatelolco), 14 February 1967, Article 30; African Nuclear Weapon Free Zone Treaty (Treaty of Pelindaba), 11 April 1996, Article 20; South Pacific Nuclear Free Zone Treaty (Treaty of Rarotonga), 6 August 1985, Article 13.

by one depends on continued performance by all. This form of reciprocity is absent both from bilateralizable multilateral treaties, for which violation of the treaty is relevant only for the injured State and not for all other prties, and from integral-type treaties, which will be examined next. The case of interdependent multilateral treaties indicates that reciprocity is not synonymous with strict equality of undertaking but can subsist where different parties have different obligations. Further, it is applicable not only in obligations that operate bilaterally but also in those where rights and obligations under the treaty apply collectively.

3.4.3 *Multilateral Treaties of the Integral Type*

While there is little dispute that reciprocity can apply collectively where interdependent obligations are concerned, it is multilateral treaties of the integral type that are most often held as examples of the limits of reciprocity in international law, and considered nonreciprocal in nature.[134] In the case of integral obligations, relations under the treaty cannot be split into a set of bilateral relationships by virtue of which States perform their obligations under the instrument toward one other State party only, nor do they establish obligations that depend on observance by all parties. Treaties of the integral type instead regulate or create a *collective* interest.[135] As will be seen in this section, however, that does not mean that reciprocity does not apply to this type of obligation. Instead, as demonstrated by the functioning of human rights treaties, it is instead the existence of a "vertical" legal relationship between States and other subjects of international law (i.e. individuals) that dictates where reciprocity is less relevant in integral-type treaties.

The birth of human rights treaties after 1945 in particular led to an increase in the number of agreements where States' undertakings were not so much made toward another State party but rather took on the appearance of a unilateral engagement, which aimed to protect an

[134] See ie. Sicilianos, "Classification of Obligations," p. 1135; E. Klein, "Denunciation of Human Rights Treaties and the Principle of Reciprocity," in U. Fastenrath, ed., *From Bilateralism to Community Interest: Essays in Honour of Judge Bruno Simma*, Oxford, Oxford University Press, 2011, p. 477.

[135] ILC, Sixth report on the content, forms and degrees of international responsibility (Part Two of the draft articles); and "Implementation" (mise en oeuvre) of international responsibility and the settlement of disputes (part three of the draft articles), W. Riphagen, Special Rapporteur, Doc. No. A/CN.4/389 and Corr.1& Corr.2, *Yearbook of the International Law Commission, 1985*, vol. II, Part One, p. 8; Campiglio, "Principio di reciprocità," p. 128.

interest under the treaty. A similar rationale underpins multilateral environmental agreements, with the common interest in this case being not the rights of individuals but the protection of a truly collective good, namely, the environment. Therefore, rights and obligations under "integral treaties" do not operate in a manner whereby a breach affects only one State, as will be seen further in Chapter 5. They are instead usually considered to operate *erga omnes* or *erga omnes partes*, according to the distinction famously made by the ICJ in the *Barcelona Traction* case; these are "obligations of a State toward the international community as a whole [...] all States can be held to have a legal interest in their protection."[136]

3.4.3.1 Integral Treaties as an Objective Order?

The view that considers integral treaties to be nonreciprocal is based on a plurality of arguments and underpinned by an understanding of reciprocity as a synallagma. One such argument considers that this type of treaty creates an objective order, in the nature of a public order; and as reciprocity is subjective and relational in nature, it therefore should have no place in an objective regime. This has notably been the position of the ECtHR in *Austria* v. *Italy* and *Ireland* v. *UK*.[137] The ECtHR in *Ireland* v. *UK* said that

> unlike international treaties of the classic kind, the Convention comprises more than mere reciprocal engagements between contracting States. It creates, over and above a network of mutual, bilateral undertakings, objective obligations which, in the words of the Preamble, benefit from a "collective enforcement." By virtue of Article 24, the Convention allows contracting States to require the observance of these obligations without having to justify an interest.[138]

136 *Barcelona Traction, Light and Power Company, Limited*, Judgment of 5 February 1970, ICJ Reports 1970, p. 32, para. 33.

137 Both these cases were inter-State complaints, which, as will be seen in Chapter 6, require reciprocity in the acceptance of jurisdiction, unlike complaints by individuals. The Commission in *Austria* v. *Italy* said "the purpose of the High Contracting Parties in concluding the Convention was not to concede to each other reciprocal rights and obligations in pursuance of their individual national interest but to realise the aims and ideals of the Council of Europe, as expressed in its Statute, and to establish a common public order of the free democracies of Europe." *Austria* v. *Italy*, European Commission of Human Rights, Application No. 788/60, Decision on Admissibility, 11 January 1961, p. 18.

138 *Ireland* v. *the United Kingdom*, ECtHR, Application No. 5310/71, Judgment of 18 January 1978, para. 239.

Theoretically, a treaty that establishes an objective order – in the case of human rights treaties, for the benefit of individuals – does not imply the possibility of denunciation or withdrawal, according to VCLT Article 56.1(b). This was the position taken by the UN when the DPRK attempted to withdraw from the ICCPR in 1997.[139] The HRC also stated in its General Comment No. 26 that "the Covenant does not have a temporary character typical of treaties where a right of denunciation is deemed to be admitted, notwithstanding the absence of a specific provision to that effect" and "once the people are accorded the protection of the rights under the Covenant, such protection devolves with territory and continues to belong to them."[140] However, this is not the case with all human rights treaties. Even the European Convention on Human Rights (ECHR), which the ECtHR deems to constitute an "objective order," provides for the possibility of denunciation.[141] The same is true for the ACHR.[142] Both provisions, however, have a temporal condition attached: the effect of a denunciation does not release the State from its obligations in respect of acts occurring before the denunciation. It seems therefore that the fact of protecting a community interest makes no difference as to whether a State can terminate its obligations, although some residual protection will still attach to those individuals that acquired rights under the treaty.[143]

The point that human rights are inherent in the human person, and therefore must simply be respected by States,[144] is not invalidated by the fact that it is possible for States to denounce or withdraw from certain human rights treaties. Many human rights obligations are customary in nature; States therefore have an obligation to respect these whether they are parties to a treaty or not.[145] It does not emerge clearly, however, that

[139] Denunciation of the International Covenant on Civil and Political by the Democratic People's Republic of Korea, Letter of the Minister of Foreign Affairs of the DPRK of 23 August 1997 and Aide-Mémoire of the United Nations Under-Secretary-General for Legal Affairs of 23 September 1997, United Nations Doc. C.N.467.1997.TREATIES-10 (Annex).

[140] Human Rights Committee, General Comment 26: Issues Relating to the Continuity of Obligations to the International Covenant on Civil and Political Rights, CCPR/C/21/Rev.1/Add.8/Rev.1, 8 December 1997, paras. 3–4.

[141] ECHR, Article 58. [142] ACHR, Article 78.

[143] Klein, "Denunciation of Human Rights Treaties," p. 485.

[144] Application of the Convention on the Prevention and Punishment of the Crime of Genocide (*Croatia* v. *Serbia*), Judgment of 3 February 2015, Dissenting Opinion of Judge Cançado Trindade, para. 58.

[145] This point was set out by the ICJ with respect to the prohibition of the use of force, stating that "there are no grounds for holding that when customary international law is

treaties that establish integral obligations create an "objective" order, nor that this means that integral treaties escape the operation of reciprocity. This may better be answered by looking at the structure of undertakings in integral-type treaties.

3.4.3.2 Integral Obligations as Unilateral Undertakings?

A further argument used to point to the nonreciprocal nature of integral-type multilateral treaties considers undertakings in this type of treaty to be unilateral in nature: a State engages itself in absolute terms without any expectation of counter-performance. In human rights treaties, rather than inter-State obligations, States parties undertake to respect a specific set of rights that are possessed by individuals under their jurisdiction, without having to fulfill any condition of nationality.[146] According to this view, there is no obvious engagement toward any other State. Therefore, as there is no bilateral relationship arising under the treaty,[147] any violation or nonobservance of the treaty provisions will not directly injure another State, but – depending on one's view – it will injure either none or all of the other parties. On the narrow view, a violation might not injure any other State, and therefore strong centralized mechanisms are required to enforce rights under this type of treaty, as is the case for human rights courts or treaty bodies.

On the wider view, violation of an integral-type treaty by one State injures the rights of all other States. However, this presupposes that a form of collective reciprocity underlies integral treaties. It would simply not be possible for all other States to be injured in their legal rights if not for the fact that their duties under the treaty find a correlative in the right of all other States parties to see the treaty respected. If one accepts that reciprocity can be collective, integral treaties are reciprocal. Were this not the case, it would not be possible for States to bring complaints for violations of integral-type treaties by other States parties when they have not been directly injured, as is the case under all human rights

comprised of rules identical to those of treaty law, the latter 'supervenes' the former, so that the customary international law has no further existence of its own," in *Military and Paramilitary Activities in and Against Nicaragua (Nicaragua* v. *United States of America)*, Merits, Judgment of 27 June 1986, paras. 175, 177–179.

146 See, for example, International Covenant on Civil and Political Rights, 16 December 1966, 99 U.N.T.S. 171, Article 3, European Convention on Human Rights, Article 1.

147 Application of the Convention on the Prevention and Punishment of the Crime of Genocide (*Croatia* v. *Serbia*), Judgment of 3 February 2015, Dissenting Opinion of Judge Cançado Trindade, para. 29.

instruments, and as exemplified by the Gambia bringing a case against Myanmar for violations of the Genocide Convention at the ICJ.[148]

With regards to human rights treaties, which confer rights to individuals under the jurisdiction of States parties, the question remains whether there is still an inter-State dimension and the same form of collective reciprocity. Undoubtedly, the existence of rights owed to individuals, and not just other States, under this type of treaty, presents a difference in structure. The best way these treaties may be understood is as being triangular in nature.

This idea of a dual nature of human rights treaties emerges from the words of the ECtHR in *Ireland* v. *UK* cited above, when it explains that "the Convention ... creates, *over and above* a network of mutual, bilateral undertakings, objective obligations which, in the words of the Preamble, benefit from a 'collective enforcement'."[149] This implies that both mutuality and objectivity subsist within the Convention. The HRC in its General Comment 31 similarly said that "the contractual dimension of the treaty involves any State party being obligated to every other State party to comply with its undertakings,"[150] before recognizing that "beneficiaries of the rights recognized in this Covenant are individuals."[151]

The point that a form of collective reciprocity exists, by virtue of which the rights of all parties are injured by a breach of treaty obligations, reconciles the objective and relative or inter-State dimensions of human rights treaties without requiring recourse to concepts of contractualism or bilateralism. This inter-State dimension is also recognized explicitly within the treaties. One example is the mechanism of inter-State complaints, which will be examined in Chapter 6.[152] Interestingly, the ICCPR also requires a State availing itself of the right of derogation from specific rights under the Covenant to notify all other States parties.[153]

[148] Application of the Convention for the Prevention and Punishment of the Crime of Genocide (*The Gambia* v. *Myanmar*), Request for Provisional Measures, Order of 23 January 2020, paras. 25–31.

[149] *Ireland* v. *UK*, para. 239 (emphasis added).

[150] Human Rights Committee, General Comment 31 [80]: The Nature of the General Legal Obligation Imposed on States Parties to the Covenant, CCPR/C/21/Rev.1/Add.13, Adopted on 29 March 2004, para. 2.

[151] Ibid., para. 9. This has also been noted by some commentators: Klein, "Denunciation of Human Rights Treaties," p. 481; Campiglio, "Principio di reciprocità," pp. 124–125, 128.

[152] See, for example, ICCPR Article 41.1, ECHR Article 33, CEDAW Article 29.2, ACHR Article 45.2.

[153] ICCPR, Article 4.3.

The inter-State dimension is therefore clearly present and coexists with the nonreciprocal dimension of human rights, which principally characterizes the relationship between States and individuals – as will be seen in Chapter 6, human rights complaints mechanisms function outside the purview of reciprocity when complaints are made by individuals rather than States. The State–individual relationship under human rights treaties is based on legal inequality and a lack of correlation between the rights of individuals and States under the treaty; the nonreciprocal elements of how human rights treaties function may be seen to stem from the vertical relationship between the State and the individual.

Human rights treaties are not the only category of treaty in which there may be limits to reciprocity.[154] This point has been argued for other treaties, such as those establishing territorial regimes, and multilateral environmental treaties. However, the structure of rights and obligations in integral treaties shows that, even in this type of multilateral agreement, reciprocity continues to play an important role as the basis on which States can uphold the respect of their legal rights to have treaties respected, even if not directly injured by the conduct of another party.

3.5 Treaties Establishing Differentiated Obligations

A further class of agreement that can be considered as being "nonreciprocal" is that in which different obligations exist for different parties, or groups of parties. As seen above in the case of the NPT, a condition of reciprocity can still be clearly found even where parties may have different obligations. However, the point of whether an absence of equality in undertaking equates to a lack of reciprocity, used as a byword for a lack of equality in undertakings,[155] requires further examination.

3.5.1 *Inequality in Treaties: Historical Examples*

A discussion of differentiated obligations in treaties should start by looking at "unequal" treaties. Historically, the main categories of "unequal" or "nonreciprocal" treaties were considered to be peace

[154] A. Pellet and D. Müller, "Reservations to Treaties: An Objection to a Reservation Is Definitely Not an Acceptance," in E. Cannizzaro, ed., *The Law of Treaties beyond the Vienna Convention*, Oxford, Oxford University Press, 2011, p. 535.

[155] See, for example, the use of the term by L. Caflisch, "Unequal Treaties," *German Yearbook of International Law*, vol. 35, 1992, p. 68.

treaties and treaties of colonial expansion.[156] The concept has existed since the institution of *foedera iniqua* (or unequal alliances) in Roman times. As the name suggests, in these agreements, allied nations would recognize the superior power of Rome and restrict their own power to wage war independently.[157]

More recently, the expression "unequal treaty" was used to designate those treaties concluded between European states and States of the Far East in which the latter unilaterally granted concessions.[158] The regime of capitulations, particularly with the Ottoman Empire, meant that foreigners continued to be subject to the laws of their own States when residing abroad;[159] while initially this built upon local merchant custom, such concessions eventually became irrevocable – with, for example, the non-European party to the agreement losing the right to appoint consuls.[160] In essence, these treaties were unequal not only because they contained an imbalance in obligations but because, similarly to the *foedera iniqua* of Roman times, they required recognition of the superiority of the Western power concerned.[161] The inequality inherent in such agreements therefore concerned inequality of legal *status* rather than only an inequality of substantive obligations.[162]

The concept of "unequal treaty" was also invoked in the twentieth century, primarily by the USSR and China, to justify nonobservance of specific treaties.[163] This may have more than a little to do with the emphasis on principles of coexistence and State consent in the Soviet view of international law. Treaties deemed unequal were considered to be invalid under international law. In China, this inequality was understood in terms of strict nonreciprocity: that is, treaties were considered unequal if only one party undertook obligations and the other party only

[156] Preiswerk, "Réciprocité dans les négociations entre pays," p. 8.

[157] A. Nussbaum, "The Significance of Roman Law in the History of International Law," *University of Pennsylvania Law Review*, vol. 100, no. 5, 1952, p. 679.

[158] Ibid., p. 670.

[159] H. Chiu, "Comparison of the Nationalist and Communist Chinese Views of Unequal Treaties," in J. A. Cohen, ed., *China's Practice of International Law: Some Case Studies*, Cambridge, MA, Harvard University Press, 1972, p. 243.

[160] C. H. Alexandrowicz, "Treaty and Diplomatic Relations between European and South Asian Powers in the Seventeenth and Eighteenth Centuries," *Collected Courses of the Hague Academy of International Law*, vol. 100, 1960, pp. 250–252, 265.

[161] Ibid., p. 280. [162] Ibid., p. 281.

[163] W. Friedmann, *The Changing Structure of International Law*, London, Stevens & Sons, 1964, p. 335.

enjoyed rights.[164] However, China itself did not apply this criterion entirely coherently.[165] Examples of what might constitute "unequal treaties" for the USSR included those in which developing countries were put in a particularly weak position; for example, obtaining privileges from a developing country in exchange for aid that could be easily withdrawn; or making independence conditional on relinquishment of control over economic or financial resources.[166]

3.5.2 *The Meaning of Equality*

These examples – indeed, the term "unequal treaty" itself – highlight the main issue at play, which is how the equality of the parties is impacted by inequality within a treaty. In his writings on the topic, Vattel did not view equality of undertakings as an essential condition for treaties but rather as a standard that could be deviated from in specific circumstances; relevant factual circumstances could constitute a consideration capable of restoring the equality of the treaty.[167] This also applied in the case of treaties of alliance whose contents were unequal but the parties to which were equal. The two conditions that made treaties unequal were therefore, first, an inequality in the status of the parties (or their

164 Chiu, "Comparison of the Nationalist and Communist Chinese Views of Unequal Treaties," p. 249; Caflisch, "Unequal Treaties," pp. 61, 64. See the example of China's appraisal of the treaty between Switzerland and the United States, Caflisch, "Unequal Treaties," p. 62, and China's concessions to the USSR in Manchuria, P. Ardant, "Chinese Diplomatic Practice during Cultural Revolution," in J. A. Cohen, ed., *China's Practice of International Law: Some Case Studies*, Cambridge, MA, Harvard University Press, 1972, p. 239, as well as the example of the Nuclear Test Ban Treaty, see Chiu, "Comparison of the Nationalist and Communist Chinese Views of Unequal Treaties," pp. 249, 261–264.

165 Chiu, "Comparison of the Nationalist and Communist Chinese Views of Uneuqual Treaties," p. 264.

166 For example, for the representative of the Ukrainian Soviet Socialist Republic in the Sixth Committee of the United Nations General Assembly, that concept included: (1) cases in which a "developed" State had extracted quasi-colonial privileges from a developing country in return for development assistance that could be withdrawn at any time; (2) agreements relating to military bases which granted foreign armed forces privileges incompatible with the sovereignty of the State; and (3) treaties which made the independence of a nation conditional upon the latter's abandoning control over its mineral resources, its trade or its finances (Caflisch, "Unequal Treaties," p. 65.)

The latter category is interesting considering the particular mechanism of CBDR seen below which gives technical or financial assistance to developing countries in exchange for access to genetic resources (as in the CBD) or reduction in emissions – a requirement that places restrictive effects on economic development. The difference is that in the case of CBDR, the exchange is legally protected and built into the treaty as a condition of participation.

167 Vattel, *Law of Nations*, p. 347 (Book II, Chapter XII, para. 173).

"dignity"), or second, imposing more substantive burdens on the weaker party.[168] For Vattel, therefore, inequality in treaties was only really a problem if it affected the legal equality of the parties or imposed disproportionate obligations by imposing a greater burden upon the party whose material conditions were worse.

These historical examples of treaties considered unequal show that there are two possible explanations to account for why the inequality introduced by such agreements was considered problematic. The first would be to focus on the content of the obligation. A treaty that conditions independence of a State upon relinquishment of control over its natural resources could be seen as creating a relationship of inequality, or nonreciprocity, because of the *content* of the obligation; requiring one party to give up control of its natural resources is so onerous that there cannot be any reciprocity within such an agreement. Another explanation instead would see the lack of reciprocity as residing within the effects of the treaty on the legal *status* of the parties. To enter into such an agreement in the first place implies that the parties are not legally equal, or that the obligation affects the legal equality of the parties to such an extent that no reciprocity is possible; the obligations contained within it have the effect of creating legal inequality between the parties.

Given that material conditions are not equal in all States, differentiation in treaty obligations may be a way of introducing compensatory inequality. A link here exists with principles of justice, equity,[169] and proportionality. The principle of common but differentiated responsibilities (CBDR), and differentiated obligations in multilateral environmental agreements (MEAs) for States that have different socioeconomic conditions, is a case in point; even more so with treaties such as the Paris Agreement, where a dynamic element is introduced into differentiation, such that the obligations of States parties evolve with the evolution of their concrete economic conditions.[170] However, this still does not solve the problem of determining whether a treaty is "unequal." Imbalances to the detriment of one party to a treaty may be offset in another instrument that provides for converse unilateral benefits.[171] It is very hard to establish what States' interests are in signing a treaty; indeed, as seen

[168] Ibid., p. 349 (Book II, Chapter XII, para. 175).

[169] Horn, *Reservations and Interpretative Declarations*, p. 150.

[170] See L. Rajamani, "Ambition and Differentiation in the 2015 Paris Agreement: Interpretative Possibilities and Underlying Politics," *International and Comparative Law Quarterly*, vol. 65, April 2016, p. 508.

[171] Caflisch, "Unequal Treaties," pp. 58–59.

above, it is often difficult to even establish what the precise burden of rights and obligations is concretely and how these fall on the parties. One party may benefit from the treaty in the future or the projected benefits may not turn out as they were expected to at all.[172]

There are in fact no provisions of the law of treaties, nor of general international law, setting out that an imbalance in treaty obligations is a reason for nullity of the agreement.[173] The rules in the VCLT regarding invalidity of treaties exclude the legal effect of treaties concluded by coercion of a State representative or threat or use of force,[174] but this does not include political or economic pressure. This is despite claims for inclusion of a provision on the invalidity of unequal treaties, or those concluded under economic or political pressure, by some governments before the ILC,[175] which resulted in a declaration adopted by the UN Conference on the Law of Treaties in which it "*[s]olemnly condemns* the threat or use of pressure in any form, whether military, political, or economic, by any State in order to coerce another State to perform any act relating to the conclusion of a treaty in violation of the principles of the sovereign equality of States and freedom of consent."[176] As the law of treaties enshrines the sovereign equality of parties to the treaty, this point is already taken care of by general rules on conclusion of treaties, without having to look at the substance of their provisions. States may decide to accept more or fewer rights and obligations than other contracting parties in a treaty. The question to turn to now is whether treaties establishing highly differentiated obligations may be considered reciprocal at all.

172 M. Lachs, "Le développement et les fonctions des traité multilatéraux," *Collected Courses of the Hague Academy of International Law*, vol. 92, 1957, p. 273; Paulus, "Reciprocity Revisited," p. 117; Tomuschat, "Obligations Arising for States," p. 361.

173 Caflisch says that there is "no rule according to which international treaties [. . .] rest on legal or factual reciprocity." However, this is an unclear use of the term reciprocity, as it is unclear whether he is referring to equality of exchange or merely the existence of some form of consideration. Caflisch, "Unequal Treaties," pp. 68–69; Paulus, "Reciprocity Revisited," p. 119.

174 VCLT Articles 51 and 52.

175 See ILC, Law of Treaties: Comments by Governments on the Draft Articles on the Law of Treaties, Drawn up by the Commission at Its Fourteenth, Fifteenth and Sixteenth Session, Doc. Nos. A/CN.4/182 and Corr. 1&2 and Add. 1, 2/Rev.1 & 3, *Yearbook of the International Law Commission 1966*, vol. II, Comments of the Government of Czechoslovakia, p. 286.

176 Declaration on the Prohibition of Military, Political or Economic Coercion in the Conclusion of Treaties, Final Act of the United Nations Conference on the Law of Treaties, UN Doc. A/CONF.39/26 (Annex).

3.5.3 *Reciprocity and Differentiated Obligations*

Multilateral environmental agreements (MEAs) are of particular interest in examining the effect of differentiated obligations on reciprocity as an example of an integral treaty, as truly multilateral agreements aimed at protecting a common interest – the environment – both within and beyond areas under State jurisdiction. One characteristic of MEAs that has also emerged since the 1970s is the principle of common but differentiated responsibilities (CBDR).

The concept of CBDR as it exists in contemporary international environmental law is expressed in Principle 12 of the Stockholm Declaration[177] and has since been incorporated into most MEAs since the 1970s, most notably for present purposes in the United Nations Framework Convention on Climate Change (UNFCCC). The latter states in its Article 3.1 that "[t]he Parties should protect the climate system for the benefit of present and future generations of humankind, on the basis of equity and in accordance with their common but differentiated responsibilities and respective capabilities."[178] The UNFCCC, and its Kyoto Protocol, established a system in which developed and developing countries had highly differentiated obligations to limit their emissions of greenhouse gases (GHGs), with developed countries required to meet mandatory targets, and developing country parties not subject to any binding emissions limits.[179] This reflects the factual differences that exist between States in terms of their economies, and therefore differing capabilities to address climate change, and their historical responsibilities as large emitters of GHGs and size of their contribution to the problem itself. CBDR therefore

[177] "Resources should be made available to preserve and improve the environment, taking into account the circumstances and particular requirements of developing countries and any costs which may emanate from their incorporating environmental safeguards into their development planning and the need for making available to them, upon their request, additional international technical and financial assistance for this purpose," Declaration of the United Nations Conference on the Human Environment (Stockholm Declaration), 16 June 1972.

[178] C. D. Stone, "Common but Differentiated Responsibilites in International Law," *The American Journal of International Law*, vol. 98, no. 2, April 2004, p. 279; United Nations Framework Convention on Climate Change, 9 May 1992, Article 3(1).

[179] R. Lyster and A. Bradbrook, *Energy Law and the Environment*, Cambridge, Cambridge University Press, 2006, pp. 53–54; P. Minnerop, "Climate Protection Agreements," in R. Wolfrum, ed., *The Max Planck Encyclopedia of Public International Law*, Oxford University Press, 2008–, online edition, [www.mpepil.com], para. 10; Rajamani, "Ambition and Differentiation," p. 506.

is intended to provide a way to take into account both these factors while pursuing a common interest.[180] This is reflected in the Rio Declaration of 1992, according to whose Principle 7 "States have common but differentiated responsibilities. The developed countries acknowledge the responsibility that they bear in the international pursuit to sustainable development in view of the pressures their societies place on the global environment and of the technologies and financial resources they command." A similar mechanism exists in the Kigali Amendment to the Montreal Protocol on substances that deplete the Ozone layer, which calculates baselines and reductions for countries differently depending on whether they are developed or developing.[181]

Provisions embodying CBDR may be considered "differential norms," that is, norms that on their face provide "different, presumably more advantageous, standards for one set of States than for another set."[182] CBDR has been considered both as setting aside the principle of sovereign equality,[183] and as embodying nonreciprocal arrangements that are intended to increase equality between States whose material situations are characterized by disparities.[184] Differential norms have therefore been characterized as a manifestation of equity,[185] and an exception or derogation from the sovereign equality and reciprocity-based system of international law[186] to reflect the material inequalities that exist between States.[187]

CBDR is not the only example of norms that apply differently for different sets of States. To follow the distinction set out by Magraw, this would also include "contextual" norms, which "on [their] face provide identical treatment to all States affected by the norm, but the application of which requires (or at least permits) consideration of characteristics

[180] D. Bodansky, "The Paris Climate Change Agreement: A New Hope?," *American Journal of International Law*, vol. 110, no. 2, p. 302; E. Hey, "Common but Diffrentiated Responsibilities," in R. Wolfrum, ed., *The Max Planck Encyclopedia of Public International Law*, Oxford University Press, 2008–, online edition, [www.mpepil.com], para. 1.

[181] Minnerop, "Climate Protection Agreements," para. 38.

[182] D. B. Magraw, "Legal Treatment of Developing Countries: Differential, Contextual, and Absolute Norms," *Colorado Journal of International Environmental Law and Policy*, vol. 69, 1990, p. 73.

[183] P. Cullet, "Differential Treatment in International Law: Toward a New Paradigm of Inter-state Relations," *European Journal of International Law*, vol. 10, no. 3, 1999, pp. 551–554.

[184] Ibid., pp. 551, 573. [185] Ibid., p. 556. [186] Ibid., p. 574.

[187] Ibid., p. 582, Hey, "Common but Differentiated Responsibilities," para. 12.

which might vary from country to country."[188] Indeed, it is not easy to find treaties that provide exactly the same costs and benefits for all States parties. Because no two States are the same, no two treaty obligations will have exactly the same effect. As Stone points out, the difference is that more usually, these differences occur in ways "which preserve formal equality within the instrument." Examples include reservations, unilateral declarations, informally differentiated commitments, and clauses that are "formally equal, but known to be uneven in impact."[189] The difference with CBDR is that the latter addresses differences in setting out obligations, in order to ensure that the *impact* of obligations is the same for all States, taking into account their developmental and socioeconomic conditions. It is therefore eminently proportional and does away with formal equality in treaty obligations to ensure substantive equality – using differentiation to reach similar outcomes to bilateral energy agreements outlined above. Article 3.2 of the UNFCCC states that "[t]he specific needs and special circumstances ... of those Parties, especially developing country Parties, that would have to bear a *disproportionate or abnormal* burden under the Convention, should be given full consideration."[190] These considerations are taken into account to establish both how much each State can contribute to the reduction of greenhouse gases, and what it requires to ensure economic growth.[191] It is a principle that is therefore also linked to equity.[192]

Reciprocity is not therefore absent from MEAs, even those that contain highly differentiated obligations. The implementation of CBDR in actual fact resembles a bargain between developed and developing countries; in many agreements, the implementation of the latter's obligations is indicated as "depending on" obligations of developed countries, usually concerning transfer of technology. This is notably the case in the Paris Agreement, where a more nuanced form of CBDR was chosen by con-

[188] Magraw, "Legal Treatment of Developing Countries," p. 74. For examples of such types of norms, Magraw cites the Convention on Liability for Damage Caused by Space Objects; see ibid., p. 85

[189] See Stone, "Common but Differentiated Responsibilites in International Law," p. 300.

[190] Emphasis added.

[191] UNFCCC Article 4.2(a), with flexibility granted to this end UNFCCC Article 4.6(a).

[192] Hey, "Common but Differentiated Responsibilities," para. 12; Magraw, "Legal Treatment of Developing Countries," p. 78; Stone, "Common but Differentiated Responsibilites in International Law," p. 300.

tracting parties, with a significant emphasis on technology transfer from developed to developing States.[193]

The implementation of CBDR does not stop at incorporating flexibility but may be implemented by a very specific mechanism based on a true exchange. The crucial formula is "will depend on": UNFCCC Article 4.7 sets out that "[t]he extent to which developing country Parties will effectively implement their commitments under the Convention *will depend on* the effective implementation by developed country Parties of their commitments under the Convention related to financial resources and transfer of technology."[194] The same formulation is present in the Convention on Biological Diversity Article 20.4, and a similar formulation is used in Article 5.5 of the Montreal Protocol on Substances that Deplete the Ozone Layer. This is a perfect example of a provision embodying legal reciprocity, understood as interdependence of obligations; while obligations might differ, performance thereof is still dependant on other parties doing their part.

Technology transfer is used in these agreements as a way to, in the words of Cullet, "entice" developing countries into ratification. In the case of climate change agreements, technology and financing are offered in exchange for a reduction in emissions that would otherwise be deleterious to developing countries' economic growth. In the case of the Convention on Biological Diversity, technology and financing are offered in exchange for access to genetic resources held by developing countries. The wider effect, perhaps understandably given the close link between the two fields, is to introduce economic considerations, and an economic exchange, into environmental matters – something that should theoretically be the antithesis of the commonly held view of MEAs as protecting the commons.[195] And yet, CBDR is still used as a means of ensuring the protection of a common resource.

The above shows that reciprocity is not absent from agreements or rules that aim to protect or regulate a collective interest. Furthermore, it also illustrates how reciprocity requires proportionality and an interdependence of legal obligations, rather than strict equality of undertaking. This point emerges even more clearly in trade agreements.

[193] See Minnerop, "Climate Protection Agreements," especially paras. 18–20 and 24–27; Rajamani, "Ambition and Differentiation," pp. 508, 510, 512.

[194] Emphasis added.

[195] M. Waibel and W. Alford, "Technology Transfer," in R. Wolfrum, ed., *The Max Planck Encyclopedia of Public International Law*, Oxford University Press, 2008–, online edition, [www.mpepil.com], para. 54.

3.5.4 *Equality and (Non-)Reciprocity in Trade Agreements*

International trade law and particularly the General Agreement on Tariffs and Trade (GATT) / World Trade Organization (WTO) system, is explicitly based on States entering into "reciprocal and mutually advantageous arrangements."[196] Reciprocity in the system of international trade law works as a basis for cooperation for States to extend trade concessions in a system that tends toward progressive reduction of tariffs and nontariff barriers to trade. It has a specific meaning in this context, is synallagmatic, and amounts to an equal factual exchange.

Differentiated obligations and nonreciprocity for less developed states are also a key characteristic of the system – GATT Article XXXVIII(8) explicitly states that "developed contracting parties do not expect reciprocity for commitments made by them in trade negotiations to reduce or remove tariffs or other barriers to the trade of the less-developed contracting parties" – and a feature of trade agreements between developed and developing States. A further example may be found in the treaties between the European Economic Community (EEC) / European Commission (EC) / EU and ex-colonies of European States. The first such trade agreement was concluded between the EEC and African States in Yaoundé in 1963. In Article 2, associated States[197] benefited from progressive abolition of customs duties and equivalent charges in EEC member States for their products but in Articles 3 and 4 retained the right to levy duties to address their development needs. Article 6 similarly allowed associated States to retain the right to impose quantitative restrictions for development needs. EEC member States agreed to provide financial and technical assistance to associated States, particularly in matters related to trade, to offset the difficulties that associated States could be exposed to by trade liberalization. Associated States, however, were required to grant a right of establishment to nationals of EEC member States under Title III of the treaty, on a basis of nondiscrimination and most-favored nation (MFN) treatment.

[196] General Agreement on Tariffs and Trade 1986, Preamble, but also Article XXVIII(2).

[197] Convention of Association between the European Economic Community and the African and Malagasy States Associated with that Community, signed at Yaoundé on 20 July 1963 (Yaoundé Convention). Associated States were: Burundi, Cameroon, the Central African Republic, Chad, Congo (Brazzaville), Congo (Léopoldville – now Democratic Republic of the Congo), Republic of Dahomey (now Benin), Gabon, Ivory Coast, Madagascar, Mali, Mauritania, Niger, Rwanda, Senegal, Somalia, Togo, and Republic of the Upper Volta (now Burkina Faso).

The Yaoundé Convention has been seen as formally reciprocal in nature, but providing for a set of exceptions to general rules relating to tariff abolition, with obligations weighing on EEC States only as far as financial cooperation is concerned, and on associated States only regarding right of establishment.[198] In this respect, the Yaoundé Convention could be seen to retain some form of exchange, as well as general obligations for all States parties, some of which allow for differential application and exceptions, and some that weigh only on one side and not the other.[199]

The next stage in EU–ACP (African, Caribbean, and Pacific countries) cooperation was the Lomé Convention, signed in 1975.[200] Article 1 clearly states that the object of the Convention is promoting trade "taking into account the respective levels of development" of contracting parties. The Fourth Lomé Convention was signed in 1990 and significantly expands on mechanisms for cooperation between EC and ACP States. Its Article 1 confirms the special character of relations between EC and ACP States "based on their reciprocal interest" and posits as basic principles "equality between partners, respect for their sovereignty, mutual interest and interdependence."[201] At the same time, Article 25 states that the general trade arrangements "in view of the ACP States' present development needs ... shall not comprise any element of reciprocity for those States as regards free access." A similar provision is incorporated in Article 174, which sets out that the ACP States "shall not be required for the duration of this Convention to assume ... obligations corresponding to the commitment entered into by the Community under this chapter in respect of imports of the products originating in the ACP States." The latter provision, speaking of "corresponding obligations," therefore also excludes any interpretation that might require ACP States to undertake the same commitments in respect of imports from EC countries as EC countries do in respect of imports from ACP States. Lomé IV therefore explicitly excludes reciprocity for certain obligations relating to trade liberalization under the treaty, while maintaining general provisions on

198 Preiswerk, "Réciprocité dans les négociations entre pays," pp. 21–24.

199 See Dero, *Réciprocité et le droit*, p. 273.

200 Lomé II was signed in 1979 and introduced minor changes; Lomé III was signed in 1984, and Lomé IV in 1990, and was programmed to last ten years. For a brief outline of the history of EU–ACP cooperation and the main agreements pertaining thereto, see http://ec.europa.eu/development/body/cotonou/lome_history_en.htm.

201 Article 2, Fourth ACP-EEC Convention, signed at Lomé on 15 December 1989 (Lomé IV).

nondiscrimination,[202] with the aim of promoting trade between EC and ACP States while taking account of their different levels of development and securing "effective additional advantages" for ACP States.[203]

The world trade system is based, at least in theory, upon nondiscrimination and reciprocity in tariff concessions.[204] However, the GATT, in Article XVIII, recognizes that "it may be necessary" for developing country parties to maintain tariff protection and quantitative restrictions and "deviate temporarily from the provisions of the other Articles." Part IV of GATT sets out both the principle that developed contracting parties do not expect reciprocity for commitments on tariff reduction from developing countries in Article XXXVI.8, and, in Article XXXVII, measures that give special regard to the needs and interests of developing countries.

Subsequent WTO agreements have also recognized differential treatment for developing country parties. The Waiver – Generalized System of Preferences allows preferential treatment to be accorded to products originating in developing countries.[205] The Enabling Clause also recognizes that "contracting parties may accord differential and more favourable treatment to developing countries, without according such treatment to other contracting parties."[206] Paragraph 5 of the Enabling Clause explicitly states that "developed countries do not expect reciprocity for commitments made by them in trade negotiations." This absence of the expectation of reciprocity is explained further in the paragraph as not expecting developing countries "to make contributions which are inconsistent with their individual development, financial and trade needs."

Differential treatment is also accorded to developing countries in other WTO agreements. For example, Article 15 of the Anti-dumping Agreement speaks of "special regard" for developing country parties;[207] the Technical Barriers to Trade agreement speaks of "differential and more favourable" treatment for developing country parties, which is

[202] For example, Articles 25 and 64. [203] Article 167 as amended in Lomé bis.

[204] Preiswerk, "Réciprocité dans les négociations entre pays," p. 28.

[205] Decision on Generalized System of Preferences, Decision of 25 June 1971 ("Waiver – GSP"), para. (a).

[206] Differential and More Favourable Treatment, Reciprocity and Fuller Participation of Developing Countries, Decision of 28 November 1979 (Enabling Clause), para. 1.

[207] Agreement on Implementation of Article VI of the General Agreement on Tariffs and Trade 1994, 15 April 1994 ("Anti-dumping Agreement").

articulated by taking account of developing country needs, and the possibility for the Committee on Technical Barriers to Trade to "grant, upon request, specified, time-limited exceptions in whole or in part from obligations under this Agreement."[208] Similarly, the Subsidies and Countervailing Measures (SCM) Agreement makes an exception for specifically listed developing country parties, and a temporary exception for other developing countries, to the prohibition on subsidies contingent on export performance and domestic use.[209] Delayed implementation of some provisions for developing country parties is also available under Article 65.2 of the Agreement on Trade-Related Aspects of Intellectual Property Rights (TRIPs).[210]

The WTO system therefore establishes differential treatment for developing countries, dividing groups of States parties into different categories, similarly to the NPT. Unlike the NPT, however, the designation of developed/developing does not have the intention of crystallizing differences but rather of providing some preferential treatment for those parties who find themselves in a given factual situation, with a specific aim: of ensuring that, at some point in the future, the same parties will emerge from the situation that requires preferential treatment in the first place. The temporary character of exceptions can be seen in the specific conditions attached to the exceptions in GATT Article XVIII.4, Article 27 of the SCM Agreement, and Article 65.2 of TRIPs.

The WTO system therefore allows its underlying principles of reciprocity in concessions and nondiscrimination to be tempered to make allowances for temporarily different material conditions. Therefore, while reciprocity in the content of concessions and treatment may be restricted in a specific context – that is, regarding a specific product, a specific party, or for a specific amount of time – it is still a characteristic of the system. Exceptions thereto in response to different social conditions are intended to provide balance and tend toward material equality rather than instituting a system in which there is any permanent exception to reciprocity.

208 Article 12.8, Agreement on Technical Barriers to Trade, 15 April 1994 ("TBT Agreement").

209 Article 27, Agreement on Subsidies and Countervailing Measures, 15 April 1994 ("SCM Agreement").

210 Agreement on Trade-Related Aspects of Intellectual Property Rights, 15 April 1994, Article 65.2.

3.5.5 *Differential Treatment and Equality*

The question that arises is to what extent nonreciprocal obligations in such agreements may amount to a lack of reciprocity of the treaties themselves. Some authors have considered differential obligations of the type examined here to constitute a derogation from sovereign equality.[211] At the same time, there is a great insistence upon equality in the law of development; it is this very insistence on equality in advantages accruing from the operation of the treaties that requires differentiation of obligations.[212] Differential treatment in trade law therefore bears all the hallmarks of a form of distributive justice and, indeed, of an application of equity to the basic principles of nondiscrimination that underlie the WTO system.[213] The principle of reasonableness seems to apply here: that is, equality should be recognized, and cooperation should be based on fair reciprocity – "that all who cooperate should share in the benefits and burdens of cooperation in some appropriate fashion as judged by a suitable benchmark."[214] If reciprocity is considered in this sense as the equal value of a given end for all participants,[215] and indeed the reversibility of the position of participants to a system, then it can also be considered to cover the examples of "nonreciprocity" in trade agreements.

There are therefore two meanings of reciprocity in trade agreements: the strictly equal mutual extension of concessions within the framework of the overall system, which can have exceptions for developing states, and the overall interdependence of differentiated but proportional obligations under a treaty between States that have different material conditions.

Differentiated obligations in treaties may therefore constitute an exception to *specific* reciprocity of treatment (in the extension of concessions), but insofar as the crucial element in legal reciprocity is the interdependence of legal obligations, the fact that States may not undertake exactly the same obligations will not signify that the agreement in question is automatically nonreciprocal. In fact, these kinds of

211 Dupuy, Communauté internationale et disparités de développement," p. 123.

212 Virally, "Panorama du droit international contemporain," p. 325; Wils, "Concept of Reciprocity in EEC Law," p. 249.

213 Preiswerk, "Réciprocité dans les négociations entre pays," p. 38.

214 O. Suttle, "Equality in Global Commerce: Toward a Political Theory of International Economic Law," *The European Journal of International Law*, vol. 25, no. 4, 2014, p. 1054, citing Rawls, p. 528.

215 Ibid., p. 1061.

agreement, often dealing with economic or resource issues, can have a strong element of exchange, as is the case of trade agreements, and indeed represent a case of collective reciprocity in regulating a common interest, as is the case of MEAs. The key elements here, too, are the interdependence and proportionality of obligations.

3.6 International Organizations

If it were correct to say that reciprocity pertains to classical, bilateral international law, and that a communitarian system of international law entails a move away from reciprocity, then intuitively, the institutionalization inherent in international organizations should put in place a collective and centralized decision-making mechanism that reduces the importance of the inter-State dimension and, consequently, of reciprocity. Whereas integral treaties safeguard and regulate a collective interest, in international organizations a centralized mechanism pursues the collective interest of the States constituting the organization. So, the greater the degree of centralization and institutionalization of the international organization, the lesser should be the place occupied by reciprocity. Furthermore, in forming an international organization, States endow it with international personality.[216] Acts of the organization are therefore not merely the acts of its member States.

At the same time, institutionalization in the sphere of international law is not the same as institutionalization in domestic legal systems; international organizations and institutions do not change the fundamental legal equality of States or the horizontal nature of international law. International organizations continue to be based on treaties, and it is these treaties that set out their competences and powers.[217] Firstly, the agreement, or agreements, instituting international organizations continue to be based on the reciprocity inherent in the law of treaties, as examined above. Secondly, the States members of an international organization have the same rights and obligations under the treaty.[218]

[216] Dupuy, "Unité de l'ordre juridique international," p. 148. The ICJ famously stated in the *Reparations* Advisory Opinion that "fifty States, representing the vast majority of the members of the international community, had the power, in conformity with international law, to bring into being an entity possessing objective international personality, and not merely personality recognized by them alone, together with capacity to bring international claims." *Reparations for Injuries Suffered in the Service of the United Nations*, Advisory Opinion of 11 April 1949, ICJ Reports 1949, p. 185.

[217] Virally, "Panorama du droit international contemporain," p. 257.

[218] Poch de Caviedes, "De la clause 'rebus sic stantibus'," p. 120.

This section will therefore analyse the examples of the EU and UN, in particular the United Nations Security Council (UNSC), to establish whether reciprocity is absent from institutionalized areas of international law, or whether it continues to subsist.

3.6.1 *Treaty-Based Institutions: The Example of the EU*

The prime example of an international organization with a high degree of institutionalization is that of the EU. If the degree of institutionalization of an organization is the principal factor that excludes the operation of reciprocity, then we should expect mechanisms of reciprocity to be absent from the operation of the EU. Indeed, the European Court of Justice (ECJ) has consistently rejected the excuse of nonperformance – that is, a form of reciprocity in execution – invoked by States confronted by violations of treaty rules by other member States.[219] This may be explained by the existence of a *lex specialis* within the EU treaty system, which puts in place a specific institutional response mechanism to address violations rather than leaving responses to breaches to the bilateral relations between member States. However, the availability or unavailability of the exception of nonperformance does not of itself mean that obligations under the treaty are not reciprocal.

There are, however, other indications from the ECJ that point to a special nature of the EU and the obligations that weigh on its member States. In *Van Gend en Loos*, the Court stated that "[t]he objective of the EEC Treaty, which is to establish a Common Market, the functioning of which is of direct concern to interested parties in the Community, implies that this treaty is more than an agreement which creates mutual obligations between contracting states."[220] There is therefore a communitarian aspect to the institutional setup of the EU (at the time, the EEC)

[219] Wils, "Concept of Reciprocity in EEC Law," p. 257. The ECJ stated in *Commission* v. *Germany* that

> a Member State cannot, in any circumstances, plead the principle of reciprocity and rely on a possible infringement of the Treaty by another Member State in order to justify its own default. Nor, therefore, can a Member State rely on the principle of reciprocity to contest the admissibility of an action brought against it for failure to fulfil its obligations (*Commission of the European Communities* v. *Federal Republic of Germany*, Case No. 325/82, Judgment of 14 February 1984, para. 11.)

Similar arguments were made in *Commission of the E.E.C.* v. *Grand Duchy of Luxembourg and Kingdom of Belgium*, Cases Nos. 90 and 91/63, Judgment of 13 November 1964, p. 631.

[220] *Van Gend en Loos* v. *Netherlands Inland Revenue Administration*, Case No. 26/62, Judgment of 5 February 1963, para. 12.

which, similarly to what was found by the ECtHR in *Ireland* v. *UK*, puts in place a system of obligations going beyond mere reciprocity. However, it is interesting to note how this is explained by the Court, which states that

> this view is confirmed by the preamble to the treaty which refers not only to governments but to peoples. The Community constitutes a new legal order of international law for the benefit of which the states have limited their sovereign rights, albeit within limited fields, and the subjects of which comprise not only Member States, but also their nationals .... Community law therefore not only imposes obligations upon individuals but is also intended to confer upon them rights which become part of their legal heritage.[221]

While the unavailability of the exception of nonperformance may be explained by the high degree of institutionalization and centralization within the EU, the extent to which it may be seen as a system that is not *only* based on reciprocal, inter-State relations is explained by the Court as being due to the fact that it is not only States that are bearers of rights and obligations under the treaties but individuals too. Similarly to human rights treaties, there is a vertical dimension to EU legal obligations.

3.6.2 *Particularities: The International Labour Organization*

The International Labour Organization (ILO) is a particularly interesting example with which to address the persistence of reciprocity and its mechanisms within international organizations. The obligations of member States of the ILO are recognized as being indivisible and not susceptible of being split into bilateral pairings. That is, they are obligations *erga omnes partes*.[222]

The impossibility of making reservations to ILO conventions would seem therefore to flow from the particular nature of the organization.[223] Further, similarly to the case of the EU, this limitation to reciprocity is justified by the peculiar legal character of the treaties in question, which stems from their adoption by the International Labour Conference, which includes not only representatives of States, but also of non-State

[221] Ibid.

[222] K. Keith, "Bilateralism and Community in Treaty Law and Practice," in U. Fastenrath, ed., *From Bilateralism to Community Interest: Essays in Honour of Judge Bruno Simma*, Oxford, Oxford University Press, 2011, p. 765.

[223] Campiglio, "Principio di reciprocità," p. 193.

actors, that is, of employers and workers; further, the object of the labor conventions requires that they be uniformly applied.[224]

There are mechanisms for flexibility built into the acceptance of international labor conventions. Firstly, the so-called *clauses de souplesse* allow for the obligations assumed by States to be diversified to some extent. Those conventions whose ratification depends on a declaration being made by States may allow for the exact scope of obligations assumed to be outlined in the declarations. In some cases, declarations are only required when the State wishes to avail itself of some exception or modification in the scope of its obligations.[225] In form, these declarations are similar to a reservation: they are made at the moment at which a State ratifies a labor convention (not after) and specify the extent to which the State accepts the obligations contained in the instrument. However, unlike reservations, other member States cannot invoke these declarations in their own respect.[226] They therefore function unilaterally.

It is also possible for some States to subject their ratification to a condition that it only comes into effect when specific third States have also ratified the conventions. The ILO director general specified that these are conditions rather than reservations, in that they do not modify the scope of the obligations assumed.[227] However, this possibility illustrates how adherence by States to labor conventions is not merely a unilateral act; it is permissible for such ratification to come into force only on condition that other States equally ratify, and to modify the scope of obligations to the extent permitted by way of a declaration. Further, there is a limit to what States may not accept; declarations made by States may "not render null and void the principal obligations assumed by that State and particularly onerous the obligations assumed by other States which had accepted the Convention as a whole and did not thereby obtain reciprocal advantages."[228] Obligations under

[224] Harvard Draft on the Law of Treaties, "Article 13. Use of the Term 'Reservation'," *The American Journal of International Law*, vol. 29, Supplement: Research in International Law, 1935, pp. 843–844.

[225] International Labour Organization, *Handbook of Procedure Relating to International Labour Conventions and Recommendations*, Geneva, International Labour Office, 2012, pp. 13–15.

[226] Horn, *Reservations and Interpretative Declarations*, p. 167.

[227] *Memorandum du Directeur du Bureau International du Travail*, "Faculté de formuler des reserves dans les conventions générales" Soumis au Conseil le 15 juin 1927, *Journal officiel de la Société des Nations*, July 1927, Annex 967a, pp. 882–884, Doc. No. C.212.1927. V; Horn, *Reservations and Interpretative Declarations*, p. 863.

[228] League of Nations Doc. No. C.66.N.24.1924.II, p. 123.

international labor conventions may be described as being essentially integral, while allowing for some differentiation, as long as the latter is proportional.

Aside from the requirement for more than one State to ratify for labor conventions to enter into force, ILO conventions also require States to reciprocally accord national treatment.[229] Within the Constitution of the ILO, there is also a provision for entry into force of labor conventions, even when they do not pass with a two-thirds majority of votes, among members of the organization inter partes.[230] Therefore, conventions not passed by the International Labour Conference may still apply on a basis of reciprocity. There also exists a mechanism for States to file complaints with the International Labour Office if they deem any other member not to be securing effective observance of any labor convention.[231] Similarly to human rights treaties, therefore, the consent of States to the ILO is predicated on other members carrying out their obligations under the treaties. Obligations are owed to other States rather than merely undertaken unilaterally toward a centralized body. The objective of achieving uniform standards for the protection of conditions of labor requires mutuality and equality of undertaking among member States.[232]

The limitations that do exist to reciprocity, notably in the availability of reservations and therefore the possibility of bilaterally modifying the application of labor conventions, may also be understood by reference to the tripartite structure of the ILO.[233] This was specifically the explanation given by the ILO's Director General, who explained the consent necessary to establish a reservation as "unobtainable" in the case of international labor conventions, as these are "not drawn up by contracting States alone [but] the International Labour Conference in which there are non-governmental representatives, and hence the acceptance of a reservation by all States concerned would not suffice."[234] In this case, it is therefore the inequality in the status of parties to the Conference that explains the unavailability of reservations, and consequently constitutes a limit to reciprocity.

[229] Campiglio, "Principio di reciprocità," pp. 135–136.

[230] Constitution of the International Labour Organization, 1 April 1919, Article 21.1.

[231] Ibid., Article 26.1. [232] Harvard Draft on the Law of Treaties, "Article 13," p. 844.

[233] This is set out in Constitution of the ILO, Article 7.1.

[234] *Memorandum du Directeur du Bureau International du Travail*, Doc. No. C.212.1927.V; Harvard Draft on the Law of Treaties, "Article 19," p. 843.

3.6.3 *The United Nations and Peace and Security*

The veto power of the five permanent members of the UNSC under Chapter VII of the UN Charter (UNC) has been seen as undermining the sovereign equality of States as set out in Article 2.1 of the UNC.[235] According to this view, the fact that five members of the UN have more rights than others and can enforce respect for international law – and that they are effectively removed from the reach of this enforcement power, because they can stop enforcement action being taken against themselves – means that there is a fundamental lack of reciprocity at the heart of the institutional setting of the most important and universal international organization in contemporary international society. The situation of the five permanent members of the UNSC is not meant to compensate a material inequality for the difference in rights and obligations, as is normally the case of differential treatment, as examined above; the five permanent members simply have a decision-making power that is more extensive than that of other members of the UNSC, and indeed all other UN member States.

The first point to note is that this is set out in the Charter of the UN. Therefore, as with the rest of the obligations under the Charter, the rules concerning the Security Council are, according to Article 2.1, based on the sovereign equality of UN member States. The aim of this provision was to allay fears that the organization was to be a form of super-State, instead confirming it as not being placed above its members.[236] Further, these powers are set out in a treaty, which member States must accept, a point that is consistent with the formal equality of States under the treaty.[237] In response to the argument that the UNSC derogates from sovereign equality, it may be said that member States of the organization may elect to distribute powers and responsibilities among its members and organs as they see fit, without this affecting their formal equality.

At the same time, there is also a temporal element involved that reinforces the inequality between the permanent members of the UN Security Council and other member States. It is possible for any State to be elected a member of the Security Council for a given amount of time; however, the power of five States to effectively veto decisions is

[235] Dupuy, "Unité de l'ordre juridique international," p. 224.

[236] M. G. Kohen, "Article 2 Paragraphe 1," in J.-P. Cot and A. Pellet, eds., *La Charte des Nations Unies: Commentaire article par article*, vol. I, 3rd ed., Paris, Economica, 2005., 2005, pp. 411–412.

[237] J. Crawford, "Multilateral Rights and Obligations in International Law," *Collected Courses of the Hague Academy of International Law*, vol. 319, 2006, p. 411.

effectively temporally unlimited as, according to Article 108 of the Charter, acceptance on the part of all permanent members would be necessary to amend the Charter and remove the power of veto. The situation of inequality of power is not therefore temporary, nor does it make up for any material inequality with a view to reestablishing equality between States.

This inequality does not translate to the whole of the UN. States have equal votes in the General Assembly, the principal legislative organ. The remit of the UNSC does not extend beyond maintenance of peace and security – a specific, although important, field of UN activity. Therefore the UNSC cannot be equated to a general decision-making organ, as its competence is restricted to a given subject matter as set out in the Charter. At the same time, the scope of the maintenance of international peace and security is undeniably wide, a point whose significance is reinforced by the fact that the Security Council may subjectively decide what falls within its competences, under Article 39 of the Charter.

The effect of the requirement that the permanent members vote concurrently in decision-making effectively means that no enforcement measures can be taken against them without their consent – something that is not available to other members of the Security Council or of the UN. Yet, the UNSC is also a body distinct to the States that compose it. It is not the special nature of the permanent members *as States* that gives binding force to UNSC resolutions, but the binding power of its resolutions comes from the fact that it is acting within its powers as set out in the Charter. The UNSC can also only impose obligations on members of the UN, and not on third States. The five permanent members, as States, are also still bound by the resolutions of the Security Council, and to the same extent.

Furthermore, an element of reciprocity may also be seen to exist in the security guarantee that is provided by the UNSC, perhaps in a manner similar to that of the NPT system. There has been an equal and mutual renunciation to the right to use force in international relations by all member States under the UNC; it is not that the five permanent members of the UNSC retain the right to use force unilaterally against any other State. All States therefore benefit equally from this renunciation, and from its correlative right, which is the protection offered by the organization, and notably the UNSC, in maintaining peace and security in the case of a violation of the prohibition on the use of force by any State.[238]

[238] Virally, "Panorama du droit international contemporain," p. 289.

There is an argument to be made for seeing the UNSC, similarly to other institutional organs in the EU and WTO, as having the aim of eliminating self-help, or the application of reciprocity in execution, for the use of force in international relations. This is further highlighted by the mechanism originally envisaged, in Articles 43–47 of the Charter, for the UNSC to have armed forces placed at its disposal by member States. This degree of centralization never occurred, with resort instead being made to authorizations for States to take "all necessary measures."[239] Therefore it is not the UNSC itself that can use force, but it can allow member States – *any* member States, although in practice these will usually be those having sufficient military resources – to do so. Importantly, the permanent members cannot unilaterally decide to authorize themselves to use force in response to a threat to international peace and security but must do so on the basis of a positive vote in the Council.

It is also worth noting the significance of the nature of the UN Charter as a treaty. If the organization came to an end, the customary prohibition on the use of force in international relations would still subsist.[240] The effect would be that no State could have recourse to the use of force in international relations, except in situations of self-defense. The institutional mechanism allowing a centralized response would therefore disappear.

Therefore, it is true that the UNSC does escape reciprocity to a certain extent, the differentiated obligations it establishes for five States effectively giving these States a power that others do not have that is temporally unlimited. It is not however so much the difference in what the permanent members may do – authorize use of force – as what may not be done to them, which is to subject them to the same enforcement measures that they may impose on other States, that highlights this lack of reciprocity. However, this is tempered by the character of the UNSC as a treaty-based institutional mechanism, which deals with a specific (although effectively broad) subject matter, and the fact that, when the Security Council as a body takes measures under Articles 41 and 42 of the Charter, its decisions also bind the permanent members in the same manner as other members of the UN. Further, the permanent members

[239] First used in Security Council Resolution 678 on the Iraqi invasion of Kuwait, S/Res/678 (1990), para. 2. See also, for example, Security Council Resolution 1973 on the situation in Libya, at para. 4, S/Res/1973 (2011).

[240] See Military and Paramilitary Activities in and Against Nicaragua (*Nicaragua* v. *United States of America*), Merits, Judgment of 27 June 1986, paras. 175, 177–179.

only have a privileged position by virtue of their membership in the UN on the basis of acceptance by all other member States.

3.6.4 *The WTO: Institutionalized Reciprocity*

While the international organizations mentioned so far are characterized by varying degrees of centralization and institutionalization on the basis of the formal equality of their members expressed in a treaty, each entailing some form of limitation to reciprocity without completely escaping the relativity of obligations under the instrument in question, the case of the WTO is interesting because, as briefly outlined above, it essentially institutionalizes reciprocity in its strictest sense as a *do ut des* or exchange of concessions.[241] This shows that reciprocity and institutionalization are not necessarily antithetical.

One of the main purposes of the WTO is to be a forum for negotiation[242] that will allow States to reach the "reciprocal and mutually advantageous" concessions and agreements that they are bound to reach according to the provisions of the GATT, the main agreement regulating world trade.[243] Reciprocity is important not only in negotiations to this end but also by multilateralizing and ensuring uniformity in the benefits reached through the operation of the MFN clause.[244] This distinguishes the WTO from most other international institutions and organizations, where the point is instead to provide for a collective and centralized form of decision-making.[245]

Although they are agreed multilaterally, the obligations stemming from WTO agreements apply essentially in a bilateral fashion. Each member decides on its own tariff schedule, and in practice is required to apply a specific standard of treatment to imports originating from

[241] Frigo, "Reciprocità nell'evoluzione," p. 458; A. T. Guzman and J. Pauwelyn, *International Trade Law*, New York, Wolters Kluwer Law & Business, 2009, pp. 86–87; *Portugal v. Council*, Case No. C-149/96, Judgment of 23 November 1999, para. 42.

[242] Marrakesh Agreement establishing the World Trade Organization (with final act, annexes, and protocol), 15 April 1994, 1867 U.N.T.S. 4, Article III.2; Guzman and Pauwelyn, *International Trade Law*, p. 80.

[243] General Agreement on Tariffs and Trade, 30 October 1947, 55 U.N.T.S. 194, Preamble, Articles XXVIII.2, XXVIIIbis; J. Wouters and B. De Meester, *The World Trade Organization: A Legal and Institutional Analysis*, Antwerp/Oxford, Intersentia, 2007, p. 19.

[244] Guzman and Pauwelyn, *International Trade Law*, p. 288; Wouters and De Meester, *World Trade Organization*, pp. 25–26.

[245] This point is also reflected in the fact that it is the WTO members as a whole that take major decisions by consensus; Marrakesh Agreement establishing the World Trade Organization, Article IV; Guzman and Pauwelyn, *International Trade Law*, p. 89; Wouters and De Meester, *World Trade Organization*, pp. 186–187.

each of the other members taken individually. The difficulties in ensuring material reciprocity through equality of concessions may be obviated by turning to bilateral agreements. However, reciprocity is still a fundamental aspect of the functioning of trade agreements, both multilateral and bilateral.

There is a further important element of institutionalization to the WTO, which is the attribution of the capacity to react to breaches of trade rules to the organization itself, rather than to States on a bilateral basis.[246] This is done through its highly institutionalized, automatic, and compulsory dispute settlement mechanism (DSU).[247] The DSU allows for the establishment of a panel to pronounce on whether there has been any violation, and if this decision is appealed, a review by an appellate body. The dispute settlement mechanism is truly institutionalized, and therefore differs from other dispute settlement mechanisms under international law, which generally apply between two States.[248] This therefore limits the possibility for States to take reciprocal measures on a bilateral basis to ensure execution of WTO obligations.

However, it does not completely eliminate the possibility for members to take bilateral measures. If the offending member does not implement the panel or appellate body report, it may request compensation. If this is not forthcoming, a request may be made to the Dispute Settlement Body to suspend concessions as retaliation, which is authorized in thirty days unless there is consensus to the contrary.[249] Such suspensions must be equivalent to the initial damage caused by the violating measures – again demonstrating concern with reciprocity.[250] Members may also choose to respond to a prohibited subsidy not by taking a case before the DSU but

[246] Campiglio, "Principio di reciprocità," p. 298.

[247] Annex 2 to the Marrakesh Agreement.

[248] Guzman and Pauwelyn, *International Trade Law*, pp. 119–124.

[249] Agreement on Subsidies and Countervailing Measures, 15 April 1994 (SCM Agreement), Articles 10–23; Guzman and Pauwelyn, *International Trade Law*, p. 124. States may also take countermeasures against WTO members who grant prohibited subsidies and do not comply with the recommendations of the WTO's Dispute Settlement Body (DSB), upon authorization of the DSB: Agreement on Subsidies and Countervailing Measures, 15 April 1994 (SCM Agreement), Article 4.10.

[250] See, for example. *European Communities – Measures Concerning Meat and Meat Products (Hormones)*, Original Complaint Filed by the United States, Recourse to Arbitration by the European Communities under Article 22.6 of the DSU, Decision by Arbitrators, 12 July 1999, WT7DS26/ARB, paras. 16–22; Wouters and De Meester, *World Trade Organization*, pp. 249–251.

by applying a countervailing duty,[251] or impose anti-dumping measures in response to dumping.[252]

The WTO is an example of an institution that institutionalizes reciprocity, which still remains at the basis of how it functions, including in the enforcement of rules. Indeed, the analysis above shows that reciprocity is not absent from institutionalized international law; while reciprocity does have limitations, aside from the particular case of the UNSC, these coincide with the existence of subjects with rights within the organization that are not States.

3.7 Treaty Effects beyond the Parties

In theory, treaties whose effects reach beyond the mere rights and obligations existing between the parties would escape the effects of reciprocity, as they would place obligations on States that are not parties, without granting corresponding rights – or, conversely, granting rights without imposing any corresponding obligations. Two such cases will be looked at here. The first is that of objective regimes, often used to describe treaties relating to a particular territorial regime that has an objective existence outside its subjective effect for the parties, and the second is that of treaty effects for third States, which concerns the scope of the principle *pacta tertiis nec nocent nec prosunt* and how, indeed whether, treaties can establish rights and obligations for third States.

3.7.1 *Treaties Establishing Objective Regimes*

The expression "objective regime" is usually used to refer to a treaty, whether bilateral or multilateral, which has a purported validity *erga omnes*; that is, its dispositions no longer bind only the parties but must be respected by all States. The regimes in question are usually, but not necessarily, territorial regimes,[253] such as territorial settlements in

[251] Guzman and Pauwelyn, *International Trade Law*, p. 407; Wouters and De Meester, *World Trade Organization*, p. 84.

[252] Agreement on Implementation of Article VI of the General Agreement on Tariffs and Trade 1994, 15 April 1994 (Anti-dumping Agreement), Article 7; Guzman and Pauwelyn, *International Trade Law*, p. 434; Wouters and De Meester, *World Trade Organization*, p. 88.

[253] S. P. Subedi, "The Doctrine of Objective Regimes in International Law and the Competence of the United Nations to Impose Territorial or Peace Settlements of States," *German Yearbook of International Law*, vol. 37, 1994, pp. 167, 172, 175, 181, 192. This was recognized by the ILC in the Fifth Report on the Law of Treaties (Treaties and Third States), by Sir Gerald Fitzmaurice, Special Rapporteur, Doc. No. A/CN.4/130, *Yearbook of*

peace treaties and boundary treaties. The notion of an objective treaty was defined in Waldock's third report on the Law of Treaties to the ILC:

> When it appears from its terms and from the circumstances of its conclusion that the intention of the parties is to create in the general interest general obligations and rights relating to a particular region, State, territory, locality, river, waterway, or to a particular area of sea, sea-bed, or air-space; provided that the parties include among their number any State having territorial competence with reference to the subject matter of the treaty, or that any such State has consented to the provision in question.[254]

The consequence of a treaty constituting an objective regime is that the regime thus created becomes opposable to States that are not parties to the treaty.[255]

3.7.1.1 Examples: Territorial and Nonterritorial Regimes

Specific examples include neutralization,[256] boundary treaties to which the exception of *rebus sic stantibus* does not apply, which are not affected by State succession,[257] and which may alter the territorial scope of obligations entered into with third States,[258] specific territorial regimes,[259] and demilitarization.[260]

the International Law Commission 1960, vol. II, pp. 5, 78; Vienna Convention on Succession of States in Respect of Treaties, 23 August 1978, Articles 11 and 12.

254 ILC, Third Report on the Law of Treaties, Doc. No. A/CN.4/167, p. 26. See also P. Cahier, "Le problème des effets des traits à l'égard des états tiers," *Collected Courses of the Hague Academy of International Law*, vol. 143, 1974, p. 661.

255 Cahier, "Problème des effets des traités," p. 662; C. Rousseau, *Droit international public*, 11e ed., 1987, Paris, Dalloz, p. 68.

256 Subedi, "Doctrine of Objective Regimes," pp. 176–177.

257 Vienna Convention on Succession of States in Respect of Treaties, 23 August 1978, 1946 U.N.T.S. 3, Article 11.

258 Virally, "Panorama du droit international contemporain," p. 150; ILC, Law of Treaties: Comments by Governments on the Draft Articles on the Law of Treaties, Drawn up by the Commission at Its Fourteenth, Fifteenth and Sixteenth Session, Doc. Nos. A/CN.4/182 and Corr. 1&2 and Add. 1, 2/Rev.1 & 3, *Yearbook of the International Law Commission 1966*, vol. II, Comments of the Government of the Netherlands, p. 321.

259 Subedi gives the example of the 1988 Afghan settlement agreement, "Doctrine of Objective Regimes" at p. 178; see also Fitzmaurice's Fifth Report on the Law of Treaties, Doc. No. A/CN.4/130, pp. 79–80, but also the example of Mandates and Trusteeship in Waldock's Third Report to the ILC, Doc. No. A/CN.4/167, p. 30.

260 The example given by Subedi is of the Iraqi–Kuwaiti border, "Doctrine of Objective Regimes," pp. 179 and 197, although this was not imposed by treaty but by a resolution of the UNSC. The best example is the demilitarization of the Aaland Islands, given in Fitzmaurice's Fifth Report on the Law of Treaties, Doc. No. A/CN.4/130, pp. 97–98.

The Antarctic Treaty is one example of a treaty that is considered to have established a regime that all States, and not only parties to the Washington Convention, must respect.[261] The Antarctic Treaty regime provides for joint use of Antarctica for purposes of scientific research and exploration, and despite not imposing any obligations upon non-parties, any State not party to the Washington Convention would be regarded as bound by its provisions in carrying out activities in Antarctica.[262] Unlike the case of a boundary treaty or neutralization, in which the regime is established by the State having jurisdiction over the territory, and therefore having some title to decide the status of the territory (one of the conditions for an objective regime initially recognized by the ILC), none of the States parties to the Washington Convention have sovereignty over Antarctica. In fact, the Treaty freezes their claims to sovereignty.[263] The Treaty was also not adopted under the aegis of an international conference but by a small group of States "[r]ecognizing that it is in the interest of all mankind that Antarctica shall continue forever to be used for peaceful purposes."[264]

The Treaty sets out a number of obligations and rights for all States, according to the Preamble, "in the interest of all mankind." It sets out the prohibition of the use of Antarctica for any measures of a military nature in Article I, the obligation not to explode nuclear weapons or dispose of radioactive material in Article V, and an obligation of cooperation and exchange of information in scientific matters in Article III. On the other hand, the Treaty sets out the freedom of scientific investigation, and contracting parties have the right to designate observers in Article VII. Of course, to enjoy this freedom of scientific research, States must have the capacity to organize scientific expeditions and respect the obligations under the Treaty in the first place. States that do not have such a capacity remain bound by the obligations put in place by the Treaty, without the possibility of enjoying access to the continent for purposes of scientific research.

261 Subedi, "Doctrine of Objective Regimes," p. 183.

262 B. Simma., "The Antarctic Treaty as a Treaty Providing for an 'Objective Regime,'" *Cornell International Law Journal*, vol. 19, 1986, p. 197; Fitzmaurice, Fifth Report on the Law of Treaties, Doc. No. A/CN.4/130, pp. 93–94.

263 The Antarctic Treaty, 1 December 1959, Article 4; Simma, "Antarctic Treaty," p. 201; M. G. Kohen, *Possession Contestée et Souveraineté Territoriale*, Paris, PUF, 1997, p. 107. It may of course be considered that States Parties to the Washington Convention considered themselves to in fact have territorial competence over the given portions of Antarctica which they claim.

264 Antarctic Treaty, Preamble.

The second example is that of international waterways, which are also often considered objective regimes.[265] In using an international waterway, third States can avail of the regime established by the treaty without actually having to become parties to it.[266] At the same time, States must conform to the conditions for use set out in the treaty governing the waterway in question.[267] Unlike the case of Antarctica, the question of waterways conforms to the conditions set out by Fitzmaurice, in that it is the territorial State that has the right to lay down conditions for use of the waterway.[268] Third States therefore exercise their right to use the waterway on condition that they subject themselves to these conditions of use.[269] The existence of objective regimes has been put forward not only for territorial matters but also for matters such as preservation of fish stocks, regulating international communication,[270] and marine cemeteries.[271]

3.7.1.2 Explaining "Objective Regimes"

Many explanations have been put forward as to how a treaty may become an objective regime, generally underpinned by an argument that certain treaties reach beyond their merely contractual dimension;[272] some authors have gone so far as to say that treaties establishing "objective" regimes "are the only tool available to fill the normative gaps of the international legal order."[273] This is generally based either on a

265 Fitzmaurice, Fifth Report on the Law of Treaties, Doc. No. A/CN.4/130, p. 87; Comments by Governments on the Draft Articles on the Law of Treaties, Drawn up by the Commission at Its fourteenth, fifteenth and sixteenth session, Comments of the Government of Portugal, p. 334; see also PCIJ, *Case of the S.S. "Wimbledon,"* Judgment of 17 August 1923, PCIJ, No. A01.

266 Fitzmaurice, Fifth Report on the Law of Treaties, Doc. No. A/CN.4/130, p. 92.

267 Ibid.; E. David, "Article 34: General Rule regarding Third States," in O. Corten and P. Klein, eds, *The Vienna Convention on the Law of Treaties: A Commentary*, Oxford, Oxford University Press, 2011, p. 891.

268 ILC, Summary Records of the Second Part of the Seventeenth Session, 3–28 January 1966, *Yearbook of the International Law Commission*, 1966, vol. I, Pt. I, p. 229; Cahier, "Problème des effets des traits," p. 687.

269 Cahier, "Problème des effets des traités," p. 695.

270 F. Salerno, "Treaties Establishing Objective Regimes," in E. Cannizzaro, ed., *The Law of Treaties beyond the Vienna Convention*, Oxford, Oxford University Press, 2011, p. 228.

271 Klabbers, "Cimetières marins sont-ils établis comme des regimes objectifs?," pp. 121–133.

272 *International Status of South West Africa*, Advisory Opinion, ICJ Reports 1950, Separate Opinion by Sir Arnold McNair, p. 154; Subedi, "Doctrine of Objective Regimes," p. 191.

273 Salerno, "Treaties Establishing Objective Regimes," p. 241.

"constitutional" or "public order" explanation of objective regimes, seen as examples of States legislating in the general interest.[274]

A further set of explanations focuses instead on the nature of the rights at issue and on analogies from private law. The first argument was raised before the PCIJ in the *Wimbledon* case, and considers rights arising from such objective regimes to be a form of servitude; that is, a limitation to the property rights of one State in favor of allowing usage rights to others, and one that is "exercisable not only against a particular owner of tenement but against any successor to him in title."[275] In the case of the *Wimbledon*, this would have meant a limitation upon Germany's sovereign rights to regulate navigation in the Kiel Canal. The Court did not feel it necessary to pronounce on what it considered to be a question of a "very controversial" nature.[276] This question is linked to the problem of whether objective regimes could be considered to establish real as opposed to personal rights – rights *in rem* rather than *in personam*. This was the view put forward by McNair in his Separate Opinion in the South West Africa cases: rights *in rem* have "a greater degree of permanence than personal rights"[277] and, differently to personal rights, which would bind only another State, real rights operate *erga omnes* and bind "the whole world."[278] Any change, therefore, in the person holding the right would leave the right unaffected; such would have been the case for the Mandate in the South West Africa cases or, one would presume, a change in legal personality of a State. Once again, the emphasis is placed on the opposability of such rights to all other States, rather than only the States parties to the treaty in question.

The practice relating to treaties establishing objective regimes is also inextricably linked to the historical role of Great Powers. This was clearly set out by Lord McNair in his Separate Opinion to the Advisory Opinion on the *International Status of South West Africa*.

274 Simma, "From Bilateralism to Community Interest," 1994, pp. 360–361. See, for example, A. Frowein, "Reactions by Not Directly Affected States to Breaches of International Law," *Collected Courses of the Hague Academy of International Law*, vol. 248, 1994, p. 361.

275 M. Fitzmaurice, "Third Parties and the Law of Treaties," *Max Planck Yearbook of the United Nations*, vol. 6, 2002, p. 68, cit. J. L. Brierly, *Law of Nations: An Introduction to the International Law of Peace*, Oxford, Clarendon, 1963, p. 191.

276 PCIJ, *Case of the S.S. Wimbledon*, pp. 23–24.

277 *International Status of South West Africa*, Separate Opinion by Sir Arnold McNair, p. 157.

278 Z. Douglas, *The International Law of Investment Claims*, Cambridge, Cambridge University Press, 2012, pp. 203–205, cit. T. W. Merrill and H. E. Smith, "The Property/Contract Interface," *Columbia Law Review*, vol. 101, no. 4, 2001, pp. 776–777; Fitzmaurice, Fifth Report on the Law of Treaties, Doc. No. A/CN.4/130, pp. 69–70.

> From time to time it happens that a group of great Powers, or a large number of States both great and small, assume a power to create by a multipartite treaty some new international regime or status, which soon acquires a degree of acceptance and durability extending beyond the limits of the actual contracting parties, and giving it an objective existence.[279]

In a negative sense, this means that accepting the possibility of treaties becoming "objective regimes" also means accepting the possibility that some States may be "more equal" than others, simply by virtue of their intention to put in place a regime whose validity must be recognized by all.[280]

If this role as a public power could have been seen to reflect the functioning of international society until the era of the League of Nations, with the Charter of the United Nations, and its emphasis on sovereign equality and universality, resistance to this possibility has increased. Because of the principle of sovereign equality of States, such legislative competence by a limited group of States would not be possible. This may raise the question as to whether, in this case, the UN could not be said to have the capacity to impose territorial settlements that gain objective validity, including for States that are not directly involved in the territorial settlement.

The example has been given of the demilitarization zone imposed by the UN on the Iraq–Kuwait border,[281] which could be considered "objective" because it established a boundary that all States have an obligation to respect, whether UN members or not. Iraq – the State with territorial competence – was also bound to observe the conditions imposed by the Security Council in its Resolution 687 of 8 April 1991. However, when it comes to the UN, the imposition of administrations or regimes on a given territory is generally carried out in the context of the maintenance of international peace and security. The scope of the Security Council's discretion in Chapter VII of the UNC as to which measures it may put in place in furthering the maintenance of international peace and security does not of itself exclude the imposition of a territorial regime or administration.

Secondly, as long as the UN and its organs are acting within their competences under the Charter, the point whether the State responsible

[279] *International Status of South West Africa*, Separate Opinion by Sir Arnold McNair, p. 153.

[280] Chinkin, *Third Parties in International Law*, p. 26; Cahier, "Problème des effets des traités," p. 644.

[281] Subedi, "Doctrine of Objective Regimes," pp. 179, 197.

for the territory has consented to the particular regime is not relevant. In the example given above, Iraq does not have to respect the demilitarized zone because the latter has an "objective" existence, but merely because Iraq is bound to comply with the decisions of the UNSC by virtue of its membership of the organization.[282] It is clear that, firstly, because of the principle of sovereign equality in contemporary international law (a principle which has if anything been strengthened over the decades since the UN came into existence), no State has the power to impose, without more, any form of objective regime on others; secondly, the role of the UN in administering territory cannot be compared to that of the Great Powers in the past, but rather flows from its organizational competence.[283]

There are other mechanisms by which treaties could have effects beyond their parties. The first of these is that third States acquiesce in the regime created.[284] The second is that a tacit agreement may exist between third States and parties to the treaty (one of the explanations given for the regimes of international waterways).[285] There is therefore a correlation between the third State's usage right under a given treaty, and its obligation to respect its provisions; by exercising navigation rights, it is also agreeing to submit to the treaty's obligations.[286]

Another explanation considers that treaty regimes can gain a wider effect through a customary lawmaking process.[287] For example, with

282 Ibid., pp. 201, 205.

283 In fact, even in McNair's Separate Opinion on the *Legal Status of South West Africa*, he considered that it was "every State which was a Member of the League at the time of its dissolution" that had a legal interest in the exercise of the Mandate (*International Status of South West Africa*, Separate Opinion by Sir Arnold McNair, p. 158).

284 Subedi, "Doctrine of Objective Regimes," p. 194.

285 Fitzmaurice, Fifth Report on the Law of Treaties, Doc. No. A/CN.4/130, p. 92.

286 P. Braud, "Recherches sur l'état tiers en droit international public," *Revue générale de droit international public*, vol. 72, 1968, p. 75; Fitzmaurice, Fifth Report on the Law of Treaties, Doc. No. A/CN.4/130, pp. 72–73. This view is backed up by the Court's finding in the *Oder* case that the Treaty of Versailles could not have effects without ratification: PCIJ, *Case Relating to the Territorial Jurisdiction of the International Commission of the River Oder*, Judgment of 10 September 1929, PCIJ, No. A23, p. 21.

287 Klabbers, "Cimetières marins sont-ils établis comme des regimes objectifs?," p. 126; Comments by Governments on the Draft Articles on the Law of Treaties, Drawn up by the Commission at Its Fourteenth, Fifteenth and Sixteenth Session, Comments of the Government of Portugal, p. 334; Fitzmaurice, Fifth Report on the Law of Treaties, Doc. No. A/CN.4/130, pp. 67, 81–82; David, "Article 34," p. 895; G. Gaja, "Article 38: Rules in a Treaty Becoming Binding on Third States through International Custom," in *The Vienna Convention on the Law of Treaties: A Commentary*, Oxford, Oxford University Press, 2011, p. 958; Kohen, *Possession contestée et souveraineté territoriale*, p. 108.

respect to the Antarctic Treaty, the explanation has been put forward that practice existed before the Treaty was concluded, that the States concluding the Treaty were specially affected, and that there were no objections to the Treaty upon its conclusion.[288] On the other hand, it may be objected that the silence of other States cannot be taken as evidence of *opinio juris* and that the contracting parties did not intend to give the treaty any effect beyond its contractual dimension.[289] This position essentially would view the Antarctic regime as not being an objective regime at all but rather one whose obligations are accepted by third States that use Antarctic territory.

Finally, perhaps the most compelling explanation of the effects of treaties *erga omnes* has to do with a simple principle, which is that it is not possible to contest the valid acts of other States. Therefore, third States are simply held to not impede the performance of the rights arising under a validly concluded treaty and to recognize the legal situation resulting from it. This is essentially a consequence of the principle of good faith[290] and an act of noninterference in the rights and obligations set out by third States in a treaty. Once States conform to the requirements of a regime, they enter into a form of tacit agreement based on usage and, indeed, on reciprocity.

3.7.2 *Treaty Effects for Third States*

As the expression "objective regime" does not provide a clear category of agreement that escapes the operation of reciprocity, it will be of interest to examine further the related question of the effects of treaties for third States. If it were possible for treaties to grant rights or impose obligations on third States, this would mean an escape from not only the requirement of consent but also the reciprocity of rights and obligations under treaty law; it may mean that rights could be granted without any correlative obligations, or that a State, without its consent, could be held to comply with a certain obligations without however enjoying either a correlative right or being able to expect performance from others.

3.7.2.1 Pacta tertiis nec nocent nec prosunt

The general rule recognized in Article 34 of the VCLT is that "[a] treaty does not create either obligations or rights for a third State without its

[288] Simma, "Antarctic Treaty," p. 202. [289] Ibid., p. 204.

[290] Cahier, "Problème des effets des traités," p. 675; C. Laly-Chevalier, "Article 35: Treaties Providing for Obligations for Third States," in *The Vienna Convention on the Law of Treaties: A Commentary*, Oxford, Oxford University Press, 2011, pp. 909–910.

consent." This may be considered a formulation of the principle of Roman law that *pacta tertiis nec nocent nec prosunt*. As explained by Sir Humphrey Waldock in his Third Report on the Law of Treaties, the reason why in international law treaties cannot create rights or obligations for States not parties to them without the latter's consent is the fact of the sovereign equality and independence of States.[291] This principle therefore recognizes that treaties have a relative effect.[292] It has notably been recognized in ICJ case law on maritime delimitation that taking into account the existence of the coasts and entitlements of third States to effect a delimitation does not in any way affect the legal interests of those third States.[293] The Court has also noted that agreements between one party to a maritime delimitation case and third States cannot affect the rights and obligations of the other party to the case.[294]

If a treaty were to impose rights or obligations on third States without their consent, this would be an exception not only to the relative effect of treaties but also to the principle of sovereign equality of States. The two are intertwined; the relativity of rights and obligations under international law, which entails the reciprocity of rights and obligations, stems from the legal equality of States. It would amount to one group of States legislating for others.

The question that has troubled doctrine over whether it is possible for States to agree in a treaty to confer a benefit upon a third State without the latter having to consent – in other words, making a *stipulation pour autrui* – arose most notably before the PCIJ in the *Free Zones* case.[295]

[291] ILC, Third Report on the Law of Treaties, Doc. No. A/CN.4/167, p. 18; ILC, Draft Articles on the Law of Treaties, with Commentaries, pp. 226–227, Chinkin, *Third Parties in International Law*, p. 26; A. Aust, *Modern Treaty Law and Practice*, 3rd ed., Cambridge, Cambridge University Press, 2013, p. 227; D. Murray, "How International Humanitarian Law Treaties Bind Non-State Armed Groups," *Journal of Conflict and Security Law*, vol. 20, no. 1, 2015, pp. 110–111; Salerno, "Treaties Establishing Objective Regimes," p. 230; Laly-Chevalier, "Article 35," p. 904; Cahier, "Problème des effets des traités," p. 609.

[292] David, "Article 34," pp. 887–888; Cahier, "Problème des effets des traités," pp. 612, 614; ILC, Law of Treaties: Comments by Governments on the Draft Articles on the Law of Treaties, ... Comments of the Government of Czechoslovakia, p. 287.

[293] Land, Island and Maritime Frontier Dispute (El Salvador/Honduras), Application to Intervene, Judgment, ICJ Reports 1990, p. 124, para. 77; Maritime Delimitation in the Black Sea (*Romania* v. *Ukraine*), Judgment, ICJ Reports 2009, p. 100, para. 114.

[294] Territorial and Maritime Dispute (*Nicaragua* v. *Colombia*), Judgment, ICJ Reports 2012, pp. 684–685, paras. 161–162.

[295] Although a number of treaties may be seen as making *stipulations pour autrui*, such as Articles 109 and 358 of the Treaty of Versailles. See ILC, Draft Articles on the Law of Treaties, with Commentaries, p. 228; Cahier, "Problème des effets des traités," p. 621.

Whereas some authors recognize such a possibility,[296] in actual fact the PCIJ did not find it necessary to decide upon the question; it did however mention that there is nothing to prevent States making such a stipulation, but that such a creation of a right in favor of a third State "cannot be lightly presumed," and that in any case the assent of the third State in question was required.[297] While in the early work of the ILC the notion gained some traction,[298] the point is now settled in the VCLT: rights, similarly to obligations, cannot be conferred upon States without their consent.

3.7.2.2 Distinguishing Effects from Rights and Obligations

The creation of rights or obligations for third States should however be distinguished from the question of the *effects* of a treaty for third States. It could be said that most treaties have some kind of effect for third States.[299] The most obvious example is that of MFN treatment, which allows for the provisions of a treaty to be invoked by a third party by virtue of its own agreement requiring MFN treatment with one of the States parties to the third treaty. But a State may also be a party to a convention requiring it to dispose of toxic waste in a specific manner, meaning it will not be able to enter into arrangements for waste disposal with other States. Economic flows under one free trade agreement may be affected by the conclusion of another free trade agreement. In territorial matters, the scope of application of one treaty may be changed because one of the parties has concluded a treaty with another State by which the latter cedes a portion of its territory.

One must therefore be careful to distinguish the incidental effects of treaties on third States from their creating rights and obligations. A State cannot object to a treaty concluded by third States merely on the basis that the latter has some adverse effects for it.[300] In the words of

[296] Such as J.-P. Jacqué, "A propos de la promesse unilatérale," in D. Bardonnet et al., eds., *Mélanges offerts à Paul Reuter*, Paris, Pedone, 1981, pp. 330, 334.

[297] PCIJ, *Case of the Free Zones of Upper Savoy and the District of Gex*, Judgment of 7 June 1932, PCIJ, No. A/B46, pp. 147–148; Waldock, Third Report on the Law of Treaties, Doc. No. A/CN.4/167, pp. 23–24, Fitzmaurice, "Third Parties and the Law of Treaties," p. 52.

[298] Fitzmaurice, Fifth Report on the Law of Treaties, Doc. No. A/CN.4/130, p. 81.

[299] Tomuschat, "Obligations Arising for States," p. 257.

[300] Fitzmaurice, Fifth Report on the Law of Treaties, Doc. No. A/CN.4/130, pp. 73–74, 81; Klabbers gives the example of the agreement on the wreck of the *MV Estonia*, "Cimetières marins sont-ils établis comme des regimes objectifs?," pp. 124–125; Salerno, "Treaties Establishing Objective Regimes," p. 233; Laly-Chevalier, "Article 35," p. 909; ILC, Report on the Law of Treaties by Mr. H. Lauterpacht, p. 154.

Fitzmaurice, "the fact that a treaty may result in creating a liability or disability for a third State, or may operate to the disadvantage or detriment of that State, or in a manner contrary to its interest, is not per se a ground on which the parties can, inter se, refuse to carry out the treaty."[301] Whereas no legal relationship arises if the third State merely obtains an advantage under the treaty, in the case of the conferral of a right, this right is owed to the third State by one or more of the treaty parties.[302] Once again, rights entail corresponding obligations. Where there are no rights or obligations for third States, these may still be "objects" of a treaty, but all rights and obligations will only arise between the parties.[303]

3.7.2.3 The Requirement of Consent

Indeed, for all the talk of the effects of "objective" treaties and regimes for third States, there are no examples of these treaties actually being enforced against third States without their consent;[304] the ICJ and PCIJ, for example, have always been careful to speak of States "accepting" an obligation under a treaty before finding it to be enforceable. Rights and obligations flow from this consent by the third State, which is bound by its own acceptance, rather than by the treaty in question. So even though a State may accept the rights and obligations that the treaty sets out, it does not actually become a party to the treaty.[305]

This makes sense considering that a treaty is a formal agreement and will itself set out the conditions for accession, if any. It would make this mechanism redundant to accept that merely by accepting a specific right by unilateral declaration, a third State could become a treaty party. The third State's consent therefore effectively creates a collateral agreement

301 Fitzmaurice, Fifth Report on the Law of Treaties, Doc. No. A/CN.4/130, p. 77.

302 P. D'Argent, "Article 36: Treaties Providing for Rights for Third States," in *The Vienna Convention on the Law of Treaties: A Commentary*, Oxford, Oxford University Press, 2011, p. 933; Cahier, "Problème des effets des traités," p. 681.

303 Fitzmaurice, Fifth Report on the Law of Treaties, Doc. No. A/CN.4/130, p. 84. An example of this is given by Simma regarding the Antarctic Treaty: Simma, "Antarctic Treaty," p. 204.

304 David, "Article 34," p.890; ILC, Third Report on the Law of Treaties, Doc. No. A/CN.4/167, p. 20; Laly-Chevalier, "Article 35," pp. 903, 906–907; Cahier, "Problème des effets des traités," p. 677.

305 Fitzmaurice, Fifth Report on the Law of Treaties, Doc. No. A/CN.4/130, pp. 91, 104; Cahier, "Problème des effets des traités," pp. 603–604; Waldock, Third Report on the Law of Treaties, Doc. No. A/CN.4/167, p. 26; Aust, *Modern Treaty Law and Practice*, p. 228.

between it and the parties to the treaty.[306] Therefore, the third State enjoys the rights the parties to the treaty have granted it and is bound by the obligations related to those rights; equally, the parties to the treaty are bound to grant the third State the rights extended to it in the treaty, but only those. Although the agreement of the third State is connected to the treaty, it is not equal to an acceptance of the entirety of its terms, and the treaty therefore cannot be opposed to it in its entirety.

Regarding revocability of the rights or obligations of third States to a treaty, the conditions in the VCLT are slightly different. Whereas under Article 37.1 the consent of both the parties to the treaty and the third State are required to revoke an obligation under a treaty, under Article 37.2 the parties to the treaty may revoke a right unless it can be established that "[it] was intended not to be revocable or subject to modification without the consent of the third State." It is more likely that the third State would wish to revoke its acceptance of an obligation under the treaty than the parties themselves; therefore, the consent of all concerned is required.[307]

The underlying rationale reflects the reciprocity of rights and obligations inherent in the collateral agreement by which a State assumes obligations or rights under a treaty. This is reflected in the discussions taking place in the ILC on the conditions for revocation of rights or acceptance of obligations by third States.[308] States parties to a treaty should not be able to unilaterally revoke the rights they have extended. Accepting and exercising rights "invariably involve(s) corresponding obligations"[309] and it should therefore be envisaged that States parties to a treaty should not be able to terminate the rights they have granted where these were not intended to be revocable without consent of the third State. The mechanism of reciprocity is all the more obvious in respect of obligations; in the case of obligations for third States, consent cannot be unilaterally revoked by the third State unless there is an agreement to the contrary; instead, the consent of the treaty parties is required. Again, accepting an obligation means that the State also gains corresponding rights, and it cannot simply revoke its consent to the

[306] ILC, Summary Records of the Eighteenth Session, p. 227; ILC, Draft Articles on the Law of Treaties with Commentaries, p. 227; Laly-Chevalier, "Article 35," p. 916.

[307] ILC, Summary Records of the Eighteenth Session, p. 230.

[308] ILC, Summary Records of the First Part of the Seventeenth Session, 3 May–9 July 1965, *Yearbook of the International Law Commission*, vol. I, 1965. See Comments by Rosenne, p. 87; and Paredes, p. 88.

[309] Ibid., Comments by Paredes, p. 88.

obligations at will. Interestingly, in discussions before the ILC, Paredes referred to "considerations of justice and fairness" as supporting this view.[310] In any case, in the face of "almost non-existent"[311] practice the point remains one of mostly theoretical interest.

These issues perfectly illustrate the link that exists between rights and obligations in international law. Acceptance of a right, which is implied also by the exercise of that right, entails corresponding obligations. Otherwise, it would be possible for such rights and obligations to be withdrawn at will. The example of treaties on international waterways is instructive in this regard. If such treaties can be regarded as extending rights of use to third States, the exercise of such rights by third States using a waterway also entails the respect of the obligations set out in the treaty.[312]

3.7.2.4 Article 2.6 of the UN Charter: An Exception?

Article 2.6 of the UN Charter is often taken as an example of a treaty provision that is binding on third States. It reads: "The Organization shall ensure that States which are not Members of the United Nations act in accordance with these Principles so far as may be necessary for the maintenance of international peace and security." One interpretation of this provision suggests that this means that the UNSC is able to impose obligations on third States. This would entail either recognizing a legislative role for the UNSC, or understanding the Charter as an example of a public interest treaty according to which, in matters relating to the maintenance of peace and security, nonparties are also held to observe the decisions of the Security Council.

In support of this interpretation, reference is made to the statement of the ICJ in its *Namibia* Advisory Opinion that "it is for non-member States to act in accordance with those [Security Council] decisions."[313] However, a look at the paragraph preceding this sentence gives a better idea of the Court's position. It first recognizes that nonmember States are "not bound" by Articles 24 and 25 of the UN Charter; it then goes

[310] Ibid. [311] Laly-Chevalier, "Article 35," p. 918.

[312] Fitzmaurice, Fifth Report on the Law of Treaties, Doc. No. A/CN.4/130, pp. 91–92; in general, Chinkin, *Third Parties in International Law*, p. 135 and Laly-Chevalier, "Article 35," p. 913. The example has also been given of Part XI of UNCLOS: Fitzmaurice, "Third Parties and the Law of Treaties," p. 113.

[313] Legal Consequences of the Continued Presence of South Africa in Namibia (South West Africa) notwithstanding Security Council Resolution 276 (1970), Advisory Opinion of 21 June 1971, ICJ Reports 1971, para. 126. This is the view espoused by Murray, "How International Humanitarian Law Treaties Bind," p. 116.

on to note that nonmember States have been called upon in UNSC Resolution 276

> to give assistance in the action which has been taken by the United Nations with regard to Namibia. In the view of the Court, the termination of the Mandate and the declaration of the illegality of South Africa's presence in Namibia are opposable to all States in the sense of barring *erga omnes* the legality of a situation which is maintained in violation of international law: in particular, no State which enters into relations with South Africa concerning Namibia may expect the United Nations or its Members to recognize the validity or effects of such relationship, or of the consequences thereof.

The decision of the UNSC does not therefore directly create rights and obligations for third States. However, it is considered "opposable" to third States: this means that nonmember States cannot expect their relations with South Africa concerning Namibia to have any effects vis-à-vis UN member States. This paragraph in effect restates the principle that States must recognize the effects of valid legal acts.

Perhaps a better interpretation of UNC Article 2.6 is that it imposes obligations upon the UN member States themselves rather than upon third States.[314] This is also the interpretation put forward by Switzerland, which was not a UN member State until 2002, in its attitude toward UNSC resolutions. Switzerland reserved the right to carry out or not carry out resolutions of the UN Security Council on the basis that Article 2.6 does not imply any legal obligation for nonmember States; it could voluntarily decide to apply UNSC resolutions, but this did not imply any legal obligation to do so on its behalf. The Swiss Federal Council stated: "*le Conseil de Sécurité peut exiger d'États non membres qu'ils adoptent une attitude solidaire des sanctions des Nations Unies, mais sans pouvoir les y obliger juridiquement.*"[315] [an exchange of services of the same nature between the two contracting States, who mutually concede to each other fishing rights in sectors within their respective jurisdiction.] Article 2.6 of the UN Charter cannot therefore be seen as imposing obligations on third States in the manner of international legislation.

3.7.2.5 Reciprocity as a Mechanism to Extend Application of a Treaty to Nonparties

Reciprocity can also play a role in providing a basis for cooperation in the absence of legal obligations, and it may be used as a basis on which to

[314] Lauterpacht, Report on the Law of Treaties, 1953, p. 93; David, "Article 34," pp. 892–893.

[315] David, "Article 34," p. 893; Cahier, "Problème des effets des traits," p. 716; L. Caflisch, "Pratique Suisse," *Annuaire Suisse de Droit International*, vol. XXVI, 1969–1970, pp. 85–88.

extend the applicability of a treaty to third States. This may concern only specific provisions or the entirety of the treaty.[316] The possibility is notably present in the Geneva Conventions of 12 August 1949 under Common Article 2: "Although one of the Powers in conflict may not be a party to the present Convention, the Powers who are parties thereto shall remain bound by it in their mutual relations. They shall furthermore be bound by the Convention in relation to the said Power, if the latter accepts and applies the provisions thereof." This principle was also applied earlier: the 1929 Geneva Convention on Prisoners of War was applied on the basis of reciprocity between the United States and Japan following an exchange of communications between the two parties.[317]

Article 6 of the 1926 International Convention for the Unification of Certain Rules Relating to the Immunity of State-Owned Vessels also states that "[t]he provisions of the present Convention may be applied in each Contracting State for the benefit of non-Contracting States and their nationals only on the basis of reciprocity." The provision was analyzed in *Vernicos* v. *U.S.*, where the United States Court of Appeals found that "the parties to a treaty, each of whom makes a sacrifice for a countervailing benefit, do not want the other party to extend the same benefit to a State not making such sacrifices."[318] The fact that both States were prepared to allow suits by the nationals of the other State to be brought was sufficient to fulfill this requirement of reciprocity. This is similar to the extension of rights and obligations to third States under Article 36.1 of the VCLT, which provides that "[a] right arises for a third State from a provision of a treaty if the parties to the treaty intend the provision to accord that right [. . .] and the third State assents thereto. Its assent shall be presumed so long as the contrary is not indicated, unless the treaty otherwise provides." In the case of the extension of the operation of a treaty on the basis of reciprocity, there is still an acceptance on the part of the third State through its conduct.[319]

3.8 Conclusion

Reciprocity underlies the conclusion of treaties, as well as the operation of the rules on the law of treaties, notably those on reservations. These recognize that States parties to a treaty cannot require performance of

316 Chinkin, *Third Parties in International Law*, p. 50.
317 Provost, "Reciprocity in Human Rights," p. 390.
318 *Vernicos Shipping Co.* v. *United States*, United States, Court of Appeals, Second Circuit, 21 June 1965, 42 ILR 186, at 188.
319 Chinkin, *Third Parties in International Law*, p. 51.

greater obligations than they are themselves prepared to accept. The underlying interdependence and correspondence of rights and obligations in treaties applies to both bilateral and multilateral treaties, even those of the "integral" type, and both in treaties where there is an obvious exchange, and where parties take on obligations in unilateral terms. Reciprocity is also evident in how treaty rights and obligations may be extended to third States, and in the absence of any clear cases of "objective regimes."

Some limitations to reciprocity are also encountered. This is notably the case for reservations to human rights treaties. An examination of how the ILO works also shows that the reason reservations are inapplicable to international labor conventions may be put down to the fact that it is not only States, but also individuals, which draw up the conventions in question. If we add to this the justification given by the ECJ in *Van Gend en Loos*, it appears that limitations to reciprocity exist when a treaty also extends rights to subjects that are not States. There is a close link, in international law, between the applicability of reciprocity and the legal equality of the subjects involved in a legal relationship.

Further, some limitations to reciprocity in execution exist in the case of international organizations. The institutionalization inherent in such organizations, and the fact that they have an international personality distinct to that of their member States, means that obligations under these systems cannot be suspended on a basis of reciprocity of execution, through mechanisms of countermeasures or the exception of nonperformance.

Limitations on reciprocity cannot however be explained by the *substance* of the obligations – that they aim to protect a community interest or that they pertain to a specific area of international law. Instead, it appears that limitations arise when there are different legal subjects than States having rights under the treaty. Chapter 4 will therefore look in greater detail at the particular issue of reciprocity and the treatment of individuals in international law.

4 Treatment of Individuals

We have seen that the differences between the role reciprocity plays in "classic" bilateral treaties and in treaties that are meant to embody community values are not as easy to draw as is usually suggested. However, the examination of treaties in Chapter 3 indicates that there is a difference, in terms of the reciprocity of rights and obligations, between treaties that only set out rights and obligations for States and those that confer rights directly on individuals. This chapter will therefore focus in particular on the treatment of individuals in international law, assessing how reciprocity functions differently depending on who rights are owed to in different substantive areas of law.

The matter of international regulation of the treatment of individuals began long before the advent of human rights. Bilateral treaties of friendship, commerce, and navigation (FCN) concluded from the end of the eighteenth century, covered a wide range of areas of regulation, and concerned how States were to treat each other's citizens. FCN treaties were very much based on reciprocity of treatment between the two States parties, a prime example of classical international law.[1] A significant development in how international law regulated treatment of individuals occurred with the progressive abolition of the slave trade in the late eighteenth and nineteenth centuries, both in the domestic laws of nations such as Great Britain, France, and Denmark, and in international instruments.[2]

[1] Virally, "Principe de réciprocité," p. 6.

[2] Such as the Declaration of the Eight Powers relative to the Universal Abolition of the Slave Trade, annexed as Act XV to the 1815 General Treaty of the Vienna Congress, 8 February 1815, 63 C.T.S. 473; Treaty for the Suppression of the African Slave Trade, 20 December 1841, 73 C.T.S. 32; J. Alcaide Fernández, "*Hostes Humani Generis*: Pirates, Slavers, and Other Criminals," in B. Fassbender et al., eds., *The Oxford Handbook of the History of International*

After World War I, regulation by international treaty of the rights of workers began, through the conventions of the International Labour Organization and treaties on minorities.[3] In its Advisory Opinion on *Jurisdiction of the Courts of Danzig* in 1928, the PCIJ held that individuals could enjoy rights under treaties.[4] After World War II, and the adoption of the Universal Declaration on Human Rights, regional human rights conventions in Europe, the Americas, and Africa,[5] and the two Covenants (ICCPR and ICESCR), a system came into being in which individuals could have direct rights under treaties, irrespective of whether they were nationals or foreigners in the State in which they were present, merely by virtue of their quality as humans.[6]

Law, Oxford, Oxford University Press, 2012, p. 132; D. Weissbrodt, "Slavery," in R. Wolfrum, ed., *The Max Planck Encyclopedia of Public International Law*, Oxford University Press, 2008–, online edition, [www.mpepil.com], para. 26.

3 Judge Jessup, in his Separate Opinion in the South West Africa cases, placed these treaties in the category of treaties that States concluded

> in order to protect general interests of an economic, political or humanitarian nature, by means of obligations the uniformity and general observance of which are of the essence of the agreement. The interdependence of international relations frequently results in States having a vital interest in the maintenance of certain rules and principles, although a modification or breach of these principles in any particular single case is not likely to affect adversely some of them at all or at least not in the same degree ....
> (cit. Note by "H. L." in 1935 *British Yearbook of International Law*, p. 165)

South West Africa (Liberia v. *South Africa)*, Judgment of 21 December 1962, Separate Opinion of Judge Jessup, p. 430.

4 PCIJ, *Jurisdiction of the Courts of Danzig*, Collection of Advisory Opinions, 3 March 1928, PCIJ, Series B, No. B/15; see in this sense K. Parlett, "The PCIJ's Opinion in *Jurisdiction of the Courts of Danzig*. Individual Rights under Treaties," *Journal of the History of International Law*, vol. 10, 2008, pp. 119–145.

5 European Convention on Human Rights, Rome, 4 November 1950, and American Convention on Human Rights, 22 November 1969, later followed by the African Charter on Human and Peoples' Rights, 27 June 1981.

6 Simma considers human rights to have "superseded and supplemented" the preexisting system based on rules on the treatment of aliens, Simma, "From Bilateralism to Community Interest," p. 243. There are some interesting areas in which this change materialized, such as agreements relating to the rescue of astronauts. The following are the words of the Chairman in discussions at the ILC:

> Obviously, it would be contrary not only to logic but also to the fundamental duties owed by all to those men who ventured into space to expose them to the risks resulting from the exclusion of any areas of the world from the operation of a convention of a humanitarian character. To do so would expose astronauts to the danger of being left helpless if they landed in certain areas, merely because, for political reasons, some States happened not to recognize other States. Ultimately, the real beneficiary of an agreement on assistance to astronauts and the return of spacecraft would be man himself. The life of an astronaut, the protection of basic rules of international law and

The different approaches to these rights are exemplified by the arguments of the United States and Germany in the *LaGrand* case before the ICJ. The United States in this case claimed that the rights in the Vienna Convention on Consular Relations (VCCR) were not individual rights; it advanced the argument that Germany's submissions were "inadmissible on the ground that Germany seeks to have a standard applied to the United States that is different from its own practice."[7] Therefore, the United States made an argument on the basis of reciprocity in application for why it could not be held to a higher standard than Germany. Germany instead claimed that individual rights were at issue.[8]

4.1 Standards of Treatment and Protection

The analysis will begin from the more traditional standards of treatment of aliens, that is, those based explicitly on reciprocity of treatment and the international minimum standard, before moving on to the two relative standards of national treatment and the most-favored nation clause. Although the latter two may also be used to regulate the treatment that goods must receive when entering a State, as is the case under the GATT, they will be analyzed here specifically in relation to the treatment of individuals. In reality, reciprocity underlies all these standards of treatment, although in different ways, depending on what specific rules require.

4.1.1 *Treatment of Aliens Based on Reciprocity*

An important means of regulating the treatment of aliens is explicitly based on, that is, conditional upon, reciprocity. The reciprocal treatment can either be required by law, or not, and can either be set out in internal law or in a treaty.[9]

Treatment of foreigners on the basis of reciprocity incorporated in domestic legislation generally has the purpose of ensuring that a similar standard of treatment will be granted to citizens of the receiving State as

their implementation were more important than the passing interests and policies of individual States.

(ILC, Summary Records of the First Part of the Seventeenth Session, 3 May–9 July 1965, *Yearbook of the International Law Commission*, vol. I, 1965, 795th meeting, p. 137)

[7] *LaGrand (Germany* v. *United States of America)*, Judgment of 27 June 2001, ICJ Reports 2001, para. 62.

[8] Ibid. Although Germany still replied to the point on admissibility by explaining that it did observe the standards in question. The Court limited itself to noting that the evidence presented by the United States did not justify its contention, at para. 63.

[9] Lagarde distinguishes these as "diplomatic" and "legislative" reciprocity, Lagarde, "Réciprocité en droit international privé," pp. 129–130.

the receiving State grants to citizens of the foreign State.[10] Rights or material treatment are therefore granted to citizens of other States internally, on condition that equal rights or treatment are granted to one's own citizens.[11] When it is not required by international law, this may be considered the extension of a privilege to citizens of another State,[12] which may be useful in encouraging the extension of a certain standard of treatment when there is no other basis for cooperation or legal obligation in place.

A related area of application of reciprocity as a condition can be found in certain, particularly older, treaties and rules of private international law. Reciprocity in this sense has been defined as "le fait pour un Etat de faire dépendre le traitement qu'il donnera aux problèmes de droit international privé qui se posent dans son territoire du traitement donné par les Etats étrangers à des problèmes identiques qui se posent dans leur territoire."[13] [an exchange of services of the same nature between the two contracting States, who mutually concede to each other fishing rights in sectors within their respective jurisdiction.] This condition effectively falls into the category of reciprocity in execution. Because actual performance is required in order to assess whether the condition of reciprocity is fulfilled,[14] the mechanism eventually comes to have something of a retaliatory nature.[15] It is this retaliatory aspect that, according to Lagarde, makes reciprocity unsuitable for regulating the treatment of individuals: While it is States that make concessions, it is individuals who suffer the consequences of retaliatory acts.[16]

While reciprocity in execution can play an important role in avoiding the detrimental effects of noncooperation, it becomes an imperfect means of ensuring cooperation where it is individuals, and not States directly, that are affected by any suspension of benefits. This may help to

[10] Childs, "Shaky Foundations: Criticism of Reciprocity," p. 229.

[11] E. Schneeberger, "Reciprocity as a Maxim of International Law," *Georgetown Law Journal*, vol. 37, 1948–1949, p. 29; Conforti, *Diritto Internazionale*, p. 368.

[12] Nolan et al., *Black's Law Dictionary*, p. 1269. Such provisions give a salient role to the domestic judge, to whom it will fall to analyze whether there is in fact reciprocity between the two States, by assessing whether the acts of the other State are sufficient to fulfill this condition. On this point, see Lenhoff, "Reciprocity," p. 620. On the role of administrative judges in deciding whether reciprocity exists, *Mme Cheriet-Benseghir*, req. no. 317747, France, Conseil d'Etat, 9/07/2010.

[13] Lagarde, "Réciprocité en droit international privé," p. 111.

[14] Niboyet, "Notion de réciprocité," p. 275; see also the definition of reciprocity used by the United States, in Keohane, "Reciprocity in International Relations," p. 3.

[15] Dero, *Réciprocité et le droit*, p. 63, Lagarde, "Réciprocité en droit international privé," p. 112.

[16] Ibid., p. 190.

explain why there has been a shift, in private international law, toward uniform law conventions, which function in the same way as any other treaty, with reciprocity of rights and obligations ensured by ratification by States parties, without requiring analysis of whether equal treatment has been granted in a similar circumstance.[17] Fundamentally, the aim of uniform law conventions, of ensuring that actual equal treatment is extended throughout all contracting States, is the opposite to that of treatment based on a condition of reciprocity, which in fact establishes discrimination between foreign nationals, by taking as a point of reference a bilateral relationship and establishing standards of treatment exclusively on the basis of nationality.[18]

Where reciprocity of treatment is required by a treaty, the response to a given treatment will be an actual obligation imposed upon States. Treaties may also not specifically mention reciprocity but may simply contain an obligation to ensure equality of treatment between citizens of the two contracting States. This was the case in *Filleting within the Gulf of St Lawrence*, in which Article 4(b) of the treaty between Canada and France established that French and Canadian trawlers could fish in each other's waters "*sur un pied d'égalité.*"[19]

Requiring reciprocity in the treatment of nationals of the other State therefore adds an element of conditionality and a focus on actual treatment, rather than a mere reciprocal obligation – reciprocal in a general sense as implying correlative rights and obligations – between States parties to the treaty.[20]

[17] See, for example, Campiglio, *Principio di reciprocità*, pp. 101–102, Niboyet, "Notion de réciprocité," p. 316.

[18] Tellingly, Article 7 of the Statelessness Convention exempts stateless persons from the requirement of reciprocity, ensuring that they are granted the same rights as "aliens generally," without any limitations based on reciprocity. The reason, as explained in one commentary, is that because they are not nationals of any State, stateless persons cannot qualify for treatment accorded on the basis of reciprocity; see Commentary to Article 7 in: N. Robinson, *Convention Relating to the Status of Stateless Persons: A Commentary*, World Jewish Congress 1955, Reprinted by the Division of International Protection of the United Nations High Commissioner for Refugees, 1997. Without the guarantee in Article 7.1 of the Statelessness Convention of being accorded "the same treatment as is accorded to aliens generally," stateless persons could simply be treated at the discretion of the State, at least at the time in which treatment of aliens, indeed of all persons, was not regulated by universal human rights instruments but by mechanisms based on reciprocity of treatment.

[19] Accord du 27 mars 1972 relatif aux relations réciproques entre le Canada et la France en matière de pêche, Filleting in the Gulf of St. Lawrence, para. 2.

[20] This sense of reciprocity as a condition, implying actual equality of treatment, is the sense in which "reciprocity" is often employed but is not its only meaning.

4.1.2 *The Minimum Standard of Treatment*

A minimum standard of treatment for aliens was advanced by capital-exporting States in the early twentieth century.[21] The standard was supposed to be equal to that applied by "civilized nations"; it encountered some opposition, notably by States in Latin America, who disagreed with the fact that a minimum standard of treatment would end up granting foreigners better treatment than a State's own nationals, a point, they argued, incompatible with State equality.[22] Opposition was based on the Calvo Doctrine, which considered that, by virtue of the equality of States, aliens should not have rights or privileges not accorded to nationals, and therefore that the State should be free to reduce protection for alien property when it likewise reduced protection for nationals.[23] These objections were again raised by the Newly Independent States in the 1960s.[24] However, by the end of World War II, the minimum standard was accepted as customary international law.[25]

As far as the content of the minimum standard is concerned, this remains unclear. Today, most investment treaties incorporate a standard of "fair and equitable treatment" (FET). The North American Free Trade Agreement (NAFTA) States parties indicated in a binding Note of Interpretation that they intended FET to be interpreted as a reference to the minimum standard, after a number of investment arbitration tribunals found FET to provide more extensive rights than the minimum standard.[26] There is however no real consensus as to whether these two standards require the same level of treatment.[27] There are views that consider that some rules included in the minimum standard encompass

[21] S. Hobe, "The Development of the Law of Aliens and the Emergence of General Principles of Protection under Public International Law," in M. Bungenberg et al., eds., *International Investment Law*, C. H. Beck/Hart/Nomos, Munich, Oxford, 2015, p. 9.

[22] Ibid.

[23] C. Calvo, *Droit international: Théorie et pratique*, 1896, p. 3, cited in R. Dolzer and C. Schreuer, *Principles of International Investment Law*, Oxford, Oxford University Press, 2008, p. 12; P. Juillard, "Calvo Doctrine/Calvo Clause," in R. Wolfrum, ed., *The Max Planck Encyclopedia of Public International Law*, Oxford University Press, 2008–, online edition, [www.mpepil.com], para. 3; M. Paparinskis, *The International Minimum Standard and Fair and Equitable Treatment*, Oxford, Oxford University Press, 2013, pp. 23–24, 27.

[24] P. Dumberry, "The Minimum Standard of Treatment in International Investment Law: The Fascinating Story of the Emergence, the Decline and the Recent Resurrection of a Concept," *Proceedings of the Conference "International Law and Time,"* Geneva, 2015, p. 11.

[25] Ibid., pp. 1, 3. [26] Ibid., p. 2.

[27] UNCTAD, "Dispute Settlement: Investor-State," UNCTAD Series on Issues in International Investment Agreements, United Nations, New York, Geneva, 2003, UNCTAD/ITE/IIT/30, p. 73.

what may today be considered human rights, such as procedures in case of detention, the right to legal personality, and some of the rules regarding conditions for expropriation.[28]

Indeed, similarly to human rights, the international minimum standard is not a relative standard: It applies regardless of the treatment a State extends to its own nationals, or to nationals of other States, and regardless of how other States treat its nationals.[29] It means that the treatment of aliens is governed by international law; as such, this standard of treatment is a truly inter-State obligation[30] rather than conferring any rights on individuals; aliens are considered not *as* individuals but *as* nationals of a State. The obligations, however, operate in the same way as any other rule of customary international law, with a correlation between rights and obligations, but without it being necessary to fulfill any specific condition of reciprocity.

4.1.3 *National Treatment*

National treatment and most-favored nation treatment are the two main standards of treatment used in current practice, specifically in the areas of trade and investment. National treatment requires that foreigners receive at least the same level of treatment as nationals of the host country.[31] Generally, therefore, according foreign persons a level of treatment more favorable than that accorded to nationals will not be in breach of the standard.[32] Some agreements specifically provide for treatment of foreigners that is "the same as" rather than "no less favorable," or speak of "equal footing." Such formulations do not explicitly prohibit States parties from according treatment to foreign nationals that is more favorable than that accorded to their own citizens; however, foreigners have no right to such preferential treatment, and nationals of the State may challenge measures that are more favorable to foreigners than to themselves.[33]

28 Hobe, "Development of the Law of Aliens," p. 14; Douglas, *International Law of Investment Claims*, p. 7.

29 H. Lauterpacht, *International Law and Human Rights*, London, Brandon & Dickens, 1950, p. 121. A parallel is drawn by Provost with international labor conventions, which establish minimum labor standards, Provost, "Reciprocity in Human Rights," p. 385.

30 R. Pisillo Mazzeschi, "The Relationship between Human Rights and the Rights of Aliens and Immigrants," in U. Fastenrath, ed., *From Bilateralism to Community Interest: Essays in Honour of Judge Bruno Simma*, Oxford, Oxford University Press, 2011, p. 554.

31 UNCTAD, "Dispute Settlement: Investor-State," p. 72.

32 Ibid., p. 72.

33 UNCTAD, "National Treatment," *UNCTAD Series on Issues in International Investment Agreements*, New York, Geneva, United Nations, 1999, UNCTAD/ITE/IIT/11 (Vol. IV), p. 35.

National treatment provides a minimum, relative standard of treatment, and is usually found with other standards such as fair and equitable treatment, or most-favored nation treatment. While these standards are distinct from national treatment, they may still determine the level of treatment accorded to the investor and result in more favorable treatment being accorded to the alien. National treatment is perhaps the most universally accepted standard of treatment, more so, at least historically, than the international minimum standard.[34]

Reciprocity has also historically played a role in national treatment, particularly in domestic legislation. In the United States, until 1909 reciprocity was a condition for the extension of national treatment.[35] National treatment is also not only reserved for the context of economic activities: In 1793, France passed a decree establishing that sick and wounded soldiers of other States would be entitled to the same care received by French soldiers, an internal provision that eventually became international law through its reciprocal acceptance.[36]

National treatment is a relative standard, in requiring a comparison of concrete treatment in concrete circumstances between nationals and foreigners, but without by itself prescribing any specific content to this treatment.[37] This has led some authors to characterize national treatment as an example of formal, or abstract, reciprocity.[38] National treatment also does not aim to introduce any substantive equality or wider nondiscrimination between nationals and foreigners, nor between nationals of third States themselves, and in this sense is an inward-looking standard. Its key difference with, for example, human rights is that nationality is the key criterion for its application. The standard of treatment therefore depends on an individual being a citizen of a specific State.

[34] Habachy gives the example in Muslim law, "Property, Right, and Contract," p. 452; the national treatment standard was advanced by Latin American States that did not want to accept a customary rule imposing a minimum standard of treatment. See, for example, H. Dickerson, "Minimum Standards," in R. Wolfrum, ed., *The Max Planck Encyclopedia of Public International Law*, Oxford University Press, 2008–, online edition, [www.mpepil.com], para. 5.

[35] A. Lenhoff, "Reciprocity in Function: A Problem of Conflict of Laws, Constitutional Law, and International Law," *University of Pittsburgh Law Review*, vol. 44, 1953–1954, p. 50; by the same author, "Reciprocity," p. 624.

[36] Lenhoff, "Reciprocity," p. 625. [37] UNCTAD, "National Treatment," p. 7.

[38] Lenhoff, "Reciprocity in Function," p. 5; Niboyet, "Notion de réciprocité," p. 285; Preiswerk, "Réciprocité dans les négociations entre pays," p. 9.

4.1.4 The Most-Favored Nation Clause

While national treatment ensures nondiscrimination between nationals and foreigners, the aim of most-favored nation (MFN) treatment is instead to ensure that no discrimination occurs *between* nationals of third States in the receiving State. A standard formulation found in bilateral investment treaties (BITs) is the obligation to accord "treatment no less favourable" to the investors or investments of the other party than that which is accorded to investors or investments of a third State. The formulation may be left general or may specify to which treaty provisions it applies.[39] MFN provisions therefore "oblige the State granting MFN treatment to extend to the beneficiary State the treatment accorded to third States."[40]

MFN clauses are now mostly unconditional,[41] in that they do not require any specific treatment to be granted in order to apply, which is considered to better guarantee equality of treatment; however, this was not always the case. MFN initially required a specific counterperformance or concession.[42] It is nowadays reciprocal only in the sense that it equally binds the parties to a treaty, allowing the extension of advantages to third parties automatically and without the need to fulfill any condition of reciprocity.[43]

One important limitation to the scope of MFN treatment is that of the *ejusdem generis* principle. This limits the treatment that may count for comparison under MFN. For example, persons benefiting from MFN must be in the same category as those of the third State whose treatment is being analyzed.[44] This means that an MFN clause in an investment treaty could not cover treatment accorded in a treaty relating to

[39] Canada 2004 Model BIT, Art. 4.1; German Model Treaty 2008 Concerning the Encouraging and Reciprocal Protection of Investments, Article 3; see also ILC, Final Report, Study Group on the Most-Favoured Nation Clause, 29 May 2015, Document A/CN.4/L.852, p. 7.

[40] S. Schill, *The Multilateralization of International Investment Law*, Cambridge, Cambridge University Press, 2014, p. 121.

[41] Ibid.; see comment by US Secretary of State Hughes, in ibid., p.131, and in general, ibid., p.132.

[42] Schill, *Multilateralization of International Investment Law*, p. 130; Virally, "Panorama du droit international contemporain," p. 306. The 1978 ILC draft articles demonstrate the preoccupation with the conditionality of the MFN clause; see ILC, Draft Articles on Most-Favoured Nation Clauses with Commentaries, *Yearbook of the International Law Commission*, vol. II, 1978, Part Two, especially Article 13, pp. 33, 36–39, and the ILC's 2015 report on the MFN clause, p. 6.

[43] Virally, "Panorama du droit international contemporain," p. 306.

[44] ILC, Final Report on the MFN Clause 2015, p. 8.

immunity. The wording of the clause may also limit which matters are susceptible of MFN treatment, which may be narrower than the original treaty.[45]

Exceptions to the provision may also be made, often including sectors in which States require reciprocity of treatment, such as taxation.[46] This allows for the specificities of bilateral relationships to be maintained in areas where a specific counterperformance is still required. There may also exist situations in which it is only possible for one of the parties to a treaty to offer MFN, such as is the case of a landlocked State party to a treaty granting MFN treatment to ships. In this case, either concessions will be made in a different area or the application of the clause will simply be a unilateral advantage for one of the parties, with reciprocity at the level of rights and obligations not translating into a true exchange.[47]

In fact, although it may "draw in" the provisions granted in a treaty between one State party and a third party, MFN is not actually, in terms of rights and obligations, anything more than a bilateral exchange and does not create rights or obligations for third States without their consent.[48] The only two parties upon whom the clause confers rights and obligations are the parties to the treaty containing the MFN standard.[49]

Similarly to national treatment, MFN does not impose a specific content for the standard of treatment.[50] This may, although it is far less likely than with national treatment, be less than the international minimum standard. MFN does work better than national treatment at ensuring equality; although a State may be free to accord an individual better treatment than it accords nationals of third States, this may mean that it

[45] Schill, *Multilateralization of International Investment Law*, p. 154; ILC, Draft Articles, p. 29; ILC, Final Report on the MFN Clause 2015, p. 12.

[46] UNCTAD, "Most-Favoured Nation Treatment," *UNCTAD Series on Issues in International Investment Agreements*, United Nations, New York, Geneva, 1999, UNCTAD/ITE/IIT/10 (Vol. III), pp. 98–99, 104.

[47] ILC, Draft Articles, p. 19; Decaux, *Réciprocité en droit international*, p. 189.

[48] ILC, Final Report on the MFN Clause 2015, p. 7.

[49] UNCTAD, "Most-Favoured Nation Treatment," pp. 2, 22. This is one of the reasons used by arbitral tribunals to deny the application of the MFN clause to jurisdictional clauses in BITs, in line with the ICJ's decision in *Anglo-Iranian Oil Co.: Tecnicas Mediambientales Tecmed S.A.* v. *the United Mexican States*, ICSID Case No. ARB (AF)/00/02, Award, 29 May 2003, para. 69, in UNCTAD, "Most-Favoured Nation Treatment," pp. 61–62.

[50] ILC, Draft Articles, p. 24, commentary to Article 7: "The general duty not to discriminate between States is not breached by treating another State, its nationals, ships, products, etc., in a particularly advantageous way"; A. Reinisch, "Most Favoured Nation Treatment," in M. Bungenberg et al., eds., *International Investment Law*, Oxford, Hart/Munich, Nomos, 2015pp. 808–809; UNCTAD, "Most-Favoured Nation Treatment," p. 23.

will be under an obligation to extend this more favorable treatment to another individual, depending on how the MFN standard is worded in the relevant treaties.[51] While the purpose of MFN is to ensure nondiscrimination between nationals of third States,[52] functioning as it does to unify treatment in a multilateral setting, it also tends to ensure equality.[53] This explains its use in economic law, where it serves to create a "level playing field," which should ensure optimum competitive conditions.[54] Because of its aim of nondiscrimination, the ILC has also considered MFN to be linked to the principle of sovereign equality.[55]

The element of reciprocity of rights and obligations in MFN, the fact that States may invoke MFN treatment as well as having the obligation to extend it, is therefore fundamental to ensuring that the legal equality of States is translated into practice.[56] This does not however require any concrete balance or equality in its actual effects; Scelle effectively points out that this would transform a reciprocal clause (that operates multilaterally) into a synallagma, involving conditionality of obligation, as well as of treatment.[57] It is this distinction that has led authors to characterize

[51] ILC, Final Report on the MFN Clause 2015, p. 19. However, as an UNCTAD report points out, MFN is rarely used to challenge material treatment; the same report explains MFN treatment as ensuring an "additional guarantee of equality and non-discrimination," UNCTAD, "Most-Favoured Nation Treatment," pp. 1, 17.

[52] Reinisch, "Most Favoured Nation Treatment," p. 824: Cottier and Schneller explain MFN and national treatment as being what nondiscrimination "essentially consists of," T. Cottier and L. Schneller, "The Philosophy of Non-discrimination in International Trade Regulation," in A. Kamperman Sanders, ed., *The Principle of National Treatment in International Economic Law: Trade, Investment, and Intellectual Property*, Cheltenham, Elgar, 2014, pp. 5, 7; it is important to note that the criterion of nationality is the yardstick against which the existence of discrimination is measured, UNCTAD, "Most-Favoured Nation Treatment," pp. 27, 100.

[53] Schill, *Multilateralization of International Investment Law*, p. 124, cit. *Rights of Nationals of the United States of America in Morocco (France* v. *United States)*, Judgment of 27 August 1952, I.C.J. Reports 1952, p. 192; Wils, "Concept of Reciprocity in EEC Law," p. 258.

[54] Schill, *Multilateralization of International Investment Law*, pp. 123, 129. This is particularly ensured by the use of the unconditional MFN clause, ibid., pp. 131, 174; ILC, Final Report on the MFN Clause 2015, p. 12; UNCTAD, "Most-Favoured Nation Treatment," p. 13.

[55] ILC, Final Report on the MFN Clause 2015, p. 12.

[56] Cottier and Schneller, "Philosophy of Non-discrimination," p. 6; Scelle points out that a "unilateral" MFN clause, that is, one in which a State must accord MFN without having a correlative right to such treatment, has been imposed in the case of some peace treaties, which tended toward a reestablishment of equality of rights in any case, Scelle, "Doctrine de Léon Duguit," pp. 463–464. The ILC in 1978 considered the reciprocity of rights and obligations in granting MFN as the clause's "essential ingredient," ILC, Draft Articles, p. 37.

[57] Scelle, "Doctrine de Léon Duguit," p. 464.

the reciprocity inherent in MFN as "abstract" or formal reciprocity. The tribunal in *Siemens* v. *Argentina* pointed out that

> [t]his understanding [that the claim of a benefit under an MFN clause triggers application of the whole treaty only to the extent that it is advantageous to the beneficiary of the clause] does not mean that the investor in Argentina will enjoy a more favorable treatment than the investor in Chile. The MFN clause works both ways. The investor in Chile will be able to claim similar benefits under the Chile BIT.[58]

Reciprocity in the operation of the MFN clause is crucial to what some authors[59] see as its multilateralizing function. The clause allows bilateral treaties to create a set of multilateral relations in order to realize generalized nondiscrimination.[60] It can not only multilateralize treatment but also "freeze" the ability of a State to contract out of the most favorable level of treatment it has granted.[61] It can therefore constitute an exception to the bilateral negotiation that occurs in treaty-making.[62]

By virtue of this, MFN also affects the balance of rights and obligations in treaties, presupposing a separability of the provisions of third treaties. On the one hand, therefore, there is the view that bilateral treaties especially, and above all bilateral investment treaties, contain a package of interdependent rights and obligations, based on reciprocity of rights and obligations, that affects how they are interpreted. On the other hand, reciprocal

[58] *Siemens* v. *Argentina*, ICSID Case No. ARB/02/8, Decision on Jurisdiction, 3 August 2004, para. 108. This formal, or legal, reciprocity as opposed to reciprocity of treatment seems to be at the basis of Cottier and Schneller's confusion of the two concepts, explaining the functioning of MFN as reflecting the "political idea of reciprocity" but that "reciprocity is consistent only with the doctrine of conditional MFN," "Philosophy of Non-discrimination," p. 9. See the explanation in ILC, Draft Articles, p. 16.

[59] See, for example, Schill, *Multilateralization of International Investment Law*, p. 123; S. Schill, "Ordering Paradigms in International Investment Law: Bilateralism – Multilateralism – Multilateralization," in Z. Douglas, J. Pauwelyn, and J. E. Viñuales, eds., *The Foundations of International Investment Law: Bringing Theory into Practice*, Oxford, Oxford University Press, 2014, pp. 119–121; also Cottier and Schneller, "Philosophy of Non-discrimination," p. 8. An UNCTAD report considers MFN's inherent link with multilateralism as making it a "cornerstone" of the international trade system but as having a questionable role in bilateral investment treaties, UNCTAD, "Most-Favoured Nation Treatment," p. 114, a view also supported by Virally, "Principe de réciprocité," 1967, p. 6.

[60] Schill, "*Multilateralization of International Investment Law*, p. 195, as is the case in the comparison with nationals only in the case of national treatment. See ibid., p. 129.

[61] Schill sees this as inherent in its nondiscriminatory function, although this is based on his view of international law as essentially "bilateralist," a view that is questioned here, Schill, *Multilateralization of International Investment Law*, p. 122.

[62] Schill, *Multilateralization of International Investment Law*, p. 124. "MFN clauses . . . lock States into a framework of multilateralism that is adverse to bilateral alliances," ibid., p. 196.

MFN provisions incorporated in those same treaties lead to the bilateral packages being split up, with benefits only, and not the corresponding burdens, being extended under the operation of MFN.[63] While aiming for a global reciprocity, MFN therefore adversely affects the strict reciprocity or synallagma in the bilateral treaty.[64]

4.1.5 *Reciprocity and Standards of Treatment*

Reciprocity is used as a condition for the initial extension of treatment, be this in domestic law, national treatment, or with MFN. However, the move away from conditionality has resulted in reciprocity of rights and obligations in the treaties in question not necessarily being reflected in any concrete exchange between States in their treatment of each other's nationals.

Furthermore, while in all the above examples equality and nondiscrimination are key aims of the standards, the comparison used will differ. The term of comparison to establish a standard of treatment will either look at how the State itself treats certain nationals or at the standard of treatment accorded by another State, accounting for the differences in how the standards function.

4.2 Individual Rights versus Reciprocity?

There are a number of substantive areas of international law that are concerned with how States treat individuals. These are international humanitarian law, human rights law, and investment law. In all these systems, the ultimate beneficiaries of rules are individuals or legal persons such as corporate entities.[65] There are some crucial differences among these areas of law that make the analysis of how reciprocity

[63] This was the sense of the decision in *Siemens* v. *Argentina*, paras. 108–109, cit. in UNCTAD, "Most-Favoured Nation Treatment," p. 69; also Schill, *Multilateralization of International Investment Law*, p. 159.

[64] This is one of the reasons why UNCTAD advises States to exclude all preexisting and future treaties dealing with sectors that are based on reciprocity – meaning here conditions of reciprocity – such as "aviation, fisheries and maritime matters" from the scope of MFN treatment, UNCTAD, "Most-Favoured Nation Treatment," p. 107. Virally sees the application of MFN clauses as capable of "destroy[ing] the real reciprocity of the treaty containing it, as concrete advantages may be very unequal, and will allow one of the contractants to benefit from gratuitous advantages," Virally, "Principe de réciprocité," 1967, p. 73.

[65] U. Kriebaum, "The Nature of Investment Disciplines," in Z. Douglas, J. Pauwelyn, and J. E. Viñuales, eds., *The Foundations of International Investment Law: Bringing Theory into Practice*, Oxford, Oxford University Press, 2014, p. 48.

works particularly interesting. The key distinguishing feature of human rights is that these do not regulate protection on the basis of nationality, unlike for example investment law, but instead grant rights to individuals on a territorial basis, thereby also establishing standards of treatment for individuals that are within their own State of nationality. The fact that this eliminates the strictly bilateral and inter-State dimension that one would normally find in standards that apply on the basis of nationality is what has led many authors to view human rights as qualitatively different to other standards of treatment, and as having a truly collective rationale.[66]

The question therefore is what differences exist between these substantive areas of law depending on whether the rights involved are inter-State obligations or whether they also confer direct rights on individuals, and whether these differences affect reciprocity.

4.3 International Humanitarian Law

International humanitarian law (IHL), which regulates the conduct of parties to armed conflicts, is interesting to analyze with respect to reciprocity because it is considered a prime example of an area of law based on inter-State obligations and at the same time concerns the treatment of specific categories of individuals during armed conflicts. IHL has moved from the general "law of war" to having the purpose of regulating the treatment of persons in armed conflict, and increasingly to protect individuals in armed conflict.[67] IHL also imposes specific obligations on States and their armed forces, as well as on specific groups and individuals. This section will analyze whether conditions of reciprocity in IHL still exist, before addressing the rights and obligations of non-State actors and protected persons, and key differences between IHL and human rights.

4.3.1 The Reciprocal Nature of IHL Conventions and the Problem of States Not Parties

In the context of the laws of war, the term "reciprocity" is generally used to denote violation of the rules applicable in armed conflict in response

[66] Pisillo Mazzeschi, "Relationship between Human Rights," p. 553.

[67] D. Fleck, ed., *The Handbook of International Humanitarian Law*, 3rd ed., Oxford, Oxford University Press, 2013 (Kindle ed.), pp. 101–102.

to a violation.[68] The term is used here, however, to also encompass reciprocity in the functioning and application of rules of IHL.

Views vary as to whether IHL obligations are a series of unilateral engagements by States,[69] or based on reciprocity.[70] The fact that engagements may be unilateral does not preclude the operation of reciprocity, and it is argued here that IHL conventions are both multilateral and reciprocal in nature.[71] A classic example of the correlation of rights and obligations in the domain of the law applicable in armed conflict is that of neutrality. A neutral State is one that is not participating in an armed conflict. However, such a status comes with both a set of rights and correlative duties. While the neutral State has the right not to be affected by the conflict, it also has an obligation not to support a party in the conflict, which is articulated through a number of specific obligations such as being bound to resist violations of its neutrality, not providing ammunition or materiel, or taking part in acts of war of parties to the conflict.[72] States must therefore conform themselves to certain obligations in order to enjoy the rights of neutrality.

If two States parties to a conflict are parties to humanitarian law conventions, they will also be bound in their mutual relations, without any additional condition of reciprocity, or case-by-case observance of the

[68] See, for example, M. Sassòli and Y. Shany, "Should the Obligations of States and Armed Groups under International Humanitarian Law Be Equal?," *International Review of the Red Cross*, vol. 93, no. 882, June 2011, p. 431.

[69] See, for example, C. Pilloud, J. de Preux, Y. Sandoz, and B. Zimmermann, *Commentary on the Additional Protocols of 8 June 1977 to the Geneva Conventions of 12 August 1949*, ICRC, Martinus Nijhoff, Geneva, 1987, "Article 1," para. 49.

[70] For example, F. J. Hampson, "Belligerent Reprisals in the 1977 Protocols to the Geneva Conventions of 1949," *The International and Comparative Law Quarterly*, vol. 37, no. 4, October 1988, pp. 818–843, at p. 829.

[71] Chinkin, *Third Parties in International Law*, p. 132; in an armed conflict between two High Contracting Parties as per Common Article 2 of the Geneva Conventions of 12 August 1949, the rules apply between the armed forces of two States parties, regardless of any condition of reciprocity, that is, the parties are bound by the rules regardless of their degree of compliance, Provost, "Reciprocity in Human Rights," p. 394; Jinks gives the example of the 1991 and 2003 armed conflicts between the United States and its allies and Iraq, where the Geneva Conventions were and remained applicable because they had been ratified by the parties to the conflict, despite the fact that their provisions were not observed, D. Jinks, "The Applicability of the Geneva Conventions to the 'Global War on Terror,'" *Virginia Journal of International Law*, vol. 46, 2005–2006, pp. 194–195.

[72] Fleck, *Handbook of International Humanitarian Law*, p. 1101; see also Office of the General Counsel, Department of Defense of the United States of America, *Law of War Manual*, June 2015 (Updated December 2016), p. 960; Federal Ministry of Defence of the Federal Republic of Germany, ed., *Humanitarian Law in Armed Conflicts Manual*, VR II 3, August 1992, p. 1110.

rules, being necessary.[73] This mutuality of application was not however always so clear. Until World War I, conventions on the laws of war[74] had an important limitation to their applicability in conflicts. This was the general participation clause, or *clausula si omnes*, requiring that *all* parties to a conflict be parties to a convention for it to apply. The clause was dropped from the 1929 Geneva Conventions, a change partly explained by the development of the rules on international humanitarian law and partly by the experience of World War I. Although the Convention for the Amelioration of the Condition of the Wounded and Sick in Armies in the Field of 1906 had been applied by all parties during the conflict, it technically was never in force because Montenegro, although party to the conflict, was not a party to the treaty. At the revision of the Convention in 1929, the clause was therefore abandoned[75] and replaced by a provision stating that "if one of the belligerents is not a party to the Convention, its provisions shall, nevertheless, remain binding as between the belligerents who are parties thereto."[76] The International Military

[73] See Jinks, "Applicability of the Geneva Conventions," pp. 191–193; Paulus, "Reciprocity Revisited," p. 135; the argument made by Marco Sassòli in Sassòli, Shany, "Should the Obligations ... Be Equal?," p. 431.

[74] Some examples include Convention (II) with Respect to the Laws and Customs of War on Land and its annex, The Hague, 29 July 1899, Article 2; Convention (IV) respecting the Laws and Customs of War on Land and its annex, The Hague, 18 October 1907, Article 2; Convention (VII) relating to the Conversion of Merchant Ships into War-Ships, The Hague, 18 October 1907, Article 7; Convention (XI) relative to certain Restrictions with regard to the Exercise of the Right of Capture in Naval War, The Hague, 18 October 1907, Article 9, to name but a few; see further P. Gautier, "General Participation Clause (Clausula si omnes)," in R. Wolfrum, ed., *The Max Planck Encyclopedia of Public International Law*, Oxford University Press, 2008–, online edition, [www.mpepil.com], para. 2.

[75] International Committee of the Red Cross, Commentary on the First Geneva Convention, "Article 2: Application of the Convention," 2016, available at www.icrc.org/applic/ihl/ihl.nsf/Comment.xsp?action=openDocument&documentId=BE2D518CF5DE54EAC1257F7D0036B518, para. 345, and n. 196; the Convention for the Amelioration of the Condition of the Wounded and Sick in Armies in the Field, Geneva, 6 July 1906, contained a *si omnes* clause at Article 24; Schneeberger, "Reciprocity as a Maxim of International Law," p. 34; Lenhoff, "Reciprocity," p. 625; T. Meron, "International Law in the Age of Human Rights: General Course on Public International Law," *Collected Courses of the Hague Academy of International Law*, vol. 301, 2003, pp. 33–34; R. Quadri, *Diritto Internazionale Pubblico*, 5a ed., Napoli, Liguori, 1989, p. 206; J. Pictet, ed., *Commentary to the IV Geneva Convention Relative to the Protection of Civilian Persons in Time of War*, Geneva, ICRC, 1958, p. 22; International Committee of the Red Cross, *Commentary to the Convention (III) Relative to the Treatment of Prisoners of War*, 1960, Article 2 Commentary, p. 21; Gautier, "General Participation Clause (Clausula si omnes)," para. 6.

[76] Convention for the Amelioration of the Conditions of the Wounded and Sick in Armies in the Field, Geneva, 27 July 1929, Article 25; ICRC, *Commentary to the III Geneva Convention*, 1960, p. 21.

Tribunal at Nuremberg was also confronted by the problem posed by the *clausula si omnes* but avoided having to pronounce on its applicability by finding that the rules in the Hague Convention (IV) on War on Land of 1907 "by 1939 [...] were recognized as customary law by all civilized nations" and therefore bound States even if these were not parties to the Convention. Indeed, the crystallization of the rules of the Geneva Conventions into customary international law gradually diminished the relevance of the *clausula*.[77]

The current wording of Common Article 2 of the 1949 Geneva Conventions instead reflects the fact that the Conventions apply between States, that is, that their obligations are owed from one State party to another: "Although one of the Powers in conflict may not be a party to the present Convention, the Powers who are parties thereto shall remain bound by it in their mutual relations."

Humanitarian law treaties are therefore (leaving aside the question of customary rules of international law) only binding between parties thereto. However, once this is established, their application is not dependent on reciprocity.[78] IHL is also nondiscriminatory in nature. That is, once an armed conflict exists, under IHL the question of which party is the aggressor is irrelevant, and rules apply equally to all.[79]

While the Geneva Conventions have today reached universal ratification, this was not always the case, and the Conventions make recourse to reciprocity of conduct in order to provide for their application where a conflict may involve States not parties. The last sentence of Common Article 2 of the Geneva Conventions reads "Although one of the Powers in conflict may not be a party to the present Convention, the Powers who are parties thereto shall remain bound by it in their mutual relations. They shall furthermore be bound by the Convention in relation to the said Power, if the latter accepts and applies the provisions thereof." Reciprocity of rights and obligations is therefore the key element for applicability of the conventional rules between parties; between a party and a nonparty, the latter must "accept and apply" the dispositions of the Convention for it to be applicable.

This point highlights another role reciprocity has in IHL treaties, that is, as a positive factor of enforcement. The Military Manual of the German armed forces goes so far as to make reference to the Golden

[77] International Military Tribunal (Nuremberg), Judgment and Sentences, 1 October 1946, *The American Journal of International Law*, vol. 41, no. 1, 1947, p. 248; Gautier, "General Participation Clause (Clausula si omnes)," para. 5.

[78] Fleck, *Handbook of International Humanitarian Law*, pp. 205, 1207.

[79] Ibid., pp. 101, 206.

Rule, that "soldiers must treat their opponents in the same manner as they themselves want to be treated."[80] The 1958 Commentary to the IV Geneva Convention states that "the Contracting Power must at least apply their provisions from the moment hostilities break out until such a time as the adverse party has had the time and an opportunity of stating his intentions."[81] This interpretation was put forward as a "moral" rather than "strictly legal" requirement.[82] Reciprocity is used as a pragmatic explanation for why this is a favorable course of action; an initial application of the Convention improves the chances of application by a nonparty, and removes a "pretext for non-acceptance."[83]

This essentially amounts to using reciprocity of treatment as a basis for the application of conventional standards in the absence of any conventional legal obligation. One example of this was the application of the 1929 Geneva Convention on Prisoners of War between Japan and the United States during World War II. Japan was a not a party to the Convention, but the two States exchanged communications to apply the Convention in any case, on the basis of reciprocity.[84] Therefore, Common Article 2 allows for the possibility of releasing States parties from their obligations vis-à-vis a party to a conflict that is not a party to the treaty and refuses to accept its provisions, while encouraging the continued application of the Convention by and between States parties.[85] Further, it allows the extension of the application of the Convention on the basis of reciprocity, where the nonparty applies (and thus implicitly accepts) its provisions.

Modern IHL, however, is considered nonreciprocal in nature; according to this view, States are bound by their humanitarian law obligations unconditionally, regardless of whether other belligerents observe the same convention.[86] It is true that the customary nature of many rules of IHL now makes it difficult, indeed at most times unnecessary, to determine which is the source of the rule that the State must respect.

There are also a number of indications that the mechanisms of reciprocity are limited in IHL. For example, under Article 1.1 of Additional

[80] See Federal Ministry of Defence of the Federal Republic of Germany, *Humanitarian Law in Armed Conflicts Manual*, pp. 1202, 1204.

[81] Pictet, *Commentary to the IV Geneva Convention*, p. 23. [82] Ibid.

[83] Ibid., pp. 23–24. The Commentary also notes that tacit and explicit acceptance are equally valid.

[84] Provost, "Reciprocity in Human Rights," p. 390.

[85] ICRC, *Commentary to the III Geneva Convention*, pp. 26–27.

[86] Sassòli and Shany, "Should the Obligations … Be Equal?," p. 431.

Protocol I to the Geneva Conventions, parties "undertake to respect and ensure respect for this Protocol in all circumstances," and therefore not to invoke reasons to not apply the Protocol as a whole. This also includes invoking reciprocity, or the fact that another party has not respected the Protocol, as grounds for nonapplication.[87] The Commentary to the Additional Protocol notes that this prohibition on invoking reciprocity "to shirk the obligations of humanitarian law is absolute." Humanitarian protection cannot, in other words, be made subject to compliance by another party in the conflict.[88] No condition of reciprocity, that is, of any actual respect of the rules of IHL as a necessary precondition for the respect of the rules by the other party to the conflict, should be read into contemporary IHL.

IHL treaties are, further, exempt from the provisions on material breach of treaties in the VCLT, whose Article 60.5 provides that the its provisions on material breach being grounds for terminating or suspending operation of a treaty "do not apply to provisions relating to protection of the human person contained in treaties of a humanitarian character, in particular to provisions prohibiting any form of reprisals against persons protected by such treaties." The reason for the existence of this provision is closely linked to the existence of reprisals as a mechanism within IHL.

4.3.2 *The Issue of Reprisals*

A number of mechanisms of reciprocity, outlined above, do not apply in international humanitarian law, which has, with certain limits, its own enforcement mechanism: that of reprisals. Reprisals are acts made by and toward States or other entities possessing international personality, as a retort to a previous act by the addressee that the actor "can reasonably consider a violation of international law." The act of reprisal itself must amount to a violation of an identical or other norm of international law, whose purpose must be to coerce the addressee of the act to change its policy, and must respect the conditions and limits laid down in international law, notably objectivity, subsidiarity, and proportionality.[89] Reprisals should therefore be distinguished from retortion, which may be an unfriendly act but is not one that breaches a rule. Modern

[87] Pilloud et al., *Commentary on the Additional Protocols*, "Article 1," para. 49; Fleck, *Handbook of International Humanitarian Law*, p. 1402.

[88] Pillou et al., *Commentary on the Additional Protocols*, "Article 1," para. 51; Fleck, *Handbook of International Humanitarian Law*, p. 1219.

[89] F. Kalshoven, *Belligerent Reprisals*, Leiden, Nijhoff, 2005, p. 33.

State practice further require reprisals to be in response to serious violations, having the purpose to compel respect of the law of armed conflict, and only to put a stop to an illegality once all other means have been exhausted. The fact that reprisals have a function of coercing return to respect of a rule of international law also requires them to be publicized, as well as being proportionate to the original wrong. The seriousness of the recourse to reprisals is demonstrated by the condition, set out in many military manuals, for the decision to take a reprisal to be authorized at the highest levels.[90] These conditions are considered to be customary international law.[91]

The reciprocal nature of reprisals is reflected in the requirement that these be directed against the State that carried out the original wrongful act; that is, reprisals are limited to being taken against the State with which legal relations in an international armed conflict were entered into. Reprisals are built in to the system of IHL, with the purpose of acting as a deterrence tool to dissuade parties from breaching the law;[92] they can be considered the flip side of the positive role of reciprocity, which encourages observance and respect for the rules by parties to an armed conflict.

However, the existence of this specific mechanism of reciprocity should not be equated to a generalized reciprocity of observance as a condition for respect of IHL. Reprisals are a mechanism of reciprocal enforcement available to parties, a specific solution in a specific area of international law. They do not amount to suspension of rules in the case of a breach of IHL but rather excuse the illegality of certain acts that would otherwise be themselves illegal.

The expansion of categories of protected persons in IHL has set a number of limits to the taking of reprisals. In the Geneva Conventions and Additional Protocol I, it is prohibited to carry out reprisals against the wounded, sick, and shipwrecked; medical and religious personnel and facilities; prisoners of war; civilians and certain categories of civilian property and objects indispensable to the survival of the civilian

[90] See, for example, Office of the Judge Advocate General, *Canada National Defence Joint Doctrine Manual – Law of Armed Conflict at the Operational and Tactical Levels*, Doc. B-GJ-005-104/FP-02, sections 15-3 to 15-6; Federal Ministry of Defence of the Federal Republic of Germany, *Humanitarian Law in Armed Conflicts Manual*, paras. 477–478; Kalshoven, *Belligerent Reprisals*, p. 332; Hampson, "Belligerent Reprisals," p. 823.

[91] Y. Dinstein, *The Conduct of Hostilities under the Law of International Armed Conflict*, 3rd ed., Cambridge, Cambridge University Press, 2016, p. 290.

[92] Ibid.*Conduct of Hostilities*, p. 289; Fleck, *Handbook of International Humanitarian Law*, 1404.

population; but also the natural environment, works containing dangerous forces, and cultural objects.[93] The prohibition on carrying out reprisals against protected persons and objects is absolute,[94] although this has not stopped some States from making reservations in relation to the prohibition against carrying out reprisals against civilians, as shall be seen below. The effect of these prohibitions is that, in modern IHL, the taking of reprisals is limited to the armed forces and to the choice of weapons and methods of combat against military objectives.[95]

This limitation is, it is argued, not only attributable to the principle of humanity that is central to IHL[96] but also highlights the fact that these categories of protected person are right-holders under IHL. Therefore, targeting reprisals at these categories of person would fall outside the legal relationship between the wrongdoing State party to a conflict and the retaliating State. The fact that a State acted in breach of the laws of war cannot mean denying the individual rights held by protected persons.[97]

Article 51 of Additional Protocol I sets out a series of rules to be observed "in all circumstances" in order to ensure protection of the civilian population, including the prohibition of taking reprisals against civilians. The importance of the provision is such that in previous drafts of the Protocol, it was envisaged that no reservations to this provision would be permissible.[98] This did not make its way into the final text, however, and a small number of States parties have since made reservations to Article 51. These include, in the case of Egypt, reserving the right to react to all violations on the basis of reciprocity; to react against

[93] Convention (I) for the Amelioration of the Condition of the Wounded and Sick in Armed Forces in the Field, Geneva, 12 August 1949, Article 46; Convention (II) for the Amelioration of the Condition of Wounded, Sick and Shipwrecked Members of Armed Forces at Sea, Geneva, 12 August 1949, Article 47; Protocol Additional to the Geneva Conventions of 12 August 1949, and relating to the Protection of Victims of International Armed Conflicts (Protocol I), 8 June 1977, Articles 20, 51.6, 52.1, 55.2, 56.4; Convention (III) Relative to the Treatment of Prisoners of War, Geneva, 12 August 1949, Article 13.3; Convention (IV) Relative to the Protection of Civilian Persons in Time of War, Geneva, 12 August 1949, Article 33.3; Dinstein, *Conduct of Hostilities*, p. 293; Kalshoven, *Belligerent Reprisals*, p. 321; and confirming the "general prohibition of the targeting of civilians," *Prosecutor* v. *Martić*, Case No. IT-95-11-A, ICTY, Appeals Chamber, Judgment of 8 October 2008, paras. 263–267.

[94] Pilloud et al., *Commentary on the Additional Protocols*, "Article 51," para. 1984.

[95] Ibid., paras. 1985–1985; Hampson, "Belligerent Reprisals," pp. 826, 831.

[96] See Kalshoven, *Belligerent Reprisals*, p. 114.

[97] Dinstein, *Conduct of Hostilities*, p. 294. A similar argument could be applied to the prohibition of taking reprisals against the natural environment and cultural property.

[98] Pilloud et al., *Commentary on the Additional Protocols*, "Article 51," para. 1930.

serious violations with "all measures under international law," in the case of Germany, or the use of means necessary to protect the reserving States' own civilian population from grave violations, in the case of France and the UK. The UK's reservation specifically reserves the right to take "otherwise prohibited measures ... to compel to cease violation."[99] These reserving States therefore consider that the civilian population does not escape the mechanism of reciprocity inherent in reprisals. This is particularly clear from the explanation in the UK Military Manual, that "reprisals taken in accordance with [the reservation] are permissible by *and against* the United Kingdom."[100]

The fact that a small number of States have made reservations to the effect that they consider it possible to still take reprisals against civilians does not in itself mean that such a measure would be permissible under international law. The Commentary to Additional Protocol I notes that general international law, notably VCLT prohibitions on reservations incompatible with the nature and purpose of the treaty, apply.[101] Subsequent case law has also affirmed the customary nature of the prohibition of taking reprisals against civilians, notably the *Kupreškić* case, which considered that the prohibition of belligerent reprisals against civilians was now part of general international law, with reprisals against civilians being a "blatant infringement of the most fundamental principles of human rights."[102] Even authors who disagree with the customary nature of Additional Protocol I or an absolute prohibition on any targets of reprisal of a civilian nature accept that reprisals should not detrimentally affect the rights of individuals.[103]

It emerges from practice, codification, and jurisprudence, therefore, that the rise of human rights, the principle of humanity in IHL, and the rights of protected persons have placed limits on the legality of targeting

[99] The full list of reservations to Additional Protocol I is available at https://ihl-databases.icrc.org/applic/ihl/ihl.nsf/States.xsp?xp_viewStates=XPages_NORMStatesParties&xp_treatySelected=470.

[100] Emphasis added. *The Joint Service Manual of the Law of Armed Conflict*, Joint Service Publication 383, 2004 Edition, pp. 422–423; H. H. Almond and F. Kalshoven, "Reprisals: The Global Community Is Not Yet Ready to Abandon Them," *Proceedings of the Annual Meeting (American Society of International Law)*, vol. 74, 1980, pp. 196–205, at p. 205.

[101] Pilloud et al., *Commentary on the Additional Protocols*, "Article 51," para. 1930.

[102] See *Prosecutor* v. *Kupreškić et al.*, ICTY Case No. IT-95-16-T, Judgment of 14 January 2000, paras. 527–535.

[103] See Dinstein, *Conduct of Hostilities*, who takes this as "settled law," p. 295.

belligerent reprisals against civilians in IHL; these escape the inter-State, reciprocal dimension of IHL.

4.3.3 *The Problem of Reciprocity in Non-international Armed Conflicts*

In the case of non-international armed conflicts, where at least one party to the conflict is not a State, the question arises as to whether reciprocity will have the same scope and limitations, where the parties to the conflict are not legally equal under international law. Common Article 3 of the 1949 Geneva Conventions places unconditional obligations on States parties to respect certain minimum standards of treatment in non-international armed conflicts.[104] It was originally envisaged that the provision applying to non-international armed conflict should have a condition of reciprocal application, that is, that the parties to the Convention would be bound to apply it subject to the adverse party also obeying the rules. This was however dropped in 1948.[105]

This absence of any condition of reciprocity is recognized as meaning that Common Article 3 applies even when irregular groups in a non-international armed conflict do not themselves respect IHL.[106] However, the fact that the conflict is non-international does not by itself mean that there is no reciprocity of rights and obligations. All States parties to the Convention undertake to observe the rules in non-international armed conflicts on their territory and are all equally bound by the provision. However, its application in the case of a non-international armed conflict is internal, rather than external, there being no obvious exchange in material treatment between States.

As for non-State armed groups (NSAGs), these are not High Contracting Parties to the Geneva Conventions;[107] however they are recognized as having the obligation to respect Common Article 3. Non-State parties to the conflict may make a unilateral declaration consenting to be bound. But even in the absence of such a declaration, NSAGs are considered

[104] Common Article 3 of the 1949 Geneva Conventions reads as follows: "In the case of armed conflict not of an international character occurring in the territory of one of the High Contracting Parties, each Party to the conflict shall be bound to apply, as a minimum, the following provisions."

[105] International Committee of the Red Cross, Commentary on the First Geneva Convention, "Article 3: Conflicts Not of an International Character," 2016, available at: www.icrc.org/applic/ihl/ihl.nsf/Comment.xsp?action=openDocument&documentId=59F6CDFA490736C1C1257F7D004BA0EC, paras. 370–373.

[106] Ibid., para. 504; Jinks, "Applicability of the Geneva Conventions," p. 190.

[107] International Committee of the Red Cross, Commentary on the First Geneva Convention, "Article 3: Conflicts Not of an International Character," para. 505.

bound by virtue of the fact that the State on whose territory the armed conflict is taking place is a contracting party to the Conventions.[108] NSAGs are, for the purposes of Common Article 3, placed on a footing of equality with the State party to the Convention, despite the fact that the two are fundamentally legally unequal.[109] This "fiction" of equality[110] between two sides that are not in fact equal in either legal or material terms is closely linked to the idea of reciprocal compliance and, indeed, fairness, which lies at the basis of the rationale of IHL.[111] However, it is one of the reasons underpinning the difference in the rules applicable in international and non-international armed conflicts.

The first inequality is material, as States and armed groups or rebels may not have the same material capacity to respect the rules of IHL.[112] This point is made clear by the terms of Additional Protocol II of 1977, which applies only when the non-international armed conflict reaches a certain degree of intensity involving criteria such as control over territory and a degree of organization that enable the armed groups to carry out "sustained and concerted military operations" and implement the provisions of the Protocol.[113] The second inequality is legal. Armed groups, although they have to respect the provisions of IHL in non-international armed conflicts, are also, perhaps mainly, subject to obligations in domestic law, particularly domestic criminal law.[114]

[108] Ibid., para. 507; Fleck, *Handbook of International Humanitarian Law*, p. 1201.

[109] Ibid., paras. 504–505; Pilloud et al., *Commentary on the Additional Protocols*, para. 1351.

[110] The term is used by Sassòli, Sassòli and Shany, "Should the Obligations … Be Equal?," p. 431.

[111] Comments by Shany in Sassòli, Sassòli and Shany, "Should the Obligations … Be Equal?," p. 434. Another rationale for international humanitarian law is, indeed, humanitarian, that is, the protection of humanitarian values, ibid., p. 433.

[112] Sassòli and Shany, "Should the Obligations … Be Equal?," p. 429–430.

[113] Protocol Additional to the Geneva Conventions of 12 August 1949, and relating to the protection of victims of non-international armed conflicts (Protocol II), of 8 June 1977, Article 1.1; Pilloud et al., *Commentary on the Additional Protocols*, pp. 1348, 1350. It is also worth noting in this connection the possibility for the "authority representing a people" engaged in a conflict with a High Contracting Party to make a declaration undertaking to apply the provisions of the 1949 Geneva Conventions and Additional Protocol I in the context of "armed conflicts in which peoples are fighting against colonial domination and alien occupation and against racist régimes in the exercise of their right of self-determination," Protocol Additional to the Geneva Conventions of 12 August 1949, and Relating to the Protection of Victims of International Armed Conflicts (Protocol I), of 8 June 1977, Articles 1.4 and 96.3. Such a declaration was made by the Polisario Front: see https://armedgroups-internationallaw.org/2015/09/02/unilateral-declaration-by-polisario-under-api-accepted-by-swiss-federal-council/

[114] Sassòli and Shany, "Should the Obligations … Be Equal?," pp. 428, 435.

There are some problems with ensuring respect for rules in the same way by two sides that are not, in fact, equal. The lack of a footing of equality between parties to a non-international armed conflict limits the mechanisms of reciprocity at work in the applicable IHL rules. Accepting the provisions of Article 3 does not confer protected belligerent status on non-State parties to the conflict, and according to its Paragraph 4, the application of the Article's provisions "shall not affect the legal status of the Parties to the conflict." Many of the rights of combatants, therefore, remain the preserve of legally equal High Contracting Parties.

4.3.4 *The Position of Individuals in IHL*

Reciprocity is particularly limited in the case of the obligations of States with respect to protected persons.[115] There is clearly a case to be made for saying that the rules of IHL directly endow specific categories of individuals with rights and obligations. Certain authors[116] view the move away from reciprocity as a condition of application of IHL rules as intrinsically linked to the existence of individual rights. It is undeniable that IHL originally operated on a strictly inter-State level, setting out rights and obligations for States only. Regarding, for example, the treatment of prisoners of war, it was with the 1949 Convention that the existence of "rights" for individuals, and not just States, was affirmed.[117]

At the same time, some questions remain. For example, if individuals have rights under the Geneva Conventions, they should be able to waive these, yet Common Article 7 prevents individuals from renouncing the rights conferred by the Conventions because of the danger that persons in a position of weakness might be forced into such a waiver, as well as the harm that the loss of protection could cause.[118] States therefore

[115] See Protocol Additional to the Geneva Conventions of 12 August 1949, and Relating to the Protection of Victims of International Armed Conflicts (Protocol I), of 8 June 1977, Articles 51 and 52; K. Parlett, *The Individual in the International Legal System*, Cambridge, Cambridge University Press, 2011, p. 184; Provost, "Reciprocity in Human Rights," p. 393; on prisoners of war, see Meron, "International Law in the Age of Human Rights," pp. 64–65; R. Sabel, "The Legality of Reciprocity in the Law against Terrorism," *Case Western Reserve Journal of International Law*, vol. 43, 2010–2011, p. 476.

[116] Jinks, "Applicability of the Geneva Conventions," p. 168.

[117] International Committee of the Red Cross, Commentary on the First Geneva Convention, "Article 7: Non-Renunciation of Rights," 2016, available at: www.icrc.org/applic/ihl/ihl.nsf/Comment.xsp?action=openDocument&documentId=7C6EB1D1D7A71575C1257F7D0035EAB5, para. 1000; ICRC, *Commentary to the III Geneva Convention*, pp. 90–91.

[118] International Committee of the Red Cross, Commentary on the First Geneva Convention, "Article 7: Non-Renunciation of Rights," paras. 990, 992–993; ICRC,

cannot release themselves from obligations toward protected persons, nor can the latter dispose of their rights under the Conventions.[119] Interestingly, the Commentary to the III Geneva Convention also considers that individuals themselves have the obligation to ensure respect for their own inalienable rights, with the non-renunciation clause therefore also containing obligations for individuals correlative to the rights it confers.[120] Means of ensuring that individual rights under the Conventions are respected also exist, with procedural mechanisms available for individuals to uphold their rights by appeal to Protecting Powers and the ICRC, under Article 30.[121]

While therefore individuals, or more generally non-State actors, have rights and obligations directly under IHL, there are some fundamental differences with human rights. While IHL may also be considered to embody rights and obligations that are *erga omnes* in nature,[122] the two fields have very different rationales. IHL is not concerned with how a State treats individuals on its territory in general but with humanitarian concerns that arise during wartime.[123] While the customary nature of many IHL rules has rendered some considerations around participation in treaties less relevant, unlike human rights law, IHL does not require States to apply the Conventions vis-à-vis States that are not parties and do not apply the Conventions themselves. IHL retains a strong inter-State dimension, underpinned by reciprocity. Human rights are instead

Commentary to the III Geneva Convention, Commentary to Article 7, p. 88; Pictet, *Commentary to the IV Geneva Convention*, pp. 72–74; Parlett, *Individual in the International Legal System*, p. 185; Fleck, *Handbook of International Humanitarian Law*, section 539.

119 P. D'Argent, "Non-Renunciation of the Rights Provided by the Convention," in A. Clapham et al., eds., *The 1949 Geneva Conventions: A Commentary*, Oxford, Oxford University Press, 2015, p. 146.

120 ICRC, *Commentary to the III Geneva Convention*, p. 92; Pictet, *Commentary to the IV Geneva Convention*, explicitly states that "rights entail obligations," pp. 79–80.

121 International Committee of the Red Cross, Commentary on the First Geneva Convention, "Article 7: Non-Renunciation of Rights," para. 1001; Pictet, *Commentary to the IV Geneva Convention*, pp. 78–79; D'Argent, "Non-Renunciation of the Rights," p. 151. The existence of individual obligations under IHL is backed up by the emergence of individual international criminal responsibility for grave breaches, which however may be seen as being a separate set of rules to those in humanitarian law treaties.

122 Frowein, A., "Reactions by Not Directly Affected States to Breaches of International Law," *Collected Courses of the Hague Academy of International Law*, vol. 248, 1994, p. 396; Meron, "International Law in the Age of Human Rights," sees this nature as giving the possibility for all States to take steps in response to breaches of the Geneva Convention, at p. 36.

123 D'Argent, "Non-Renunciation of the Rights," pp. 150–151.

concerned with a vertical relationship between individuals and the State under whose jurisdiction they find themselves.

4.4 Human Rights

The particularities of human rights treaties have been outlined in Chapter 3, and will be the object of further attention in Chapter 6. However, it will be useful here to recall some of the factors distinguishing how human rights operate for other standards of treatment being examined here. Human rights do not depend for their application upon a criterion of nationality.[124] Nor do human rights attach to specific categories of individuals, in the same manner as IHL or investment law. Instead, *all* individuals present in the territory of a State or under its jurisdiction or control enjoy human rights, without distinction.

It is also widely accepted that human rights belong properly to individuals.[125] This has led to the view that human rights are nonreciprocal in nature.[126] This point of view is closely linked to the applicability of human rights internally within States to all individuals without distinction of nationality, which removes or minimizes their inter-State dimension.[127] This section will however set out that human rights are still by nature reciprocal, despite this reciprocity being limited by the existence of a relationship of legal inequality between the State and the individual.

It is undeniable that human rights are not subject to any condition of reciprocity, in the sense that there is no requirement for a certain standard of conduct to be taken by the beneficiary of the right in order for the rules to apply.[128] This fact is however not limited to rules on

124 Virally, "Panorama du droit international contemporain," p. 120; Dupuy, "Unité de l'ordre juridique international," p. 36.

125 Kriebaum, "Nature of Investment Disciplines," p. 49; Virally distinguishes human rights from IHL on this basis, Virally, "Panorama du droit international contemporain," p. 358.

126 Dupuy, "Obligation en droit international," p. 223 and Dupuy, "Unité de l'ordre juridique international," p. 36.

127 Dupuy, "Unité de l'ordre juridique international," p. 379; Provost, "Reciprocity in Human Rights," pp. 388, 453; this was also the position taken by the ACHR in Inter-American Court of Human Rights, Advisory Opinion OC-2/82, of 24 September 1982 "The effect of reservations on the entry into force of the American Convention on Human Rights (Arts. 74 and 75)," paras. 27, 29, 33; A. Drzemczewski, "The Sui Generis Nature of the European Convention on Human Rights," *The International and Comparative Law Quarterly*, vol. 29, no. 1, January 1980, pp. 54, 61–62.

128 Provost, "Reciprocity in Human Rights," pp. 398, 404.

human rights and does not mean that, only because there is no *condition* of reciprocity, that the rules do not apply in a reciprocal manner.

Human rights provisions in treaties are subject not only to the reciprocal concessions that occur in treaty negotiation[129] but also to the operation of reciprocity in treaties more generally,[130] particularly as a condition of engagement and in their application.[131] The fact that obligations in human rights treaties operate *erga omnes partes* – or even that customary rules on human rights operate *erga omnes* – does not exclude reciprocity but in fact is a product of it. It is the fact that each State party owes obligations to all others and that every other State party may require compliance (as will be seen further in Chapter 5) that allows human rights standards to actually be upheld.

Human rights grant direct rights to individuals, who can access international instances in order to uphold them. Their obligations function both between State and State, and between State and individual. Insofar as obligations operate between States, the relationship is horizontal. When individual rights are concerned, the relationship is instead vertical, asymmetrical and nonreciprocal; an individual that holds a right under a human rights treaty does not have a correlative obligation toward the State under the treaty. These dual relationships, State–State and State–individual, are best highlighted by the possibility for both States and individuals to bring claims under human rights treaties,[132] and the differences between the two types of procedure.

As the ECtHR explained in *Ireland* v. *UK*, whereas individuals must be victims of a violation of Convention rights in order to bring a claim before the Court, States may bring claims for any alleged breach by any other State party.[133] In an inter-State human rights complaint, the violation alleged does not have to relate to a specific violation of an individual's rights but may also be general in nature, relating to any form of nonobservance. This inter-State enforcement is possible exactly

[129] Simma, From Bilateralism to Community Interest, p. 375, sees this as the only way in which reciprocity is relevant to human rights treaties.

[130] Provost, "Reciprocity in Human Rights," p. 453. [131] Ibid., p. 454.

[132] A. Roberts, "State-to-State Investment Treaty Arbitration: A Hybrid Theory of Interdependent Rights and Shared Interpretive Authority," *Harvard International Law Journal*, vol. 55, no. 1, 2014, p. 34; Byers, *Power and the Power of Rules*, p. 200; Pisillo Mazzeschi, "Relationship between Human Rights," p. 570; Kriebaum, "Nature of Investment Disciplines," p. 49 cit. Simma. See Chapter 7.

[133] *Ireland* v. *the United Kingdom*, ECtHR, Application no. 5310/71, Judgment of 18 January 1978, paras. 239–240.

because the obligations are owed by each party to all other States parties, in view of a common interest to ensure that treaty provisions are respected.

4.5 International Investment Law

The field of international investment law is another area in which the standards of treatment applied to individuals are of interest from the point of view of reciprocity. The explosion in investor–State arbitration in the twenty-first century has led to the nature of the rights in investment law being greatly scrutinized and to a debate over whether the rights of individuals (in this case, investors) under investment agreements are direct, that is, that they belong to the individuals, or derivative, that is, that they are State rights whose enforcement is "delegated" to individuals, in what might be seen as a form of reverse diplomatic protection. At the same time, the rights and standards of treatment of investors are seen as greatly different to those of human rights.

The differences between rights of investors and human rights are generally considered to rest on the reciprocity inherent in investment agreements, as opposed to the nonreciprocity inherent in human rights treaties, whose obligations are integral in nature.[134] What in particular distinguishes investor rights under international investment agreements is the requirement of nationality to enjoy protection.[135]

This reliance on nationality necessarily creates an inter-State dimension to protection under BITs, different to the internal operation of human rights, which do not imply any inter-State relationship as far as the enjoyment of the rights themselves is concerned. However, further than this, the "reciprocity" of investment agreements has been explicitly

[134] Gourgourinis gives the example of the impossibility of making an argument based on estoppel by reason of the representations made by one party in a case concerning human rights, A. Gourgourinis, "Investors' Rights *qua* Human Rights? Revisiting the 'Direct'/'Derivative' Rights Debate," in M. Fitzmaurice and P. Merkouris, eds., *The Interpretation and Application of the European Convention on Human Rights: Legal and Practical Implications*, Leiden, Boston, Nijhoff, 2013, p. 181, and this because of the consensual nature of investment agreements, p. 182; Kriebaum, "Nature of Investment Disciplines," pp. 50, 72; Z. Douglas, J. Pauwelyn, and J. E. Viñuales, eds., *The Foundations of International Investment Law: Bringing Theory into Practice*, Oxford, Oxford University Press, 2014, p. 80.

[135] Roberts, "State-to-State Investment Treaty Arbitration," p. 38; Meron, "International Law in the Age of Human Rights," p. 337.

stated in treaty provisions[136] and in the decisions of tribunals, emphasizing the mutuality and equality of obligations undertaken by States parties.[137] In BITs, "reciprocity" has also been equated to a synallagma, or a quid pro quo,[138] which, as seen in Chapter 2, is not strictly the same thing.[139] The reciprocal nature of BITs has also had an impact upon how decisions have been made. In *Daimler*, the tribunal used an argument based on reciprocity to deny the removal of an eighteen-month waiting period to access arbitration, stating that "there is no indication that – despite the reciprocal and bilateral nature of the rest of the treaty – Germany consciously consented to proceed directly to binding international arbitration with Argentine investors in circumstances in which similarly situated German investors would not be entitled to proceed directly to binding international arbitration against Argentina."[140] However, despite claims to equality and reciprocity, investment treaties do not reflect the fundamental imbalance that can often be found between parties in terms of investment flows; although treaties are phrased in language that emphasizes reciprocity of obligations, in actual fact their provisions will generally be invoked in one direction only.[141]

[136] For example, Article 1115 of the North American Free Trade Agreement, 1 January 1994, reads "this Section establishes a mechanism for the settlement of investment disputes that assures both equal treatment among investors of the Parties in accordance with the principle of international reciprocity and due process before an impartial tribunal."

[137] Gourgourinis, "Investors' Rights *qua* Human Rights?," p. 171, cites *Kardassopoulos* v. *Georgia*; the Tribunal in *Kardassopoulos* actually set aside the relevance of reciprocity, as it "involves a relationship of mutuality whereby what is done by one party is a reaction to or dependent upon what is done by the other. In the present context the Tribunal sees no such relationship between the operation of the domestic law of the two States; rather, the two domestic laws are self-standing legal systems applying independently of each other," *Ioannis Kardassopoulos* v. *Georgia*, ICSID Case No. ARB/05/18, Decision on Jurisdiction, 6 July 2007, para. 226. Schill, *Multilateralization of International Investment Law*, p. 261.

[138] Schill, *Multilateralization of International Investment Law*, p. 24; Schill also sees bilateralism and "specific reciprocity," or quid pro quo, as a competing paradigm to the tendency to multilateralism, embodying "diffuse reciprocity," in international investment law, Schill, "Ordering Paradigms in International Investment Law," p. 100. It is submitted here that in reality the concept of "reciprocity" covers both these types of relation. *Daimler Financial Services AG* v. *Argentine Republic*, ICSID Case No. ARB/05/1, Award, 22 August 2012, para. 162.

[139] See above, Section 2.2.

[140] *Daimler*, para. 266. Douglas sees investor–State arbitration as an essential part of the "bargain," given in exchange for entry of capital into the host State's economy, Douglas, *International Law of Investment Claims*, p. 161.

[141] Sykes, "When Is International Law Useful?," p. 29. An interesting case is that of the Canada–China BIT, which does not provide for exactly equal rights for investors of the

4.5.1 *The Nature of Rights: Comparing International Investment Law and Human Rights*

Fundamentally, investors do not have any inherent rights to protection aside from their human rights. States must agree to grant each other's investors specific rights if they wish protection to be afforded to their nationals – a rationale that differs from that of human rights, which are considered to inhere in the human person.[142] There are, however, also some similarities between human rights and investment protection. Both provide substantive rights for individuals,[143] and a breach of both types of rule involves consequences for the State toward the investor or individual.[144]

Further, both types of treaty provide for some residual protection for individuals in the case of their unilateral termination[145] or denunciation. For example, the ECHR provides, in its Article 58.2, that "a denunciation shall not have the effect of releasing the High Contracting Party concerned from its obligations under this Convention in respect of any act which, being capable of constituting a violation of such obligations, may have been performed by it before the date at which the denunciation became effective." In both human rights and investment treaties, States cannot unilaterally terminate their obligations with respect to individuals who acquired rights under the treaty.[146]

two parties: G. Van Harten, "Canada's Non-Reciprocal BIT with China: Would the US or Europe Do the Same?," *Columbia FDI Perspectives*, No. 136, 8 December 2014.

142 A. Roberts, "Triangular Treaties; the Extent and Limits of Investment Treaty Rights," *Harvard International Law Journal*, vol. 56, no. 2, 2015, pp. 368, 402; *Daimler*, para. 164.

143 M. Paparinskis, "Analogies and Other Regimes of International Law," in Z. Douglas, J. Pauwelyn, and J. E. Viñuales, eds., *The Foundations of International Investment Law: Bringing Theory into Practice*, Oxford, Oxford University Press, 2014, p. 79.

144 Z. Douglas, "The Hybrid Foundations of Investment Treaty Arbitration," *British Year Book of International Law*, vol. 74, no. 1, 2003, p. 185.

145 Paparinskis, "Analogies and Other Regimes," pp. 96–99; for example, the 2008 German Model BIT reads at Article 13.3, "in respect of investments made prior to the date of termination of this Treaty, the provisions of the above Articles shall continue to be effective for a further period of twenty years from the date of termination of this Treaty." Article 13 of the UK–Belize BIT reads, "in respect of investments made whilst the Agreement is in force, its provisions shall continue in effect with respect to such investments for a period of ten years after the date of termination and without prejudice to the application thereafter of the rules of general international law."

146 A recent question that has arisen, particularly with the recent policy of termination of intra-European BITs, is whether there is any such residual protection for investors when the treaty is terminated by mutual agreement between States parties, either outright, or by previously amending it when it does not originally provide for mutual termination. See the example of the Czech Republic, L. Peterson, "Czech Republic

The question remains however as to what accounts for differences in the extent to which both types of treaty are "reciprocal." This issue is directly connected to the conceptual – but also practical – problem of whether investors have direct, substantive rights under investment agreements that they can enforce – similarly to individuals under human rights treaties – or only derived rights, in which case they are essentially beneficiaries of the rights of States.[147]

It could be contended that as investor rights are conferred by treaty, then investors are only beneficiaries, rather than holders, of rights.[148] However, the consequences of finding against a State in an investor–State arbitration seem to point in a different direction. Such awards do not create a new set of consequences on the inter-State plane[149] but rather only give certain rights to the investor as against the host State. This has consequences, including on the availability of countermeasures. In *Corn Products International* v. *Mexico* (*CPI*), Mexico argued that the wrongfulness of its measures taken against CPI was precluded because the only rights at issue were those of the United States, the State of nationality of CPI, and Mexico.[150] The tribunal, however, found that "the doctrine of countermeasures ... is not applicable to claims under Chapter XI of NAFTA,"[151] as the very purpose of Chapter XI was "to remove such claims from the inter-State plane and to ensure that investors could assert rights directly against a State,"[152] and that "Mexico owed obligations to CPI under Chapter XI of NAFTA which were separate from the obligations it owed to the United States under the NAFTA as a whole."[153] A crucial aspect of the existence of direct rights is that investors have the capacity to bring cases against host States parties to an investment agreement, acting directly in defense of their rights, and removing the dispute from the control of their home State.[154]

Terminates Investment Treaties in Such a Way as to Cast Doubt on Residual Legal Protection for Existing Investments," www.iareporter.com, 1 February 2011.

147 For an overview of the differences between the two approaches, see Douglas, "Hybrid Foundations of Investment Treaty Arbitration," pp. 163–164; Gourgourinis, "Investors' Rights *qua* Human Rights?," pp. 149–154, and on the approaches of tribunals which generally endorse the direct theory, p. 157.

148 M. Paparinskis, "Investment Treaty Arbitration and the (New) Law of State Responsibility," *The European Journal of International Law*, vol. 24, no. 2, 2013, p. 624.

149 Douglas, "Hybrid Foundations of Investment Treaty Arbitration," pp. 181, 192.

150 *Corn Products International, Inc.* v. *United Mexican States*, ICSID Case No. ARB(AF)/04/01, Decision on Responsibility, 15 January 2008, para. 151.

151 *CPI* v. *Mexico*, para. 161. 152 Ibid., paras. 161–169. 153 Ibid., para. 176.

154 See Meron, "International Law in the Age of Human Rights," pp. 338–340; Douglas, "Hybrid Foundations of Investment Treaty Arbitration," pp. 169–170, 191; Douglas,

The best way of understanding the rights of investors is, similarly to human rights, as having a "triangular" structure, in which both an inter-State and individual–State legal relationship exist within the same instrument,[155] with States conferring direct rights upon individuals in parallel to inter-State obligations.[156] Similarly to human rights treaties, there subsists in investment agreements the possibility to have recourse to inter-State dispute settlement,[157] and the consequences of the breaches of individual and State rights are distinct.[158] Inter-State arbitration may relate to interpretation or application of the treaty in general, whereas investor–State arbitration will relate to a specific violation of the rights of a specific investor, or those arising out of a specific investment[159] – similarly to the case of human rights treaties. In allowing investor–State arbitration, States parties also waive their right to exercise diplomatic protection over their investors,[160] a point that underlines the separation between the inter-State and the individual–State dimensions of BITs.

While BITs do grant direct rights to investors, and allow the possibility of bringing claims against host States for violation of their rights, the inter-State dimension of investor protection is evident; investment agreements are framed as exchanges between contracting States, in keeping with their economic nature. The reason investors enjoy rights under these instruments is because their State of nationality has agreed to a

International Law of Investment Claims, pp. 18–19; Parlett, *Individual in the International Legal System*, pp. 106–107.

155 This view is support by Kriebaum, "Nature of Investment Disciplines," p. 72; Douglas mentions the "triangular relationship" in differentiating investment arbitration from diplomatic protection, Douglas, "Hybrid Foundations of Investment Treaty Arbitration," p. 182.

156 Roberts, "Triangular Treaties," p. 357.

157 UNCTAD, "Dispute Settlement: State-State," p. 56; Roberts, "State-to-State Investment Treaty Arbitration," p. 3.

158 Douglas, "Hybrid Foundations of Investment Treaty Arbitration," pp. 189–191.

159 Roberts, "State-to-State Investment Treaty Arbitration," pp. 3, 5–6, 52.

160 Roberts also considers investment agreements to be both horizontal and vertical insofar as they address the relationship between States and non-State actors, "Triangular Treaties," p. 374. The ICSID Convention also clearly excludes the possibility for States to use the inter-State dispute settlement mechanism for disputes arising out of specific investments. Article 64 of the ICSID Convention allows for "[a]ny dispute arising between Contracting States concerning the interpretation or application of this Convention which is not settled by negotiation" to be referred to the International Court of Justice, whereas the jurisdiction of ICSID under Article 25 extends to "any legal dispute arising directly out of an investment" between a Contracting State and a national of another Contracting State"; UNCTAD, "Dispute Settlement: State-State," p. 58.

mutual exchange of investor protection with another State. This accounts also for the reciprocal nature of these agreements, and constitutes their key distinction with human rights, whose underlying rationale is instead to be found in the collective engagement by States to ensure a series of rights that inhere in the human person.

4.6 Diplomatic Protection

It is particularly interesting to ask whether, and how, the increasing number of individual rights in international law has changed diplomatic protection from the classical view of a State upholding its *own* rights in the injury of a national to a State espousing the individual rights of its national.

The classical view of diplomatic protection is set out in the *Mavrommatis* judgment of the PCIJ:

> It is an elementary principle of international law that a State is entitled to protect its subjects, when injured by acts contrary to international law committed by another State, from whom they have been unable to obtain satisfaction through the ordinary channels. By taking up the case of one of its subjects and by resorting to diplomatic action or international judicial proceedings on his behalf, a State is in reality asserting its own rights – its right to ensure, in the person of its subjects, respect for the rules of international law.[161]

Once a State exercises diplomatic protection, the legal relationship at issue becomes purely inter-State.[162] The State "makes the claim its own,"[163] and the injury to the individual becomes an injury to its State of nationality.[164] The two States therefore enter into a bilateral relationship that is based on reciprocity of rights and obligations; the State allegedly committing the violation owes an obligation to the State of nationality of the individual, which holds a right to have the rules in question respected.[165]

With this move to the inter-State level, the individual effectively loses control over the claim, which is pursued at the discretion of the State of

[161] PCIJ, *Mavrommatis Palestine Concessions*, Judgment of 30 August 1924, Series A, No. A/2, p. 12.

[162] Douglas, *International Law of Investment Claims*, p. 11.

[163] United States/Germany Mixed Claims Commission, Administrative Decision No. V, 31 October 1924, *RIAA* Vol. VII, Anderson, p. 126.

[164] Schill, *Multilateralization of International Investment Law*, pp. 246–247.

[165] Pisillo Mazzeschi, "Relationship between Human Rights," p. 555.

nationality.[166] The rationale of diplomatic protection therefore differs clearly from that of human rights, where the nationality of the individual is of no relevance.[167] In diplomatic protection, it is "in reality" the State's rights that are being upheld.

4.6.1 *Recent Developments and the Impact of Individual Rights*

Where individuals have direct rights, and procedural rights to bring claims against States under international instruments, it is not as easy to see why the rights in question should "in reality" be the rights of the State.[168] When an individual brings a claim before an investment tribunal, for example, they waive the right for their State of nationality to exercise diplomatic protection over them.[169] This change led the ILC in its commentary to the Draft Articles on Diplomatic Protection to state that "[a] State does not 'in reality' – to quote *Mavrommatis* – assert its own right only. 'In reality' it also asserts the right of its injured national."[170]

A parallel may be drawn with the possibility, which will be further analyzed in Chapter 5, for a State to claim the violation by another of an *erga omnes* obligation. In both cases, the State may have suffered no specific injury, but it will still be able to bring a claim on the basis that the rights are owed to it, as well as to the individual (in the case of diplomatic protection) or the individually injured State (in the case of an obligation owed *erga omnes*).

Diplomatic protection may therefore be seen as a counterpart to individual claims against States when considering, as confirmed by international jurisprudence, that it may also be exercised where individual, and specifically human, rights are at stake – as was the case in the *Diallo*

166 Parlett, *Individual in the International Legal System*, p. 54; ILC, First Report on Diplomatic Protection, by Mr. John R. Dugard, Special Rapporteur, Document A/CN.4/506 and Add. 1, Doc. No. A/CN.4/506 and Add. 1, 7 March and 20 April 2000, p. 222; Pisillo Mazzeschi, "Relationship between Human Rights," p. 555; *United States/Germany Mixed Claims Commission, Administrative Decision No. V*, p. 126.

167 S. Garibian, "Vers l'émergence d'un droit individuel à la protection diplomatique?," *Annuaire français de droit international*, vol. 54, 2008, p. 128.

168 ILC, Preliminary Report on Diplomatic Protection by Mr. Mohamed Bennouna, Special Rapporteur, Doc. No. A/CN.4/484, 4 February 1998, p. 314; ILC, First Report on Diplomatic Protection, pp. 221–222.

169 ILC, Preliminary Report on Diplomatic Protection by Mr. John R. Dugard, Special Rapporteur, Doc. No. A/CN.4/506 and Add. 1, 7 March and 20 April 2000, p. 315.

170 ILC, Draft Articles on Diplomatic Protection with Commentaries, *Yearbook of the International Law Commission*, vol. II, 2006, Part Two, p. 25.

case before the ICJ.[171] In the *LaGrand* case,[172] Germany's position was that it was upholding *both* its own rights, which the United States owed it under the VCCR, and the rights its nationals held directly under the treaty as individuals.[173]

The ability for a State to bring a claim on the basis of the violation of the human rights of its national is an important one, from the point of view of not only the individual but also the law of human rights. Despite the universality of many human rights instruments, access for individuals to instances before which they can bring claims of violation by a State are very limited and depend on State consent.[174] Therefore, these *erga omnes* obligations may require the strictly bilateral mechanism of diplomatic protection – despite the imperfections inherent in its discretionary nature and reliance on a link of nationality – to be upheld at the international level. Diplomatic protection has not been rendered obsolete by the advent of individual rights, and is in a sense supplementary to them.[175]

It has been put forward by States making diplomatic protection claims that two types of injury arise: direct injury to the State's own rights and indirect injury by virtue of the violation of the rights of its national.[176] This emphasizes the point that the relations at issue have a dual

[171] The *Diallo* case is especially interesting from this point of view, in which claims were based on the ICCPR and the African Charter on Human and People's rights, *Case Concerning Ahmadou Sadio Diallo (Republic of Guinea* v. *DRC)*, Judgment of 30 November 2010, para. 63, finding a breach by the Republic of Congo of its obligations under these instruments, as well as the VCCR, at para. 160; see also ILC, Seventh Report on Diplomatic Protection, by Mr. John R. Dugard, Special Rapporteur, Document A/CN.4/567, p. 6.

[172] *LaGrand, Memorial of the Federal Republic of Germany*, vol. I (text of the Memorial), 16 September 1999, paras. 4.11 and 4.14.

[173] While finding that Article 36.1 of the Vienna Convention on Consular Relations creates individual rights, the Court did not pronounce on whether these rights had the character of human rights, *LaGrand (Germany* v. *United States of America)*, Judgment of 27 June 2001, ICJ Reports 2011, paras. 77–78.

[174] ILC, First Report on Diplomatic Protection, pp. 213–214; ILC, Draft Articles on Diplomatic Protection with Commentaries, p. 26; this was the argument used by Parker in the *United States/Germany Mixed Claims Commission, Administrative Decision No. V*, p. 149.

[175] ILC, Draft Articles on Diplomatic Protection with Commentaries, p. 86; ILC, Seventh Report on Diplomatic Protection, p. 6.

[176] See the position of Germany in LaGrand, LaGrand, Memorial of the Federal Republic of Germany, vol. I (text of the Memorial), 16 September 1999, section 4, and public sitting held on Monday 13 November 2000, at 10 am, at the Peace Palace in the LaGrand case (*Germany* v. *United States of America*), oral pleadings of Prof. Simma.

nature;[177] if the fiction of *Mavrommatis* were carried through to its logical conclusion, then the only direct injury would be to the rights of the State; but this is not possible where the individual is recognized as a holder of substantive rights.[178] This point highlights the fact that in all individual rights there can, and still does, subsist an inter-State dimension.

At the same time, the advent of individual rights in international law has had no, or little, impact upon the obligation for a State to exercise diplomatic protection vis-à-vis the individual. Diplomatic protection remains a discretionary right of the State.[179] The most that the ILC managed to obtain was to include a recommendation that a State should consider exercising diplomatic protection and transfer any damages to the individual;[180] however, no further evolution has occurred. Diplomatic protection still remains controlled by the State and is exercised at its own discretion.[181]

4.7 Conclusion

This overview of the various standards of treatment of individuals shows how reciprocity in its various manifestations – as a basis of treatment, as a condition, and as a correlation of legal rights and obligations – is relevant in all areas of regulation concerning the treatment that States must grant individuals. In the absence of a preexisting international legal obligation weighing upon a State, a condition of reciprocity may be a basis on which to extend treatment to foreign nationals or ensure the extension of given rules – for example, States not parties to the 1949 Geneva Conventions "accepting and applying" their provisions. Reciprocity bears a close link to ensuring equality in the context of

[177] B. K. Schramm, *La fiction juridique et le juge: Contribution à une autre herméneutique de la Cour internationale de Justice*, Bruxelles, Bruylant, 2018, pp. 210–211.

[178] Pisillo Mazzeschi, "Relationship between Human Rights," p. 571, cit. Avena.

[179] Garibian, "Vers l'émergence d'un droit individuel," pp. 133, 141; Schill, *Multilateralization of International Investment Law*, p. 247.

[180] ILC, Draft Articles on Diplomatic Protection with Commentaries, Article 19, pp. 95–99.

[181] ILC, First Report on Diplomatic Protection, p. 223. There are some signs in State practice of a shift toward an obligation to exercise diplomatic protection, but these cannot be considered to have crystallized in any way that changes the traditional approach to the doctrine, ILC, First Report on Diplomatic Protection, p. 225; ILC, Preliminary Report on Diplomatic Protection, p. 316; Pisillo Mazzeschi, "Relationship between Human Rights," p. 572.

treatment of individuals, in the same way as for inter-State relationships, notably illustrated by the functioning of the MFN clause.

There is a close link between reciprocity and nationality as a relevant criterion for granting treatment. Where nationality is the basis on which rules are applied, there will be a notable inter-State dimension to the obligations, implying a bilateral relationship and reciprocity of rights and obligations. Where individual rights exist, such as is the case for investment and human rights law, individual procedural rights against a State remove the individual's claim from the inter-State plane. This is the case unless or until the State of nationality of the individual exercises diplomatic protection over the individual. Indeed, the continued relevance of diplomatic protection shows that in the enforcement of individual rights, there still subsists an inter-State dimension. This is the case even where standards apply internally, where a State must ensure it extends a given treatment to all individuals in its territory, including its own nationals. Where there is no bilateral inter-State relationship involved – as is the case for human rights, which apply regardless of a link of nationality, and for the provisions of humanitarian law applicable in non-international armed conflicts, such as Common Article 3 of the 1949 Geneva Conventions, and Additional Protocol II of 1977 – then the obligations will be owed *erga omnes* or *erga omnes partes*. Reciprocity in rights and obligations therefore becomes collective.

5 Reciprocity in the Enforcement of International Law

Previous chapters have addressed the operation of reciprocity within rules of international law. This chapter will instead address the operation of reciprocity in what may be loosely termed the enforcement of international law. It will look at the roles reciprocity may play in the consequences of a breach of international law. It will look at how reciprocity is articulated into various mechanisms for enforcement of international law, analyzing the exception of nonperformance and State esponsibility.

The examination of State responsibility is particularly important to establish what role reciprocity plays in international law. After all, rules of responsibility are fundamental for the existence of any legal system; if there are no consequences arising from the breach of an obligation, then there is not really any obligation to speak of.[1] State responsibility therefore gives international law its character as law and shows most clearly of all international law's own particular nature.

5.1 The Exception of Nonperformance

While it is concerned with the enforcement and execution of obligations, the exception of nonperformance in contemporary public international law is part of the law of treaties, and not of State responsibility.[2] Closely

[1] ILC, Report of the International Law Commission on the Work of Its Thirty-First Session, Doc. No. A/CN.4/SER.A/1979/Add. 1 (Part 2), *Yearbook of the International Law Commission*, 1979, Volume II, Part Two, p. 107; P.-M. Dupuy, "Le fait générateur de la responsabilité internationale des Etats," *Collected Courses of the Hague Academy of International Law*, vol. 188, 1984, p. 21; Dupuy, "Unité de l'ordre juridique international," p. 101.

[2] There were debates in the ILC as to whether to also include a version of the exception in the Articles on State Responsibility, on the basis that the formulation of the rule in Article 60.5 of

linked to the *exceptio* in contract law, it applies to treaties only,[3] and relates specifically to the grounds for terminating or suspending a treaty, rather than giving rise to the other legal consequences that stem from the commission of an internationally wrongful act in the law of State responsibility.[4] This section will therefore first address the function and content of the exception of nonperformance, and the extent to which it applies in international law, before looking at "exceptions to the exception," that is, obligations that may not be suspended on the basis of prior nonperformance by another State.

5.1.1 *Article 60 of the VCLT*

Article 60 of the VCLT sets out the conditions under which a State may terminate or suspend a treaty on the basis of prior nonperformance by another party. This is commonly accepted to be an expression of the *exceptio non adimpleti contractus*,[5] examined in detail in Chapter 2. While the two most notable international cases in which it was invoked, *Diversion of Water from the Meuse* case before the PCIJ and *Application of the Interim Accord of 13 September 1995 (FYROM* v. *Greece)* ("*FYROM* v. *Greece*"), were inconclusive as to its nature or content, codification

the VCLT was too narrow as it required "material" breach, but the proposal to include an article entitled "Non-compliance caused by prior non-compliance by another State" was eventually rejected. It was considered that the formulation in the Articles brought together too many concepts, and did not fall within the category of circumstances precluding wrongfulness. See the debates in ILC, Report of the International Law Commission on the Work of Its Fifty-First Session, 3 May–23 July 1999, Official Records of the General Assembly, Fifty-Fourth Session, Supplement No. 10, Doc. No. A/54/10, *Yearbook of the International Law Commission 1999*, vol. II, Part Two, pp. 78–79; ILC, Draft Articles on Responsibility of States for Internationally Wrongful Acts, with commentaries, *Yearbook of the International Law Commission, 2001*, vol. II, Part Two, p. 72. See also comments by Simma in his Separate Opinion to Application of the Interim Accord of 13 September 1995 (the *Former Yugoslav Republic of Macedonia* v. *Greece*), para. 27, and D. Azaria, "Exception of Nonperformance," in R. Wolfrum, ed., *The Max Planck Encyclopedia of Public International Law*, Oxford University Press, 2008–, online edition, para 9.

3 ILC, Third Report on State Responsibility, Gaetano Arangio-Ruiz, Special Rapporteur, A/CN.4/440 and Add.1, *Yearbook of the International Law Commission*, vol. II, 1991, Part One, p. 13.

4 ILC, Draft Articles on Responsibility of States, pp. 117, 141; Separate Opinion of Judge Simma in Application of the Interim Accord of 13 September 1995 (the *Former Yugoslav Republic of Macedonia* v. *Greece*), para. 20; J. Crawford, "Multilateral Rights and Obligations in International Law," *Collected Courses of the Hague Academy of International Law*, vol. 319, 2006, p. 426.

5 ILC, Draft Articles on the Law of Treaties, Report of the International Law Commission on the Work of Its Eighteenth Session, 4 May–19 July 1966, Official Records of the General Assembly, Twenty-First Session, Supplement No. 9 (A/6309/Rev.1), *Yearbook of the International Law Commission*, vol. II, 1966, p. 253.

debates at the ILC rejected the existence of any general exception of nonperformance. In the *Namibia* Advisory Opinion of 1970, the ICJ found that Article 60 of the VCLT could be considered customary law.[6] It therefore would seem that the exception of nonperformance in international law is exhausted by what is codified in Article 60 of the VCLT, with no wider exception having been accepted since.[7] Article 60 allows for "material breach" to be invoked as a ground for terminating or suspending the operation of a treaty in whole or in part. This applies both to bilateral treaties, in Article 60.1, and multilateral treaties, in Article 60.2.

5.1.2 *The Exception of Nonperformance and Reciprocity*

In its most raw form, the exception of nonperformance can be seen as a form of "self-enforcement" of treaties.[8] This is why its relevance in international law is often justified by reference to the latter's low degree of institutionalization.[9] It would however be more accurate to understand the exception as flowing from the reciprocity of rights and obligations.[10] Rather than being a characteristic of a less developed form of law, the exception of nonperformance is simply linked to a certain type of reciprocal obligation. This also accounts for why the exception still exists in national law, arguably the most institutionalized form of law there is.[11] The exception of nonperformance seeks to preserve equality between subjects, which makes it particularly important in a horizontal legal system such as international law.[12]

6 Legal Consequences of the Continued Presence of South Africa in Namibia (South West Africa) notwithstanding Security Council Resolution 276 (1970), Advisory Opinion of 21 June 1971, I.C.J. Reports 1971, para. 94.

7 Separate Opinion of Judge Simma in *FYROM* v. *Greece*, para. 10.

8 P.-M. Dupuy gives the example of the treaty of Kadesh, Dupuy, "Unité de l'ordre juridique international," pp. 83–84.

9 For example, see the Separate Opinion of Judge Simma in Application of the Interim Accord of 13 September 1995 (the *Former Yugoslav Republic of Macedonia* v. *Greece*), para 10.

10 This was the position of Greece in *FYROM* v. *Greece*, see the Separate Opinion of Judge Simma, para. 4; Hudson in the Meuse case spoke of "identical or reciprocal" obligations, PCIJ, *Diversion of Water from the Meuse*, p. 77, similarly to Niboyet, "Notion de réciprocité," p. 298, and Campiglio, "Principio di reciprocità," p. 289.

11 See the examples given by Hudson in *Diversion of Water from the Meuse*, p. 77.

12 This position is set out by Dupuy, "Unité de l'ordre juridique international," p. 101, and De Luna in debates at the ILC, Summary Records of the Second Part of the Seventeenth Session, 831st meeting, p. 62; Campiglio, "Principio di reciprocità," p. 288. See also M. M. Gomaa, *Suspension or Termination of Treaties on Grounds of Breach*, The Hague/Boston, M. Nijhoff, 1996, pp. 119, 183, and ILC, Summary Records of the Eighteenth Session, p. 255.

Therefore, while ILC drafts on the Law of Treaties explicitly based the exception of nonperformance on the "principle" of reciprocity,[13] it is instead more accurate to see it as one of the consequences of the reciprocity of rights and obligations in international law, a concrete mechanism into which an abstract characteristic is transformed. This explains why some authors see the exception of nonperformance as something that is so intrinsically linked to the nature of the obligations at issue in the specific instrument that to suspend performance by virtue of a failure by the other party to fulfill its obligation is part and parcel of the principle *pacta sunt servanda*.[14] In order to determine the accuracy of this position, however, an analysis must first be made of the actual scope of the exception of nonperformance in international law.

5.1.3 *The Regime in Article 60 of the VCLT*

Under Article 60 of the VCLT, in the case of a "material breach" of a bilateral treaty by one party, the other party may "invoke the breach as a ground for terminating the treaty or suspending its operation in whole or in part." In the case of a multilateral treaty, the same possibility is open to all parties "by unanimous agreement"; by a "specially affected State" in its bilateral relations with the defaulting State; or by any party "if the treaty is of such a character that a material breach of its provisions radically changes the position of every party with respect to the further performance of its obligations under the treaty." Article 60 therefore distinguishes between bilateral, multilateral, and what may be termed "interdependent" obligations, in the case of paragraph 2(c). Termination or suspension is not automatic but must be "invoked" and respect the procedural conditions set out in Article 65 VCLT,[15] which apply indistinctly regardless of whether the treaty is being suspended or terminated.

The exception in the VCLT is essentially restrictive; only a "material" breach may result in suspension or termination, and is defined in Article 60.3 as a "repudiation of the treaty not sanctioned in the present

[13] Simma uses this terminology, Separate Opinion of Judge Simma in *FYROM* v. *Greece*, para. 10, as does Fitzmaurice, ILC, Fourth Report on the Law of Treaties, Sir Gerald Fitzmaurice, p. 46; Arangio-Ruiz equates it to reciprocity in a treaty context, ILC, Third Report on State Responsibility, Gaetano Arangio-Ruiz, Special Rapporteur, A/CN.4/440, p. 13.

[14] J. Nisot, "L'exception 'non adimpleti contractus' en droit international", *Revue générale de droit international public*, vol. 74, 1970, p. 668; Niboyet, "Notion de réciprocité," p. 350.

[15] Gomaa, *Suspension or Termination of Treaties*, p. 97, F. L. Kirgis Jr., "Some Lingering Questions about Article 60 of the Vienna Convention on the Law of Treaties," *Cornell International Law Journal*, vol. 22, 1989, pp. 557–558.

Convention" or a "violation of a provision essential to the accomplishment of the object or purpose of the treaty."[16]

While Article 60 permits suspension or termination "in whole or in part," it does not limit *which* obligations may be suspended. As seen in Chapter 2, the exception of nonperformance generally permits non-execution of obligations that are somehow directly correlated with, or in a synallagmatic relationship to, those breached; to suspend what has been given in exchange for the performance originally stipulated. This was the argument used by Greece in the case brought by the FYROM.[17] However, despite Fitzmaurice's assertion in discussions at the ILC that nonperformance be "equivalent and corresponding,"[18] no such limitation exists in Article 60, aside from the suspension or termination being limited to the entirety or part of the same treaty that has been breached.[19] Treaties are therefore considered as a whole; the exception of nonperformance in international law is not therefore limited to the other "end" of a synallagmatic obligation.

5.1.4 *The Distinction between Types of Obligation in Article 60.2*

Article 60 also operates a distinction between types of treaty obligation. Paragraph 1 sets out that any party to a bilateral treaty may invoke its material breach as a ground for termination or suspension. This reflects the fact that under a bilateral treaty, obligations will obviously arise bilaterally.[20] However, the article also "bilateralizes" obligations within multilateral conventions, in Article 60.2(b), according to which a party specially affected by the breach of a multilateral treaty may invoke the exception of nonperformance and suspend the treaty in its bilateral relations with the defaulting State.[21] Obviously, it is not possible for one party to single-handedly terminate a multilateral treaty,[22] however,

16 Kirgis analyses the threshold of "material breach" with respect to the Algiers Accords, "Some Lingering Questions," pp. 551–555.

17 Application of the Interim Accord of 13 September 1995 (the *Former Yugoslav Republic of Macedonia* v. *Greece)*, para. 115. Interestingly, one of the reasons the Court rejected this argument, aside from the absence of breach, was the absence of any factual connection between the action taken by Greece and the FYROM's alleged breaches; ibid., para. 161.

18 ILC, Fourth Report on the Law of Treaties, Sir Gerald Fitzmaurice, Doc. No. A/CN.4/120, p. 50.

19 Gomaa, *Suspension or Termination of Treaties*, p. 118.

20 A. Yahi, "La violation d'un traité: l'articulation du droit des traités et du droit de la responsabilité internationale," *Revue Belge de droit international*, vol. 2, 1993 p. 442.

21 Gomaa, *Suspension or Termination of Treaties*, p. 103.

22 ILC, Fifth Report on the Law of Treaties by Sir Humphrey Waldock, Special Rapporteur, Doc. No. A/CN.4/183 and Add.1-4, p. 3; Crawford, "Multilateral Rights and Obligations," p. 430.

the breach gives the State it specially affects the option not to fulfill its obligations.

The reason why only the specially affected State may suspend the operation of the treaty is that most of the time, a breach of a multilateral treaty will not necessarily affect all States parties.[23] However, there are two exceptions. The first is, under Article 60.2(a), when all States party to the treaty may unanimously decide to suspend or terminate its operation; the second is the case of interdependent obligations in Article 60.2(c), where any party other than the defaulting State may suspend the operation of the treaty when a material breach "radically changes the position of every party with respect to further performance." In these types of obligation, "a breach by one party tends to undermine the whole regime of the treaty as between all the parties."[24] In previous ILC drafts, this type of obligation was also referred to as "reciprocal."[25]

Previous drafts also limited obligations whose performance could be refused to those "which consist in a reciprocal interchange between the parties of rights, benefits concessions or advantages, or of a right to particular treatment in some field with respect to a particular matter," and those "which have been the subject of the breach, and which are of such a kind that, by reason of the character of the treaty, their performance by any party is necessarily dependent on an equal or corresponding performance by all the other parties,"[26] explicitly excluding the possibility of suspending obligations on the basis of a fundamental breach in treaties where "the juridical force of the obligation is inherent, and not dependent on a corresponding performance by the other parties to the treaty."[27] The ILC finally chose not to differentiate between "general law-making" and other types of multilateral treaty.[28]

[23] Gomaa, *Suspension or Termination of Treaties*, p. 65.

[24] ILC, Draft Articles on the Law of Treaties, 1966, A/6309/Rev.1, p. 255. As seen in Chapter 3, examples of this type of treaty include disarmament treaties.

[25] ILC, Second Report on the Law of Treaties by Mr. G. G. Fitzmaurice, Special Rapporteur, Doc. No. A/CN.4/107, p. 31; ILC, Summary Records of the Fifteenth Session, 6 May–12 July 1963, *Yearbook of the International Law Commission*, vol. I, 1963, 692nd meeting, p. 127; Campiglio, "Principio di reciprocità," p. 273.

[26] ILC, Second Report on the Law of Treaties by Mr. G. G. Fitzmaurice, Special Rapporteur, Doc. No. A/CN.4/107, p. 31.

[27] ILC, Second Report on the Law of Treaties by Mr. G. G. Fitzmaurice, Special Rapporteur, Doc. No. A/CN.4/107, p. 31; this reflects the distinction between bilateral and unilateral contracts.

[28] ILC, Draft Articles on the Law of Treaties, 1966, A/6309/Rev.1, p. 255.

5.1.5 *The Raison d'Être of the Exception of Nonperformance*

The particularities of the exception in international law – the fact that it applies to the entirety of a treaty, and not only to the obligations correlated to the breach, and the procedural conditions that must be fulfilled – may also be traced back to the usefulness of the exception as a means of self-enforcement of sorts in a legal system that lacks a centralized enforcement structure.

However, the exception of nonperformance may not be equated to a countermeasure. First of all, the exception as codified in Article 60 forms part of the law of treaties, and countermeasures belong to the law of State responsibility. As the ICJ stated in the *Gabčíkovo-Nagymaros* case,

> A determination of whether a convention is or is not in force, and whether it has or has not been properly suspended or denounced, is to be made pursuant to the law of treaties. On the other hand, the evaluation of the extent to which the suspension or denunciation of a convention, seen as incompatible with the law of treaties, involves the responsibility of the State which proceeded to it, is to be made under the law of State responsibility.[29]

Article 60 of the VCLT sets out the conditions under which parties to a treaty may invoke a material breach as a ground for suspension or termination. Taking a countermeasure, instead, does not terminate the obligation; it merely precludes the wrongfulness of nonperformance, while the primary rule itself continues in force. To put it otherwise, countermeasures form part of the secondary rules of international law, that is, they are part of the legal consequences of a breach of an international obligation. The exception of nonperformance, instead, relates to the question of whether a primary rule is still in force.[30]

Second, countermeasures may suspend any rule that is applicable between the responsible and injured States, and not only the treaty that has been breached. Third, the exception of nonperformance applies only to treaties,[31] whereas international obligations of any source may

[29] *Gabcikovo-Nagymaros Project (Hungary/Slovakia)*, Judgment of 25 September 1997, ICJ Reports 1997, para. 47. See further P.-M. Dupuy, "Droit des traités, codification et responsabilité internationale," *Annuaire français de droit international*, vol. 43, 1997, particularly pp. 19–20, 23–25.

[30] That is, the two mechanisms belong to the spheres of secondary and primary rules respectively, in the sense employed by Roberto Ago: "[I]t is one thing to define a rule and the content of the obligation it imposes, and another to determine whether that obligation has been violated and what should be the consequences of the violation," ILC, Draft Articles on Responsibility of States, p. 31.

[31] ILC, Report of the International Law Commission on the Work of Its Fifty-First session, A/54/10, pp. 165, 168; Kirgis, "Some Lingering Questions," p. 567.

be suspended in taking countermeasures. But there is a further difference. The exception of nonperformance is aimed at giving grounds for suspending or terminating obligations because a material breach compromises the equality of the parties, and as such is linked mainly to considerations of fairness; it reflects the correlation between international rights and obligations in a specific treaty instrument, and therefore the reciprocity that underpins all treaties. Countermeasures, in contrast, are meant to ensure that compliance resumes after a breach.[32]

5.1.6 *Restrictions*

Article 60 sets out some limitations to obligations that can be suspended or terminated on the basis of nonperformance. First of all, Article 60.4 sets out that "the foregoing paragraphs are without prejudice to any provision in the treaty applicable in the event of a breach." The possibility of suspending a treaty in response to material breach by a party is therefore residual in nature, and a treaty itself may specify that it cannot be suspended or terminated on the basis of nonperformance. For example, suspension of obligations as a response to material breach is not available in the EU treaties, where an institutional apparatus exists to regulate the consequences of a breach.[33]

While treaties of an integral type are not explicitly excluded from the applicability of Article 60, Article 60.2(b) sets out a structural limitation of similar effect. According to this subparagraph, a party to a multilateral treaty can invoke the suspension of the operation of all or part of the treaty "in its relations between itself and the defaulting State." This provision requires that the obligations in question actually be bilateralizable. If they are not, it is Article 60.2(a) that becomes applicable, in which the material breach entitles "the other parties by unanimous agreement to suspend the operation of the treaty in whole or in part or to terminate it" either between themselves and the defaulting State, or between all the parties. In other words, States may not bilaterally with-

[32] Provost, "Reciprocity in Human Rights," p. 399; D. Azaria, *Treaties on Transit of Energy via Pipelines and Countermeasures*, Oxford, Oxford University Press, 2015, p. 144; ILC, Draft Articles on the Law of Treaties, 1966, A/6309/Rev.1, p. 255.

[33] Consolidated Versions of the Treaty on European Union and of the Treaty Establishing the European Community, 2002, *Official Journal of the European Communities*, 2002/C 325/01, Article 35.7, Articles 235–237, Article 292 ("Member States undertake not to submit a dispute concerning the interpretation or application of this Treaty to any method of settlement other than those provided for therein"). Dero, *Réciprocité et le droit*, pp. 30, 342–343; Campiglio, "Principio di reciprocità," pp. 76, 236, 301, 307–308.

hold performance of a treaty whose obligations operate *erga omnes partes*.[34] It is also obviously not possible for States to suspend peremptory norms on the basis of a prior nonperformance, by virtue of their inderogable nature.

Furthermore, there is an explicit, substantive limitation to the applicability of Article 60 in its paragraph 5, according to which the right to invoke a material breach as grounds for termination or suspension does "not apply to provisions relating to the protection of the human person contained in treaties of a humanitarian character, in particular to provisions prohibiting any form of reprisals against persons protected by such treaties." The reference to treaties of a "humanitarian character" would seem to include treaties of humanitarian law, as well as the Genocide Convention, refugee conventions, and human rights treaties.[35]

This provision was introduced at the Vienna Conference on the Law of Treaties on the initiative of Switzerland. The main rationale was to safeguard the provisions of the Geneva Conventions prohibiting reprisals against protected persons, as well as other agreements or declarations registered with a neutral intermediary by States expressing the wish to observe their principles, which "should not be exposed to termination or suspension that would endanger human life."[36] These, however, were not the only agreements taken into consideration; so were "other equally important conventions concerning the status of refugees, the prevention of slavery, the prohibition of genocide and the protection of human rights in general" because "in no event should their violation by one party result in injury to innocent people."[37]

34 This seems to be what the ICJ affirmed in the Genocide Convention (*Bosnia-Herzegovina* v. *Serbia*) case; Application of the Convention on the Prevention and Punishment of the Crime of Genocide (*Bosnia and Herzegovina* v. *Yugoslavia*), Counter-Claims, International Court of Justice, Order of 17 December 1997, ICJ Reports 1997, para. 35, commented by Meron, "International Law in the Age of Human Rights," p. 302.

35 ILC, Third Report on State Responsibility, Gaetano Arangio-Ruiz, Special Rapporteur, A/CN.4/440 and Add.1, p. 33.

36 Comments by Mr. Bindschedler (Switzerland), United Nations Conference on the Law of Treaties, First Session, Vienna, 26 March–24 May 1968, Summary records of the plenary meetings and the meetings of the Committee of the Whole, Doc. No. A/CONF.39/11, p. 354.

37 Comments by Mr. Ruegger (Switzerland), United Nations Conference on the Law of Treaties, Second Session, Vienna, 9 April–22 May 1969, Summary records of the plenary meetings and the meetings of the Committee of the Whole, Doc. No. A/CONF.39/11/Add.1, p. 112; M. G. Kohen, "La codification du droit des traités: quelques éléments pour un bilan global," *Revue générale de droit international public*, vol. 104, no. 3, 2000, p. 591.

However, the question is whether this includes *any* provision relating to protection of the human person – which, it has been indicated, could apply to a wide variety of treaties, including on matters such as development.[38] Meron takes the position that the limitation in Article 60.5 "leaves intact the right of a State to suspend those provisions which do not relate to the protection of human rights and humanitarian norms and do not constitute *jus cogens* in response to a material breach of a humanitarian or human rights treaty."[39] Considering also the examples given by the Swiss delegate at the Vienna Conference, this seems to be a correct appraisal; the prohibitions of genocide and slavery are clearly peremptory norms of international law. Indeed, the general rationale for the inclusion of the restriction was that "[t]he absence of a proviso on the fundamental rules for the protection of the human person would be dangerous"; the humanitarian restriction "would simply be a saving clause to protect human beings."[40]

Despite the lack of practice on the issue, it is therefore justified to consider that the restriction in Article 60.5 is intended to cover fundamental rules concerning protection of the human person. This limit may be considered a substantive one, in the sense that it is not a question of the impossibility of suspending or terminating treaties under which individuals have direct rights, nor *any* treaty concerning the treatment of individuals. For example, treaties concerning protection of investments, although they concern treatment of individuals, would still be liable to suspension or termination on grounds of material breach. It also does not make sense to rely on any "nonreciprocal" nature of these treaties as a discerning factor,[41] as Article 60 does not distinguish between treaties on such a basis. Even a strictly inter-State agreement would fall under the Article 60.5 exception if its provisions were of a humanitarian nature and their suspension or termination caused injury to individuals.

5.1.7 *Conclusion*

The exception of nonperformance cannot be seen as a general principle that applies in all areas of international law, nor as allowing any

[38] ILC, Third Report on State Responsibility, Gaetano Arangio-Ruiz, Special Rapporteur, A/CN.4/440 and Add.1, p. 33.

[39] Meron, "International Law in the Age of Human Rights," p. 40.

[40] Comments by Mr. Ruegger (Switzerland), United Nations Conference on the Law of Treaties, Second Session, Doc. No. A/CONF.39/11/Add.1, p. 112.

[41] As Combacau does: Combacau and Sur, *Droit International Public*, p. 391.

obligation to be suspended or terminated by virtue of any breach. It is instead limited to a particular ground for terminating or suspending treaties in whole or in part under specific conditions. While it undeniably stems from reciprocity, there is no "principle of reciprocity" on the basis of which treaty obligations, or indeed general international law, may be suspended or terminated in response to a breach. It is, rather, one of the mechanisms applicable in the execution of obligations of international law that reflects the reciprocity of rights and obligations. As the next section will address, this reciprocity of rights and obligations also lies at the basis of the law of State responsibility.

5.2 Reciprocity in the Law of State Responsibility

State responsibility, the set of secondary rules that sets out the legal consequences of breaches of international law, is also the area that tells us most as to the structure of international law in general. In fact, the main distinction between "contemporary" international law and "classical" international law is generally taken to be the existence, in the latter, of obligations *erga omnes* and peremptory norms, or *jus cogens*.[42] Chapter 3 analyzed the various types of bilateral, integral, and interdependent obligation with respect to reciprocity. This section will complete that analysis by looking at whether there are structural differences in the consequences that stem from violation of peremptory or *erga omnes* rules – and specifically, whether these consequences escape the operation of reciprocity.

State responsibility may be defined as the new legal relations arising from the breach of a rule of international law.[43] Unlike the exception of nonperformance, which, as codified in Article 60 of the VCLT, provides a ground of suspension or termination of a treaty, the aim of State responsibility is for compliance with an obligation that has been breached to resume where possible.[44] Under the law of State responsibility, the main obligation arising from a breach is for the responsible State to make reparation for the injury it has caused.[45] International responsibility arises when two objective conditions are met: when there is a breach

[42] Crawford terms these the "*grandes verticales*" of international law, "Multilateral Rights and Obligations," p. 397.

[43] ILC, Draft Articles on Responsibility of States, pp. 32–33.

[44] Ibid., p. 87.

[45] Ibid., GA Res. 56/83 of 12 December 2001, Art. 31; this goes as far back as Hugo Grotius, *Rights of War ... book 2*, Chs. 1–2; Book 3, Chs. XIX, XV–XVIII. On the role of damage in Roman law, see Dupuy, "Fait générateur," p. 22.

of an obligation and when that breach may be attributed to a State.[46] State responsibility is also nonpunitive in nature. These characteristics point toward an expectation that reciprocity should play an important role in State responsibility, which is intersubjective, and tends toward a reestablishment of balance between responsible and injured States.

5.2.1 *The Nature of Obligations in the ILC Articles*

The law of State responsibility is set out in the ILC's Articles on the Responsibility of States for Internationally Wrongful Acts (referred to henceforth by the acronym "ARSIWA," or as "ILC Articles"), the fruit of a four-decade codification effort. The ILC Articles are, however, residual in nature and States can decide to establish different, specific consequences for the breach of certain rules.[47] The ARSIWA also do not cover the entirety of the consequences of breaches of international law, as they only concern States, and not individuals or international organizations.[48]

The rules of State responsibility form a unitary system; that is, there is no distinction on the basis of the source of the rule being breached. The consequences are the same regardless of whether it is a treaty rule, customary law, a unilateral act, or any other possible source of obligation, and whether it is bilateral or multilateral in nature.[49]

5.2.1.1 Bilateral Obligations

Bilateral obligations are not necessarily only those set out in bilateral treaties, bilateral custom, or unilateral acts and promises but are those owed to a State "individually." This may also include obligations arising under a multilateral treaty "where particular performance is incumbent under the treaty as between one State party and another,"[50] that is, those that have been previously referred to as "bilateralizable" multilateral treaties. The legal relationship arising from a breach of a bilateral

[46] ILC, Articles on Responsibility of States for Internationally Wrongful Acts, Art. 2.

[47] Ibid., Art. 55, commentary, p. 32. See the example of the EU given by Dero, *Réciprocité et le droit*, pp. 12, 24, 30, 43, 63–64.

[48] ILC, Articles on Responsibility of States for Internationally Wrongful Acts, Arts. 57–58, commentary pp. 87–88. A set of articles on the responsibility of International Organizations was also drafted by the ILC in 2011, available in *Yearbook of the International Law Commission*, 2011, vol. II, Part Two.

[49] ILC, Articles on Responsibility of States for Internationally Wrongful Acts, commentary, pp. 55–56.

[50] ILC, Articles on Responsibility of States for Internationally Wrongful Acts, commentary, p. 118; Chinkin, *Third Parties in International Law*, p. 1; Sicilianos, "Classification of Obligations," p. 1133.

obligation will therefore only link the two States between which it operates, that is, the State violating the obligation and the State to which the obligation breached is owed. No other State will be legally concerned by the consequences of such a breach.[51]

Bilateral obligations are those in which it is perhaps easiest to see the operation of reciprocity, and these obligations are often referred to as "reciprocal" or "synallagmatic."[52] However, this is something of a misnomer, as not all bilateral obligations will have their performance conditioned upon execution by another party. This is notably the case of rules of customary international law such as those relating to innocent passage, where a breach involves two States, yet the existence of the rule does not depend on any bilateral condition of performance but rather on its acceptance by all States.[53]

5.2.1.2 Interdependent and Integral Obligations

Obligations whose operation in case of a breach cannot be reduced to a bilateral legal relationship are divided in the ARSIWA into two categories, reflecting the division in Article 60 VCLT: interdependent and integral obligations. Both of these concern obligations that are owed to a plurality of States.[54]

Interdependent obligations are those whose observance is conditioned upon performance by all other parties.[55] In ARSIWA Article 42(b)(ii), an "injured State" also includes one of a group of States among which an obligation operates whose breach "is of such a character as radically to change the position of all other States to which the obligation is owed with respect to [. . .] further performance" (a formulation that is identical to Article 60 VCLT). Interdependent obligations are synallagmatic, due to their reliance on performance by all parties. If one of the parties breaches an obligation of this nature, all other States parties to the treaty

[51] Chinkin, *Third Parties in International Law*, p. 292.

[52] See for example the use of these three terms made interchangeably by Cassese, *International Law in a Divided World*, pp. 28–29.

[53] Azaria identifies innocent passage as a "reciprocal" obligation in this sense, a good example of how an obligation may be bilateral and reciprocal, in the sense that there is a correlation between the right and obligation in question, but no relationship of conditionality. Azaria, *Treaties on Transit of Energy*, p. 114.

[54] ILC, Fourth Report on State Responsibility, by Mr. Gaetano Arangio-Ruiz, Special Rapporteur, Doc. No. A/CN.4/444 and Add. 1-3, *Yearbook of the International Law Commission*, vol. II, 1992, Part Two, p. 44.

[55] See Azaria giving the example of pipeline agreements, *Treaties on Transit of Energy*, pp. 115–116.

will be "injured States," because future performance is fundamentally compromised.[56]

The third kind of obligation envisaged by the ILC Articles is that of "integral" obligations. While some confusion in terminology occurred during debates at the ILC, the manner in which the two types of obligation function is essentially opposite. Multilateral obligations of the integral type apply regardless of how and whether they are executed by other parties. A breach therefore does not "radically change" the position of all other States to whom the obligation is owed. The best examples of such obligations are probably those relating to human rights. Because these apply internally within the State and with respect to individuals regardless of their nationality, performance is not dependant on respect of the same obligations by other States.[57] This "vertical" dimension in their application removes the possibility of a condition of reciprocity being a successful means of ensuring their observance.[58]

This type of obligation is covered by Article 42(b), that is, obligations owed to "a group of States" or "the international community as a whole." Under Article 42(b)(i), an injured State can be specially affected by the breach of an integral obligation,[59] while Article 48 outlines the action that may be taken by other States to whom the obligation is owed.

[56] P.-M. Dupuy, "Quarante ans de codification du droit de la responsabilité des etats: un bilan," *Revue générale de droit international public*, t. 107, 2003, p. 333; Sicilianos, "Classification of Obligations," pp. 1133–1135; ILC, Articles on Responsibility of States for Internationally Wrongful Acts, commentary, p. 119; Crawford, "Multilateral Rights and Obligations," p. 448; Dupuy, "Unité de l'ordre juridique international," p. 138; C. J. Tams, "Individual States as Guardians of Community Interests," in U. Fastenrath, ed., *From Bilateralism to Community Interest: Essays in Honour of Judge Bruno Simma*, Oxford, Oxford University Press, 2011, p. 385; ILC, Second Report on the Law of Treaties by Mr. G. G. Fitzmaurice, Special Rapporteur, Doc. No. A/CN.4/107, pp. 53–54.

[57] Dupuy, "Unité de l'ordre juridique international," p. 139; B. Simma, "Bilateralism and Community Interest in the Law of State Responsibility," in Y. Dinstein, ed., *International Law at a Time of Perplexity: Essays in Honour of Shabtai Rosenne*, Boston, Nijhoff, 1989, p. 823.

[58] Sykes, "When Is International Law Useful?," p. 448; ILC, Second Report on the Law of Treaties by Mr. G. G. Fitzmaurice, Special Rapporteur, Doc. No. A/CN.4/107, p. 54. Picone does not limit this to human rights but also includes other objects that are external to States, such as the environment, P. Picone, "Obblighi reciproci e obblighi erga omnes degli Stati nel campo della protezione internazionale dell'ambiente marino dall'inquinamento," in V. Starace, ed., *Diritto internazionale e protezione dell'ambiente marino*, Milano, Giuffrè, 1983, p. 33; Paulus, "Reciprocity Revisited," p. 119; ILC, Third Report on State Responsibility, James Crawford, Special Rapporteur, Doc. No. A/CN.4/507, 15 March 2000, p. 39.

[59] ILC, Articles on Responsibility of States for Internationally Wrongful Acts, Commentary, p. 127.

Taking reciprocity as the correlation of legal rights and obligations, integral obligations can be seen as a form of "global" reciprocity.[60] The very fact that they are owed to a group of States, or all States in the international community, highlights this fact. International legal obligations, even those owed to the international community, are not undertaken in the abstract; they are owed to other States, and all States have a right to see the obligations performed.[61]

The type of "integral" obligation envisaged in the articles can be further subdivided into two categories, reflected in Article 42(b) and 48.1. The first is an obligation owed to a group of States, which may also be termed *erga omnes partes*, and the second is owed to the international community as a whole, or *erga omnes*.[62]

The question arises as to what is meant by "international community as a whole." The international community does not have legal personality.[63] Instead, it is best seen as being composed of *all*

[60] Wyler and Papaux explain these as "*obligations assumées*," reciprocal in the recognition of values that are common to States, "Mythe structurant de l'humanité," 184. Frigo sees solidarity as a form of "generalised and multilateral reciprocity," Frigo, "Reciprocità nell'evoluzione," p. 475. P.-M. Dupuy takes the view that the characteristic of integral obligations is that reciprocity does not apply to the consequences of their violation, but as we shall see reciprocity may be seen as applicable in the consequences of their breach, "Unité de l'ordre juridique international," pp. 140–142.

[61] Klein, "Denunciation of Human Rights Treaties," p. 481; Paulus, "Reciprocity Revisited," p. 126; Gaja gives the example of the obligation to respect human rights still existing toward other States, G. Gaja, "*Jus Cogens* beyond the Vienna Convention," *Collected Courses of the Hague Academy of International Law*, vol. 172, 1981, p. 294; ILC, Fourth Report on State Responsibility, by Mr. Gaetano Arangio-Ruiz, Special Rapporteur, Doc. No. A/CN.4/444 and Add. 1-3, pp. 43–44; giving the example of the UN charter, Crawford, "Multilateral Rights and Obligations," p. 404; Byers, *Custom, Power and the Power of Rules*, p. 197.

[62] The first use of the term "obligations *erga omnes*" was made by the ICJ in its judgment in *Barcelona Traction*, defined as "obligations of a State toward the international community as a whole" where "in view of the importance of the rights involved, all States can be held to have a legal interest in their protection," *Barcelona Traction, Light and Power Company Lmited*, Judgment of 5 February 1970, I.C.J. Reports 1970, p. 32. The distinction between obligations *erga omnes* and *erga omnes partes* was also included in Institut de Droit International, "Resolution on Obligations *Erga Omnes* in International Law," Krakow Session, 2005; C. Dominicé, "The International Responsibility of States for Breaches of Multilateral Obligations," *European Journal of International Law*, vol. 10, no. 2, 1999, pp. 355–356; L.-A. Sicilianos, "L'influence des droits de l'homme sur la structure du droit international, Première partie: Les droits de l'homme et la hiérarchisation de l'ordre juridique international," *Revue générale de droit international public*, vol. 116, 2012, p. 9.

[63] E. K. Proukaki, *The Problem of Enforcement in International Law*, Abingdon, Routledge, 2010, p. 25; A. L. Vaurs-Chaumette, Ch. 70: The International Community as a Whole," in

States,[64] as well as, arguably, other subjects such as international organizations and individuals.[65] However, international organizations will be able to react to breaches of obligations only according to the terms of their constituent treaties, with the same being the case for individuals, who are only granted procedural rights under specific treaties in the case of a breach of their rights. The reference to the international community simply means that in the case of *erga omnes* obligations, all other States are right-holders.[66] This is also the point that distinguishes *erga omnes* obligations from peremptory norms.[67]

The requirement in Article 48.1(a) is that the "group" to which an *erga omnes partes* obligation is owed be "established for the protection of a collective interest." The existence of this collective interest is therefore what pushes against the bilateralizable nature of the obligations.[68]

J. Crawford, A. Pellet, and S. Olleson, eds., *The Law of International Responsibility*, Oxford, Oxford University Press, 2010, p. 1023.

64 ILC, Articles on Responsibility of States for Internationally Wrongful Acts, Commentary, p. 127.

65 ILC, Fourth Report on State Responsibility, by Mr. James Crawford, Special Rapporteur, Doc. No. A/CN.4/517 and Add. 1, p. 10; Crawford, "Multilateral Rights and Obligations," p. 447.

66 Vaurs-Chaumette, "Ch. 70: The International Community," 1025.

67 This distinguishes *erga omnes* obligations from peremptory norms. Whereas the two categories will in fact overlap in most cases the point of *erga omnes* obligations is not their inderogability. Crawford, "Multilateral Rights and Obligations," p. 412; ILC, Fourth Report on State Responsibility, by Mr. James Crawford, Special Rapporteur, Doc. No. A/CN.4/517 and Add. 1, p. 13. There are other differences, such as the fact a treaty that derogates from *erga omnes* obligations is not in itself void, as would be the case for a treaty derogating from a *jus cogens* norm: Gaja, "*Jus Cogens* beyond the Vienna Convention," p. 281, although because an *erga omnes* obligation is owed to all States, the effect of States derogating from it would still be a wrongful act as regards those not agreeing to sign the new treaty. The one point to make is that consent to derogate from an *erga omnes* obligation is not precluded, whereas consent does not apply as a circumstance precluding wrongfulness to peremptory norms; this is set out in Article 26 of the ILC Articles; Proukaki, *The Problem of Enforcement in International Law*, p. 50; Byers explains *jus cogens* as simply "a description of certain characteristics" of given norms, rather than reflecting any structural difference, *Custom, Power and the Power of Rules*, p. 195.

68 ILC, Sixth Report on the Content, Forms and Degrees of International Responsibility (Part Two of the draft articles); and "Implementation" (mise en oeuvre) of international responsibility and the settlement of disputes (part three of the draft articles), Riphagen, Special Rapporteur, Doc. No. A/CN.4/389 and Corr.1& Corr.2, p. 8; Sicilianos, "Influence des droits de l'homme," p. 249; ILC, Fourth Report on State Responsibility, by Mr. Gaetano Arangio-Ruiz, Special Rapporteur, Doc. No. A/CN.4/444 and Add. 1-3, p. 44. Dero sees the ECHR as excluding reciprocity because it creates a collective obligation, *Réciprocité et le droit*, p. 46. There is an argument to be made that it is not only "integral" obligations that are meant to protect a collective interest. Crawford gives the example of

All States are therefore legally affected by a breach of an *erga omnes* obligation, and all States may take action of some form in response to a breach. Interestingly, the ILC had originally envisaged the possibility of all States being defined as "injured" by the breach of an *erga omnes* obligation.[69] *Erga omnes* obligations demonstrate a form of generalized reciprocity, according to which all States may take some form of action in response to a breach and request compliance with the obligations.[70]

The reason for this may be seen in connection with two seemingly opposite phenomena. The first is international law's structure, based on sovereign equality and lacking any centralized enforcement mechanism, which leaves it up to States to deal with breaches of obligations, even those owed to the international community as a whole.[71] The second is the increasing factual interdependence of States,[72] which increases the need for collective regulation and therefore the spread of collective obligations.

5.2.1.3 Correlation between Rights and Obligations

The analysis so far illustrates a fundamental point that is connected to the horizontal structure of international society. That is, obligations in international law are relative, and not absolute. Obligations do not exist in the abstract, but only in relation to other subjects of international law, which may on occasion be individuals but are in general States. This is

diplomatic relations, rules concerning which may be seen to protect not only specific interests of States but a fundamental collective interest of all States, "Multilateral Rights and Obligations," p. 449. P.-M. Dupuy cites the "collective interest" as one reason why this kind of obligation is not reciprocal, "Unité de l'ordre juridique international," pp. 138, 142.

69 See ILC, Third Report on State Responsibility, James Crawford, Special Rapporteur, Doc. No. A/CN.4/507, pp. 40–41; ILC, Fourth Report on State Responsibility, by Mr. Gaetano Arangio-Ruiz, Special Rapporteur, Doc. No. A/CN.4/444 and Add. 1-3, pp. 44–45; Crawford, "Multilateral Rights and Obligations," p. 433.

70 Picone, "Obblighi reciproci e obblighi erga omnes," pp. 27, 55, 59, 87–88; Crawford, "Multilateral Rights and Obligations," p. 413; Byers, *Custom, Power and the Power of Rules*, pp. 196–197; *East Timor (Portugal* v. *Australia)*, Judgment of 30 June 1995, ICJ Reports 1995, Dissenting Opinion of Judge Weeramantry, p. 172, explains the operation of *erga omnes* obligations in this manner as between pairs of States; at p. 216, he states that "the current state of international law requires that violations of the concept be followed through to their logical and legal conclusion." The position of all other States in the case of a violation of an *erga omnes* obligation is not therefore that of "third States," as it would be were the obligations at issue only bilateral: Sicilianos, "Influence des droits de l'homme," p. 248.

71 Picone, "Obblighi reciproci e obblighi erga omnes," p. 74; Crawford, "Multilateral Rights and Obligations," pp. 344–346.

72 Dupuy, "Fait générateur," p. 110.

sometimes referred to as the "bilateral" structure of international law;[73] however it is more accurate to see it as the reciprocal basis of international law: Every obligation is owed to another State, which holds the correlative right to see the obligation performed, and every right entails an obligation.[74]

This is so as a consequence of a structural factor, namely the sovereign equality of States. Without any legally superior centralizing institution in the international system, responsibility is only conceivable in terms of subjective rights and obligations.[75] The domestic and international legal systems are quite simply completely different – this is why State responsibility is not civil or criminal, but simply international. This principally horizontal structure of international society explains why State responsibility functions the way it does. Introducing truly vertical elements in the international legal order would require the existence of an entity placed above States – but discussions on the desirability of such a structure can only fall outside the scope of law and into that of political philosophy.

5.3 State Responsibility and the Reciprocity of Rights and Obligations

While all international legal obligations have, in the end, a correlative right-bearer in a relationship of legal equality with the State holding the obligation, there are different degrees to which States may be concerned by the obligation in question and the extent to which they may be injured by a breach. This section will therefore address the differing extent of injury in the ILC Articles, and whether this differentiation has any significance for the reciprocity of international legal obligations.

[73] See ie. Proukaki, *The Problem of Enforcement in International Law*, p. 12; Picone, "Obblighi reciproci e obblighi erga omnes," p. 22.

[74] ILC, Articles on Responsibility of States for Internationally Wrongful Acts, Commentary, p. 35; Crawford, "Multilateral Rights and Obligations," pp. 243, 433; ILC, Second Report on State Responsibility, by Roberto Ago, Special Rapporteur, Doc. A/CN.4/233, pp. 181, 183, 192–193; see also comment by the government of Canada, ILC A/CN.4/19 1950, p. 197; ILC, Third Report on State Responsibility, James Crawford, Special Rapporteur, Doc. No. A/CN.4/507, pp. 33, 37.

[75] A. Ollivier, "Ch. 49: International Criminal Responsibility of the State," in J. Crawford, A. Pellet, and S. Olleson, eds., *The Law of International Responsibility*, Oxford, Oxford University Press, 2010, p. 705; Arangio-Ruiz spoke of the lack of centralization being particularly keenly felt in the law of State responsibility, ILC, Third Report on State Responsibility, Gaetano Arangio-Ruiz, Special Rapporteur, A/CN.4/440 and Add.1, p. 7.

5.3.1 *Injured States under Article 42*

The circumstances in which a State may be considered "injured" by a breach of an international obligation are set out in Article 42 of the ARSIWA. As mentioned above, this covers not only States to whom an obligation is owed individually, in Article 42(a), as is the case for a bilateral obligation, but also States that are specially affected by the breach of an integral obligation (*erga omnes* or *erga omnes partes*) in Article 42(b)(i), or any State in the context of the breach of an interdependent obligation, in Article 42(b)(ii).

A State specially affected by the breach of an *erga omnes* or *erga omnes partes* obligation, though not defined in the articles, may be considered "affected to a special extent, over and above the position of other States parties."[76] For example, in the case of a breach of the prohibition of aggression in international law, the specially affected State would be the State against whom the act of aggression is carried out. A similar case arising from a treaty rule could be the obligation to prevent, reduce, or control pollution of the seas in Article 194 UNCLOS. In case of a breach, the specially affected State is the one on whose coasts the pollution has occurred, even though the obligation to prevent pollution is still owed to all States under the treaty. Similarly, if the pollution in question were to spread to the shores of more than one other country, there may be a number of States injured by the same breach.[77]

An injured State does not therefore only have a legal interest in the obligation. The primary obligation must have been violated in its own respect, and not just the right it has to see that obligation observed by other States. For example, by virtue of their being parties to the Genocide Convention, all States have the right to see the obligation to prevent genocide observed by all other States parties, and this can give rise to a right for States to demand performance of their obligations by other States parties, even if they are not injured, as clearly seen in the case brought by the Gambia against Myanmar at the ICJ.[78] However, unless genocide is committed by one State party on the territory of another, or

[76] Crawford, "Multilateral Rights and Obligations," p. 428.

[77] ILC, Third Report on State Responsibility, James Crawford, Special Rapporteur, Doc. No. A/CN.4/507, p. 45.

[78] Application of the Convention on the Prevention and Punishment of the Crime of Genocide (*The Gambia* v. *Myanmar*), Provisional Measures, Order of 23 January 2020, I.C.J. Reports 2020, p. 3.

for example targeting its nationals, other States parties will not be injured by a breach in the sense of Article 42.[79]

An injured State has the right to invoke the responsibility of the State breaching the obligation. Invocation is a formal set of steps and should be distinguished from mere protest or calls for observation of the obligation. No particular entitlement is required to protest against breaches of international law.[80] Invocation involves making a specific claim "such as for compensation for a breach affecting it, or specific action such as the filing of an application before a competent international tribunal, or even the taking of countermeasures."[81] It should be recalled that the obligation of a State responsible for an internationally wrongful act to make reparation for the injury is not contingent on any State invoking its responsibility, but this obligation arises directly from the commission of the wrongful act.[82] The extent to which any entities that are not States will be able to invoke the responsibility of the State is instead set out in the specific primary rule.[83]

5.3.2 Other than Injured States under Article 48

In earlier drafts of the ILC Articles, it had been envisaged that all States could be considered injured by breaches of *erga omnes* obligations.[84] Eventually, the recognition that States could be injured differently by the same breach was reflected in the "other than an injured State" category in Article 48. States parties to an *erga omnes* obligation remain affected by its breach, whether or not there is an injured State in the sense of Article 42, and have a right to see the obligation performed.[85]

[79] See the distinction with legal interest in See ILC, Articles on Responsibility of States for Internationally Wrongful Acts, Commentary, p. 117.

[80] Ibid.; E. Brown Weiss, "Invoking State Responsibility in the Twenty-First Century," *The American Journal of International Law*, vol. 96, no. 4, 2002, p. 800; ILC, Third Report on State Responsibility, James Crawford, Special Rapporteur, Doc. No. A/CN.4/507, p. 46.

[81] ILC, Articles on Responsibility of States for Internationally Wrongful Acts, Commentary, p. 117.

[82] Ibid., Article 31; ILC, Third Report on State Responsibility, James Crawford, Special Rapporteur, Doc. No. A/CN.4/507, p. 15.

[83] ILC, Articles on Responsibility of States for Internationally Wrongful Acts, Commentary, p. 115.

[84] ILC, Fourth Report on State Responsibility, by Mr. Gaetano Arangio-Ruiz, Special Rapporteur, Doc. No. A/CN.4/444 and Add. 1-3, pp. 45–49.

[85] G. Gaja, "Ch. 62: The Concept of an Injured State," in J. Crawford, A. Pellet, and S. Olleson, eds., *The Law of International Responsibility*, Oxford, Oxford University Press, 2010, p. 947; Crawford, "Multilateral Rights and Obligations," p. 443; Brown Weiss, "Invoking State Responsibility," p. 803; Gaja, "Ch. 62," p. 941.

"Other than injured" States under Article 48 can invoke the fulfillment of cessation, assurances of nonrepetition if applicable, and reparation. However, this invocation of responsibility is not for their own benefit, in the same way it is for an injured State. They may not insist on reparation toward themselves but "only in the interest of the injured State or the beneficiaries of the obligation breached."[86] This reflects the fact that many *erga omnes* obligations may be owed to entities that are not States, such as individuals, in the case of human rights, or peoples, in the case of the right to self-determination; or they may protect areas that are beyond national jurisdiction. Without this generalized standing in Article 48, the breach of an *erga omnes* obligation would not have any consequences aside from the responsible State having the obligation to resume performance and provide reparation, as set out in ARSIWA Articles 29, 30 and 31[87] – an obligation, however, that would only exist in the abstract. The rights of individuals and other entities in international law therefore still depend for enforcement on the horizontal, reciprocal structure of international obligations.

5.3.3 *The Rejection of the Concept of "Crimes"*

The 1996 draft of the ILC Articles contained the notorious Article 19, which set out the category of "crime" of State. This was an internationally wrongful act "which results from the breach of an international obligation so essential for the protection of fundamental interests of the international community that its breach is recognized as a crime." The nature of international crime did not however only attach to given categories of norms but also depended on the seriousness of the breach.[88] In the case of a "crime," all States were to be considered

[86] ILC, Articles on Responsibility of States for Internationally Wrongful Acts, Aricle 48.2(b); ILC Commentary, p. 126; ILC, Report of the International Law Commission to the General Assembly on the Work of Its Fifty-Second Session, Doc. No. A/CN.4/SER.A/2000/Add.1 (Part 2)/Rev.1, *Yearbook of the International Law Commission*, 2000, Vol. II, Part Two, p. 33; Sicilianos, "Influence des droits de l'homme," p. 249, speaking of the Genocide case before the ICJ, or see the analysis of the South West Africa cases by Crawford, "Multilateral Rights and Obligations," p. 437.

[87] ILC, Report of the International Law Commission to the General Assembly on the Work of Its Fifty-Second Session, Doc. No. A/CN.4/SER.A/2000/Add.1 (Part 2)/Rev.1, pp. 57–58; ILC, Articles on Responsibility of States for Internationally Wrongful Acts, Commentary, p. 127; ILC, Third Report on State Responsibility, James Crawford, Special Rapporteur, Doc. No. A/CN.4/507, pp. 48–49; Gaja, "Ch. 62," pp. 958, 961.

[88] Draft Articles on State Responsibility Adopted by the International Law Commission on First Reading, January 1997, Doc. No. A/CN.4/L. 528/Add. 2, Article 19.

injured.[89] The concept was abandoned in the final Articles:[90] As well as a reticence to accept a concept as loaded as that of a "crime," it was not possible to establish what the generally recognized legal consequences of such a "crime" would be.[91]

Such a differentiation could have had important consequences for international law, depending on how it was to be implemented. The concept was meant to be a move away from the "bilateralist" system of State responsibility.[92] However, the only manner in which it could have made a significant difference in the structure of State responsibility would have been if there had been a general, centralized, and institutional response in the case of crimes, which would have introduced an element of verticality that would have distinguished the "horizontal" and intersubjective response to regular internationally wrongful acts, or "delicts," from an institutionalized and centralized response to serious breaches of fundamental rules, or "crimes."[93] Had there been an institutional expression of the international community to provide this response, it would have been possible to say that a part of the law of State responsibility, and indeed international law, escaped the operation of reciprocity, its implementation not being left to the inter-State plane.

The need to recognize that not all internationally wrongful acts are the same is to some extent reflected in Chapter III of Part Two of the ILC

[89] Draft Articles on State Responsibility with Commentaries thereto Adopted by the International Law Commission on First Reading, January 1997, Report of the International Law Commission on the Work of Its Forty-Eighth Session, 6 May–26 July 1996, Official Records of the General Assembly, Fifty-First session, Supplement No. 10, *Yearbook of the International Law Commission*, 1996, vol. II(2), Doc. No. A/51/10; Crawford, "Multilateral Rights and Obligations," pp. 433–434; Proukaki, *The Problem of Enforcement in International Law*, p. 77.

[90] The concept of crime of State was rejected by the ICJ in the Bosnian Genocide case, Application of the Convention on the Prevention and Punishment of the Crime of Genocide (*Bosnia and Herzegovina* v. *Serbia and Montenegro*), Judgment, ICJ Reports 2007, para. 170.

[91] ILC, Fourth Report on the Content, Forms and Degrees of International Responsibility (Part Two of the draft articles), Riphagen, Special Rapporteur, Doc. No. A/CN.4/366 and Add. 1 & Add/Corr.1, p. 11.

[92] M. Spinedi, "From One Codification to Another: Bilateralism and Multilateralism in the Genesis of the Codification of the Law of Treaties and the Law of State Responsibility," *European Journal of International Law*, vol. 13, no. 5, 2002, p. 1116; A. Frowein, "Reactions by Not Directly Affected States to Breaches of International Law," *Collected Courses of the Hague Academy of International Law*, vol. 248, 1994, p. 413.

[93] E. Wyler, "From 'State Crime' to Responsibility for 'Serious Breaches of Obligations under Peremptory Norms of General International Law,'" *European Journal of International Law*, vol. 13, no. 5, 2002, p. 1148, explains that "previous Drafts [...] had failed in establishing a legal system specifically tailored to international crimes."

Articles. Under Article 40, breaches of peremptory norms involving a "gross or systematic failure by the responsible State to fulfil the obligation" place an obligation on all States to cooperate to bring such a breach to an end, and to not recognize the lawfulness of the situation or render aid or assistance in maintaining it. Nonrecognition has long been employed to debar any legal consequences arising from the commission of such acts – although this specification is unnecessary when speaking of peremptory norms, which cannot be derogated from in any case, including through explicit acceptance. Recognition would not have any legal effect in such a situation anyway. If the breach is ongoing, then States would most likely not be able to render aid or assistance without incurring responsibility under Article 16 of the ARSIWA. There are therefore no further specific consequences for serious breaches of peremptory norms. The duty to cooperate itself seems to be a piece of progressive development by the ILC and cannot in any case be equated to a centralized response. There is therefore no real difference in terms of the legal consequences of a serious breach of a peremptory norm and of any other internationally wrongful act, and no aggravated obligations weighing on a State that has committed such a serious breach; the consequences set out in Article 41 apply only to other States.[94]

5.4 Countermeasures

Countermeasures are measures of self-help taken by States,[95] defined as "act[s] of State not in conformity with an international obligation" under Article 22 of ARSIWA. When such action is taken toward a State responsible for an internationally wrongful act, in accordance with the conditions set out in Articles 49–54, its wrongfulness is precluded. Countermeasures do not have the effect of terminating the obligation they violate but only temporarily excuse its nonperformance.[96]

The term "countermeasure" is often confused, or used interchangeably with, the notions of "sanction," "reprisal," and "retortion." Sanctions may

94 Wyler, "From 'State Crime' to Responsibility," p. 1151.

95 ILC, Articles on Responsibility of States for Internationally Wrongful Acts, Commentary, p. 134.

96 Ibid., p. 71; H. Lesaffre, "Ch. 33.4: Circumstances Precluding Wrongfulness in the ILC Articles on State Responsibility: Countermeasures," in J. Crawford, A. Pellet, and S. Olleson, *The Law of International Responsibility*, Oxford, Oxford University Press, 2010, p. 473; Lenhoff, "Reciprocity," p. 629; Proukaki, *The Problem of Enforcement in International Law*, p. 2; ILC, Report of the International Law Commission on the Work of Its Thirty-First Session, Doc. No. A/CN.4/SER.A/1979/Add. 1 (Part 2), p. 109.

be distinguished from countermeasures insofar as they imply a punitive action, and the term is considered more applicable to measures taken in an institutional setting.[97] "Retortion" is a response of unfriendly conduct that does not amount to a breach of international law.[98] It is always open to States to take retortionary measures. For example, the withdrawal of privileges that go beyond the treatment required by law would be an act of retortion rather than a countermeasure.[99]

"Reprisal" is the term that comes closest to the meaning of "countermeasure." The Institut de Droit International defined reprisals as

> Des mesures de contrainte, dérogatoires aux règles ordinaires du Droit des Gens, prises par un Etat à la suite d'actes illicites commis à son préjudice par un autre Etat et ayant pour but d'imposer à celui-ci, au moyen d'un dommage, le respect du droit."[100]

> [Coercive measures, derogating from the ordinary rules of the Law of Nations, taken by a State following illicit acts committed against it by another State and with the aim of imposing upon the latter, by means of an injury, respect for the law.]

The concept of "reprisal" is also very much tied to the context of the laws of war.[101] "Countermeasure" was considered more neutral by the ILC and was the terminology eventually retained.[102]

The taking of a countermeasure is linked to reestablishing equality between the parties upon the violation of an obligation.[103]

[97] ILC, Third Report on State Responsibility, Gaetano Arangio-Ruiz, Special Rapporteur, A/CN.4/440 and Add.1, p. 10, although it was indicated in ILC debates that even the UN does not speak of "sanctions," ILC, Report of the International Law Commission on the Work of Its Fifty-First Session, Doc. No. A/54/10, p. 163.

[98] ILC, Articles on Responsibility of States for Internationally Wrongful Acts, Commentary, p. 128; A. D. Mitchell, "Does One Illegality Merit Another? The Law of Belligerent Reprisals in International Law," *Military Law Review*, vol. 170, 2001,p. 156. The discussion in the ILC Articles also addressed the question whether the definition should be limited to unfriendly responses to unlawful, rather than just unfriendly, acts, ILC, Third Report on State Responsibility, Gaetano Arangio-Ruiz, Special Rapporteur, A/CN.4/440 and Add.1, p. 10.

[99] Notably in international humanitarian law, See Pictet, *Commentary to the IV Geneva Convention*, p. 227.

[100] Institut de Droit International, Session de Paris, 1934, "Régime des représailles en temps de paix," Article premier.

[101] Mitchell, "Does One Illegality Merit Another?," p. 157.

[102] ILC, Third Report on State Responsibility, Gaetano Arangio-Ruiz, Special Rapporteur, A/CN.4/440 and Add.1, p. 11.

[103] Proukaki, *The Problem of Enforcement in International Law*, p. 2; E. Zoller, *Peacetime Unilateral Remedies: An Analysis of Countermeasures*, Dobbs Ferry, Transnational, 1984, p. 14.

Countermeasures are also nonpunitive in nature,[104] their aim being to induce the State committing the breach to resume compliance with the rule.[105] The very existence of countermeasures is a consequence of the decentralized, horizontal structure of international law.[106] The question arises whether the rise of individual rights in international law has made any difference to the "classical" concept of countermeasure and what the role of countermeasures can be in ensuring respect for obligations owed to the international community as a whole.

5.4.1 *The Debate around Countermeasures and the Difference with Measures of Reciprocity*

Reciprocity appears to lie at the basis of the three types of consequences of a breach that may arise in international law: nonperformance, countermeasures, and retortion.[107] In discussions before the ILC, however, it was initially suggested to distinguish "reciprocity" as a separate, independent response, amounting to suspension or nonperformance of the *same* obligation violated in the case of certain specific reciprocal obligations. This differed to the case of countermeasures, in which *any* international obligation could be suspended.[108]

In the end, however, it was accepted that countermeasures covered both those measures that could be considered "reciprocal" insofar as they concerned only the nonperformance of the same obligation and

[104] D. Alland, "Countermeasures of General Interest," *European Journal of International Law*, vol. 13, no. 5, 2002, p. 1226; Ollivier, "Ch. 49: International Criminal Responsibility of the State," p. 707; ILC, Fourth Report on State Responsibility, by Mr. Gaetano Arangio-Ruiz, Special Rapporteur, Doc. No. A/CN.4/444 and Add. 1-3, p. 7.

[105] ILC, Articles on Responsibility of States for Internationally Wrongful Acts, Commentary, p. 131; ILC, Fourth Report on State Responsibility, by Mr. Gaetano Arangio-Ruiz, Special Rapporteur, Doc. No. A/CN.4/444 and Add. 1-3, p. 6.

[106] Virally, "Principe de réciprocité," 1967, p. 52; L.-A. Sicilianos, "Ch. 80: Countermeasures in Response to Grave Violations of Obligations Owed to the International Community," in J. Crawford, A. Pellet, and S. Olleson, eds., *The Law of International Responsibility*, Oxford, Oxford University Press, 2010, p. 1140; Paulus, "Reciprocity Revisited," pp. 120–121; Mitchell, "Does One Illegality Merit Another?," p. 175, avoiding a situation in which one State is bound to respect a rule that another State would benefit from without having to observe it, as in the laws of war, at 160.

[107] Simma, "Reciprocity," para. 14; Zoller, *Peacetime Unilateral Remedies*, p. 27; ILC, Third Report on State Responsibility, Gaetano Arangio-Ruiz, Special Rapporteur, A/CN.4/440 and Add.1, pp. 12–13.

[108] ILC, Third Report on State Responsibility, Gaetano Arangio-Ruiz, Special Rapporteur, A/CN.4/440 and Add.1, p. 11; ILC, Report of the International Law Commission on the Work of Its Fifty-First Session, 3 May–23 July 1999, Official Records of the General Assembly, Fifty-Fourth Session, Supplement No. 10, Doc. No. A/54/10, p. 142.

those that concerned nonperformance of a distinct obligation.[109] While a measure of "reciprocity" may be used as a descriptive term, there is no separate regime to that of countermeasures.

5.4.2 *The Legal Regime of Countermeasures*

Countermeasures are part of general international law and are general in character. Specific treaty regimes may exclude countermeasures from the mechanisms for enforcement of their obligations.[110]

A specific chapter of the ILC Articles is devoted to the conditions applying to countermeasures. The first condition, specified in Article 49.1, is that "a State may *only* take countermeasures against a State which is responsible for an internationally wrongful act" (emphasis added). This is therefore a built-in limitation of countermeasures: The wrongfulness of the conduct is only precluded in relation to the responsible State. Wrongfulness is not precluded against any third States that may also be owed the obligation subject of a countermeasure.[111] By definition, if by way of countermeasure a State does not perform a non-bilateralizable multilateral obligation – that is, an interdependent obligation, obligation *erga omnes* or *erga omnes partes* – the wrongfulness of this nonperformance will not be precluded with respect to States other than the responsible State.[112]

[109] ILC, Articles on Responsibility of States for Internationally Wrongful Acts, Commentary, p. 129; ILC, Report of the International Law Commission to the General Assembly on the Work of Its Fifty-Second Session, Doc. No. A/CN.4/SER.A/2000/Add.1 (Part 2)/Rev.1, p. 51; Proukaki, *The Problem of Enforcement in International Law*, p. 69.

[110] ILC, Articles on Responsibility of States for Internationally Wrongful Acts, Commentary, p. 133; see EC/EU case-law: *Commission of the E.E.C.* v. *Grand Duchy of Luxembourg and Kingdom of Belgium*, Cases Nos. 90 and 91/63, Judgment of 13 November 1964, p. 631; *Commission of the European Communities* v. *Federal Republic of Germany*, Case No. 325/82, Judgment of 14 February 1984, Separate Opinion of Judge Roemer, para. 183; Conforti, *Diritto Internazionale*, p. 367, at least unless and until the treaty mechanism itself breaks down, Proukaki, *The Problem of Enforcement in International Law*, p. 223.

[111] ILC, Articles on Responsibility of States for Internationally Wrongful Acts, Commentary, pp. 75, 129–130; ILC, Report of the International Law Commission to the General Assembly on the Work of Its Fifty-Second Session, Doc. No. A/CN.4/SER.A/2000/Add.1 (Part 2)/Rev.1, p. 52; ILC, Sixth Report on the Content, Forms and Degrees of International Responsibility (Part Two of the draft articles); and "Implementation" (mise en oeuvre) of international responsibility and the settlement of disputes (part three of the draft articles), Riphagen, Special Rapporteur, Doc. No. A/CN.4/389 and Corr.1& Corr.2, p. 12.

[112] S. Borelli and S. Olleson, "Ch. 84: Obligations Relating to Human Rights and Humanitarian Law," in J. Crawford, A. Pellet, and S. Olleson, eds., *The Law of International Responsibility*, Oxford, Oxford University Press, 2010, p. 1186; ILC, Third Report on State

The question also arises as to whether this condition would mean that wrongfulness is not precluded for measures suspending the direct international rights of individuals. Article 49.1 specifies that countermeasures "may only be taken against a State which is responsible" – this would therefore seem to exclude the possibility of taking countermeasures that suspend rights that are owed directly to individuals; the formulation in Article 49.1 indicates that the condition is exhaustive.[113] This may be read in two ways. One is to exclude the possibility of taking *any* measure that suspends *any* individual rights. However, the extensive State practice in taking measures against individuals, particularly affecting their right to property, such as freezing assets, would indicate that this view is not congruous with international practice.

The second possible interpretation is that suspending individual rights *as a direct response* to a violation by a State does not constitute a valid countermeasure. This would make sense; as countermeasures are intersubjective, suspending rights that are not owed to the responsible State would simply not fall within their definition. For example, let us imagine that State A, in breach of a bilateral treaty of friendship with State B, somehow intervenes in State B's internal affairs in breach of its international obligations. In response, State B stops complying with its obligations under a regional human rights treaty (to which, to simplify things, we shall say that State A is not a party) to respect the right to privacy of individuals, justifying this action as a countermeasure against State A's breach. This would not be a valid countermeasure, as it is not taken "against" State A, the responsible State, but "against" individuals that have the right to privacy under a specific human rights convention. The same also seems to be maintained by some authors[114] and by the ILC.[115]

This position appears to be confirmed by findings, such as in *CPI v. Mexico*, that a State cannot take countermeasures against the rights of investors.[116] However, there still remains the problem of the suspension

Responsibility, Gaetano Arangio-Ruiz, Special Rapporteur, A/CN.4/440 and Add.1, p. 25, although Arangio-Ruiz appears to use the term "integral" in the sense of "interdependent."

113 This was reflected in debates at the ILC: Report of the International Law Commission to the General Assembly on the Work of Its Fifty-Second Session, Doc. No. A/CN.4/SER.A/2000/Add.1 (Part 2)/Rev.1, p. 52.

114 Yahi, "La violation d'un traité," p. 459; Provost, "Reciprocity in Human Rights," p. 451.

115 ILC, Articles on Responsibility of States for Internationally Wrongful Acts, Commentary, p. 129.

116 See ibid., p. 202.

of property rights of nationals of responsible States. This kind of action reflects the fiction that human rights are also State rights; in taking such measures, the injured State is "in reality" taking action against the rights of the responsible State. This link to diplomatic protection explains the two elements of practice highlighted above. The first is that in taking countermeasures, States do not suspend rights *in general* under a treaty, but only with regard to nationals, even specific individuals, of the responsible State. The second explains why the justification that could apply for suspending property rights of nationals of the responsible State could not possibly be used for suspending investor rights, as was the case in *CPI* v. *Mexico*, in regards of which diplomatic protection is excluded.

The nonpunitive nature of countermeasures is set out in Article 49.1, where the object of countermeasures is stated as "to induce th[e] State to comply with its obligations." Countermeasures are not therefore intended to punish wrongful conduct but to secure a return to compliance. Outside this, countermeasures are no longer lawful. Article 49 also sets out that countermeasures must be "limited to the nonperformance *for the time being* of international obligations" (emphasis added), and "shall, as far as possible, be taken in such a way as to permit the resumption of performance of the obligation in question." Countermeasures must therefore be temporary and reversible;[117] they cannot bring about a fundamental change of circumstances, nor cause irreparable prejudice to the rights they affect.

5.4.3 *Limitations to Countermeasures*

The ILC Articles go on to set out, in Article 50.1(d), a series of obligations that may not be affected by countermeasures. Obviously enough, peremptory norms cannot be the object of countermeasures; as they are non-derogable in nature, by definition States cannot be excused for breaching them.[118] Article 50.1(a) also includes the obligation to refrain from the threat or use of force as embodied in the UN Charter. As Article

[117] ILC, Articles on Responsibility of States for Internationally Wrongful Acts, Commentary, pp. 129–130.

[118] Ibid., Article 50.1(d); commentary, pp. 129–132; Yahi, "La violation d'un traité," p. 459; ILC, Sixth Report on the Content, Forms and Degrees of International Responsibility (Part Two of the draft articles); and "Implementation" (*mise en oeuvre*) of international responsibility and the settlement of disputes (part three of the draft articles), Riphagen, Special Rapporteur, Doc. No. A/CN.4/389 and Corr.1& Corr.2, p. 11. Riphagen explains this by reason of rules of *jus cogens* being nonreciprocal. As they are all obligations of the *erga omnes* type, this is not entirely correct, as all States will have both an obligation to

2.4 of the Charter may be safely considered to be customary international law, and a peremptory norm of international law, this can be considered to fall within the same category as Article 50.1(d). The explicit inclusion of the prohibition of the threat or use of force as an obligation that cannot be affected by countermeasure is further connected to the explicit exclusion of forcible reprisals from the definition of countermeasures.

Another category that is excluded from the taking of countermeasures is that of "obligations for the protection of fundamental human rights" in Article 50.1(b). As for the other restrictions under Article 50.1, this paragraph does not only indicate which rights may not be themselves suspended by way of countermeasure but also which may not be *affected* by countermeasures – even if only incidentally. "Obligations for the protection of fundamental human rights" have been considered to coincide with the rights that may not be derogated from in human rights treaties.[119] The provision stems from the formulation in the *Naulilaa* arbitration that countermeasures must be limited by "basic considerations of humanity."[120] This restriction is not based on any structural factor, that is, whether the rights are owed to individuals or to States, but rather on what they aim to protect.

The adjective "fundamental" therefore qualifies those rights that may not be affected by way of countermeasure. Suspension of property rights, freezing of assets and the like are liable to derogation in human rights treaties, and not considered to fall under the "fundamental" heading.[121] This provision also does not mean that *any* detrimental effects on human

comply and the right to expect compliance from all other States and to invoke the responsibility of any State breaching such an obligation.

119 ILC, Fourth Report on State Responsibility, by Mr. Gaetano Arangio-Ruiz, Special Rapporteur, Doc. No. A/CN.4/444 and Add. 1-3, p. 31. The ECtHR has found that ECHR obligations cannot be suspended by way of countermeasure, as they are "objective," but as seen in Chapter 4 above, it is not clear what meaning this term practically has.

120 "[La représaille] est limitée par les expériences de l'humanité et les règles de la bonne foi, applicables dans les rapports d'État à État," [an exchange of services of the same nature between the two contracting States, who mutually concede to each other fishing rights in sectors within their respective jurisdiction.] Responsabilité de l'Allemagne à raison des dommages causés dans les colonies portugaises du sud de l'Afrique (sentence sur le principe de la responsabilité) (Portugal contre Allemagne), 31 July 1928, RIAA, vol. II, p. 1026.

121 Arangio-Ruiz indicated such "fundamental" rights as not allowing violations of the right to life, or "torture, slavery or other indignity," ILC, Third Report on State Responsibility, Gaetano Arangio-Ruiz, Special Rapporteur, A/CN.4/440 and Add.1, p. 32; this therefore excludes the right to property, Borelli and Olleson, "Ch. 84: Obligations," p. 1180.

rights are inconsistent with the taking of countermeasures. However, countermeasures must not seriously impact upon obligations protecting fundamental human rights,[122] a point reflected in State practice.[123] The concern with considerations of humanity may also be considered inherent to the nonpunitive character of countermeasures; taking measures that reduce the population of a State to starvation would, for example, clearly be a punitive measure and not one aimed at reestablishing equality between States.

Finally, a criterion for the legality of countermeasures is proportionality, set out in Article 51.[124] This has been interpreted and accepted in practice and by the ILC as a test of "disproportionality" that relies on both quantitative and qualitative measures, including the importance of the obligation involved.[125] This is again linked to the nature of countermeasures as nonpunitive and aiming to restore equality.

Other restrictions in Article 50.2 are intended to ensure the good functioning of international relations. These relate to the non-suspension of dispute settlement procedures by way of countermeasure and respect for the inviolability of diplomatic or consular agents,[126] that is, "not so much the substantive character of the obligation but its function in

[122] Borelli and Olleson, "Ch. 84: Obligations," p. 1182; Committee on Economic, Social and Cultural Rights, Seventeenth Session, General Comment No. 8 (1997), "The Relationship between Economic Sanctions and Respect for Economic, Social and Cultural Rights," Doc. No. E/C.12/1997/8, especially paras. 7, 16.

[123] See the example given by Arangio-Ruiz concerning the exception made for living and medical expenses of individuals who had their assets frozen by the UK during the Falklands/Malvinas crisis, ILC, Fourth Report on State Responsibility, by Mr. Gaetano Arangio-Ruiz, Special Rapporteur, Doc. No. A/CN.4/444 and Add. 1-3, p. 30, and similar exceptions made by France in regard to measures against the personal guard of the Central African Republic Head of State Bokassa; see Provost, "Reciprocity in Human Rights," p. 444.

[124] ILC, Articles on Responsibility of States for Internationally Wrongful Acts, Commentary, p. 134. Proportionality was described as a "sine qua non for legality," ILC, Report of the International Law Commission to the General Assembly on the Work of Its Fifty-Second Session, Doc. No. A/CN.4/SER.A/2000/Add.1 (Part 2)/Rev.1, p. 53; ILC, Fourth Report on State Responsibility, by Mr. Gaetano Arangio-Ruiz, Special Rapporteur, Doc. No. A/CN.4/444 and Add. 1-3, pp. 22–23.

[125] Air Services Agreement of 27 March 1946 case (United States/France), *18 R.I.A.A. 416*, Award of 9 December 1978, para. 83; taken up by the ILC, see ILC, Articles on Responsibility of States for Internationally Wrongful Acts, Commentary, pp. 134–135.

[126] Described as being of a "functional" character in ILC, Articles on Responsibility of States for Internationally Wrongful Acts, Commentary, p. 134, but we can also consider this to fall within the area of "*les règles de la bonne foi, applicables d'Etat à Etat,*" in the *Naulilaa* arbitration, 31 July 1928, *RIAA*, vol. II, p. 1026.

relation to the resolution of the dispute which has given rise to the threat or use of countermeasures."[127] Article 52.3(b) also prohibits countermeasures from being taken if the dispute is pending before a court or tribunal.

Allowing States to take unilateral action to suspend provisions that are capable of settling their disputes would effectively render almost all forms of dispute settlement meaningless.[128] When there is jurisdiction to bring a dispute before a body that may settle it, this obligation must be performed, and a specific avenue of redress is open to the States in dispute; therefore, the specific mechanism of reciprocity that is the taking of a countermeasure is unavailable. The other side of the equation is that countermeasures also obviate the lack of compulsory dispute settlement in international law; where no means of judicial settlement is available for the specific dispute, then the State affected may take countermeasures against the responsible State.

5.4.4 *Taking of Countermeasures by States other than an Injured State*

Article 54 of the ARSIWA states that "[t]his Chapter does not prejudice the right of any State, entitled under Article 48, paragraph 1 to invoke the responsibility of another State, to take lawful measures against that State to ensure cessation of the breach and reparation in the interest of beneficiaries of the obligation breached." If the wording is cloudy, this is because that is what was explicitly intended by the ILC.[129]

It is not clear whether a legal interest of the type an "other than injured State" has under the law of State responsibility entitles it to take countermeasures. The kind of breach to which Article 54 action would apply would be the breach of an *erga omnes* obligation, that is, where all

[127] ILC, Articles on Responsibility of States for Internationally Wrongful Acts, Commentary, p. 133.

[128] ILC, Articles on Responsibility of States for Internationally Wrongful Acts, Commentary, p. 133.

[129] "[T]he current state of international law on countermeasures taken in the general or collective interest is uncertain . . . chapter II includes a saving clause which reserves the position and leaves the resolution of the matter to the further development of international law," ILC, Articles on Responsibility of States for Internationally Wrongful Acts, Commentary, p. 139; see also ibid., p. 76, and the reasons given in ILC, Report of the International Law Commission to the General Assembly on the Work of Its Fifty-Second Session, Doc. No. A/CN.4/SER.A/2000/Add.1 (Part 2)/Rev.1, p. 60. There is a question relating to the meaning of "lawful measures" and whether this could simply include retortion, but considering that a State does not need any particular justification for taking measures of retortion, it is a more reasonable interpretation to consider the article as referring to countermeasures; Sicilianos, "Ch. 80: Countermeasures," pp. 1145, 1147.

States are owed the obligation. Allowing for such a possibility would be another example of the functioning of reciprocity in the context of multilateral obligations. However, under Article 54, it is "any State" that can react, with no obligation to act in concert with others.[130] How could proportionality be maintained when a number of States are taking countermeasures? A series of perfectly proportionate acts could result in manifest disproportionality, resulting in a wrongful situation without any wrongdoing State. In the face of these problems, therefore, the ILC preferred to leave the question open than either open the door to a series of individual measures by States for any breach of an *erga omnes* obligation or attempt to impose some form of collective action that was clearly not available in general international law outside specific treaty-based structures such as the UN. The reticence of the ILC in formulating any permissive rule to this end, and the reticence of governments in accepting it, is therefore understandable.

It has, however, been argued that States do in fact take such measures, and that the practice is representative enough to amount to a rule of customary international law.[131] Actions that could be characterized as countermeasures taken by States other than the injured State were, for example, taken by the European Union in 1982 during the Falklands/Malvinas conflict, taking economic measures against Argentina such as suspending imports.[132] Even more striking an example, because the State affected by the breach was not a member State of the EU, were the measures taken by the EU against Russia in response to the latter's violation of the sovereignty and territorial integrity of Ukraine in 2014.[133] The measures involve restrictions on financial transactions, the export of arms and materiel, and the transfer of technologies relating to deep water oil exploration and production.[134]

130 Alland, "Countermeasures of General Interest," p. 1228.

131 See the comprehensive overview and analysis of State practice in this regard in Proukaki, *The Problem of Enforcement in International Law*, pp. 103–201.

132 Council Regulation (EEC) No. 877/82 of 16 April 1982 relating to suspending imports of all products originating in Argentina, *Official Journal of the European Communities*, No. L 102/1.

133 Although the EU and its member States were of course closely concerned by the conflict, first because the Ukraine had been close to signing an Association Agreement with the EU, and second, because of the downing of a civilian airliner that had departed from Amsterdam on 17 July 2014, with many EU nationals on board while overflying Ukraine.

134 Council Decision 2014/512/CFSP of 31 July 2014, concerning restrictive measures in view of Russia's actions destabilizing the situation in Ukraine, *Official Journal of the European Union*, L 229/13; Council Regulation (EU) No. 833/2014 concerning restrictive

Logically, if each State is owed performance of an *erga omnes* obligation, then each State should be entitled to take countermeasures under the conditions of Article 54. Allowing for such action might also be justifiable in the face of the violation of obligations owed to individuals and peoples. Otherwise, short of any institutional action, for example at the UN level, there would be no mechanism in international law that could induce a State to cease its wrongful conduct against, for example, individuals within its jurisdiction, and provide reparation.

5.5 Conclusion

The structure and mechanisms of international responsibility demonstrate the persisting essentially reciprocal nature of international law and the structural limitations its horizontal nature poses to establishing specific consequences for breaches of community obligations. This is not to say that it does not take into account the features of contemporary international law, namely the existence of peremptory norms and rights *erga omnes*, as well as the existence of individual rights. However, these are taken into account within the relational structure of international law.

Even breaches of fundamental, peremptory norms find their consequences within the reciprocal structure of international law; *erga omnes* obligations bestow rights on all States to call for their respect. Without such a mechanism, in the absence of generalized standing for non-State right-holders such as individuals and peoples, violations of rules whose beneficiaries are not States are left without consequences unless the primary rule itself empowers individuals to invoke the responsibility of the responsible State.

Reciprocity lies at the heart of this structure. State responsibility tends to the reestablishment of the legal equality that is the basis of international law, and the return to compliance with those obligations – not in the abstract, but toward other States, who hold the right to see those obligations fulfilled. Reciprocity itself, though, as a "raw" mechanism to curtail rights in response to breaches, is itself absent from the law of State responsibility. It is not accurate to speak of "measures of reciprocity," and they certainly do not have any independent legal effect. Reciprocity has been tamed and institutionalized in the enforcement of international law.

measures in view of Russia's actions destabilizing the situation in Ukraine, *Official Journal of the European Union*, L 229/1.

6 Reciprocity and the Jurisdiction of International Courts and Tribunals

This chapter looks at the role reciprocity plays in the jurisdiction of international courts and tribunals, and the differences in the role reciprocity plays in inter-State dispute settlement, and in dispute settlement procedures that involve non-State entities such as individuals. The analysis will first focus on the International Court of Justice (ICJ) and the well-developed role that reciprocity plays in its jurisdiction. Secondly, the analysis will turn to the system of compulsory dispute settlement in the United Nations Convention on the Law of the Sea (UNCLOS). The final three instances analyzed all concern individuals, but in all of them, being treaty-based, an inter-State dimension subsists: the International Criminal Court; human rights courts and complaint mechanisms; and investment tribunals, specifically the issue of the extension of jurisdiction on the basis of an MFN clause.

6.1 Acceptance of the Jurisdiction of the International Court of Justice

The system of acceptance of the jurisdiction of the ICJ is a natural starting point as it is the inter-State judicial settlement body *par excellence*. Although the Statute of the ICJ is an integral part of the Charter of the United Nations, this does not mean that any State party to the UN or to the Statute automatically submits to the jurisdiction of the Court;[1] instead, an additional act of consent is required by both parties to the case in question. There is also a further requirement: consent must be reciprocal. That is, the parties to a dispute must accept the jurisdiction of

[1] C. Tomuschat, "Article 36," in A. Zimmermann, et al., eds., *The Statute of the International Court of Justice: A Commentary*, 2nd ed., Oxford, Oxford University Press, 2012, p. 647.

the Court in the same manner, regardless of the heading of jurisdiction the dispute falls under, whether this is a special agreement, a compromissory clause in a treaty, or a declaration of acceptance of the Court's compulsory jurisdiction under Article 36.2 of the Statute. To this may be added a more specific mechanism of reciprocity, which relates to the scope of States' acceptance of the jurisdiction of the Court, and specifically the manner in which States may invoke restrictions to their acceptance of the Court's jurisdiction under Article 36.2.

6.1.1 *Jurisdiction of the Court under Article 36.1*

Article 36.1 of the Statute of the Court provides that the jurisdiction of the Court "comprises all cases which the parties refer to it and all matters provided for in the Charter of the United Nations or in treaties and conventions in force." Under this paragraph, the Court may have jurisdiction on the basis of general dispute settlement treaties, compromissory clauses in treaties, special agreements between States, or *forum prorogatum*.[2] Reciprocity is inherent in all these types of jurisdiction, both in general and specific terms.

6.1.1.1 General Dispute Settlement Treaties and Compromissory Clauses

The Court may have jurisdiction on the basis of a treaty; this can be either a general dispute settlement treaty or a treaty that contains a compromissory clause that confers jurisdiction on the Court. The States parties to the dispute must be parties to the treaty. Perhaps the most-used general dispute settlement treaty conferring jurisdiction on the ICJ is a regional treaty, the American Treaty on the Pacific Settlement of Disputes, or Pact of Bogotá, and specifically its Article XXXI.[3] This provides that "[i]n conformity with Article 36, paragraph 2 of the Statute of the International Court of Justice, the High Contracting Parties declare that they recognize, in relation to any other American State, the jurisdiction of the Court as compulsory *ipso facto* [...] as long as the present Treaty is in force." Despite the reference to Article 36.2, the Pact of

[2] Reference is also made to "all matters provided for in the Charter of the United Nations," however this will not be examined here. The Court found in the *Case Concerning the Aerial Incident of 10 August 1999 (Pakistan* v. *India)* that "the United Nations Charter contains no specific provision of itself conferring compulsory jurisdiction on the Court," *Aerial Incident of 10 August 1999 (Pakistan* v. *India)*, Jurisdiction of the Court, Judgment of 21 June 2000, ICJ Reports 2000, para. 48.

[3] American Treaty on the Pacific Settlement of Disputes, Bogotá, 30 April 1948.

Bogotá constitutes a separate basis of jurisdiction to Optional Clause declarations. In *Border and Transborder Armed Actions (Nicaragua* v. *Honduras)*, the Court found that the provisions of the Pact

> together indicate that the commitment in Article XXXI can only be limited by means of reservations to the Pact itself. It is an autonomous commitment, independent of any other which the parties may have undertaken or may undertake by depositing with the United Nations Secretary-General a declaration of acceptance of compulsory jurisdiction under Article 36, paragraphs 2 and 4, of the Statute.[4]

Therefore, the conditions of consent set out in one instrument cannot be affected by the State accepting the jurisdiction of the Court in any other instrument. This general reciprocity – consent on the same basis – must exist between States parties to a dispute in order for the Court to have jurisdiction.

Reciprocity is also inherent in compromissory clauses that confer jurisdiction upon the Court. These may take a number of forms or may impose preconditions that must be fulfilled before having recourse to the Court.[5] The ICJ will have jurisdiction when the States in dispute are both parties to the treaty in question and either have not made reservations to the compromissory clause or these reservations do not exclude the dispute at hand.

Some treaties require States parties to make a specific declaration recognizing the jurisdiction of the ICJ.[6] In this case, States parties can only be considered as having consented to the Court's jurisdiction once they have made the relevant declaration. The same is true for treaties in which States must be parties to a Protocol in order to submit disputes to the Court.[7] The general requirement of reciprocity in the consent of

[4] *Border and Transborder Armed Actions (Nicaragua* v. *Honduras)*, Jurisdiction and Admissibility, Judgment, ICJ Reports 1988, para. 36.

[5] As is for example the case of Article 22 of the Convention for the Elimination of All Forms of Racial Discrimination: Application of the International Convention for the Elimination of All Forms of Racial Discrimination (*Georgia* v. *Russian Federation*), Preliminary Objections, Judgment, ICJ Reports 2011, para. 141.

[6] Convention on Biological Diversity, 5 June 1992, Art. 27.3; Basel Convention on the Control of Transboundary Movements of Hazardous Wastes and Their Disposal, 22 March 1989, Art. 20.3; United Nations Framework Convention on Climate Change, 9 May 1992, Art. 14.2.

[7] This is the case of the Vienna Convention on Diplomatic Relations, in which States must be parties to the Optional Protocol for the ICJ to have jurisdiction: Optional Protocol concerning the Compulsory Settlement of Disputes, Vienna, 18 April 1961, Article 1. This provided a basis for jurisdiction in *United States Diplomatic and Consular Staff in Tehran (United States of America* v. *Iran)*, Judgment of 24 May 1980, ICJ Reports 1980, para. 45.

States is therefore always applicable in the case of jurisdiction on the basis of treaties under Article 36.1.

It is also possible that States may have entered a reservation either excluding the compromissory clause or restricting their acceptance of the Court's jurisdiction. Specific reciprocity in consent is therefore also necessary. A further analysis must thus be made as to whether the States in question have accepted the jurisdiction of the Court over the specific dispute. Given the reciprocal functioning of reservations, it is also possible for the respondent State to invoke a reservation made by the applicant State. This notably happened in the *Aegean Sea Continental Shelf* case. Turkey objected to the jurisdiction of the Court on the basis that Greece, the applicant, had made a reservation to the General Act of 1928 on which jurisdiction was based.[8] Turkey therefore invoked the reservation to the treaty made by Greece on the basis of reciprocity, which had the effect of excluding the dispute from the jurisdiction of the Court.[9]

6.1.1.2 Special Agreements

States may also conclude a special agreement, or *compromis*, to confer jurisdiction over a specific dispute to the Court. These agreements usually take the shape of a formal instrument,[10] but it may also be sufficient for consent to be expressed in an exchange of minutes[11] or a letter,[12] as long as it is clear that the parties intended to thereby submit a dispute to the Court.[13]

8 R. Kolb, *The International Court of Justice*, Hart, Oxford, 2013, p. 424; Torres Bernárdez, "Reciprocity in the System," pp. 315–318; see for example *Aegean Sea Continental Shelf (Greece* v. *Turkey)*, Judgment of 19 December 1978, ICJ Reports 1978, especially para. 39.

9 *Aegean Sea Continental Shelf (Greece* v. *Turkey)*, Judgment of 19 December 1978, ICJ Reports 1978, para. 90.

10 For example, the Special Agreement for Submission to the International Court of Justice of the Dispute between Malaysia and Singapore Concerning Sovereignty over Pedra Branca/Pulau Batu Puteh Middle Rocks and South Ledge, Jointly notified to the Court on 24 July 2003.

11 *Maritime Delimitation and Territorial Questions between Qatar and Bahrain*, Jurisdiction and Admissibility, Judgment of 1 July 1994, ICJ Reports 1994, paras. 27, 30.

12 Application of the Convention on the Prevention and Punishment of the Crime of Genocide (*Bosnia and Herzegovina* v. *Yugoslavia*), Preliminary Objections, Judgment, ICJ Reports 1996, para. 37.

13 For example, the Court did not consider this sufficiently clear in Application of the Convention on the Prevention and Punishment of the Crime of Genocide (*Bosnia and Herzegovina* v. *Yugoslavia*), Preliminary Objections, para. 37, and Aegean Sea Continental Shelf (*Greece* v. *Turkey*), Judgment of 19 December 1978, ICJ Reports 1978, para. 107.

Because both parties to the dispute explicitly agree that it is to be submitted to the ICJ, the same ascertainments in respect of reciprocity do not have to be made in the case of jurisdiction based on a special agreement as for jurisdiction on the basis of a compromissory clause in a treaty or an Article 36.2 declaration. In concluding a special agreement, reciprocity exists in the general and specific sense, since there is one single instrument establishing acceptance of the Court's jurisdiction and, being concluded in regard to a specific dispute, the scope of jurisdiction is agreed and there are no possible variations in the scope of the parties' acceptance.

6.1.1.3 Forum Prorogatum

Forum prorogatum is a modality of acceptance of the jurisdiction of the Court according to which consent is not deduced from a treaty or an agreement but from certain acts, that is "applied when a respondent State has, through its conduct before the Court or in relation to the applicant party, acted in such a way as to have consented to the jurisdiction of the Court."[14] In the case of *forum prorogatum*, consent must be "unequivocal" and "indisputable."[15] Reciprocity of consent is given by the fact that here too the respondent State must consent in the same manner as the applicant State, by demonstrating its consent to the Court exercising jurisdiction over a specific dispute presented by the applicant. It is not sufficient for it to have consented in another manner, such as by making an Article 36.2 declaration. Here, too, reciprocity is required in the basis of both States' acceptance of jurisdiction.

While it may seem that where jurisdiction is based on *forum prorogatum*, the scope of jurisdiction is already defined by the scope of the application, a further examination is needed as to what exactly the two States have consented to. Because jurisdiction on the basis of *forum prorogatum* is essentially based on two unilateral acts, the two States may have accepted jurisdiction to varying extents. This point was at issue in *Djibouti* v. *France*,[16] where a question arose as to whether facts

[14] Certain Questions of Mutual Assistance in Criminal Matters (*Djibouti* v. *France*), Judgment, ICJ Reports 2008, para. 61; *forum prorogatum* was also the basis of jurisdiction in the *Corfu Channel* case, *Corfu Channel Case*, Judgment on Preliminary Objection of 25 March 1948, ICJ Reports 1948, pp. 26–27.

[15] Certain Questions of Mutual Assistance in Criminal Matters (*Djibouti* v. *France*), Judgment, ICJ Reports 2008, para. 62.

[16] Certain Questions of Mutual Assistance in Criminal Matters (*Djibouti* v. *France*), Judgment, ICJ Reports 2008, para. 83.

occurring after the Application was filed could be subsumed into France's acceptance. The Court stated,

> France's expression of consent must, however, be read together with Djibouti's Application to discern properly the extent of the consent given by the Parties to the Court's jurisdiction, and thereby to arrive at that which is common in their expressions of consent [. . .] when consent is given post hoc, a State may well give only partial consent, and in so doing narrow the jurisdiction of the Court by comparison with what had been contemplated in the Application.[17]

In the case of *forum prorogatum*, the Court may therefore also be faced with two acceptances of consent of varying scope and must establish the extent to which they coincide. Reciprocity will therefore be relevant in a specific sense, in order to ensure that a wider consent to jurisdiction is not opposed to a State than that which it has accepted.

6.1.2 *The Optional Clause System*

Article 36.2 of the ICJ Statute sets out the "Optional Clause" system, according to which States may declare that they accept the jurisdiction of the Court for all, or some, disputes. Here too there exists reciprocity in the general sense; the Optional Clause system only works between States having made declarations under Article 36.2. However, the entirety of the Optional Clause system is also underpinned by a rationale of specific reciprocity, most clearly understandable in terms of reversibility. Just as a State making an Article 36.2 declaration may benefit from it by being entitled to bring a case before the Court, it may also be the subject of proceedings to the extent that it has accepted the jurisdiction of the ICJ in its declaration.[18]

6.1.2.1 The Nature of Declarations under Article 36.2

In accordance with the principle of consent, States parties to the ICJ Statute are under no obligation to make a declaration under Article 36.2. The Optional Clause system may therefore be seen as creating compulsory jurisdiction, but only among those States that have agreed to it.[19] Once a declaration is made, the State is bound by its terms and

[17] Ibid., paras. 65–66.

[18] H. Thirlway, "Reciprocity in the Jurisdiction of the International Court," *Netherlands Yearbook of International Law*, vol. 15, 1984, pp. 38, 120; Case concerning Right of Passage over Indian Territory *(Portugal* v. *India)*, Preliminary Objections, Judgment of 26 November 1957, ICJ Reports 1957, p. 144.

[19] V. Lamm, *Compulsory Jurisdiction in International Law*, Elgar, Cheltenham, 2014, p. 89.

subject to the Court's jurisdiction.[20] McNair in the *Anglo-Iranian Oil Co.* case defined the system as one of "contracting-in" rather than "contracting-out";[21] in making declarations under Article 36.2, States undertake additional obligations to those already incorporated in the ICJ Statute.[22]

The nature of these declarations of acceptance was defined by the Court in *Fisheries Jurisdiction (Spain* v. *Canada)*: "A declaration of acceptance of the compulsory jurisdiction of the Court, whether there are specified limits set to that acceptance or not, is a unilateral act of State sovereignty. At the same time, it establishes a consensual bond and the potential for a jurisdictional link with the other States which have made declarations."[23] The Court has resisted applying the rules on the law of treaties directly to the modification or interpretation of Article 36.2 declarations.[24] Unlike treaties, Optional Clause declarations are not an expression of agreement between States but a free expression of will on the part of States.[25] However, they interact to create a system; obligations necessarily arise between States in concrete cases rather than existing in the abstract.[26] Regardless of what a State has stated in its declaration, its being subject to the jurisdiction of the Court will depend on, first, another State having also made a declaration under Article 36.2, and, second, the content of these declarations coinciding.[27] For example,

[20] *Anglo-Iranian Oil Co. case (United Kingdom* v. *Iran)*, Preliminary Objections, Judgment of 22 July 1952, ICJ Reports 1952, Individual Opinion of President McNair, p. 116; S. Rosenne, *The Law and Practice of the International Court, 1920–1996, Volume II: Jurisdiction*, 3rd ed., Leiden, Nijhoff, 2006, p. 829; Kolb, *International Court of Justice*, p. 448.

[21] *Anglo-Iranian Oil Co.*, Individual Opinion of President McNair, p. 116.

[22] Rosenne, *The Law and Practice of the International Court*, p. 828; V. Lamm, "Reciprocity and the Compulsory Jurisdiction of the International Court of Justice," *Acta Juridica Hungarica*, vol. 44, nos. 1–2, 2003, p. 47; Lamm, *Compulsory Jurisdiction in International Law*, p. 97.

[23] *Fisheries Jurisdiction (Spain* v. *Canada)*, Jurisdiction of the Court, Judgment of 4 November 1998, ICJ Reports 1998, para. 46.

[24] See for example the distinction made with the rules on transmitting declarations in the VCLT in *Land and Maritime Boundary between Cameroon and Nigeria*, Preliminary Objections, Judgment of 11 June 1998, ICJ Reports 1998, para. 30; C. Eckhart, *Promises of States under International Law*, Oxford, Hart, 2012, p. 74.

[25] Kolb, *International Court of Justice*, pp. 454–455.

[26] *Land and Maritime Boundary between Cameroon and Nigeria*, Preliminary Objections, Judgment of 11 June 1998, para. 43; Rosenne, *The Law and Practice of the International Court*, p. 741.

[27] *Military and Paramilitary Activities in and against Nicaragua (Nicaragua* v. *United States of America)*, Jurisdiction and Admissibility, Judgment of 26 November 1984, para. 60; Case concerning Right of Passage over Indian Territory (*Portugal* v. *India*), Preliminary Objections, Judgment of 26 November 1957, ICJ Reports 1957, p. 125, Dissenting Opinion of Vice-President Badawi, p. 155; on the "contractual" nature of declarations see Eckhart,

the fact that a State accepts the jurisdiction of the Court in "all disputes" does not mean that it can be brought before the Court by another State in regards of a dispute that the latter has excluded from the terms of its acceptance in its own declaration. It is here that reciprocity plays an important and specific role in the Optional Clause system. The language in Article 36.2 also highlights the relational nature of the Optional Clause system. It clearly concerns the subjective rights of States, applying only between States that have made a declaration, not *erga omnes*, and not exposing them to any obligation concerning disputes with subjects of international law that are not States.[28]

6.1.2.2 "Accepting the Same Obligation"

The reciprocal basis of the Optional Clause system is found in the reference to States recognizing the jurisdiction of the Court "in relation to any other State accepting the same obligation."[29] This requires it to be established that the dispute falls within the declarations of both parties to the case.[30] The fact that the requirement of "accepting the same obligation" is incorporated into Article 36.2 also means that it is irrelevant whether States explicitly mention in their declarations that they accept the jurisdiction of the Court on the basis of reciprocity.[31] The Court has interpreted the "same obligation" as meaning "no more than that, as between States adhering to the Optional Clause, each and all of them are bound by such identical obligations as may exist at any time during which the acceptance is mutually binding."[32]

Therefore, the Court only has jurisdiction over a dispute to the extent that the declarations made by the States concerned coincide; the dispute

Promises of States, pp. 70–73, and against this, insisting on the unilateral nature of declarations, Lamm, *Compulsory Jurisdiction in International Law*, p. 95.

28 Thirlway, "Reciprocity in the Jurisdiction," p. 37. See the ICJ outlining the requirement in the definition of reciprocity of proving that a subjective right has been impaired in *Right of Passage*, pp. 147–148.

29 Statute of the International Court of Justice, Article 36.2; S. A. Alexandrov, *Reservations in Unilateral Declarations Accepting the Compulsory Jurisdiction of the International Court of Justice*, Dordrecht, Nijhoff, 1995, p. 34; Kolb, *International Court of Justice*, p. 474.

30 *Military and Paramilitary Activities in and against Nicaragua*, Judgment of 26 November 1984, para. 64: in this case, Judge Mosler took this to mean that temporal conditions included in the reservation were also subject to reciprocity, Separate Opinion of Judge Mosler, p. 466; Thirlway, "Reciprocity in the Jurisdiction," p. 111; H. Briggs, H., "Nicaragua v. United States: Jurisdiction and Admissibility," *The American Journal of International Law*, vol. 79, no. 2, April 1985, p. 376; Torres Bernárdez, "Reciprocity in the System," pp. 291, 304.

31 Briggs, "Nicaragua v. United States," p. 376.

32 *Right of Passage*, p. 144.

in question must fall within *both* declarations.[33] This is where the functioning of reciprocity begins to be outlined more clearly. A State cannot, in effect, go beyond the terms of its own declaration on the basis that the dispute at issue has been accepted by the other State. The narrower acceptance of jurisdiction therefore dictates which disputes may be brought before the Court.[34] This requires absolute identity of performance.[35] The applicant State cannot take advantage of a more extensive acceptance of jurisdiction made by another State.[36] While in practice this means that a State is bound by the terms of its own declaration, the mechanism by which this is effectively carried out is referred to as "reciprocity."

The Court defined reciprocity in the context of reservations in the *Interhandel* case in the following manner: "Reciprocity in the case of Declarations accepting the compulsory jurisdiction of the Court enables a Party to invoke a reservation to that acceptance which it has not expressed in its own Declaration but which the other Party has expressed in its Declaration."[37] Reciprocity functions to allow a State to not only invoke its own reservations, but also those of the other State.[38]

This, however, raises problems as to how exactly one State may invoke a reservation made by the other. For example, in the *Norwegian Loans* case, France had excluded all disputes that it considered to come within its domestic jurisdiction.[39] By virtue of reciprocity, Norway was entitled to invoke France's reservation. However, this could have meant either

[33] *Anglo-Iranian Oil Co. case*, Judgment of 22 July 1952, p. 103; *Case of Certain Norwegian Loans (France* v. *Norway)*, Judgment of 6 July 1957, I.C.J. Reports 1957, p. 23; Kolb, *International Court of Justice*, pp. 455, 480, 506; *Anglo-Iranian Oil Co. case*, Judgment of 22 July 1952, Individual Opinion of President McNair, p. 116; Torres Bernárdez, "Reciprocity in the System," p. 304; Lamm, *Compulsory Jurisdiction in International Law*, p. 31.

[34] Briggs, "Nicaragua v. United States," p. 376; Kolb, *International Court of Justice*, pp. 476, 481. See a good example in the Court's reasoning in *Case of Certain Norwegian Loans*, p. 23.

[35] Torres Bernárdez, "Reciprocity in the System," p. 292.

[36] Thirlway, "Reciprocity in the Jurisdiction," p. 98; Lamm, *Compulsory Jurisdiction in International Law*, p. 31; Kolb, *International Court of Justice*, p. 672.

[37] *Interhandel Case (Switzerland* v. *United States of America)*, p. 23.

[38] According to the Court in *Interhandel Case*, "Reciprocity enables the State which has made the wider acceptance of the jurisdiction of the Court to rely upon the reservations to the acceptance laid down by the other Party. There the effect of reciprocity ends." *Interhandel Case (Switzerland* v. *United States of America)*, p. 23; Lamm, *Compulsory Jurisdiction in International Law*, pp. 74, 116; Tomuschat, "Article 36," p. 654; Alexandrov, *Reservations in Unilateral Declarations*, pp. 36, 55; Kolb, *International Court of Justice*, pp. 462, 476, 523; Rosenne, *The Law and Practice of the International Court*, p. 762; Thirlway, "Reciprocity in the Jurisdiction," p. 117.

[39] *Case of Certain Norwegian Loans*, p. 21.

that Norway could have invoked the reservation referring to *France's* domestic jurisdiction or that it could have invoked it as referring to its *own* domestic jurisdiction. In the end, the Court decided on the second meaning,[40] thereby giving Norway's invocation of the reservation the same effect that France's invocation would have had – the possibility of excluding disputes from the jurisdiction of the Court on the basis of a subjective appreciation of what constituted matters within its jurisdiction.[41] This focus on the effect of the reservations avoids a situation in which a reservation may be worded to only benefit one State.[42] In essence, reciprocity in this context means reversibility; it ensures balance of rights, or equality, as one State cannot claim more rights than the other.[43]

It is furthermore not possible for the respondent State to claim "double reciprocity," as was attempted by the United States in *Interhandel*; no further construction or blend of limitations from the two declarations may be made.[44] The effect of reciprocity in this context is therefore that the Court needs to be competent regardless of which State would seize it[45] – that is, reciprocity as reversibility.

There have been cases in which States have been brought before the Court by an applicant that filed an Optional Clause declaration only days before filing a case, such as in the *Right of Passage* and *Cameroon* v. *Nigeria* cases. This prompted the respondent States to raise objections on the basis of an absence of reciprocity and raised the question of when the existence of reciprocity should be established.

The Court's jurisprudence has been clear in stating that Optional Clause declarations take effect instantly and do not depend on notification to other States. As indicated by the use of the terms "*ipso facto*" in Article 36.2, declarations may be immediately relied on by other States,

40 Ibid., pp. 24, 27; Lamm, "Reciprocity and the Compulsory Jurisdiction," p. 57.

41 Thirlway, "Reciprocity in the Jurisdiction," p. 179, Rosenne, *The Law and Practice of the International Court*, p. 763; Alexandrov, *Reservations in Unilateral Declarations*, p. 81.

42 See Thirlway, "Reciprocity in the Jurisdiction," p. 180, giving the example of anti ambush clauses. This is particularly relevant in the context of automatic reservations, which work to discourage States from making such reservations, because the working of reciprocity automatically deprives them of the possibility of bringing other States before the Court: see Lamm, *Compulsory Jurisdiction in International Law* p. 58. On the irrelevance of wording, see Torres Bernárdez, "Reciprocity in the System," p. 309.

43 *Right of Passage*, p. 144.

44 *Interhandel Case (Switzerland* v. *United States of America)*, p. 23; see also Lamm, *Compulsory Jurisdiction in International Law*, p. 59; Kolb, *International Court of Justice*, p. 482.

45 Torres Bernárdez, "Reciprocity in the System," pp. 293, 306.

and rights to bring cases accrue upon making of the declaration.[46] States have in this respect argued that the instant filing of a declaration by a State that they had not realized was a party to the Optional Clause system is contrary to the principle of reciprocity because, following the argument of reversibility, they would not have been in a position to bring a case against that State.[47] However, this argument may be dispensed with not by denying the scope of the argument of reversibility but rather by indicating that reciprocity must exist *at the moment the Court is seized*. This is the moment at which the existence of "the same obligation" must be determined.[48] It is not necessary to look at what the situation was before this time, as previous to this, obligations are "in a state of flux" and it would therefore be impossible to compare the obligations established by the declarations.[49]

This also explains the exclusion of formal conditions from the reach of reciprocity, particularly those relating to the conditions of termination set out in the declaration. A State cannot invoke the formal conditions of another State's declaration on the basis of reciprocity; a State cannot claim that it has not accepted "the same obligation" as another merely because it has not reserved the right to terminate its declaration with immediate effect.[50] This would involve applying reciprocity before the

[46] *Right of Passage*, p. 146; *Land and Maritime Boundary between Cameroon and Nigeria*, Judgment of 11 June 1998, paras. 25, 27, 31.

[47] See the Dissenting Opinion of Judge Koroma in *Land and Maritime Boundary between Cameroon and Nigeria*, Judgment of 11 June 1998, pp. 389–390. This was the basis of Vice-President Weeramantry's dissent in *Cameroon* v. *Nigeria*, who relied on the contractual analogy for the Optional Clause system to explain why he considered the requirement of knowledge to be necessary for establishing jurisdiction: *Land and Maritime Boundary between Cameroon and Nigeria*, Judgment of 11 June 1998, Dissenting Opinion of Vice-President Weeramantry, pp. 362, 368, 373.

[48] Thirlway, "Reciprocity in the Jurisdiction," p. 182; Tomuschat, "Article 36," p. 684; Briggs, "Nicaragua v. United States," p. 376; Lamm, *Compulsory Jurisdiction in International Law*, pp. 62, 112; Kolb, *International Court of Justice*, pp. 481–484; *Military and Paramilitary Activities in and against Nicaragua*, Judgment of 26 November 1984, Separate Opinion of Judge Oda, p. 511.

[49] *Military and Paramilitary Activities in and against Nicaragua*, Judgment of 26 November 1984, para. 64 and para. 116.

[50] See the arguments of the United States in *Military and Paramilitary Activities in and against Nicaragua*, Judgment of 26 November 1984, paras. 55–56, and the Court's reasoning in rejecting these, at paras. 61–62; *Military and Paramilitary Activities in and against Nicaragua*, Judgment of 26 November 1984, Separate Opinion of Judge Jennings, p. 549; Alexandrov, *Reservations in Unilateral Declarations*, p. 58; Briggs, "Nicaragua v. United States," p. 377; Torres Bernárdez, "Reciprocity in the System," p. 308; Kolb, *International Court of Justice*, p. 523.

Court is seized, that is, before the bilateral nexus between the parties is formed.

6.1.2.3 The Meaning of the Express "Condition of Reciprocity" in Article 36.3

Article 36.3 goes on to specify that States may make declarations "unconditionally or on condition of reciprocity." The explanation for this wording lies in the concern of the drafters of the Statute of the PCIJ that States should be able to specify that they were bound on condition that a certain group, or certain specific States, also made declarations. In the system as it was originally conceived, States could select for which of the categories of dispute under Article 36.2 they accepted the Court's jurisdiction; Article 36.3 set out that they could also subject their declarations to the condition that other States also accept the Court's jurisdiction, or limit the temporal duration of their declarations. The paragraph is the brainchild of the Brazilian jurist Fernandes, who was concerned to avoid the situation in which the Great Powers might not accept the jurisdiction of the Court, leaving instead only small States as parties to the Optional Clause system.[51] The reference to reciprocity in this paragraph therefore only refers to an option to make a reservation *ratione personae*.[52] The provision has, in any case, lost some importance due to the recognition of the freedom of States to make the reservations, or subject their declarations to the conditions, that they please.

6.1.3 *Conclusion*

Within the Optional Clause system, reciprocity allows States to invoke reservations made by other States in order to limit the Court's jurisdiction. This is in reality the same condition that applies to cases brought on the basis of special agreement or compromissory clauses, that is, that the States must have accepted "the same obligation." Reciprocity is therefore always a condition that must be met for the Court to have jurisdiction.[53] It is also applicable regardless of the nature of the rules in question. This

[51] Thirlway, "Reciprocity in the Jurisdiction," p. 105; Tomuschat, "Article 36," p. 681; Kolb, *International Court of Justice*, pp. 461, 474; Lamm, *Compulsory Jurisdiction in International Law*, p. 98; Torres Bernárdez, "Reciprocity in the System," p. 298; Lamm, "Reciprocity and the Compulsory Jurisdiction," pp. 47–48.

[52] Thirlway, "Reciprocity in the Jurisdiction," p. 107.

[53] Ibid., p. 98; Rosenne, *The Law and Practice of the International Court*, p. 541; *Anglo-Iranian Oil Co. case*, Judgment of 22 July 1952, p. 103; Lamm, *Compulsory Jurisdiction in International Law*, p. 102; Tomuschat, "Article 36," p. 653.

has, for example, allowed the Court to specify that a reservation to the Genocide Convention would preclude it from having jurisdiction, regardless of the importance of the rules allegedly breached.[54]

The rationale for reciprocity in the jurisdiction of the Court is repeatedly stated as being the preservation of equality[55] and that the effect of applying reciprocity is that the parties are on a footing of complete equality in accepting the jurisdiction of the Court;[56] that is, each has accepted the same rights and obligations in relation to the other party and to the specific dispute.[57]

6.2 UNCLOS Part XV

The 1982 UN Convention on the Law of the Sea (UNCLOS) sets out in its Part XV a detailed mechanism for the resolution of disputes arising under the Convention. While this concerns a plurality of courts and tribunals, the functioning of the system is interesting as an example of compulsory dispute settlement for a wide substantive area of international law, as well as for the role reciprocity plays within it.

6.2.1 *The Basic Characteristics of UNCLOS Dispute Settlement*

Part XV of UNCLOS relates to the settlement of disputes concerning the interpretation or application of the Convention. The first point of note is, therefore, that there is a general reciprocity insofar as the dispute settlement mechanism only applies to States that are parties to the Convention. Part XV is a compulsory dispute settlement mechanism; aside from the exceptions that are set out below, parties to the Convention must settle their disputes, either through conciliation or, if this fails, unilaterally submitting the dispute to a court or tribunal, in accordance with UNCLOS Article 286. Article 287 provides for the possibility for States to make a declaration as to which forum they prefer. Where States' choices do not coincide, arbitration is the default means of dispute settlement.

54 Tomuschat, "Article 36," p. 263.

55 Alexandrov, *Reservations in Unilateral Declarations*, p. 29; Kolb, *International Court of Justice*, p. 482.

56 Briggs, "Nicaragua v. United States," p. 376.

57 Kolb, *International Court of Justice*, p. 483; Lamm, "Reciprocity and the Compulsory Jurisdiction," p. 65; namely, by invoking the reservation of the other State: Wyler and Papaux, "Mythe structurant de l'humanité," p. 190.

The particularity of the UNCLOS dispute settlement system is that it is not a compromissory clause of the usual nature, but it sets out a comprehensive mechanism that accounts also for the existence of other agreements that may overlap with, or implement, UNCLOS. Article 280 sets out that the application of Part XV is residual; that is, States parties may "agree at any time to settle a dispute [. . .] by any peaceful means of their own choice." However, it also remains applicable in the case that the States in question have not reached a settlement using the means of their choice, in Article 281, on condition that the possibility of settling the dispute under UNCLOS is not excluded.[58]

Article 282 addresses the place of the UNCLOS dispute settlement mechanism within the constellation of other international agreements concerning the law of the sea and providing for binding dispute settlement. The Arbitral Tribunal in the *Southern Bluefin Tuna* case interpreted this as meaning that disputes should be settled under the more specific agreement, and designed to give parties to a dispute flexibility in their choice of means[59] – an interpretation that was however criticized for meaning that States are essentially able to contract out of the supposedly compulsory UNCLOS dispute settlement system as they wish.[60]

There are two incidental proceedings for which the International Tribunal for the Law of the Sea (ITLOS) always has jurisdiction. The first

[58] UNCLOS Art. 281.1; T. Treves, "Dispute-Settlement in the Law of the Sea: Disorder or System?," in M. G. Kohen, ed., *Promoting Justice, Human Rights and Conflict Resolution through International Law / La promotion de la justice, des droits de l'homme et du règlement des conflits par le droit international: Liber Amicorum Lucius Caflisch*, Leiden, Brill, 2007, p. 932; E. D. Brown, "Dispute Settlement and the Law of the Sea: The UN Convention Regime," *Marine Policy*, vol. 21, no. 1, 1997, pp. 20, 23; N. Klein, *Dispute Settlement in the UN Convention on the Law of the Sea*, Cambridge, Cambridge University Press, 2005, pp. 32, 34, 37.

[59] *Southern Bluefin Tuna Case between New Zealand and Japan and between Australia and Japan*, Award on Jurisdiction and Admissibility, Decision of 4 August 2000, *R.I.A.A.*, vol. XXIII, pp. 38–39. In its Order on Provisional Measures, ITLOS found that it could still grant provisional measures even though there was another convention that was possibly applicable, *Southern Bluefin Tuna Cases (New Zealand* v. *Japan, Australia* v. *Japan)*, Cases Nos. 3 and 4, Requests for Provisional Measures, Order of 27 August 1999, paras. 51–55. 71; Klein, *Dispute Settlement in the UN Convention*, pp. 26–27, 34, 149; Treves, "Dispute-Settlement in the Law," p. 933; R. Churchill, "Some Reflections on the Operation of the Dispute Settlement System of the UN Convention on the Law of the Sea During Its First Decade," in D. Freestone, et al., *The Law of the Sea: Progress and Prospects*, Oxford, Oxford University Press, 2006, pp. 400, 402.

[60] For a summary of arguments, see B. Kwiatkowska, "The Australia and New Zealand v Japan Southern Bluefin Tuna (Jurisdiction and Admissibility) Award of the First Law of the Sea Convention Annex VII Arbitral Tribunal," *The International Journal of Marine and Coastal Law*, vol. 16, no. 2, 2001, pp. 254–262.

is the power to prescribe provisional measures under Article 290, even if a dispute settlement mechanism has not yet been agreed upon by States,[61] or a court or tribunal has been chosen that is different to ITLOS.[62] The second mechanism is prompt release of vessels under Article 292. Where it is alleged that a State detaining a vessel has not complied with the UNCLOS provisions on prompt release, the issue may be submitted to any court or tribunal by agreement, or if there is no such agreement within ten days, to ITLOS.[63]

Finally, a special procedure applies for disputes relating to the Area. Activities in the Area do not only involve States but also private entities and the Authority established by Part XI of UNCLOS. Under Article 188, disputes between States may be submitted by agreement to a special chamber of ITLOS, or unilaterally to an ad hoc chamber of the Sea-Bed Disputes Chamber.[64] Contractual disputes, that is, not only involving States, may be unilaterally submitted to commercial arbitration.[65] This procedure applies regardless of the choice of procedure States may have made under Article 287.[66]

6.2.2 *Declarations under Article 287*

The heart of the dispute settlement system under UNCLOS is section 2 of Part XV, which sets out the procedures available for compulsory settlement of disputes arising under the Convention. section 2 revolves around Article 287, which gives States the possibility to make a declaration by which they choose the body, or bodies, they wish to settle their disputes. The choices available under Article 287.1 are (a) ITLOS, (b) the ICJ, (c) an arbitral tribunal established in accordance with UNCLOS Annex VII, or (d) a special arbitral tribunal under Annex VIII (for disputes relating to fisheries, protection and preservation of the marine

[61] UNCLOS Article 290.5.

[62] Under UNCLOS Article 290.1, the court or tribunal having jurisdiction has the power to prescribe provisional measures. See the example of *The "Arctic Sunrise" Case (Kingdom of the Netherlands* v. *Russian Federation)*, Order on Request for the prescription of provisional measures of 22 November 2013, Case No. 22, paras. 36–37.

[63] UNCLOS Article 292.1; Brown, "Dispute Settlement," p. 20; S. Wasum-Rainer and D. Schlegel, "The UNCLOS Dispute Settlement System – Between Hamburg and The Hague," *German Yearbook of International Law*, vol. 48, 2005, p. 210; D. R. Rothwell and T. Stephens, *The International Law of the Sea*, Oxford, Hart, 2010, p. 453.

[64] UNCLOS Article 288.1.

[65] UNCLOS Article 188.2; Wasum-Rainer and Schlegel, "UNCLOS Dispute Settlement System," p. 207.

[66] UNCLOS Article 287.2; T. Treves, "The Jurisdiction of the International Tribunal for the Law of the Sea," *Indian Journal of International Law*, vol. 37, 1997, p. 410.

environment, marine scientific research, and navigation, including pollution by vessels and dumping, under Article 1 of Annex VIII).

States can make a declaration under Article 287.1 at any time. The declaration may be time-limited and may indicate a plurality of choices.[67] Unlike the Optional Clause system of the ICJ, there are a number of instances that States parties may select from. Also unlike the ICJ system, compulsory dispute settlement provisions do not apply only to States having made a declaration. If States do not make a choice, they are still subject to the jurisdiction of the residual dispute settlement mechanism, an Annex VII arbitral tribunal.[68] There is one additional important condition. The dispute may only be submitted to the instance for which States have indicated their preference under Article 287.1 if the choice of forum of the States involved coincides.[69] If there is a discrepancy in the parties' choices, then the effect is the same as if no declaration had been made, and the dispute may only be submitted to an Annex VII arbitral tribunal.[70]

[67] For example, in its Article 287 declaration, Italy "chooses the International Tribunal for the Law of the Sea and the International Court of Justice, without specifying that one has precedence over the other"; the Russian Federation

> chooses an arbitral tribunal constituted in accordance with Annex VII as the basic means for the settlement of disputes concerning the interpretation or application of the Convention. It opts for a special arbitral tribunal constituted in accordance with Annex VIII for the consideration of matters relating to fisheries, the protection and preservation of the marine environment, marine scientific research, and navigation, including pollution from vessels and dumping. It recognizes the competence of the International Tribunal for the Law of the Sea, as provided for in article 292, in matters relating to the prompt release of detained vessels and crews.

States may also explicitly state that they accept to have a specific dispute settled in their declaration, as was the case with Bangladesh and Myanmar, which declared their acceptance of the jurisdiction of ITLOS to settle their dispute regarding delimitation in the Bay of Bengal, ITLOS, *Dispute concerning Delimitation of the Maritime Boundary between Bangladesh and Myanmar in the Bay of Bengal (Bangladesh/Myanmar)*, Judgment of 14 March 2012, Case No. 16, paras. 41–50; Wasum-Rainer and Schlegel, "UNCLOS Dispute Settlement System," p. 198; Rothwell and Stephens, *The International Law of the Sea*, p. 449; Meron, "International Law in the Age of Human Rights," p. 343.

[68] UNCLOS Article 287.3; *The Bay of Bengal Maritime Boundary Arbitration (Bangladesh* v. *India)*, Award of 7 July 2014, PCA Case No. 2010-16, para. 66; *Guyana* v. *Suriname*, Award of 17 September 2007, PCA Case No. 2004-04.

[69] UNCLOS Article 287.4; see the example of the ITLOS, *Dispute concerning Delimitation of the Maritime Boundary between Bangladesh and Myanmar in the Bay of Bengal (Bangladesh/Myanmar)*; Klein, *Dispute Settlement in the UN Convention*, p. 57.

[70] UNCLOS Article 287.5; Treves, "Dispute-Settlement in the Law," p. 929; Treves, "Jurisdiction of the International Tribunal," p. 400; Brown, "Dispute Settlement,", p. 20.

States making declarations may also limit these as they see fit to specific categories of dispute. In this case, acceptance of the same instance would be limited to the specific matters for which acceptance has been given. This possibility was recognized by the ITLOS in the *M/V Louisa* case. Saint Vincent and the Grenadines had made a declaration that it accepted the jurisdiction of the ITLOS for disputes "concerning the arrest or detention of its vessels."[71] It argued that this did not constitute a limitation to its declaration, whereas Spain argued on the basis of reciprocity that the declaration did indeed limit the jurisdiction of the ITLOS.[72] ITLOS, relying extensively on the example of the Optional Clause system of the ICJ, found not only that it was open to States to introduce such limitations in their Article 287 declarations as they saw fit,[73] but, citing the *Norwegian Loans* case, that its jurisdiction existed only to the extent that the two declarations coincided.[74]

A word should finally be said concerning the role of Article 287 declarations in the case of conventions other than UNCLOS incorporating Part XV as their dispute settlement provisions. For the Straddling Stocks Convention, declarations under Article 287 apply also for disputes arising under the Convention,[75] as well as under any other "subregional, regional or global fisheries agreement relating to straddling fish stocks or highly migratory fish stocks,"[76] unless that State makes a declaration under the Straddling Stocks Convention. The same conditions apply as under Article 287 of UNCLOS.[77] This raises an interesting problem in terms of reciprocity in the case of a dispute between a State having made a declaration under UNCLOS, and one having made a declaration under the Straddling Stocks Convention.

As the effect of Article 30 is to incorporate the relevant provisions of UNCLOS, States parties to the Straddling Stocks Convention are not bound to differing extents depending on whether they are parties to UNCLOS or not. The system simply permits State consent in regard to the choice of procedure to be expressed either by a declaration already made under UNCLOS or by one applicable only under the Straddling

[71] The M/V "Louisa" (*Saint Vincent and the Grenadines* v. *Spain*), Case No. 18, Judgment of 28 May 2013, para. 75.

[72] Ibid., paras. 77–78. [73] Ibid., paras. 79–80.

[74] Ibid., paras. 81–82; M. Kawano, "Compulsory Disputes Settlement Procedures under UNCLOS: Their Achievements and New Agendas," in *The Rule of Law in the Seas of Asia: Navigational Chart for Peace and Stability*, Japan Ministry of Foreign Affairs, 2015, p. 124.

[75] Straddling Stocks Convention, Article 30.2.

[76] Ibid.; Rothwell and Stephens, *The International Law of the Sea*, p. 451.

[77] Straddling Stocks Convention, Article 30.4.

Stocks Convention.[78] If a dispute arises under the Straddling Stocks Convention, States will only be bound insofar as disputes under that Convention are concerned; it is irrelevant that one State may have, in its UNCLOS declaration, accepted or excluded jurisdiction over other matters. To the extent that the declarations coincide, they will establish the jurisdiction of a specific instance in respect of disputes arising under the Straddling Stocks Convention – a possibility States have accepted in consenting to be bound by that Convention. This therefore ensures reciprocity between the parties to the dispute.[79]

6.2.3 *Limitations and Exceptions under Articles 297 and 298*

There are a variety of inbuilt and optional exceptions in UNCLOS that exclude specific areas from the dispute settlement mechanism.

6.2.3.1 Automatic Exceptions

Article 297.1 submits disputes concerning the exercise by coastal States of their sovereign rights or jurisdiction to compulsory dispute settlement in regard to freedom of navigation, overflight or laying cables or pipelines, and other uses of the sea in Article 58 of UNCLOS, and alleged infractions of coastal State rules and regulations by States exercising these freedoms. It also reiterates jurisdiction over coastal State contravention of rules on protection and preservation of the marine environment.[80] There are automatic limitations in Article 297 that limit the applicability of dispute settlement provisions. States are not obliged to accept the compulsory submission to settlement of disputes relating to (a) marine scientific research;[81] (b) the sovereign rights of the coastal State with respect to the living resources in the exclusive economic zone (EEZ) or their exercise, "including its discretionary powers for determining the allowable catch, its harvesting capacity, the allocation of surpluses

[78] Treves gives the example of Canada, which ratified the Straddling Stocks Convention without being a party to UNCLOS, making a declaration first under the Straddling Stocks Convention, and then making another (compatible) declaration when it ratified UNCLOS, T. Treves, "A System for Law of the Sea Dispute Settlement," in D. Freestone, et al., eds., *The Law of the Sea: Progress and Prospects*, Oxford, Oxford University Press, 2006, p. 425.

[79] A point reaffirmed by the possibility for non-Parties to UNCLOS to nominate conciliators, arbitrators and experts under Article 30.4 of the Straddling Stocks Convention.

[80] UNCLOS Article 297.1(c); Treves, "Jurisdiction of the International Tribunal," p. 404; Rothwell and Stephens, *The International Law of the Sea*, p. 456; R. Rayfuse, "The Future of Compulsory Dispute Settlement under the Law of the Sea Convention," *Victoria University of Wellington Law Review*, vol. 36, no. 4, 2005, p. 686; Klein, *Dispute Settlement in the UN Convention*, pp. 213, 220.

[81] UNCLOS Article 297.2(a).

to other States and the terms and conditions established in its conservation and management laws and regulations."[82]

While certain categories of dispute are automatically excluded from the application of procedures under Part XV, they may still be unilaterally submitted to conciliation where they concern (a) specific disputes regarding marine scientific research; (b) manifest failure of the coastal State "to comply with its obligations to ensure [. . .] that the maintenance of the living resources in the exclusive economic zone [EEZ] is not seriously endangered"; (c) arbitrary refusal by the coastal State to determine the allowable catch and capacity to harvest living resources that the applicant State is interested in fishing; (d) arbitrary refusal by the coastal State to allocate to any State its declared surplus;[83] and (e) disputes over maritime delimitations having arisen after the entry into force of UNCLOS (excluding, however, consideration of sovereignty over territory). This also requires the parties to reach an agreement on their dispute, and if no agreement is reached, submit the dispute to a procedure under section 2.[84] This can be seen as an attempt to strike a balance between the sovereign rights of States over maritime areas in which they previously had none and the rights of other States to use the seas.

6.2.3.2 Optional Exceptions

Article 298 details a set of optional exceptions to compulsory dispute settlement. In order to avail of these exceptions, States must make a declaration to that effect, similarly to the system under Article 287.[85] States may make Article 298 declarations at any time and are free to exclude all or some of the matters outlined in the article. In the absence of such a declaration, disputes falling into these categories must be considered to fall within the scope of compulsory jurisdiction.[86] States may exclude three classes of dispute from compulsory dispute settlement: disputes concerning Articles 15, 74, and 83 of UNCLOS relating to maritime delimitations, or involving historic bays or titles;[87] disputes concerning military and law enforcement activities regarding the

[82] UNCLOS Article 297.3(a); Brown, "Dispute Settlement," pp. 21–22; Klein, *Dispute Settlement in the UN Convention*, p. 176.

[83] UNCLOS Articles 297.2(b), 297.3(b)(iii); see Klein, *Dispute Settlement in the UN Convention*, p. 189, who underlines that the decision relating to what constitutes allowable catch and surplus, and conditions for fishing, are the decision of the coastal State and not subject to dispute settlement, at p. 185.

[84] UNCLOS Article 298.1(a).

[85] Brown, "Dispute Settlement," p. 21.

[86] Treves, "Jurisdiction of the International Tribunal," p. 406.

[87] UNCLOS Article 298.1(a)(i).

exercise of sovereign rights or jurisdiction excluded under one of the automatic exceptions in Articles 297.2 and 297.3;[88] and, finally, disputes in respect of which the UNSC is exercising its functions under the UN Charter.[89]

The functioning of reciprocity in Article 298 is particularly interesting. First of all, Article 298.3 underlines that a State having excluded one or more classes of dispute by way of an Article 298 declaration may not then submit a dispute falling within the excepted categories to any procedure in the Convention unless the other party to the disputes so consents.[90] Under both Articles 287 and 298, the body that is settling the dispute is bound by the more restrictive consent to jurisdiction made by either State. The Article 298.3 mechanism is automatic, and it does not rest with the other State to invoke the declaration to avoid jurisdiction. Article 298 declarations may be withdrawn at any time[91] or overridden by the consent of either party to the dispute. Article 298.4 however continues to allow for a State that has made a declaration under Article 298.1(a) to be brought before a conciliation commission.[92]

The system of optional exceptions in Article 298 of UNCLOS can therefore be understood to function similarly to a set of preestablished reservations that States may make to exclude certain categories of dispute from the UNCLOS compulsory dispute settlement system. As such, it works on the basis of reciprocity. Both States parties to a dispute must have accepted to have the dispute settled to the same extent. If one has excluded the dispute by way of an Article 298 declaration, then neither one of the States involved in a dispute may bring the case before a dispute settlement mechanism as per section 2.

6.2.4 *Conclusion*

The UNCLOS is a comprehensive regime setting out the rights and obligations of States in respect of the seas, including the extension of sovereign rights to new maritime areas. The comprehensive dispute

88 UNCLOS Article 298.1(b). This means that the restriction in Article 297 should be interpreted as not including law enforcement activities in relation to the rights in question, otherwise it would not be necessary to have an Article 298.1(b); Treves, "Jurisdiction of the International Tribunal," p. 406.

89 UNCLOS Article 298.1(c). See in general Wasum-Rainer and Schlegel, "UNCLOS Dispute Settlement System," p. 200; Rothwell and Stephens, *The International Law of the Sea*, p. 454.

90 Rothwell and Stephens, *The International Law of the Sea*, p. 454.

91 UNCLOS Article 298.2.

92 M. H. Nordquist, et al., eds., *The United Nations Convention on the Law of the Sea 1982: A Commentary*, Volume V, Dordrecht, Nijhoff, 1989, p. 116.

settlement system in UNCLOS Part XV was intended to provide a safeguard to the balance of concessions made in negotiating the treaty.[93] This is also reflected in the exceptions to compulsory dispute settlement provided in the treaty, which attempt to reconcile the rights of the coastal State to regulate and manage the living resources in the maritime areas over which it has sovereign rights with the rights of third States to use of the oceans.

At the same time, the system is still very much based on consent, notably by the fact that UNCLOS is a treaty, and therefore requires consent to be bound. The system for choice of procedure under Article 287, and for optional exceptions to jurisdiction under Article 298, adds a second layer of consent, and insofar as it depends on unilateral choices of States, functions in an essentially similar manner, in terms of reciprocity, as the ICJ's Optional Clause system, albeit allowing for different choices of dispute settlement forum. UNCLOS sets out a system of jurisdiction that, with the exclusion of certain classes of dispute, is compulsory and based on reciprocity. States are bound to accept compulsory dispute settlement for specific disputes and to the same extent. However, the choice of forum of one State cannot be opposed to another State that has not so agreed; nor can a State suffer because it has accepted jurisdiction for a broader range of disputes than the other.

6.3 The International Criminal Court

While the International Criminal Court (ICC) is not a dispute settlement mechanism, but rather an international court set up to establish the international criminal responsibility of individuals, its operation is still of interest from the point of view of reciprocity, in particular the possibility for the ICC to exercise its jurisdiction over nationals of States that are not parties to the Rome Statute.[94] This has raised many questions as

[93] Klein, *Dispute Settlement in the UN Convention*, pp. 52, 140.

[94] R. D. Mancera, "The Rome Statute and Third States: Determining the Validity of the Jurisdiction of the International Criminal Court over Third-State Nationals," *Ateneo Law Journal*, vol. 51, no. 4, 2007, p. 988. For example, Rwandan nationals have been charged by the Court in relation to the situation in the Democratic Republic of the Congo, both in *The Prosecutor* v. *Callixte Mbarushimana*, Case No. ICC-01/04-01/10, and *The Prosecutor* v. *Sylvestre Mudacumura*, Case No. ICC-01/04-01/12. Rwanda is not a State party to the Rome Statute. The Office of the Prosecutor is also conducting a preliminary examination into alleged crimes in Palestine, concerning actions of both the Israeli Defence Forces and Palestinian armed groups. Palestine acceded to the Rome Statute on 2 January 2015, but Israel never ratified the Statute. If an investigation is opened, this may result in an

to whether this means that the ICC imposes obligations on third States. If it did, then this could be considered an example of a treaty creating obligations for third States, which would be bound to comply with rules without having consented and without having any connected rights.

The Court's jurisdiction is set out in Article 12 of the Statute. At the outset, it should be noted that no separate declaration is required to accept jurisdiction; when States become parties to the Statute, they thereby accept the jurisdiction of the Court.[95] The ICC has jurisdiction when the crimes in question occurred on the territory of a State party or when the individuals accused of the crimes are nationals of a State party.[96] Therefore, the first situation in which the Court may have jurisdiction over nationals of nonparties is if they have committed an international crime on the territory of a party to the Rome Statute.

States not parties to the Statute may also accept the jurisdiction of the Court by way of a declaration, another way in which the Court may have jurisdiction over individuals that are nationals of States not parties to the Statute.[97] Finally, the Security Council acting under chapter VII of the UN Charter may refer a situation to the ICC prosecutor.[98] In this situation, the jurisdiction of the Court extends to all UN member States,[99] by virtue of the effects of chapter VII and the consequent obligation for all States to carry out decisions of the Security Council taken on this basis.

In the case of crimes committed on the territory of a State party or by nationals of a State party, the fact that the crimes in question have been carried out on the territory of a State party is sufficient to grant

exercise of jurisdiction over nationals of a third State, Israel: see International Criminal Court, Office of the Prosecutor, Report on Preliminary Examination Activities (2015), 12 November 2015, pp. 11–17.

95 Rome Statute of the International Criminal Court, 17 July 1998, U.N. Doc. A/CONF.183/9, Article 12.1. This is referred to as "automatic jurisdiction," M. Inazumi, "The Meaning of the State Consent Precondition in Article 12(2) of the Rome Statute of the International Criminal Court: A Theoretical Analysis of the Sources of International Criminal Jurisdiction," *Netherlands International Law Review*, vol. 99, 2002, p. 162.

96 Rome Statute, Articles 12.2(a) and (b); Inazumi, "Meaning of the State Consent Precondition," pp. 162–163, 182, 184.

97 Rome Statute, Article 12.3.

98 D. Akande, "The Jurisdiction of the International Criminal Court over Nationals of Non-Parties: Legal Basis and Limits," *Journal of International Criminal Justice*, vol. 1, 2003, pp. 618–619.

99 Inazumi, "Meaning of the State Consent Precondition," p. 162; Mancera, "Rome Statute and Third States," p. 993 uses the words "in the world"; however, for reasons set out in Chapter 3, this may be questioned.

jurisdiction, regardless of the nationality of the individuals in question.[100] This is in reality a delegation of the criminal jurisdiction of the State; if a person commits a crime – any crime, and not just an international crime – on the territory of another State, the latter may exercise its criminal jurisdiction over that person. As the reasoning goes, if the territorial State can exercise jurisdiction in this manner, it can also delegate this exercise of jurisdiction to a body such as the ICC.[101] States of nationality do not have exclusive criminal jurisdiction over their nationals;[102] in fact, subjecting the exercise of territorial criminal jurisdiction to the consent of the State of nationality of the accused would place the two States concerned in a position of inequality, as it would limit the capacity of one State to exercise its territorial criminal jurisdiction.[103]

Therefore, the Rome Statute does not actually impose any obligations on nonparties.[104] The discomfort of some nonparty States with this system lies in the fact that their nationals may end up on trial before the Court. The ICC however does not concern itself with the responsibility of States but only of individuals. The political discomfort States may feel at the scrutiny that may arise from an international criminal trial does still not change the fact that the jurisdiction being exercised is only over individual criminal responsibility.[105] The definition of the crimes over which the ICC has jurisdiction does not depend on a finding of responsibility of the State.[106]

[100] Mancera, "Rome Statute and Third States," p. 998; Inazumi, "Meaning of the State Consent Precondition," pp. 162–163.

[101] Akande, "Jurisdiction of the International Criminal Court," p. 621; the possibility of such delegation is reflected in international practice, see ibid., pp. 622–624.

[102] Mancera, "Rome Statute and Third States," p. 1005; Inazumi, "Meaning of the State Consent Precondition," p. 165: "other states cannot oppose the ICC; just as they cannot object to that state exercising its own jurisdiction."

[103] See Inazumi, "Meaning of the State Consent Precondition," p. 192.

[104] Paulus, "Reciprocity Revisited," p.134.

[105] Rome Statute, Article 25. This is notably the case when Heads of State are charged by the ICC, as in the case of Sudan's failure to cooperate with the Court in surrendering Omar Al Bashir: see Prosecution's request for a finding of non-compliance against the Republic of the Sudan in the case of *The Prosecutor* v. *Omar Ahmad Hassan Al Bashir*, 19 December 2014, Case No. ICC-02/05-01/09, and *Request for Arrest and Surrender for Omar Hassan Al Bashir*, 15 October 2014, Case No. ICC-02/05-01/09; Akande, "Jurisdiction of the International Criminal Court," pp. 635–636, points out that the rationale of international criminal law was to separate the responsibility of an individual from that of the State in the first place.

[106] Rome Statute, Articles 5–9; Akande, "Jurisdiction of the International Criminal Court," p. 637; Mancera, "Rome Statute and Third States," p. 1004.

Further, although the nationals of a nonparty may find themselves within the jurisdiction of the Court, this fact does not impose any obligations upon the nonparty State, which is not bound in any way by obligations under the Statute, such as that of cooperating with the Court.[107] The working of the ICC, based as it is on a treaty, therefore does not escape the reciprocity of rights and obligations of States under international law, nor does it unilaterally impose any means of enforcement of international legal obligations on States that are not parties to the treaty.

6.4 The Jurisdiction of Human Rights Courts and Treaty Bodies

As seen in previous chapters, rules of international law concerning individuals do not escape the operation of reciprocity merely by virtue of their subject matter. After World War II there was an increase in treaties created for the benefit not of the entities assuming the rights and obligations – States – but of individuals.[108] However, these were not initially accompanied by any novel way of implementing those obligations. Gradually, first with the European Convention on Human Rights (ECHR) in 1950, and later the European Court of Human Rights (ECtHR) in 1959, the American Convention on Human Rights (ACHR) in 1969 and Inter-American Court of Human Rights (IACtHR) in 1979, the African Court on Human and People's Rights in 2004, and various other human rights complaint mechanisms, procedures became available for individuals to bring cases for violations of their rights directly against States parties to human rights conventions.

6.4.1 *Individual–State Complaints under Human Rights Instruments*

The most revolutionary aspect of international law's concern for individual rights in the latter half of the twentieth century is undoubtedly the rise of instances that permit individuals to enforce their rights directly against the State. These allow individuals that are under the jurisdiction of the State party to the relevant instrument, without any link of nationality being necessary, to bring a case against the State of jurisdiction before a dispute settlement body established under the treaty. As no inter-State legal relation based on sovereign equality is concerned, but

[107] Akande, "Jurisdiction of the International Criminal Court," p. 620; Mancera, "Rome Statute and Third States," pp. 1006–1007.

[108] Cassese equates this external "interest" to an example of non-reciprocity, but, again, this approach is disputed here; Cassese, *International Law in a Divided World*, p. 209.

only a legal relation between a State and an individual present on its territory,[109] without any requirement to prove a link of nationality, it could be expected that reciprocity will not be relevant in the acceptance of the jurisdiction of human rights courts for such complaints. States must, at a certain point, have given their consent to allow individuals to bring the alleged breach before a court by becoming parties to a human rights treaty that includes such a mechanism. The basic reciprocity governing the law of treaties equally governs human rights treaties.

The possibility to bring claims against a State is a unilateral right of individuals under the main human rights instruments, such as the ECHR, the ACHR, and the Protocol establishing the African Court on Human and Peoples' Rights.[110] However, there are some variations in procedure. The main difference consists in whether the State's consent to the treaty is sufficient for a case to be brought against it or whether an additional layer of consent by the State is required.

6.4.1.1 Direct Consent to the Treaty Instrument as Sufficient

First, there are a number of treaty bodies and human rights courts in which it is not necessary for States parties to express any additional consent to have individual complaints heard against themselves by the relevant Committee or court. These provisions may either be incorporated into the treaty, in which case all States parties may have complaints brought against them by individuals,[111] or be incorporated into additional protocols to the treaty. In the latter case, the procedure will only apply to States that are parties to both the original treaty and the protocol. Most such mechanisms also reiterate the point that States must be parties to the protocol in order to have complaints brought against them, or that no complaint can be heard against a State that is not a party to the protocol.[112] In these cases, therefore, there is a requirement

[109] Or over which it has jurisdiction even though outside the State's territory, as per for example the judgments of the European Court of Human Rights in, notably, *Case of Al-Jedda v. The United Kingdom*, Application no. 27021/08, Judgment of 7 July 2011.

[110] European Convention on Human Rights, Rome, 4 November 1950, as amended by Protocols Nos. 11 and 14, supplemented by Protocols Nos. 1, 4, 6, 7, 12 and 13 (ECHR), Article 34; American Convention on Human Rights, 22 November 1969, OAS Treaty Series No. 36 (ACHR), Article 44.

[111] As is the case of the ECHR, as amended, Article 34; Protocol to the African Charter on Human and Peoples' Rights on the Establishment of an African Court on Human and Peoples' Rights, Articles 5.3 and 34.6.

[112] Optional Protocol to the Convention on the Elimination of All Forms of Discrimination against Women, UN Doc. A/Res/54/4, 15 October 1999 (CEDAW Optional Protocol), Articles 2 and 3; Optional Protocol to the International Covenant on Civil and Political

for a State to consent to the individual complaints procedure upon ratification, but no further requirement of consent. Because only one State is concerned when a case is brought against it by an individual, only the consent of the State against which the complaint is being made is relevant; there is no consideration of reciprocity in acceptance of jurisdiction.

6.4.1.2 Instruments Requiring Additional Declarations

Some instruments require further unilateral declarations by a State for it to be bound by individual complaints procedures. This is the case of the African Court on Human and Peoples' Rights,[113] the Inter-American Court of Human Rights,[114] the Convention on the Protection of Persons from Enforced Disappearance (Enforced Disappearance Convention),[115] the Convention against Torture,[116] and the Convention on the Elimination of All Forms of Racial Discrimination (CERD).[117] Unless a State has made a

Rights, Adopted and opened for signature, ratification and accession by General Assembly resolution 2200A (XXI) of 16 December 1966 (Optional Protocol to the ICCPR) Article 1; Optional Protocol to the International Covenant on Economic, Social and Cultural Rights, UN General Assembly Resolution A/RES/63/117 of 10 December 2008 (ICESCR Optional Protocol), Articles 1 and 2; Optional Protocol to the Convention on the Rights of Persons with Disabilities, UN General Assembly Resolution A/Res/61/106 of 13 December 2006, Article 1. The Optional Protocol to the Convention on the Rights of the Child on a Communications Procedure, UN General Assembly Resolution A/Res/66/138 of 19 December 2011 (CROC Protocol) allows for individual communications in Article 5, but reiterates in Article 1.3 that no communication may be received regarding States not parties to the Protocol, and in Article 1.2 that communications must regard an instrument to which the State in question is a party; the Committee has competence to receive communications regarding the Convention on the Rights of the Child, the Optional Protocol on the sale of children, child prostitution and child pornography, or the Optional Protocol on the involvement of children in armed conflict.

113 Protocol to the African Charter on Human and Peoples' Rights on the Establishment of an African Court on Human and Peoples' Rights, Article 34.6: "At the time of the ratification of this Protocol or any time thereafter, the State shall make a declaration accepting the competence of the Court to receive cases under article 5 (3) of this Protocol. The Court shall not receive any petition under article 5 (3) involving a State Party which has not made such a declaration."

114 ACHR, Article 62.

115 International Convention on the Protection of Persons from Enforced Disappearance (Enforced Disappearance Convention), 20 December 2006, 2716 U.N.T.S. 3, Article 31.1.

116 Convention against Torture and Other Cruel, Inhuman or Degrading Treatment or Punishment, adopted and opened for signature, ratification and accession by UN General Assembly Resolution 39/46 of 10 December 1984 (Torture Convention), Article 22.1.

117 Convention on the Elimination of All Forms of Racial Discrimination, Adopted and Opened for Signature and Ratification by UN General Assembly Resolution 2106 (XX) of 21 December 1965 (CERD), Article 14.1.

declaration in which it accepts that individuals may bring cases against it, no complaints may be brought against it merely because it is a party to the treaty. Therefore, under these treaty instruments, there will be two sets of States that have differing obligations. While in effect individuals will have varying rights under the treaty depending on whether the State on whose territory they are present has made a declaration or not, it will still only be necessary to examine whether the State against which the complaint is being brought has accepted the possibility of an individual complaint. Because the case over which the relevant body must have jurisdiction is between an individual and a State, there are also no consequences for inter-State relations under the treaty that need to be examined. For example, in deciding whether it has jurisdiction, the IACtHR limits itself to establishing whether and when the State in question has accepted the contentious jurisdiction of the Court[118] – a different and far simpler exercise than, for example, that undertaken by the ICJ.

6.4.1.3 Irrelevance of Reciprocity

Clearly, the consent of the State is required for individuals to be able to bring complaints directly against it, either expressed through ratification of the treaty or through any additional act of consent such as ratification of an additional protocol or the making of a declaration. However, there is no further condition of reciprocity in the case of individual complaints. Again, because the criterion of nationality is not relevant in entitling an individual to bring a case under a human rights treaty, there is no need for the State of nationality of the individual making the complaint to have made an equivalent declaration. There is no need to enter into an analysis of whether reciprocity of rights and obligations exists where the jurisdiction of the human rights instance in question concerns a dispute between an individual and a State.

6.4.1.4 The Issue of Reservations

The HRC has taken the position that in human rights treaties, an invalid reservation may be "severed" from the State's consent, and the reserving State remains bound without the benefit of the reservation.[119] While the

[118] See, for example, *Fernandez Ortega* v. *Mexico*, Judgment, IACtHR, 30 August 2010, para. 14.

[119] B. Simma and G. Hernandez, "Legal Consequences of an Impermissible Reservation to a Human Rights Treaty: Where Do We Stand?," in E. Cannizzaro ed., *The Law of Treaties: Beyond the Vienna Convention*, Oxford, Oxford University Press, 2011, p. 63.

position has since been nuanced, it is worth examining the connection with the consent of States to individual complaints mechanisms. The origin of the HRC's approach comes from the case law of the ECtHR, notably in the *Belilos* case.[120]

In *Belilos*, Switzerland made what it described as an interpretive declaration in relation to Article 6.1 of the ECHR. Switzerland raised the preliminary objection that there was no jurisdiction because the application by Ms. Belilos did not relate to a right it had recognized.[121] The ECtHR first found that the interpretive declaration was in reality a reservation and then decided that the reservation was impermissible, in order to find it had jurisdiction. Clearly, Switzerland had not conditioned its participation in the treaty on its declaration, had continued to act as if it were bound by the provisions in question, and had recognized the competence of the Court to decide on the issue.[122] The Court therefore found it had jurisdiction. A similar approach was taken in *Loizidou*, where the ECtHR found that despite the impermissibility of its reservations, Turkey had in fact invoked the benefit of the application of the Convention, and the Court therefore had competence.[123] In both these cases, it could not be considered that the States concerned did not consider themselves parties to the Convention on the basis of the impermissibility of the reservation they had made.

In general, rather than a rule, severability is considered to be a rebuttable presumption for impermissible reservations to human rights treaties when the intention of the reserving State cannot be identified.[124] This still respects the principle of consent,[125] which an otherwise extensive reliance on the HRC's General Comment 24 would not. Even the HRC itself has accepted the existence of this "presumption."[126] Although

[120] *Belilos* v. *Switzerland*, ECtHR, App. No. 10328/83, Judgment, 29 April 1988, para 60. See also *Weber* v. *Switzerland*, ECtHR, Application no. 11034/84, Judgment of 22 May 1990, and *Loizidou* v. *Turkey*, ECtHR, Application no. 15318/89, Judgment of 18 December 1996. The approach was also taken by the Inter-American Court in *Hilaire, Constantine and Benjamin et al.* v. *Trinidad and Tobago*, IACtHR, Judgment of 21 June 2002.

[121] *Belilos* v. *Switzerland*, ECtHR, Application No. 10328/83, Judgment of 29 April 1988, para. 38.

[122] Ibid., para. 60; ILC, *Guide to Practice on Reservations*, p. 534.

[123] *Loizidou* v. *Turkey*, paras. 92–98; ILC, *Guide to Practice on Reservations*, p. 529.

[124] Simma and Hernandez, "Legal Consequences of an Impermissible Reservation," p. 83.

[125] ILC, *Guide to Practice on Reservations*, p. 534.

[126] Seventeenth Meeting of the chairpersons of the human rights treaty bodies, "The Practice of Human Rights Treaty Bodies with Respect to Reservations to International Human Rights Treaties," HRI/MC/2005/5, 13 June 2005, para. 37; see also ILC, *Guide to Practice on Reservations*, p. 536.

reciprocity is not relevant in individual–State complaints mechanisms under human rights treaties, State consent still is – although interpreted in a less stringent manner than in inter-State dispute settlement mechanisms.

6.4.2 *State–State Complaints under Human Rights Instruments*

In most, if not all, human rights treaties, there also exists a possibility for States parties to bring complaints against each other for alleged violations. Unlike individual complaints procedures, inter-State complaints do concern more than one State, and a greater role for reciprocity in acceptance of these obligations is to be expected. This is despite the fact that the rationale for inter-State complaints mechanisms is not for States to uphold their own subjective rights in the same manner as individuals but to ensure that all States respect the conventions in question.[127] In reality, this mechanism is either not often used or it is used in a manner akin to diplomatic protection, or at least, where there is a close link between the violation and the interests of the applicant State.[128] However, it is clear from the relevant treaties that no special interest needs to be shown aside from the fact of an alleged violation by another State party.[129] It is therefore, at least theoretically, a form of *actio popularis*.

As for individual complaints, a State must consent to the jurisdiction of inter-State complaints mechanisms. This consent may be expressed either through a simple acceptance of the relevant instrument or by making an additional declaration. The fundamental differences with individual complaints procedures arise in the latter case.

[127] Sicilianos, "Influence des droits de l'homme," pp. 11–13; Chinkin, *Third Parties in International Law*, p. 122.

[128] Meron characterizes the facts in the *Denmark* v. *Turkey*, Application no. 34382/97, Decision on Admissibility, 8 June 1999 case before the ECtHR as an example of diplomatic protection: Meron, "International Law in the Age of Human Rights," p. 312; however, Applicant States had a similar interest in both the *Austria* v. *Italy* and *Ireland* v. *UK* cases before the ECtHR. Even in such cases the Court or Commission has been at pains to underline that States are not acting in their own interest, but in the interest of the public order protected by the Convention: see notably *Austria* v. *Italy*, European Commission of Human Rights, Application no. 788/60, Decision on Admissibility, 11 January 1961, paras. 18–20.

[129] Y. Tyagi, *The UN Human Rights Committee: Practice and Procedure*, Cambridge, Cambridge University Press, 2011, p. 341.

6.4.2.1 Availability of Inter-State Complaints Procedures without Any Additional Requirement of Acceptance

Under some human rights treaties, States may bring complaints against other States parties, and vice versa, merely by becoming parties to the treaty. One example is the ECHR, which simply provides in Article 33 that "[a]ny High Contracting Party may refer to the Court any alleged breach of the provisions of the Convention and the Protocols thereto by another High Contracting Party." Although no further acceptance is necessary, Article 33 means that all States parties equally have the right to bring cases against each other for violations of the Convention, fulfilling a basic reciprocity in the mechanism.

Two other human rights instruments do not require any additional acceptance for inter-State complaints. The first is the CERD, which however sets out in its Articles 11–13 a mechanism that is more of a compulsory conciliation procedure, resulting in recommendations that States parties may accept or not. Article 22 then provides for the possibility of referring inter-State disputes on the interpretation or application of the Convention not settled by this procedure or by negotiation to the International Court of Justice.[130] A similarly elaborate mechanism is set out in the African Charter on Human and People's Rights (Banjul Charter), which provides for a system of communication and negotiation in its Articles 47–49. However, the Protocol to the African Charter on Human and Peoples' Rights on the Establishment of an African Court on Human and Peoples' Rights allows for three categories of States to submit cases to the Court: the State having made a complaint to the Commission as per Articles 47–49 of the Banjul Charter, under Article 5 (b); the State *against which* the complaint has been made, in Article 5(c); and the State party whose citizen is a victim of a human rights violation, under Article 5(d). Therefore, although no further acceptance is required to file a complaint with the African Court on the basis of the Banjul Charter, doing so entitles both complaining and complainant State to equally bring a case, as well as explicitly allowing for diplomatic protection in cases of human rights violations.

[130] This procedure was notably employed by Georgia, which brought a case against Russia before the ICJ. However, the Court found that the precondition of negotiations had not been fulfilled, and therefore declined jurisdiction, *Application of the International Convention for the Elimination of All Forms of Racial Discrimination (Georgia* v. *Russian Federation)*, Preliminary Objections, Judgment, ICJ Reports 2011, paras. 182–184.

6.4.2.2 Inter-State Complaint Mechanisms Based on Additional Unilateral Declarations

The majority of inter-State complaint mechanisms require an additional form of consent. This may be explained by the fact that inter-State complaint mechanisms are closer to traditional international dispute settlement mechanisms. States may be more reluctant to accept having a case brought against them by another State than by an individual and therefore wish to subject the functioning of inter-State complaints procedures to an additional requirement of consent. This additional consent is expressed in the form of a unilateral declaration by States parties to a treaty that they accept that other States may bring complaints against them for not fulfilling their obligations under the Convention. This is the mechanism available under the Enforced Disappearance Convention,[131] the American Convention on Human Rights (ACHR),[132] the Convention on Migrant Workers,[133] the Torture Convention,[134] the Optional Protocol to the ICESCR,[135] the ICCPR,[136] and the Optional Protocol to the Convention of the Rights of a Child on a Communications Procedure.[137]

In all cases where a declaration is required, not only must a State party have made a declaration in order to bring a case, but it may only do so against a State party that has also made such a declaration. These conditions reflect a fundamental requirement of reciprocity in order for States to bring complaints against each other before treaty bodies or courts, regardless of the fact that the interests being protected are a common interest to have human rights observed. In the same way as jurisdiction of other bodies and courts dealing with inter-State complaints, both States involved in the dispute must have accepted to be involved in the procedure to the same extent.

The ACHR in its Article 62 also provides for the possibility, with wording similar to that employed by the ICJ's Optional Clause system, for States parties to accept "ipso facto, and not requiring special agreement" the jurisdiction of the IACtHR for some or all disputes concerning

[131] Enforced Disappearance Convention, Article 32. [132] ACHR Article 45.

[133] International Convention on the Protection of the Rights of All Migrant Workers and Members of Their Families, Adopted by UN General Assembly Resolution45/158 of 18 December 1990 (Convention on Migrant Workers), Article 76.

[134] Torture Convention, Article 21. [135] ICESCR Optional Protocol, Article 10.

[136] International Covenant on Civil and Political Rights, 16 December 1966, U.N.G.A. Res 2200A (XXI), Article 41.

[137] CROC Optional Protocol, Article 12.

the interpretation or application of the ACHR. Making such declarations on "condition of reciprocity" is explicitly given as a possibility in Art. 62.1, but taking into consideration the proviso in Article 62.3 that "the States Parties to the case recognize or have recognized such jurisdiction, whether by special declaration [. . .] or by special agreement," it is clear that here again both parties to the case must have accepted the jurisdiction of the IACtHR over the specific dispute. Most treaties also contain a compromissory clause allowing for disputes to be submitted either to arbitration or the ICJ, and explicitly provide for the possibility of making reservations to this effect, as well as for the reciprocal working of such reservations.[138]

6.4.3 *Conclusion*

It is clear that the inter-State dimension of human rights treaties continues to exist and the jurisdiction of inter-State complaint mechanisms is to a great degree dependent on reciprocity.[139] In general, it is not possible for one State to bring a claim against another State that does not have this same legal capacity, either because it has not made a declaration or not become a party to a protocol or convention.

Due to the absence of any inter-State dimension, in individual–State complaint mechanisms reciprocity is not a factor; only unilateral consent by the State is necessary. However, the particular nature of individual rights has meant that, particularly in interpreting conventional obligations, courts and treaty bodies have sought to limit the possibility for States to raise arguments based on reciprocity to escape their obligations, even in inter-State cases.

A notable example is the *Austria* v. *Italy* case before the European Commission of Human Rights. Italy had argued that Austria should not have been able to bring the case because, at the time the facts occurred, Italy had no obligations toward Austria under the Convention because Austria was not a party.[140] The Commission, however, indicated that at the time the facts occurred, any other High Contracting Party could have brought a complaint in respect of Italy's conduct before the Commission,

[138] Such as Article 92.2 of the Convention on Migrant Workers, Article 30.2 of the Torture Convention, and Article 29.2 of CEDAW. The CERD does not explicitly state the possibility of making such a reservation in its dispute settlement clause in Article 22, but does allow reservations to be made in general.

[139] Combacau and Sur, *Droit International Public*, p. 392; Tyagi, *UN Human Rights Committee*, p. 342.

[140] *Austria* v. *Italy*, p. 20.

as Italy was under an obligation to respect the Convention; and therefore, once Austria became a party, "it is more consistent with the system of collective guarantee that Austria [. . .] should have the same powers under Article 24 as the other High Contracting Parties."[141] The Commission recognized that, because Austria was not bound by the ECHR obligations at the time the facts occurred, Italy could not bring a similar complaint; however, it explains that "this absence of reciprocity in regard to the element of time springs solely from the fact that before 3rd September 1958 Austria was not subject to the regime of the Convention and *not from any differential treatment of the High Contracting Parties* in Article 24 itself."[142] The Court's decision did in fact maintain reciprocity, in ensuring that all States had the same capacity to bring the case over the same facts. Obviously, Italy did not owe Austria its substantive obligations directly; these were owed to the individuals within its jurisdiction. It would not therefore compromise the equality of the contracting parties to allow Austria to bring such a case. If anything, according to the argument made by the Commission, equality was maintained by ensuring that Austria had the same legal capacity as other contracting parties. The Commission in *Austria* v. *Italy* explained that "in becoming a Party to the Convention, a State undertakes, vis à vis the other High Contracting Parties, to secure the rights and freedoms defined in section 1 to every person within its jurisdiction"[143] and not to "create subjective and reciprocal rights for the High Contracting Parties themselves."[144] These two passages accurately distinguish the kinds of obligations States have under such instruments.

6.5 Investor–State Dispute Settlement

Since the 1990s, with the upsurge in the number of bilateral investment treaties (BITs) concluded between States, there has been a parallel rise in investment arbitrations between States and individual investors. This section will therefore give a brief overview of how investor–State dispute settlement (ISDS) works in the context of BITs, before addressing the issue of the use of MFN clauses in investment agreements to establish the jurisdiction of arbitral tribunals.

[141] Ibid.
[142] Ibid., p. 21, emphasis added; Art. 24 was the old inter-State complaints procedure under the ECHR. Emphasis added.
[143] *Austria* v. *Italy*, p. 18. [144] Ibid., p. 19.

6.5.1 *How Investor–State Dispute Settlement Works*

Dispute settlement clauses incorporated into BITs concern both disputes between contracting States and between a host State and investors of the other party. State–State dispute settlement provisions usually provide for the possibility of submitting to arbitration disputes arising between the contracting parties "relating to interpretation or application" of the agreement.[145] Of greater interest for present purposes are the provisions for dispute settlement between investors and States.

ISDS provisions allow the investors of each contracting party to bring disputes arising in relation to investments against the other contracting party, that is, the host State. The rationale of including these clauses was to remove the settlement of disputes between foreign investors and States from the vagaries of diplomatic protection. BITs therefore consist of an exchange of rights and obligations between two contracting States in relation to the treatment each must offer the investors of the other party, but also provide for procedural rights for individuals that fit the definition of investors as set out in the BIT to enforce their rights directly against the other State party.

The conditions attaching to such consent vary significantly from treaty to treaty.[146] Clauses may require recourse to national courts for a certain number of months;[147] they may include temporal limitations; they may indicate which procedures must be used, such as ICSID, the International Chamber of Commerce, or UNCITRAL rules.[148] It is this difference between the conditions to access investor–State arbitration in the various BITs that has given rise to claims by investors that the MFN clauses that are included in most, if not all, BITs – examined in Chapter 4 – may be applied to the dispute settlement clauses to circumvent the conditions in their own treaty, using instead the more "favorable" conditions in other investment treaties concluded with other States.

The main thrust of the argument in favor of applying MFN clauses to jurisdiction is that access for investors to dispute settlement with the

[145] See for example the UK–Belize BIT, Article 9, or the Canada Model BIT, Article 48.

[146] And these conditions set out the jurisdiction of the tribunal: *ICS Inspection and Control Services Ltd (United Kingdom)* v. *Argentine Republic*, UNCITRAL, PCA, Case No. 2010-9, Award on Jurisdiction, 10 February 2012, para. 258.

[147] For example, the Argentina–Italy BIT, Article 8.3.

[148] German Model BIT, Article 10, and Canada Model BIT, Article 27, which set out the possible fora to which investors may have recourse.

host State is part of the "treatment" they are granted in BITs.[149] The first instance of this application was in *Maffezini* v. *Spain*.[150] There has since been considerable divergence between arbitral tribunals on the topic.[151]

6.5.2 *Use of the MFN Clause to Establish Jurisdiction*

The issue of the applicability of MFN clauses to provisions on jurisdiction is not limited to the area of individual–State investment arbitration. The issue arose in three cases before the ICJ in the early 1950s: *Ambatielos* (and particularly the subsequent arbitral award), *Rights of US Nationals in Morocco*, and *Anglo-Iranian Oil Co.*

The *Rights of US Nationals in Morocco* case is especially useful for the link made by the Court between MFN and equality, as well as for clarifying that once provisions of third treaties are no longer in force, these cannot be applied on the basis of MFN.[152] The case also recognized that the United States was entitled to exercise consular jurisdiction over its nationals in Morocco on a MFN basis,[153] thereby importing the more favorable conditions of exercise of jurisdiction incorporated in a third treaty. While relating to jurisdiction in a wider sense, this case was in fact dealing with a different issue, namely MFN at the purely inter-State

[149] ILC, Final Report, Study Group on the Most-Favoured Nation Clause, p. 23.

[150] *Maffezini* v. *Spain*, ICSID Case No. ARB/97/7, Decision on Jurisdiction, 25 January 2000; see comments in ILC, Final Report, Study Group on the Most-Favoured Nation Clause, p. 20.

[151] In favor of this use of the MFN clause: *RosInvestCo UK Ltd.* v. *Russian Federation*, SCC Case No. Abr. V 079/2005, Award on Jurisdiction, 5 October 2007; *Siemens A.G.* v. *Argentine Republic*, ICSID Case No. ARB/02/8, Decision on Jurisdiction, 3 August 2004; *Camuzzi International S.A.* v. *Argentine Republic [II]*, ICSID Case No. ARB/03/7, Decision on Objections to Jurisdiction, 10 June 2005; *Gas Natural SDG, S.A.* v. *Argentine Republic*, ICSID Case No. ARB/03/10, Decision of the Tribunal on Preliminary Questions on Jurisdiction, 17 June 2005; *Garanti Koza LLP* v. *Turkmenistan*, ICSID Case No. ARB/11/20, Decision on the Objection to Jurisdiction for Lack of Consent, 3 July 2013, among others. Declining to apply the MFN clause in this manner: *Salini Costruttori SpA and Italstrade SpA* v. *the Hashemite Kingdom of Jordan*, ICSID Case No. ARB/02/13, Decision on Jurisdiction, 9 November 2004, paras. 118–119, *Plama Consortium Limited* v. *Republic of Bulgaria*, ICSID Case No. ARB/03/24, Decision on Jurisdiction, 8 February 2005, *ICS Inspection and Control Services Limited (United Kingdom)* v. *Argentine Republic*, PCA Case No. 2010-9, Award on Jurisdiction, 10 February 2012, among others. For an overview of the different kinds of interpretation made by arbitral tribunals in applying the MFN clause to dispute settlement clauses, see ILC, Final Report, Study Group on the Most-Favoured Nation Clause, pp. 43–44.

[152] Rights of Nationals of the United States of America in Morocco (*France* v. *United States*), Judgment of 27 August 1952, ICJ Reports 1952, p. 204.

[153] Ibid., p. 190.

level, and the rights that, at the time, the State of nationality had over its nationals abroad.

The decision in *Maffezini* may instead be traced back to the *Ambatielos* case.[154] That dispute involved the question of the treatment of a Greek national before UK courts. Greece brought a case before the ICJ claiming that the United Kingdom had the obligation to submit to arbitration in respect of the claim. In order to do so, claims had to be based on a FCN treaty. The crux of the argument was whether the MFN treatment clause in the treaty could also cover issues relating to the administration of justice. The ICJ found that these were claims based on the treaty and that the United Kingdom had an obligation to submit to arbitration.[155] However, it is important to note that the issue was that of the access of Mr. Ambatielos to the *domestic* courts of the United Kingdom and his treatment there, and not whether MFN could be used to modify the conditions of consent of the State to arbitrate with the individual directly – it could not have done so, since there was no such provision in the FCN treaty. The issue of the application of the MFN clause was still in its strictly inter-State and reciprocal relation.

The final case, *Anglo-Iranian Oil Co.*, did deal with the issue of the extension of jurisdiction through application of the MFN clause between two States. In its declaration under Article 36.2 of the ICJ Statute, Iran accepted the jurisdiction of the Court "in any dispute arising after the ratification of the present declaration with regard to situations or facts relating directly or indirectly to the application of treaties or conventions accepted by Persia and subsequent to the ratification of this declaration."[156] The treaties between Iran and the United Kingdom dated from 1857 and 1903, and were therefore not subsequent to the ratification of Iran's declaration of acceptance of the Court's jurisdiction. The United Kingdom argued that the treatment in question, which was relevant by virtue of the operation of the MFN clause, was covered in a later treaty

[154] *Maffezini* v. *Spain*, ICSID Case No. ARB/97/7, Decision on Jurisdiction, 25 January 2000, para. 54. The point that "treatment" may involve dispute settlement provisions was echoed in *Siemens* v. *Argentina*, ICSID Case No. ARB/02/8, Decision on Jurisdiction, 3 August 2004, para. 102; *AWG Group Ltd.* v. *The Argentine Republic*, Decision on Jurisdiction, UNCITRAL, 3 August 2006, para. 59, but criticized by *Salini Costruttori SpA and Italstrade SpA* v. *the Hashemite Kingdom of Jordan*, ICSID Case No. ARB/02/13, Decision on Jurisdiction, 9 November 2004, paras. 111–112.

[155] *Ambatielos Case (Greece* v. *United Kingdom)*, Merits: Obligation to Arbitrate, Judgment of 19 May 1953, ICJ Reports 1953, pp. 21–22.

[156] *Anglo-Iranian Oil Co. case (United Kingdom* v. *Iran)*, Preliminary Objections, Judgment of 22 July 1952, ICJ Reports 1952, p. 103.

between Iran and Denmark that fell within the terms of Iran's Article 36.2 declaration. However, the Court found that the United Kingdom could not use the provisions in this third treaty to found its jurisdiction, as "[i]t is [the treaty containing the most-favored nation clause] which establishes the juridical link between the United Kingdom and a third-party treaty and confers upon that State the rights enjoyed by the third party."[157] MFN could not therefore be used to change the scope of the acceptance of the Court's jurisdiction.

6.5.3 *Use of the MFN Clause by Arbitral Tribunals*

Fast-forwarding fifty years, this case law has once again become relevant as investment tribunals attempt to establish whether the MFN clause contained in a BIT also applies to the provisions of the treaty on investor–State dispute settlement. The *Maffezini* tribunal had, indeed, considered that a requirement of resort to national courts by investors for eighteen months could be circumvented by application of the MFN clause.[158] It had also, however, indicated that the clause could not apply in a series of cases: where consent to arbitration was conditioned on exhaustion of local remedies, dispute settlement provisions including a "fork in the road," to resort to a different forum than that set out in the applicable BIT,[159] and where the dispute settlement system is highly institutionalized and contains precise rules of procedure.[160] Since then, however, MFN clauses have been used to modify the provisions on dispute settlement in a number of ways, and there have also been a number of criticisms leveled at this practice in decisions denying the applicability of MFN clauses to jurisdictional provisions.[161]

[157] Ibid., p. 109.

[158] *Maffezini* v. *Spain*, ICSID case No. ARB/97/7, Decision on Jurisdiction, 25 January 2000, para. 39.

[159] Although the tribunal in *Garanti Koza* used the MFN clause to allow investors to select UNCITRAL instead of ICSID arbitration, *Garanti Koza LLP* v. *Turkmenistan*, ICSID Case No. ARB/11/20, Decision on the Objection to Jurisdiction for Lack of Consent, 3 July 2013, para. 41.

[160] *Maffezini* v. *Spain*, paras. 62–63.

[161] See *Tecnicas Mediambientales Tecmed S.A.* v. *the United Mexican States*, ICSID Case No. ARB (AF)/00/02, Award, 29 May 2003, para. 69; the tribunal in *Telenor* considered that the MFN clause could not extend to procedural rights, *Telenor Mobile Communications A.S.* v. *Hungary*, ICSID Case No. ARB/04/15, Award, 13 September 2006, para. 92; *Austrian Airlines* v. *The Slovak Republic*, final award, UNCITRAL, 9 October 2009, para. 135. For an overview, see *Venezuela US, S.R.L. (Barbados)* v. *Venezuela*, PCA Case No. 2013-34, Dissenting Opinion of Professor Marcelo G. Kohen (On the respondent's objection to jurisdiction *ratione voluntatis*), 26 July 2016.

MFN clauses may be drafted in a number of ways.[162] Decisions of arbitral tribunals, and the arguments that have been raised for and against the application of MFN to dispute settlement clauses, have often turned on the precise wording of the provisions.[163] It is not therefore possible to establish one definitive interpretation of MFN clauses that may be applicable in all cases, as the interpretation will vary almost on a case-by-case, or at least BIT-by-BIT, basis.[164] States have however started to specify in their BITs whether the MFN clause applies to dispute settlement provisions or not. It may therefore be that States have clearly consented to arbitrate with investors on the basis of the conditions included in a treaty with a third State.

6.5.4 *The Problem of Consent*

Aside from the cases in which MFN is clearly made applicable to dispute settlement provisions, there are some conclusions that may be drawn regarding the general applicability of MFN to extend the jurisdiction of an arbitral tribunal. The first question is whether the rationale of MFN is supposed to cover the issue of investor–State dispute settlement. While the MFN clause has been in use, in one form or another, for hundreds of years, the introduction of international arbitration between States and investors directly, without requiring recourse to diplomatic protection, is instead a very recent development. Reciprocal MFN treatment is an obligation operating between States to provide a certain standard of treatment for the nationals of the other State in their jurisdiction, harmonized with the same treatment afforded to nationals of other States. It therefore has an equalizing function. The treatment of investors before national courts, as was the case in *Ambatielos*, may be part of this treatment.

[162] The ILC divides MFN clauses into six categories: relating to "treatment," "all treatment," "treatment" with reference to specific aspects of the investment process, specific obligations, investors or investments "in like circumstances," and those including a territorial limitation; ILC, Final Report, Study Group on the Most-Favoured Nation Clause, pp. 16–17; OECD, "Most-Favoured Nation Treatment in International Investment Law," *OECD Working Papers on International Investment*, 2004/02, OECD Publishing, http://dx.doi.org/10.1787/518757021651, p. 9.

[163] For a breakdown of the differing interpretations, see ILC, Final Report, Study Group on the Most-Favoured Nation Clause, pp. 43–44.

[164] See *Salini Costruttori SpA and Italstrade SpA* v. *the Hashemite Kingdom of Jordan*, ICSID Case No. ARB/02/13, Decision on Jurisdiction, 9 November 2004, *Siemens* v. *Argentina*, ICSID Case No. ARB/02/8, Decision on Jurisdiction, 3 August 2004.

The rationale of investor–State dispute settlement is to allow investors to not have to rely on the actions of their State once the host State has violated the rights they enjoy under the BIT. Therefore, although investors have direct rights against the host State, these rights relate to the consequences of a purported breach, and not to whether there has been discrimination in their treatment, which is within the purview of the MFN clause.

As MFN clauses work reciprocally between both parties, if both States may invoke most-favored nation treatment, then this does not affect the reciprocal nature of the engagement. It might be argued that the issue of reciprocity of consent is not relevant as between the investor and the State; the State makes a unilateral offer to the investor to arbitrate, which the latter may or may not accept. The main issue is therefore one of clarity of consent and whether the latter may be modified by applying an MFN clause absent a clear indication to that effect.[165]

An analogy may be drawn with individual complaints mechanisms under human rights treaties. The position of the HRC according to which State consent may be implied by severing an inadmissible reservation has failed to gain much traction. Even in the case law of the ECtHR, the Court has always sought to establish that the State did consent or was acting in a manner in which it demonstrated that it considered itself bound by the treaty. If this approach is taken in human rights law, in which there is no relevant inter-State dimension as far as individual complaints are concerned, then there is all the more reason to carefully establish that States did in fact wish to have the conditions of their consent to arbitration modified by the application of the MFN clause in a BIT.

Finally, the MFN clause is supposed to have an equalizing function. However, applying it to a dispute settlement provision effectively places the investors of each of the two States parties in a different position; it alters the scope of the consent for each of the two, as the relevant third treaties in which there may be more favorable conditions of access will be different for each State. The application of the MFN clause to jurisdictional provisions would therefore end up placing the investors on a footing of inequality, and consequently would mean that the States have

[165] This was the position taken by the *Plama* tribunal, *Plama Consortium Limited* v. *Republic of Bulgaria*, Decision on Jurisdiction, ICSID Case No. ARB/03/24, 8 February 2005, para. 198; ILC, Final Report, Study Group on the Most-Favoured Nation Clause, pp. 27–28.

consented to jurisdiction of a varying scope, thereby changing the balance of rights and obligations under the treaty.[166]

The MFN clause, granted reciprocally by States to ensure equality in treatment of foreign investors and indeed of their own investors with nationals of third States, therefore has a different rationale to that of direct investor–State arbitration. Rather than strictly a question of reciprocity – which may still be ensured as between the two States parties to the BIT – the problems that arise with applying the MFN clause to conditions for acceptance of jurisdiction concern the rationale of the clause and the clarity of State consent. Not only, but the effect of applying a MFN clause to the dispute settlement provisions in a BIT may have the inverse effect to that which the clause is intended to have, by not granting investors of the two States the same rights to access arbitration with the host State.

6.6 Conclusion

This survey of the operation of reciprocity in a variety of dispute settlement mechanisms and procedures has highlighted two fundamental characteristics of the concept. The first is its close connection to legal equality. Dispute settlement involving States is always based on consent, and where it involves two States, the need to preserve equality between the two gives a salient role to reciprocity. Equality requires that both States must have accepted the same obligation in the concrete case, that is, the dispute must fall within the scope of the acceptance of both States. This is evident in the working of acceptance of jurisdiction of the ICJ, as well as UNCLOS, and in inter-State complaint mechanisms under human rights treaties.

The second point is related to exactly how this equality is implemented, and that is through reversibility. States must be in a position both to bring the specific dispute before a dispute settlement body and have it brought against them. This is clear in the concrete manner in which reservations are invoked by both sides in the Optional Clause system of the ICJ, as well as in the similar system of acceptances under UNCLOS. However, it is also made explicit in inter-State complaint procedures in human rights treaties, where both States involved in the

[166] In this sense, see the point made by the tribunal in *Daimler Financial Services AG v. Argentine Republic*, ICSID Case No. ARB/05/1, Award, 22 August 2012, para. 266.

dispute must have made declarations or accepted a treaty to the same extent.

This basic requirement applies when two States are involved in the proceedings, regardless of the nature of the rules involved. The *erga omnes* nature of the rules in dispute has been considered irrelevant by the ICJ where reciprocity of consent was lacking. Even under human rights treaties, despite the fact that inter-State proceedings do not involve the subjective rights of States, but rather rights *erga omnes partes* and therefore community interests, in which the rights of States parties are limited to ensuring that all other parties observe their undertakings, reciprocity is still required in the consent of the States involved in dispute settlement. The nature of the rules involved is not therefore the determining factor in the importance of reciprocity in their existence or implementation.

However, reciprocity of acceptance is not relevant in individual–State complaint mechanisms, where cases or complaints involve only one State and an individual, and where the latter's nationality is irrelevant. The only requirement for an individual to bring a case against a State under a human rights instrument is the consent of the State against which the complaint is being brought. This is because the only rights and obligations involved are the rights of the individual and the obligations of the State under whose jurisdiction the individuals find themselves. As no other State is involved in the relationship, there is no requirement of reciprocity in consent.

This is further demonstrated by the analysis of the consequences of applying MFN clauses to investor–State dispute settlement provisions in BITs. The subsistence of a link of nationality, and the bilateral nature of the instrument in which the provision is couched, show the unbalancing effects that applying MFN clauses to conditions of acceptance of the jurisdiction of investor–State arbitral tribunals can have on the rights and obligations of States parties to a treaty.

Conclusion

This analysis has had the aim of tracing both a general picture of how reciprocity lies at the basis of public international law and of explaining some of its more precise meanings. At the end of this survey, which has purposely looked across both more traditional areas of law and those more commonly considered to relate to community interests, a few conclusions can be drawn regarding the importance of reciprocity in international law and the factors that explain it.

The first point to note may seem paradoxical: There is no such thing as a "principle of reciprocity" in international law. The phrase has been used variously to indicate either the operation of reciprocity in specific mechanisms, such as in the Optional Clause system of the ICJ, or suspending the performance of obligations upon their violation by another State. However, these indicate two different things. The first addresses reciprocity as a condition for the assumption of obligations before an international court, and the other considers reciprocity as a ground for responding to a violation of international law. The latter mechanism was, further, rejected by the ILC in its codification of the law of State responsibility.

The absence of a "principle" of reciprocity does not mean that there is no such thing as reciprocity in international law. Reciprocity is a structural factor in public international law; it is a function of, and mechanism to implement, the principle of the sovereign equality of States. As set out in Chapter 1, reciprocity is most relevant and suited to relations between equal entities. In international law, this means that reciprocity in its fullest sense exists between legally equal entities, that is, States. Individuals or international organizations have more limited legal capacity in international law and cannot be in a relationship of full reciprocity with a State.

Second, because a system based on sovereign equality is by definition decentralized, reciprocity is fundamental to the very existence of the law and its implementation, particularly as regards the consequences of a breach. This is so even in the case of breaches of obligations that are owed to the international community as a whole. Obligations are owed to States, and it is they who may invoke the responsibility of a wrongdoing State. This is because of the absence, in international law, of any centralized organ placed above States with the *general* capacity to impose consequences for the breach of international obligations. This basic structure subsists whatever the type of obligation concerned.

Describing international law as decentralized is not the same as saying that international law is based upon bilateral obligations. As the analysis here has shown, there is nothing inherent to the concept of reciprocity that only renders it applicable in a bilateral context. Reciprocity is inherent to conceptions of justice and fairness, as well as being one of the fundamental building blocks of social relations, and not only a means of obtaining private justice.

The importance of equality in reciprocity also does not mean that it requires substantive equality of undertaking. Strict equality of treatment or of obligations is possible but not required by reciprocity. There is no reason why differentiated obligations, whether in contracts or treaties, may not be reciprocal. This is illustrated by agreements of the interdependent type such as the NPT but also environmental and trade agreements that establish different categories among States parties. In fact, provisions establishing differentiated obligations in multilateral environmental agreements may take the form of conditional bargains, closer to a classical synallagma than an exception to reciprocity.

It is better to see reciprocity as requiring not symmetry but proportionality. Obligations become nonreciprocal at the point at which disproportion affects the legal equality of their subjects. Differentiated obligations in trade agreements, examined in Chapter 3, are still proportionate, insofar as they provide for exceptions for less-developed States, but they also do not affect the legal equality of the States involved. Although the material treatment that one State may have to accord is not exactly the same as that of its trading partner, States parties are still engaged toward each other, having rights and obligations *vis-à-vis* other parties.

C.1 How Reciprocity Functions in International Law

In customary international law, reciprocity amounts to the inability of one State to lay claim to more rights than another. It must accept that those same rights may be extended to all other States if it accepts them for itself. This same mechanism also exists in the law of treaties, particularly in the rules on reservations, as seen in Chapter 3. A State cannot require more performance than it is itself prepared to grant. Reciprocity therefore plays out on the intersubjective level, in the concrete obligations that arise between States. It boils down to the concepts of opposability and reversibility. As seen in Chapter 6, this is particularly evident in dispute settlement mechanisms, such as the Optional Clause system before the ICJ and UNCLOS Part XV. Reciprocity in these contexts amounts to the possibility of opposing a reservation to the State making it, and reversibility is used to allow States to invoke the reservations of the other side in order to establish whether the two States have accepted jurisdiction over the concrete dispute.

A second facet of reciprocity in international law is that the rights and obligations of States all necessarily correlate to the rights or obligations of one, some, or all other States, on which their existence depends. This is highlighted by the rules on treaties and customary law, as well as the secondary rules of responsibility underpinning the system.

C.2 Limits to Reciprocity in Public International Law

The horizontal structure of international law, and the role of reciprocity in ensuring sovereign equality, also dictate the limits of reciprocity in public international law. These will depend on *who* obligations are owed to, rather than the content of those obligations. In general, reciprocity will not be relevant where the legal relationship involved is vertical, and not horizontal. Therefore, reciprocity does not play a significant role in individual–State relations, where individuals have direct rights in international law, as seen in Chapter 4. There are however still standards of treatment of individuals that are based upon reciprocity. When an inter-State dimension reenters into the sphere of individual rights, as is the case with diplomatic protection, reciprocity once again comes into play. Conversely, in the case of human rights, there is no condition of nationality required for individuals to enjoy rights; these are undertakings made by each State party to grant certain rights to individuals within their jurisdiction.

The first concrete example of such a limitation to reciprocity is found in the matter of reservations to human rights treaties, as analyzed in Chapter 3. In the same way as reservations that are simply meant to apply internally within the State, there is no inter-State dimension to reservations relating to substantive provisions of human rights treaties that States owe directly to individuals. Therefore, there is no relationship of equality to preserve, and one State will not be able to modify the extent to which it grants rights to individuals within its jurisdiction on the basis of a similar restriction by another State party to a human rights treaty.

Structural limitations of this type also apply in the context of the law of State responsibility, particularly the taking of countermeasures, as addressed in Chapter 5. Countermeasures must be directed against the State committing the internationally wrongful act; in fact, the widespread use of measures suspending the rights of individuals in response to internationally wrongful acts is always based on their link of nationality to the responsible State. Reciprocity also, paradoxically, works to ensure that it is not possible to suspend obligations *erga omnes* or *erga omnes partes* by reason of their violation, as performance of these obligations is necessarily owed to States other than the responsible State. Reciprocity therefore both reinforces observance of community interests, by enlarging the number of States that may invoke the responsibility of a wrongdoing State, and provides a way, through the suspension of obligations owed bilaterally, to elicit resumed compliance.

C.3 Specific Meanings of Reciprocity

The term "reciprocity" is also used to refer to specific mechanisms in international law. First of all, reciprocity may be used as a basis on which to establish State conduct when there are no legal obligations in place. Treaties may also use reciprocity as a basis for States to cooperate further than the obligations they contain.

When a treaty provision contains a condition of reciprocity, the content of the obligation depends on the material treatment being granted. Predicating concessions by one party upon those of another is a good way of ensuring a relationship of equality in which the parties will make concessions to the same extent, particularly in commercial matters. Such a provision allows one State to modulate its conduct in response to the acts of another without thereby breaching a rule or having to have recourse to the mechanisms incorporated in State responsibility.

Reciprocity may also be a basis on which to extend rights and obligations to third States to a treaty on the basis of their conduct. An example of this is the extension of the 1949 Geneva Conventions to nonparties that "accept and apply" the rules of the Convention, in Common Article 2, as analyzed in Chapter 4.

Mention is often made of "reciprocity" as a reaction that a State may have to the violation of a rule of international law in its regard. However, "reciprocity" as a category was rejected by the ILC in its work on the law of State responsibility. Reciprocity however still lies at the basis of the measures that a State may take in response to a breach, whether non-performance in the case of material breach of a treaty or the possibility of taking countermeasures.

Finally, "reciprocity" is used in the context of the jurisdiction of the ICJ on the basis of declarations made under the "Optional Clause" system under Article 36.2 of the Statute of the Court. While it relates to ensuring that States appearing before the ICJ accept "the same obligation," it has taken on a specific meaning. When a case is filed against a State on the basis of Article 36.2, the respondent State is allowed to invoke not only the reservations it makes in its own declaration but also those made by the other State. Here, the meaning of "reciprocity" is therefore closely connected to reversibility.

C.4 Conclusion

The interest of reciprocity lies in both its complexity and its deceptive simplicity. Hopefully, the analysis here has shed some light on the actual simplicity of how reciprocity functions in public international law and on how the reciprocal structure of international obligations underpins the whole of international law. While there are some precise meanings of "reciprocity" that may relate to given mechanisms or functions, in general reciprocity manifests itself through correlation and interdependence of rights and obligations, and in practice through concepts such as opposability and reversibility. Limitations to reciprocity are those that may be expected from its link with legal equality; where this legal equality is missing from a relationship between two legal subjects, reciprocity will have lesser relevance. Reciprocity is not the enemy of community interests and obligations. Instead, it is simply a fact of how these obligations are implemented in international law. It is not a weak link in the respect of international obligations, but provides the very particular means through which State may create, develop, apply, and enforce international law.

Select Bibliography

Books

Axelrod, R., *The Evolution of Cooperation*, New York, Basic Books, 1984

Campiglio, C., *Il principio di reciprocità nel diritto dei trattati*, Padua, CEDAM, 1995

Cannizzaro, E., ed., *The Law of Treaties beyond the Vienna Convention*, Oxford, Oxford University Press, 2011

Cassese, A., ed., *Realizing Utopia: The Future of International Law*, Oxford, Oxford University Press, 2012

Chinkin, C., *Third Parties in International Law*, Oxford, Clarendon, 1993

Clarke, M., and Goodale, M., eds., *Mirrors of Justice: Law and Power in the Post-Cold War Era*, Cambridge, Cambridge University Press, 2010

Corten, O., and Klein, P., eds., *The Vienna Convention on the Law of Treaties: A Commentary*, Oxford, Oxford University Press, 2011

Coulée, F., *Droit des traits et non-réciprocité: Recherches sur l'obligation intégrale en droit international public*, Paris, Université Panthéon-Assas, 1999

Crawford, J., Pellet, A., and Olleson, S., *The Law of International Responsibility*, Oxford, Oxford University Press, 2010

Decaux, E., *La réciprocité en droit international*, Paris, LGDJ, 1980

Dero, D., *La réciprocité et le droit des Communautés et de l'Union européennes*, Brussels, Bruylant, 2006

Diamond, A. S., *Primitive Law Past and Present*, London, Methuen & Co., 1971

Dupuy, P.-M., *Obligations multilaterales, droit impératif et responsabilité internationale des Etats*, Paris, Pedone, 2003

Fard, S., *Reciprocity in International Law*, Abingdon, Routledge, 2016

Fastenrath, U., ed., *From Bilateralism to Community Interest: Essays in Honour of Judge Bruno Simma*, Oxford, Oxford University Press, 2011

Fitzmaurice, M., and Merkouris, P., *The Interpretation and Application of the European Convention on Human Rights: Legal and Practical Implications*, Leiden/Boston, MA, M. Nijhoff, 2013

Gomaa, M. M., *Suspension or Termination of Treaties on Grounds of Breach*, The Hague, M. Nijhoff, 1996

Hobhouse, L. T., *Morals in Evolution: A Study in Comparative Ethics*, 5th ed., New York, Henry Holt & Co., 1925

Kolb, R., *La bonne foi en droit international public*, Paris, University Press of France, 2000

Parlett, K., *The Individual in the International Legal System*, Cambridge, Cambridge University Press, 2011

Sicilianos, L.-A., *Les reactions décentralisées à l'illicite: des contre-mesures à la légitime défense*, Paris, LGDJ, 1990

Articles and Book Chapters

Alland, D., "Countermeasures of General Interest," *European Journal of International Law*, vol. 13, no. 5, 2002, pp. 1221–1239

Braud, P., "Recherches sur l'état tiers en droit international public," *Revue générale de droit international public*, vol. 72, 1968, pp. 17–96

Brown Weiss, E., "Invoking State Responsibility in the Twenty-First Century," *The American Journal of International Law*, vol. 96, no. 4, 2002, pp. 798–816

Childs, L. B., "Shaky Foundations: Criticism of Reciprocity and the Distinction between Public and Private International Law," *New York University Journal of International Law and Politics*, vol. 38, nos. 1 & 2, 2006, pp. 221–279

Cialdini, R. B. et al., "Reciprocal Concessions Procedure for Inducing Compliance: The Door-in-the Face Technique," *Journal of Personality and Social Psychology*, vol. 31, no. 2, 1975, pp. 206–215

Crawford, J., "Multilateral Rights and Obligations in International Law," in *Collected Courses of the Hague Academy of International Law*, vol. 319, Brill, 2006, pp. 1–482

Darmstädter, F., "La réciprocité et la communauté considérées comme categories juridiques," *Archives de philosophie du droit et de sociologie juridique*, nos. 3–4, 1935, pp. 92–124

Dominicé, C., "The International Responsibility of States for Breaches of Multilateral Obligations," *European Journal of International Law*, vol. 10, no. 2, 1999, pp. 353 363

Drzemczewski, A., "The Sui Generis Nature of the European Convention on Human Rights," *The International and Comparative Law Quarterly*, vol. 29, no. 1, January 1980, pp. 54–63

Dupuy, P.-M., "Quarante ans de codification du droit de la responsabilité des etats: Un bilan," *Revue générale de droit international public*, vol. 107, 2003, pp. 305–346

Dupuy, P.-M., "L'unité de l'ordre juridique international: Cours général de droit international public," in *Collected Courses of the Hague Academy of International Law*, vol. 297, Brill, 2000, pp. 1–489

Fehr, E., and Gachter, S., "Fairness and Retaliation: The Economics of Reciprocity," *The Journal of Economic Perspectives*, vol. 14, no. 3, 2000, pp. 159–181

Frigo, M., "La reciprocità nell'evoluzione del diritto del commercio internazionale," *Comunicazioni e studi*, vols. IXX–XX, 1992, pp. 407–481

Garibian, S., "Vers l'émergence d'un droit individuel à la protection diplomatique?" *Annuaire français de droit international*, vol. 54, 2008, pp. 119–141

Goldman, B., "Refléxions sur la réciprocité en droit international," *Travaux du Comité français de droit international privé*, vols. 23–25, 1965, pp. 61–101

Golsong, H., "Les reserves aux instruments internationaux pour la protection des droits de l'homme," in Université Catholique de Louvain, Centre d'études européennes, faculté de droit. Les clauses échappatoires en matière d'instruments internationaux relatifs aux droits de l'homme: quatrième colloque du département des droits de l'homme, Brussels, 1982, pp. 24–42

Gouldner, A. W., "The Norm of Reciprocity: A Preliminary Statement," *American Sociological Review*, vol. 25, no. 2, April 1960, pp. 161–178

Katzenbach, N. dB., "Conflicts on an Unruly Horse: Reciprocal Claims and Tolerances in Interstate and International Law," *The Yale Law Journal*, vol. 65, no. 8, July 1956, pp. 1087–1157

Keohane, R. O., "Reciprocity in International Relations," *International Organization*, vol. 40, no. 1, December 1986, pp. 1–27

Lenhoff, A., "Reciprocity in Function: A Problem of Conflict of Laws, Constitutional Law, and International Law," *University of Pittsburgh Law Review*, vol. 44, 1953–1954, pp. 44–72

Lenhoff, A., "Reciprocity: The Legal Aspect of a Perennial Idea," *Northwestern University Law Journal*, vol. 49, 1954–1955, pp. 619–641

Majoros, F., "Le régime de réciprocité de la Convention de Vienne et les reserves dans les Conventions de la Haye," *Journal du droit international*, vol. 101, no. 1, 1974, pp. 73–109

Meron, T., "The Humanization of Humanitarian Law," *The American Journal of International Law*, vol. 94, no. 2, 2000, pp. 239–278

Nielsen, R. A., and Simmons, B. A., "Rewards for Ratification: Payoffs for Participating in the International Human Rights Regime?," *International Studies Quarterly*, vol. 59, 2015, pp. 197–208

Nisot, J., "L'exception 'non adimpleti contractus' en droit international," *Revue générale de droit international public*, vol. 74, 1970, pp. 668–673

Parisi, F., "The Genesis of Liability in Ancient Law," *American Law and Economics Review*, vol. 3, no. 1, 2001, pp. 82–124

Parisi, F., and Ghei, N., "The Role of Reciprocity in International Law," *Cornell International Law Journal*, vol. 36, no. 1, Spring 2003, pp. 93–123

Paulus, A. L., "*Jus Cogens* in a Time of Hegemony and Fragmentation," *Nordic Journal of International Law*, vol. 74, 2005, pp. 297–334

Picone, P., "Obblighi reciproci e obblighi erga omnes degli Stati nel campo della protezione internazionale dell'ambiente marino dall'inquinamento," in V. Starace, ed., *Diritto internazionale e protezione dell'ambiente marino*, Milano, Giuffrè, 1983, pp. 17–135

Preiswerk, R., "La réciprocité dans les négociations entre pays à systèmes sociaux ou à niveaux économiques différents," *Journal du droit international*, vol. 94, no. 1, 1967, pp. 5–40

Provost, R., "Reciprocity in Human Rights and Humanitarian Law," *The British Yearbook of International Law*, vol. 65, 1994, pp. 383–454

Roberts, A., "State-to-State Investment Treaty Arbitration: A Hybrid Theory of Interdependent Rights and Shared Interpretive Authority," *Harvard International Law Journal*, vol. 55, no. 1, 2014, pp. 1–70

Roberts, A., "Triangular Treaties: The Extent and Limits of Investment Treaty Rights," *Harvard International Law Journal*, vol. 56, no. 2, 2015, pp. 353–417

Russell, M. J., "Fluctuations in Reciprocity," *International and Comparative Law Quarterly*, vol. 1, no. 2, 1952, pp. 181–195

Schneeberger, E., "Reciprocity as a Maxim of International Law," *Georgetown Law Journal*, vol. 37, 1948–1949, pp. 29–41

Sicilianos, L.-A., "The Classification of Obligations and the Multilateral Dimension of the Relations of International Responsibility," *European Journal of International Law*, vol. 13, no. 5, 2002, pp. 1127–1145

Sicilianos, L.-A., "L'influence des droits de l'homme sur la structure du droit international, Première partie: Les droits de l'homme et la hiérarchisation de l'ordre juridique international," *Revue générale de droit international public*, vol. 116, 2012, pp. 5–30

Sicilianos, L.-A., "L'influence des droits de l'homme sur la structure du droit international; Deuxième partie: Les consequences structurelles de la hiérarchisation," *Revue générale de droit international public*, vol. 116, 2012, pp. 241–273

Simma, B., "Bilateralism and Community Interest in the Law of State Responsibility," in Y. Dinstein, ed., *International Law at a Time of Perplexity: Essays in Honour of Shabtai Rosenne*, Boston, Nijhoff, 1989, pp. 821–844

Simma, B., "From Bilateralism to Community Interest in International Law," in *Collected Courses of the Hague Academy of International Law*, vol. 250, 1994, pp. 217–384

Simma, B., "Reciprocity," in R. Wolfrum, ed., *The Max Planck Encyclopedia of Public International Law*, Oxford University Press, 2008–, online edition, [www.mpepil.com]

Thirlway, H., "Reciprocity in the Jurisdiction of the International Court," *Netherlands Yearbook of International Law*, vol. 15, 1984, pp. 97–138

Torres Bernárdez, S., "Reciprocity in the System of Compulsory Jurisdiction and in Other Modalities of Contentious Jurisdiction Exercised by the International Court of Justice," in E. G. Bello and B. A. Ajibola, eds., *Essays in Honour of Judge Taslim Olawale Elias*, vol. I, Leiden, Nijhoff, 1992, pp. 291–329

Virally, M., "Le principe de réciprocité dans le droit international contemporain," *Collected Courses of the Hague Academy of International Law*, vol. 122, 1967, pp. 1–105

Virally, M., "Sur la prétendue 'primitivité' du droit international," in *Le droit international en devenir: Essais écrits au fil des ans*, Paris, Presses universitaires de France, 1990, pp. 91–101

Woodward, J., "Cooperation and Reciprocity: Empirical Evidence and Normative Implications," in H. Kincaid, ed., *The Oxford Handbook of Philosophy of Social Science*, Oxford, Oxford University Press, 2012, pp. 581–606

Index

CAMBRIDGE STUDIES IN INTERNATIONAL AND COMPARATIVE LAW

Books in the Series

173 *Reciprocity in Public International Law* Arianna Whelan
172 *When Environmental Protection and Human Rights Collide* Marie-Catherine Petersmann
171 *The International Law of Sovereign Debt Dispute Settlement* Kei Nakajima
170 *The Everyday Makers of International Law: From Great Halls to Back Rooms* Tommaso Soave
169 *The Effects of Armed Conflict on Investment Treaties* Tobias Ackermann
168 *Investment Law's Alibis: Colonialism, Imperialism, Debt and Development* David Schneiderman
167 *Negative Comparative Law: A Strong Programme for Weak Thought* Pierre Legrand
166 *Detention by Non-State Armed Groups under International Law* Ezequiel Heffes
165 *Rebellions and Civil Wars: State Responsibility for the Conduct of Insurgents* Patrick Dumberry
164 *The International Law of Energy* Jorge Viñuales
163 *The Three Ages of International Commercial Arbitration* Mikaël Schinazi
162 *Repetition and International Law* Wouter Werner
161 *State Responsibility and Rebels: The History and Legacy of Protecting Investment Against Revolution* Kathryn Greenman
160 *Rewriting Histories of the Use of Force: The Narrative of 'Indifference'* Agatha Verdebout
159 *The League of Nations and the Protection of the Environment* Omer Aloni
158 *International Investment Law and Legal Theory: Expropriation and the Fragmentation of Sources* Jörg Kammerhofer
157 *Legal Barbarians: Identity, Modern Comparative Law and the Global South* Daniel Bonilla Maldonado
156 *International Human Rights Law Beyond State Territorial Control* Antal Berkes
155 *The Crime of Aggression under the Rome Statute of the International Criminal Court* Carrie McDougall
154 *Minorities and the Making of Postcolonial States in International Law* Mohammad Shahabuddin

153 *Preclassical Conflict of Laws* Nikitas E. Hatzimihail
152 *International Law and History: Modern Interfaces* Ignacio de la Rasilla
151 *Marketing Global Justice: The Political Economy of International Criminal Law* Christine Schwöbel-Patel
150 *International Status in the Shadow of Empire* Cait Storr
149 *Treaties in Motion: The Evolution of Treaties from Formation to Termination* Edited by Malgosia Fitzmaurice and Panos Merkouris
148 *Humanitarian Disarmament: An Historical Enquiry* Treasa Dunworth
147 *Complementarity, Catalysts, Compliance: The International Criminal Court in Uganda, Kenya, and the Democratic Republic of Congo* Christian M. De Vos
146 *Cyber Operations and International Law* François Delerue
145 *Comparative Reasoning in International Courts and Tribunals* Daniel Peat
144 *Maritime Delimitation as a Judicial Process* Massimo Lando
143 *Prosecuting Sexual and Gender-Based Crimes at the International Criminal Court: Practice, Progress and Potential* Rosemary Grey
142 *Capitalism As Civilisation: A History of International Law* Ntina Tzouvala
141 *Sovereignty in China: A Genealogy of a Concept Since 1840* Adele Carrai
140 *Narratives of Hunger in International Law: Feeding the World in Times of Climate Change* Anne Saab
139 *Victim Reparation under the Ius Post Bellum: An Historical and Normative Perspective* Shavana Musa
138 *The Analogy between States and International Organizations* Fernando Lusa Bordin
137 *The Process of International Legal Reproduction: Inequality, Historiography, Resistance* Rose Parfitt
136 *State Responsibility for Breaches of Investment Contracts* Jean Ho
135 *Coalitions of the Willing and International Law: The Interplay between Formality and Informality* Alejandro Rodiles
134 *Self-Determination in Disputed Colonial Territories* Jamie Trinidad
133 *International Law as a Belief System* Jean d'Aspremont
132 *Legal Consequences of Peremptory Norms in International Law* Daniel Costelloe
131 *Third-Party Countermeasures in International Law* Martin Dawidowicz
130 *Justification and Excuse in International Law: Concept and Theory of General Defences* Federica Paddeu
129 *Exclusion from Public Space: A Comparative Constitutional Analysis* Daniel Moeckli
128 *Provisional Measures before International Courts and Tribunals* Cameron A. Miles
127 *Humanity at Sea: Maritime Migration and the Foundations of International Law* Itamar Mann
126 *Beyond Human Rights: The Legal Status of the Individual in International Law* Anne Peters
125 *The Doctrine of Odious Debt in International Law: A Restatement* Jeff King
124 *Static and Evolutive Treaty Interpretation: A Functional Reconstruction* Christian Djeffal
123 *Civil Liability in Europe for Terrorism-Related Risk* Lucas Bergkamp, Michael Faure, Monika Hinteregger and Niels Philipsen

122 *Proportionality and Deference in Investor-State Arbitration: Balancing Investment Protection and Regulatory Autonomy* Caroline Henckels
121 *International Law and Governance of Natural Resources in Conflict and Post-Conflict Situations* Daniëlla Dam-de Jong
120 *Proof of Causation in Tort Law* Sandy Steel
119 *The Formation and Identification of Rules of Customary International Law in International Investment Law* Patrick Dumberry
118 *Religious Hatred and International Law: The Prohibition of Incitement to Violence or Discrimination* Jeroen Temperman
117 *Taking Economic, Social and Cultural Rights Seriously in International Criminal Law* Evelyne Schmid
116 *Climate Change Litigation: Regulatory Pathways to Cleaner Energy* Jacqueline Peel and Hari M. Osofsky
115 *Mestizo International Law: A Global Intellectual History 1842–1933* Arnulf Becker Lorca
114 *Sugar and the Making of International Trade Law* Michael Fakhri
113 *Strategically Created Treaty Conflicts and the Politics of International Law* Surabhi Ranganathan
112 *Investment Treaty Arbitration As Public International Law: Procedural Aspects and Implications* Eric De Brabandere
111 *The New Entrants Problem in International Fisheries Law* Andrew Serdy
110 *Substantive Protection under Investment Treaties: A Legal and Economic Analysis* Jonathan Bonnitcha
109 *Popular Governance of Post-Conflict Reconstruction: The Role of International Law* Matthew Saul
108 *Evolution of International Environmental Regimes: The Case of Climate Change* Simone Schiele
107 *Judges, Law and War: The Judicial Development of International Humanitarian Law* Shane Darcy
106 *Religious Offence and Human Rights: The Implications of Defamation of Religions* Lorenz Langer
105 *Forum Shopping in International Adjudication: The Role of Preliminary Objections* Luiz Eduardo Salles
104 *Domestic Politics and International Human Rights Tribunals: The Problem of Compliance* Courtney Hillebrecht
103 *International Law and the Arctic* Michael Byers
102 *Cooperation in the Law of Transboundary Water Resources* Christina Leb
101 *Underwater Cultural Heritage and International Law* Sarah Dromgoole
100 *State Responsibility: The General Part* James Crawford
99 *The Origins of International Investment Law: Empire, Environment and the Safeguarding of Capital* Kate Miles
98 *The Crime of Aggression under the Rome Statute of the International Criminal Court* Carrie McDougall
97 *'Crimes against Peace' and International Law* Kirsten Sellars
96 *Non-Legality in International Law: Unruly Law* Fleur Johns

95 *Armed Conflict and Displacement: The Protection of Refugees and Displaced Persons under International Humanitarian Law* Mélanie Jacques

94 *Foreign Investment and the Environment in International Law* Jorge E. Viñuales

93 *The Human Rights Treaty Obligations of Peacekeepers* Kjetil Mujezinović Larsen

92 *Cyber Warfare and the Laws of War* Heather Harrison Dinniss

91 *The Right to Reparation in International Law for Victims of Armed Conflict* Christine Evans

90 *Global Public Interest in International Investment Law* Andreas Kulick

89 *State Immunity in International Law* Xiaodong Yang

88 *Reparations and Victim Support in the International Criminal Court* Conor McCarthy

87 *Reducing Genocide to Law: Definition, Meaning, and the Ultimate Crime* Payam Akhavan

86 *Decolonising International Law: Development, Economic Growth and the Politics of Universality* Sundhya Pahuja

85 *Complicity and the Law of State Responsibility* Helmut Philipp Aust

84 *State Control over Private Military and Security Companies in Armed Conflict* Hannah Tonkin

83 *'Fair and Equitable Treatment' in International Investment Law* Roland Kläger

82 *The UN and Human Rights: Who Guards the Guardians?* Guglielmo Verdirame

81 *Sovereign Defaults before International Courts and Tribunals* Michael Waibel

80 *Making the Law of the Sea: A Study in the Development of International Law* James Harrison

79 *Science and the Precautionary Principle in International Courts and Tribunals: Expert Evidence, Burden of Proof and Finality* Caroline E. Foster

78 *Transition from Illegal Regimes under International Law* Yaël Ronen

77 *Access to Asylum: International Refugee Law and the Globalisation of Migration Control* Thomas Gammeltoft-Hansen

76 *Trading Fish, Saving Fish: The Interaction between Regimes in International Law* Margaret A. Young

75 *The Individual in the International Legal System: Continuity and Change in International Law* Kate Parlett

74 *'Armed Attack' and Article 51 of the UN Charter: Evolutions in Customary Law and Practice* Tom Ruys

73 *Theatre of the Rule of Law: Transnational Legal Intervention in Theory and Practice* Stephen Humphreys

72 *Science and Risk Regulation in International Law* Jacqueline Peel

71 *The Participation of States in International Organisations: The Role of Human Rights and Democracy* Alison Duxbury

70 *Legal Personality in International Law* Roland Portmann

69 *Vicarious Liability in Tort: A Comparative Perspective* Paula Giliker

68 *The Public International Law Theory of Hans Kelsen: Believing in Universal Law* Jochen von Bernstorff

67 *Legitimacy and Legality in International Law: An Interactional Account* Jutta Brunnée and Stephen J. Toope

66 *The Concept of Non-International Armed Conflict in International Humanitarian Law* Anthony Cullen
65 *The Principle of Legality in International and Comparative Criminal Law* Kenneth S. Gallant
64 *The Challenge of Child Labour in International Law* Franziska Humbert
63 *Shipping Interdiction and the Law of the Sea* Douglas Guilfoyle
62 *International Courts and Environmental Protection* Tim Stephens
61 *Legal Principles in WTO Disputes* Andrew D. Mitchell
60 *War Crimes in Internal Armed Conflicts* Eve La Haye
59 *Humanitarian Occupation* Gregory H. Fox
58 *The International Law of Environmental Impact Assessment: Process, Substance and Integration* Neil Craik
57 *The Law and Practice of International Territorial Administration: Versailles to Iraq and Beyond* Carsten Stahn
56 *United Nations Sanctions and the Rule of Law* Jeremy Matam Farrall
55 *National Law in WTO Law: Effectiveness and Good Governance in the World Trading System* Sharif Bhuiyan
54 *Cultural Products and the World Trade Organization* Tania Voon
53 *The Threat of Force in International Law* Nikolas Stürchler
52 *Indigenous Rights and United Nations Standards: Self-Determination, Culture and Land* Alexandra Xanthaki
51 *International Refugee Law and Socio-Economic Rights: Refuge from Deprivation* Michelle Foster
50 *The Protection of Cultural Property in Armed Conflict* Roger O'Keefe
49 *Interpretation and Revision of International Boundary Decisions* Kaiyan Homi Kaikobad
48 *Multinationals and Corporate Social Responsibility: Limitations and Opportunities in International Law* Jennifer A. Zerk
47 *Judiciaries within Europe: A Comparative Review* John Bell
46 *Law in Times of Crisis: Emergency Powers in Theory and Practice* Oren Gross and Fionnuala Ní Aoláin
45 *Vessel-Source Marine Pollution: The Law and Politics of International Regulation* Alan Khee-Jin Tan
44 *Enforcing Obligations Erga Omnes in International Law* Christian J. Tams
43 *Non-Governmental Organisations in International Law* Anna-Karin Lindblom
42 *Democracy, Minorities and International Law* Steven Wheatley
41 *Prosecuting International Crimes: Selectivity and the International Criminal Law Regime* Robert Cryer
40 *Compensation for Personal Injury in English, German and Italian Law: A Comparative Outline* Basil Markesinis, Michael Coester, Guido Alpa and Augustus Ullstein
39 *Dispute Settlement in the UN Convention on the Law of the Sea* Natalie Klein
38 *The International Protection of Internally Displaced Persons* Catherine Phuong
37 *Imperialism, Sovereignty and the Making of International Law* Antony Anghie
36 *Principles of the Institutional Law of International Organizations* C. F. Amerasinghe
35 *Necessity, Proportionality and the Use of Force by States* Judith Gardam

34 *International Legal Argument in the Permanent Court of International Justice: The Rise of the International Judiciary* Ole Spiermann
33 –
32 *Great Powers and Outlaw States: Unequal Sovereigns in the International Legal Order* Gerry Simpson
31 *Local Remedies in International Law (second edition)* Chittharanjan Felix Amerasinghe
30 *Reading Humanitarian Intervention: Human Rights and the Use of Force in International Law* Anne Orford
29 *Conflict of Norms in Public International Law: How WTO Law Relates to Other Rules of International Law* Joost Pauwelyn
28 –
27 *Transboundary Damage in International Law* Hanqin Xue
26 –
25 *European Criminal Procedures* Edited by Mireille Delmas-Marty and J. R. Spencer
24 *Accountability of Armed Opposition Groups in International Law* Liesbeth Zegveld
23 *Sharing Transboundary Resources: International Law and Optimal Resource Use* Eyal Benvenisti
22 *International Human Rights and Humanitarian Law* René Provost
21 *Remedies against International Organisations* Karel Wellens
20 *Diversity and Self-Determination in International Law* Karen Knop
19 *The Law of Internal Armed Conflict* Lindsay Moir
18 *International Commercial Arbitration and African States: Practice, Participation and Institutional Development* Amazu A. Asouzu
17 *The Enforceability of Promises in European Contract Law* James Gordley
16 *International Law in Antiquity* David J. Bederman
15 *Money Laundering: A New International Law Enforcement Model* Guy Stessens
14 *Good Faith in European Contract Law* Reinhard Zimmermann and Simon Whittaker
13 *On Civil Procedure* J. A. Jolowicz
12 *Trusts: A Comparative Study* Maurizio Lupoi and Simon Dix
11 *The Right to Property in Commonwealth Constitutions* Tom Allen
10 *International Organizations before National Courts* August Reinisch
9 *The Changing International Law of High Seas Fisheries* Francisco Orrego Vicuña
8 *Trade and the Environment: A Comparative Study of EC and US Law* Damien Geradin
7 *Unjust Enrichment: A Study of Private Law and Public Values* Hanoch Dagan
6 *Religious Liberty and International Law in Europe* Malcolm D. Evans
5 *Ethics and Authority in International Law* Alfred P. Rubin
4 *Sovereignty over Natural Resources: Balancing Rights and Duties* Nico Schrijver
3 *The Polar Regions and the Development of International Law* Donald R. Rothwell
2 *Fragmentation and the International Relations of Micro-States: Self-Determination and Statehood* Jorri C. Duursma
1 *Principles of the Institutional Law of International Organizations* C. F. Amerasinghe

For EU product safety concerns, contact us at Calle de José Abascal, 56–1°, 28003 Madrid, Spain or eugpsr@cambridge.org.

www.ingramcontent.com/pod-product-compliance
Lightning Source LLC
LaVergne TN
LVHW010055220926
848484LV00005BA/1124

* 9 7 8 1 1 0 8 8 4 5 5 8 8 *